Cybernetics
and
Applied
Systems

Cybernetics
and
Applied
Systems

edited by

Constantin Virgil Negoita

Hunter College
City University of New York
New York, New York

Marcel Dekker, Inc.   **New York • Basel • Hong Kong**

Library of Congress Cataloging-in-Publication Data

Cybernetics and applied systems / edited by Constantin Virgil Negoita.
    p.   cm.
  Includes bibliographical references and index.
  ISBN 0-8247-8677-7 (alk. paper)
  1. Cybernetics.   2. Cybernetics--Social aspects.   3. System
analysis.   I. Negoita, Constantin Virgil.
  [DNLM: 1. Cybernetics.   2. Systems Theory.   Q 310 C994]
Q310.C93   1992
003'.5--dc20
DNLM/DLC
for Library of Congress   92-9995
                                                            CIP

Marcel Dekker, Inc.
270 Madison Avenue, New York, New York 10016

Current printing (last digit):
10   9   8   7   6   5   4   3   2   1

PRINTED IN THE UNITED STATES OF AMERICA

Foreword

Cybernetics, the term coined by Norbert Wiener in 1947 to represent the field of control and communication in animal and the machine, was supposed to encompass such areas as statistics, information, feedback, computing machines, and nervous systems, as well as such adjacent disciplines as economics, sociology, psychopathology, and linguistics. At that time and technological level, this was obviously an audacious venture. In the second edition of his book on cybernetics, Wiener even extended the scope of cybernetics to self-organizing and self-reproducing systems. In fact, a superscience was shaped from the very beginning.

However, cybernetics should not be considered a collection of a large number of individual disciplines but rather a way of *reasoning* in the sciences. Actually, by applying cybernetic methods, engineers and scientists can learn much about the intelligent and social behavior of living beings. The conclusions they draw should enable them to build systems behaving similarly to living organisms themselves.

Nevertheless, the high expectations for cybernetics in the 1950s and its aura as an epoch-making science and technology were in the following two decades essentially corrected: cybernetics was de facto "reduced" to computer science, or rather to its most advanced development, artificial intelligence. Observations of the intelligent behavior of human beings have led to the implementation of machine intelligence. Furthermore, the long-term study of the human brain and nervous system has led to the silicon implementation of neural networks that, as massive parallel computing systems, can, in an associative manner, "think" even faster than John von Neumann's classical "electronic brain."

Unfortunately, books on cybernetics have recently become rare. Thus, this book, which highlights the most outstanding topics of cybernetics and provides the reader with the most recent trends, is welcome to a wide number of scientists, engineers, and graduate students as an information source on the state of the art and future trends, as well as a comprehensive introduction to individual branches of cybernetics.

Dobrivoje Popovic
Department of Control and
Computer Engineering
University of Bremen
Bremen, Germany

Preface

Thirty years after Norbert Wiener published the book that gave the science of cybernetics its name, Robert Trappl contacted leading scientists all over the world about presenting the current state of the art. *Cybernetics: Theory and Applications* (1983) not only covered different areas of cybernetics but also tried to give the reader an impression of vitality, although, at the time, the center of interest was shifting toward artificial intelligence. The past few years have seen a different trend. This book is a presentation of this trend.

Artificial intelligence and cybernetics are each concerned with the application of computers to the study of complex, natural phenomena. However, each field employs the technology of computation in a different manner.

Artificial intelligence is supposedly concerned with mechanical generation of intelligent behavior. Although it looked first to natural intelligence to identify its underlying mechanisms, those mechanisms were not known. Therefore, following an initial flirtation with neural nets, artificial intelligence became wedded to the only other known tool: the technology of serial computer programming.

By contrast, workers in cybernetics had the great good fortune to note that nature is fundamentally parallel, that feedback and pullback play similar roles in a wide variety of natural and artificial systems, and that a comprehensive program of metadisciplinary research into the mechanisms operating in human systems could reveal a great deal about the functions of goal-oriented machines.

In light of the enormous interest in building intelligent systems, the purpose of this volume is to report on how far research efforts have brought us toward a revival of cybernetics. The blend of and balance among theory, applications, and methodology should make this book a valuable reference.

The authors represented in this volume share a common concern. They want to take cybernetics out of the realm of the abstract and explain how it can contribute to an improved understanding of intelligence. Of course, this question is addressed by each author in a different way.

Ernst von Glasersfeld shows that cybernetics is metadisciplinary, in that it distills and clarifies notions that open new pathways of understanding in a great many areas of experience. Astafyev, Gorsky, and Pospelov discuss homeostasis, the property of supporting constancy.

Mario Bunge analyzes why everything is a system, a component, or a part of a system, and why this holds for atoms, people, societies, and ideas. Marc Carvallo also deals with the nature of system science, developing a system science as a subjective system that includes the observer.

Sociocybernetics applies cybernetics to the study of social and sociocultural systems. Felix Geyer and Johannes van der Zouwen agree that much has happened in the field since the first volumes with that title appeared in 1978.

Rod Swenson examines the nature of evolutionary ordering. Rather than being static or purposeless, the evolutionary dynamics of the natural world are now seen to be creative and purposive. The world is in the order-production business, and this can now be understood as a spontaneous search for symmetry in terms of natural law.

The contribution of Fenton Robb is illustrative in this respect. He attempts to ground a theory of the emergence of social institutions in human conversational interactions in a theory of the evolution of orders in physical systems.

Blanning, Marsden, Pingry, and Seror are also interested in human systems, but from another angle. Their chapter examines what, if anything, one can learn about the intelligent behavior of economic and social systems from the growing body of research in cognitive science.

Three chapters are concerned with the hierarchical organization of systems. Pierre Auger, who studies the jump from a microscopic level toward a macroscopic level, is interested in the relation between an individual and a population. Yufik, Sheridan, and Venda focus their attention on the relationship between an operator and a machine. They are interested in learning. A key concept in approaching the learning mechanisms is the pullback in a categorical structure. In my chapter, purpose by pullback can be seen as a cybernetical approach to knowledge manipulation, one that recognizes the importance of parallel processing.

Alex Andrew is also interested in the highly parallel operation of the brain and notes that the past decade has seen a strong revival of interest in neural computing.

Roman Swiniarski presents an introduction to neural networks, and Constantine Manikopoulos gives details about their application in image coding. J. J. Buckley studies the idea of control in a linguistic framework. Fuzzy controllers prove to be a striking example of parallel processing.

Markus Peschl uses arguments from computer science, philosophy, and epistemology, as well as from semiotics, to make explicit the inadequacies, insufficiencies, and problems of the traditional approach to cognitive science: the reduction to symbol manipulation.

In the final chapter, Takuji Kobori offers an outstanding example: the information transmitted from ground motion sensors functions to counteract the destructive force of earthquakes. To achieve this, buildings change their own structural dynamic characteristics. In other words, with a cybernetic approach, a building can become intelligent.

I am sure that after reading all these outstanding contributions, the reader will pull back and see the shape of the whole, one that provides a thought-provoking insight into a key issue of the past decade.

I had two audiences in mind. The first consists of science majors in the early phases of their careers. Students at this stage tend to evaluate cybernetics with artificial intelligence based on symbol manipulation because that is essentially all they have seen. Yet cybernetics is much more than artificial intelligence. People need to be exposed to the breadth of the subject. My second audience is composed of students, scientists, and engineers of other fields who are seeking literacy, which I loosely define as the ability to distinguish between science and science fiction.

Constantin Virgil Negoita

Contents

Contributors

Alex M. Andrew   Viable Systems, Devon, United Kingdom

Vsevolod I. Astafyev   FARUS, Yakutsk, Russia

Pierre Auger   University of Bourgogne, Dijon, France

Robert W. Blanning   Vanderbilt University, Nashville, Tennessee

James J. Buckley   University of Alabama at Birmingham, Birmingham, Alabama

Mario Bunge   McGill University, Montreal, Quebec, Canada

Marc E. Carvallo   State University of Groningen, Groningen, The Netherlands

R. Felix Geyer   Netherlands Universities' Institute for Coordination of Research in Social Sciences (SISWO), Amsterdam, The Netherlands

Yuri M. Gorsky   Academy of Sciences, Irkutsk, Russia

Takuji Kobori   Kajima Corporation, Tokyo, Japan

Constantine N. Manikopoulos   New Jersey Institute of Technology, Newark, New Jersey

James R. Marsden   University of Kentucky, Lexington, Kentucky

Constantin Virgil Negoita   Hunter College, City University of New York, New York, New York

Markus F. Peschl   University of Vienna, Vienna, Austria

David E. Pingry   University of Arizona, Tucson, Arizona

Dmitri A. Pospelov   Academy of Sciences, Moscow, Russia

Fenton F. Robb   The University of Edinburgh, Edinburgh, Scotland

Ann C. Seror   Laval University, Ste-Foy, Quebec, Canada

Thomas B. Sheridan   Massachusetts Institute of Technology, Cambridge, Massachusetts

Rod Swenson   University of Connecticut, Storrs, Connecticut

Roman Swiniarski   San Diego State University, San Diego, California

Valery F. Venda   University of Manitoba, Winnipeg, Canada

Johannes van der Zouwen   Vrije Universiteit, Amsterdam, The Netherlands

Ernst von Glasersfeld   University of Massachusetts, Amherst, Massachusetts

Yan M. Yufik   Institute of Medical Cybernetics, Inc., Washington, D.C.

Cybernetics
and
Applied
Systems

1
Cybernetics

Ernst von Glasersfeld   University of Massachusetts, Amherst, Massachusetts

DECLARATION OF THE AMERICAN SOCIETY FOR CYBERNETICS

Cybernetics is a way of thinking, not a collection of facts. Thinking involves concepts: forming them and relating them to each other. Some of the concepts that characterize cybernetics have been about for a long time, implicitly or explicitly. Self-regulation and control, autonomy and communication, for example, are certainly not new in ordinary language, but they did not figure as central terms in any science.

Self-regulation was ingeniously implemented in water clocks and self-feeding oil lamps several hundred years B.C. In the scientific study of living organisms, however, the concept was not introduced until the nineteenth century and the work of Claude Bernard. It has a long way to go yet, for in psychology, the dogma of a passive organism that is wholly determined by its environment, or by its genes, is still frequently accepted without question.

It is much the same with the concept of autonomy, which potentates and politicians have been using ever since the days of Sparta; but the structural and functional balance that creates organismic autonomy has only recently begun to be studied (Maturana, Varela). And there is another side to the concept of autonomy: the need to manage with what is available. That this principle governs the construction of human knowledge, and therefore lies at the root of all epistemology, was first suggested at the beginning of the eighteenth century by Vico and then

1

forcefully argued by Kant. The implications of that principle are only today being pursued in some of the sciences.

As for communication, its case is perhaps the most extreme. We are told that the serpent communicated with Adam and Eve shortly after they had been made. Moses communicated with God. And ordinary people have been communicating with one another all along. A "mathematical theory of communication" was born a mere 40 years ago, when cybernetics began (Wiener, Shannon). It was, however, still an observer's theory and said nothing about the requisite history of social interactions from which alone the communicators' meaning could spring.

Cybernetics arose when the notions of self-regulation, autonomy, and hierarchies of organization and functioning inside organisms were analyzed theoretically: that is, logically, mathematically, and conceptually. The results of these analyses have turned out to be applicable in more than one branch of science. Cybernetics, thus, is metadisciplinary (which is different from interdisciplinary) in that it distills and clarifies notions and conceptual patterns that open new pathways of understanding in a great many areas of experience.

The investigation of self-regulation, autonomy, and hierarchical arrangements led to the crystallization of concepts such as circular causality, feedback, equilibrium, adaptation, control, and, most important perhaps, the concepts of function, system, and model. Most of these terms are popular, some have become fashion words, and they crop up in many contexts. But let there be no mistake about it: the mere use of one or two or even all of them must not be taken as evidence of cybernetical thinking. What constitutes cybernetics is the systematic interrelation of the concepts that have been shaped and associated with these terms in an interdisciplinary analysis which, today, is by no means finished.

Whenever something is characterized by the particular interrelation of several elements, it is difficult to describe. Language is necessarily linear. Interrelated complexes are not. Each of the scientists who have initiated, shaped, and nourished this new way of thinking would describe cybernetics differently, and each has defined it on a personal level. Yet they are all profoundly aware that their efforts, their methods, and their goals have led them beyond the bounds of the traditional disciplines in which they started, and that, nevertheless, there is far more overlap in their thinking than individual divergence.

It was Norbert Wiener, a mathematician, engineer, and social philosopher, who adopted the word "cybernetics." Ampère, long before, had suggested it for the science of government, because it derives from the Greek word for steersman. Wiener, instead, defined cybernetics as the science of control and communication in the animal and the machine. For Warren McCulloch, a neuroanatomist, logician, and philosopher, cybernetics was experimental epistemology concerned with the generation of knowledge through communication within an observer and between observer and environment. Stafford Beer, industrial analyst and management consultant, defined cybernetics as the science of effective organization. The anthropologist Gregory Bateson stressed that whereas science had previously dealt with matter and energy, the new science of cybernetics focuses on form and patterns. For the educational theorist Gordon Pask, cybernetics is the art of manipulating defensible metaphors, showing how they may be constructed and what can be inferred as a result of their construction. And we may add that Jean Piaget, late in his life, came to see cybernetics as the endeavor to model the processes of cognitive adaptation in the human mind.

Two major orientations have lived side by side in cybernetics from the beginning. One is concerned with the conception and design of technological developments based on mechanisms of self-regulation by means of feedback and circular causality. Among its results are industrial robots, automatic pilots, all sorts of other automata, and of course computers. Computers, in turn, have led to the development of functional models of more or less intelligent processes. This has created the field of artificial intelligence, a field that today comprises not only systematic studies in problem solving, theorem proving, number theory, and other logicomathematical areas but also sophisticated models of inferential processes, semantic networks, and skills such as chess playing and the interpretation of natural language.

Other results of this essentially practical orientation have been attained in management theory and political science. In both these disciplines cybernetics has elaborated principles that clarify and systematize the relations between the controller and the controlled, the government and the governed, so that today there is a basis of well-defined theories of regulation and control (Ashby, Conant, Powers).

The other orientation has focused on the general human question concerning knowledge and, placing it within the conceptual framework of self-organization, has produced, on the one hand, a comprehensive biology of cognition in living organisms (Maturana, Varela) and, on the other, a theory of knowledge construction that successfully avoids both the absurdities of solipsism and the fatal contradictions of realism (von Foerster, McCulloch, von Glasersfeld).

Any attempt to know how we come to know is obviously self-referential. In traditional philosophy and logic, crude manifestations of self-reference have always been considered to be an anomaly, a paradox, or simply a breach of good form. Yet, in some areas, processes in which a state reproduces itself have been domesticated and formally encapsulated; and they have proven extremely useful (e.g., eigenvalues in recursive function theory, certain topological models derived from Poincaré, condensation rules in logic, and certain options in programming languages for computers, especially for application to nonnumeric computations such as in knowledge engineering and expert systems). The formal management of self-reference was dramatically advanced by Spencer Brown's calculus of indications, in which the act of distinguishing is seen as the foundation of all kinds of relationships that can be described, including the relationships of formal logic.

Recent studies, building on that foundation and extending into various branches of mathematics, have thrown a new light on the phenomenon of self-reference (Varela, Goguen, Kauffman).

The epistemological implications of self-reference have an even wider range of influence in the cybernetical approach to the philosophy of science. Here there is a direct conflict with a tenet of the traditional scientific dogma, namely the belief that scientific descriptions and explanations should, and indeed can, approximate the structure of an "objective" reality, a reality supposed to exist as such, irrespective of any observer. Cybernetics, given its fundamental notions of self-regulation, autonomy, and the informationally closed character of cognitive organisms, encourages an alternative view. According to this view, reality is an interactive conception because observer and observed are a mutually dependent couple. "Objectivity in the traditional sense," as Heinz von Foerster has remarked, "is the delusion that it is not a delusion. It is the cognitive version of the physiological blindspot: we do not see what we do not see. Objectivity is a subject's delusion that observing can be done without him. Invoking objectivity is abrogating responsibility, hence its popularity."

Observer–observed problems have surfaced in the social sciences with the emergence of the notion of "understanding." In anthropology, for example, it has been realized that it is a sterile undertaking to analyze the structure of a foreign culture unless a serious effort is made to understand that culture in terms of the conceptual structures that have created it. Similarly, in the study of foreign or historical literature, the "hermeneutic" approach has been gaining ground. Here, again, the aim is to reconstruct "meaning" in terms of the concepts and the conceptual climate at the time and the place of the author. The emerging attitude in these disciplines, though traditionalists may be reluctant to call it scientific, is in accord with cybernetical thinking.

The most powerful and encouraging corroboration of the cybernetician's disengagement from the dogma of objectivity, however, comes from the "hardest" of the sciences. In physics, the problem of the observer reared its head early in this century. The theories of relativity and quantum mechanics almost immediately raised the question of whether they actually pertained to an objective reality or, rather, to a world determined by observation. For some time the question was not answered definitively. Einstein was hoping that the realist interpretation would eventually lead to a homogeneous view of the universe. Heisenberg and Bohr tended the other way. The most recent in the long series of particle experiments have lessened the chances of realism. Realism in this context was the belief that particles, before anyone observes them, are what they are observed to be. Physics, of course, is not at an end. New models may be conceived, and the notion of an objective, observer-independent reality may once more come to the fore. But at present, the physicists' theories and experiments confirm the cybernetician's view that knowledge must not be taken to be a picture of objective reality but rather as a particular way of organizing experience.

In the few decades since its inception, cybernetics has revolutionized large areas of engineering and technology. Self-regulation has moved from the refrigerator into the cars we drive and the planes we fly in. It has made possible the launching of satellites and explorers of our solar system. It has also saddled us with target-seeking missiles, and it has brought about the computer age with its glories and its dangers. For many of us, however, this explosion of gadgetry is not the most significant feature. The wheel, the harnessing of electricity, the invention of antiseptics and the printing press have all had somewhat similar effects on the mechanics of living. Cybernetics has a far more fundamental potential. Its concepts of self-regulation, autonomy, and interactive adaptation provide, for the first time in the history of Western civilization, a rigorous theoretical basis for the achievement of dynamic equilibrium between human individuals, groups, and societies. Looking at the world today, it would be difficult not to conclude that a way of thinking which, rather than foster competition and conflict, deliberately aims at adaptation and collaboration may be the only way to maintain human life on this planet.

ACKNOWLEDGMENT

The following people have contributed ideas, formulations, and critical suggestions to this document: Stuart Umpleby, Paul Trachtman, Ranulph Glanville, Francisco Varela, Joseph Goguen, Bill Reckmeyer, Heinz von Foerster, Valentin Turchin, and my wife Charlotte. I alone, however, should be held responsible for the shortcomings of this draft.

2
Homeostatics

Vsevolod I. Astafyev   FARUS, Yakutsk, Russia

Yuri M. Gorsky   Academy of Sciences, Irkutsk, Russia

Dmitri A. Pospelov   Academy of Sciences, Moscow, Russia

I. INTRODUCTION

Long before cybernetics appeared, Claude Bernard formulated the concept of homeostasis as the property of living organisms to support some constancy of internal parameters. This concept, developed by W. Cannon, R. Hartly, V. Dillman, and many others, appeared to be very productive for analyzing physiological processes for the needs of medicine. R. Ashby, who described a specific control system (which he called "Homeostat"), capable of maintaining constancy of output parameters under substantial variations of inputs, made a valuable contribution to this concept.

Later on, the notions homeostasis and homeostat came into wide usage in cybernetics, ecology, and sociology. Furthermore, very soon it became obvious that only the unity of homeostasis and variability as the system capability of adaptation and development constitute the conditions necessary for normal functional activity of large-scale systems (including both living organisms and social systems).

Recently, the classical principal circuit diagram of the Ashby's homeostat underwent variations. This was the result of postulation of "the information unit of living matter" as a definite controlling structural element (also homeostat), its principal element (unlike that in Ashby's homeostat) being the controlled internal contradiction [1,2]. Gorsky [3] demonstrated that in the case of homeostatic systems we deal with some seldom-known sides of the law of unity and conflict of

7

opposites. It was demonstrated that controlled internal contradiction between competitive sides is the means of improving the quality of a systems operation and also the means of its ultrastability under superlarge disturbances.

Investigations of living organism homeostats and homeostatic simulation, including the experiments that involved "sticking" homeostats into hierarchical nets (which introduced the possibility of "sticking antagonists into stable systems—the synthesis of "compensatory" homeostats) [2,4], proved the universal character of the approach and allowed us to speak about the expediency of elaborating homeostatics as a branch of cybernetics. Investigations of the mechanisms of maintenance and control of homeostatic variations in diverse-nature systems under internal and external disturbances was accepted as the principal objective of homeostatics.

This chapter discusses some of the major problems of homeostatic control, analyzes some results of simulation of homeostatic control structures, and presents information about applications of homeostatic principles to the problems of technics, medicine, artificial intelligence, and linguistics. The terminology of homeostatics (see ref. 5) is used in the subsequent description.

II. ON HOMEOSTATIC PRINCIPLES OF CONTROL IN LIVING MATTER

It is well known that the basic principle of living activity of all organisms consists of functional interaction of the sets of cells, each one being considered to be the material unit of living matter, and that growth and development of organisms on the cellular level proceed in accordance with universal laws. Even so, we are still unable to understand the fundamental differences between living and nonliving matter. If living cells are constructed of molecules, which are initially nonliving, then how can one explain the substantial difference between living and nonliving matter?

Probably, the answer is to be sought in the mechanisms of control in living matter, which organize the processes of development, operation, restoration, and reproduction, the rhythms and behavior, and also mutual correlation of these processes, thus ensuring the existence of a living system as an interconnected whole in variable environment. All these processes reflect both cooperative and competitive relations between the parts of living matter in an organism on all its levels. Competitive relations are defined by internal contradictions found throughout living matter—in every aspect of an organism in which one can detect relations of antagonists[1] (sympathetic and parasympathetic nervous systems, hormones of op-

---

[1]Antagonism in living matter differs substantially from that in society. In the latter case it entails the conflict initiating the decadence of a social formation. Antagonism in living matter is a mutually oppositive and at the same time intercorrelated effect of two or more stimuli, providing some definite parameters of homeostasis.

posite effect, etc.). But traditional control theory ignored that contradictions may exist and may be used for certain aims in systems controlling objects. It seems that control models admitting contradictions may appear only because our knowledge about the controlled objects is insufficient and that one of the aims of control consists of excluding these models from the final version of the control system.

We demonstrate here that in homeostatic control structures the internal contradiction, which is also controlled, give us the idea of the principal role of contradiction in homeostats. A living organism is a system of interconnected control structures operating in accordance with their functional intention. Gorsky [4] has showed that any organism can be subdivided into four functionally different control systems responsible for (1) development (genetic code: execution of development and dying programs), (2) internal operation (control of cycles and synchronization, protection and renovation, and internal functions), (3) external operation (i.e., behavior), and (4) reproduction. Obviously, homeostatic principles are employed in control systems providing the internal operation.

III. STRUCTURES OF HOMEOSTATS AND THEIR MODELS

A. Homeostatics: Principal Types of Homeostats

When creating cybernetics, Norbert Wiener proceeded from the analogy between control in technical systems and control in living matter, while considering the latter to be "black boxes." The "black box" approach to control problems was rather productive for its time. Since new knowledge concerning optimal homeostatic control structures has appeared, however, it is reasonable to proceed to, say, the "gray box" principle as the next stage in representation of fundamentals of homeostatics.

We have subdivided homeostats into four main types by their intention: (1) homeostats of maintaining constancy of parameters (e.g., blood pressure, body temperature), (2) "pulsing" homeostats of maintaining assigned rhythms (cardiac and respiratory system homeostats), (3) homeostats for control of given development programs, and (4) "compensatory" homeostats [2,4]. All these homeostats have life cycles comprised of the following stages: initial formation ("birth" and self-organization), "childhood," "youth," "maturity," and "dying."

B. Block Diagram and Simulation Model of the Homeostat

As the invariant "information unit of living matter," the organism homeostat is implemented on different material messengers (nervous, endocrine, immune,

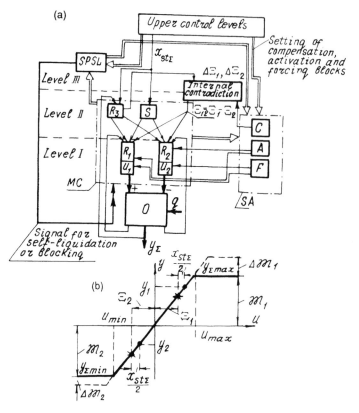

Figure 1 (a) Block diagram of the competitive homeostat of an organism: O, object; MC, main control circuit; SA, system adaptation; SPSL, protection circuit; q, perturbation; other symbols defined in text. (b) Generalized output of the homeostat.

etc.), on different levels (cell, tissue, organ); its characteristic property is the internal contradiction between competitive parts of the system (e.g., in case of two antagonists—Ξ_{12}), which serves as an "emergency reserve" for the compensation of contradictions (Ξ_d) caused by large external perturbations [1–4]. Pospelov [6] postulated a specific principle of the constancy of contradictions $\Xi_{12} + \Xi_d = \text{const}$, which means that to maintain homeostasis under large external perturbations, the internal contradiction Ξ_{12} is decreased exactly by the value of the externally caused contradiction Ξ_d.

The block diagram of an elementary one-parameter homeostat (Fig. 1a) includes three hierarchical levels: the lower level, consisting of two competitive controllers or "actuators" (R_1, R_2), and the second level, the controller "manager"

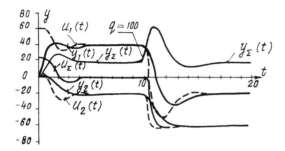

Figure 2 Behavior of the homeostat under large perturbation (jump $q = 110$ at $t = 10$ s).

(R3),[2] which form the main control circuit of the homeostat (MC). The second level also includes the circuit of additional adaptation (SA), which is responsible for the mechanism of activation and stress. The circuit of self-protection and self-annihilation (SPSA) is the top control level [1–5]. In addition, there is the internal contradiction between R_1 and R_2 (Ξ_{12}) (see the MC circuit) forming the "emergency reserve" for the homeostat. Control of this reserve and also correction of jobs for R_1 and R_2 are executed by R_3, to maintain homeostasis $y\Sigma = x_{st}\Sigma$, where $x_{st}\Sigma$ is the input (job) and $y\Sigma$ is the system output. In such a structure it is necessary to take account of material–energetic restrictions for the actuators R_1 and R_2, which in our case are characterized by the top values of the output generalized curve of the homeostat $\mathcal{M}_1$ and $\mathcal{M}_2$ (Fig. 1b). The work points for R_1 and R_2 on this line correspond to $\Xi_1 + x_{st}\Sigma/2$ and $\Xi_2 - x_{st}\Sigma/2$, where $\Xi_1 + \Xi_2 = \Xi_{12}$ is the stored internal contradiction of the homeostat. In the first phase of stress there is a short-term rise of the output top values by $\Delta\mathcal{M}_1$ and $\Delta\mathcal{M}_2$. For the homeostat main circuit we constructed a system of seventh-order ordinary differential equations, which is minimally sufficient for the simulation of main processes in a homeostatic system that includes pathological processes [3,4].[3] Investigations of the model corroborated high degrees of adaptivity, noise immunity, and survivability of such homeostats [2,4].

Figures 2 and 3 present computer oscillograms of transient processes to illustrate some properties of the main homeostat circuit when impulse perturbation is applied to the controlled object (the detected parameters correspond to the nota-

---

[2]In the general case, on account of the nature of the system under consideration, as R_3 we have a controlling structure—for living organisms, in the case of a small human collective either a human-controller (leader) or some accepted behavior rules [6]—which is to regulate relations within the collective.

[3]Computer simulation experiments were executed by O. Popova. The accepted system of equations is minimum sufficient with respect to the control principles employed and sufficient to demonstrate the work of the mechanisms.

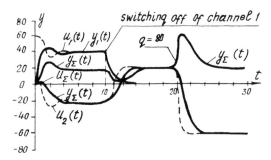

Figure 3   Switching off the first channel at t = 10 s and application of a large perturbation at t = 20 s.

tion in Fig. 1a; the first part of each oscillogram corresponds to the time of stabilization of the regime. At t = 10 seconds, Figure 2 shows some perturbation ultimate with respect to the stability reserve (here q = 110), and homeostasis is quickly restored. In Figure 3, at t = 10 seconds, we see that one of competitive controllers or "actuators" (here R_{10}) is switched out: homeostasis is restored, but survivability decreases—the top value of the perturbation is decreased to q = 80.

Impulse homeostats are generally more complex, since in this case it is necessary to maintain constancy of a few parameters (e.g., frequency, phase, ratio of positive to negative parts of the signal). The block diagram of such a homeostat is given in reference 4, which also analyzes its properties. The impulse homeostat maintains the frequency and phase given by the general generator of rhythms, which in its turn adjusts to the rhythm of the external environment. Hybrid structure is the principal characteristic of this homeostat (generation of periodic signals at the output and control of its parameters—phase, frequency, amplitude—by variation of constant levels). This homeostat type is of particular interest for non-traditional medicine, since it may be assumed that human biofields are controlled by impulse homeostats, and the ability of humans, who possess extra sensory potentials, to increase their biofield could probably be explained as a result of somehow artificially caused resonance of a large number of impulse homeostats.

The problems of adaptivity and noise immunity for all homeostats are of major significance for understanding control mechanisms. Hence, we will comment these in detail.

C.   On Adaptivity of the Homeostat

When the environmental situation changes, a set of adaptation problems is solved in the three homeostat circuits, providing high stability and good quality of control. We choose the following six principal problems.

A_1 Dynamic variation (by R_3) of jobs for R_1 and R_2 to improve the quality of the transient process.

A_2 Dynamic variation (by R_3) of internal contradictions Ξ_1 and Ξ_2 (whereas Ξ_{12} is unchanged within the linear zone); this allows an increase in the quality of the transient process and stability of operation under large perturbations.

A_3 Activation[4] of parameters regulating R_1 and R_2 by block A (Fig. 1a), which ensures the operation of the mechanism of nonspecific adaptation to stress and also of R_1 and R_2 with a low level of activation, when there are no large perturbations.

A_4 Temporary elevation of top control parameter values for R_1 and R_2 by $\Delta \mathcal{M}_1$ and $\Delta \mathcal{M}_2$ with the help of block F; this ensures the operation of the mechanism of nonspecific adaptation.

A_5 Slow decrease of Ξ_{12} for signals of block C to ensure normal operation of R_1 and R_2 in the linear area in the case of decrease of their energetic–material potentials.

A_6^1 Decrease of activation of R_1 and R_2, when there is a threat of their destruction under overload—the form of self-protection at the level of a single homeostat.

A_6^2 Application of the signal to initiate either the process of self-annihilation or the blockage of a homeostat that has become pathological and dangerous from the viewpoint of survival of the whole system (system level protection).

Algorithms of solving these adaptation problems for the homeostat simulation model are easily implemented. At the same time, these mechanisms explain stress mechanisms and mechanisms of organism adaptive resource variation in the coming of age. The two opposite adaptation problems A_6^1 and A_6^2 are of particular interest: overload protection of the homeostat if it operates properly (the aim being to preserve a single homeostat) or application of the signal to annihilate (isolate) a subsystem if its operation is pathological or dangerous for the existence of the whole (self-sacrifice to protect the whole system).

The postulated homeostat structure and its adaptation principles can be of interest for constructing technical control systems. On one hand, homeostatic control can be realized by fairly simple algorithms, and on the other hand, very good parameters of stability and quality of transient processes can be provided. Furthermore, such control structures possess the property of noise immunity with respect to external disturbances. Let us consider this significant property in detail.

---

[4]As activation (e.g., for the proportional-integral control law $F(t) = k\Delta(t) + 1/T \int_0^t \Delta(t)dt$, where $\Delta(t) = y - x$ is the displacement, k is the amplification, T is the integration constant) we consider the increase of $\tau = k/T$. As one knows, when τ is increased (the rest parameters being the same), it is possible to raise the rate of control, but at the same time this will lead to the loss-of-stability boundary.

D. On the Noise Immunity of the Homeostat

Since the outputs of controllers R_1 and R_2 are connected to the same point, the synphase noise $\xi(t)$ applied to their inputs is subtracted at the output. The equality of transfer functions for R_1 and R_2 in the channels, where the noise passes [i.e., $W_{1\xi}(\bar{\bar{p}}) = W_{2\xi}(\bar{\bar{p}})$] is the condition of complete compensation $\xi(t)$.

The ability of homeostats to compensate the noise probably may be considered to be the cause for Nature's evolutionary selection of homeostatic control principles for living matter. It is noteworthy that our analysis of compensatory mechanisms permits an explanation of the necessity for biologically active points (BAPs) on the bodies of animals and human beings.

In accordance with the hypothesis [4,7], BAPs are the aid of matching the channels with respect to the noise, thus ensuring that $W_{1bap}(\bar{\bar{p}})W_{1\xi}(\bar{\bar{p}}) = W_{2bap}(\bar{\bar{p}})W_{2\xi}(\bar{\bar{p}})$. Such a mechanism is necessary, since living systems homeostats are generally asymmetric, and the values of $W_{1\xi}(\bar{\bar{p}})$ and $W_{2\xi}(\bar{\bar{p}})$ can vary in course of their living activity.

Investigation of principles of self-compensation of external noise on homeostatic systems is important in connection with employing similar principles in technical controlling systems and providing a scientific basis for the acupuncture methods in medicine.

E. The Concept of Homeostatic Nets

Homeostats of living organisms are interconnected (in accordance with some principle) into nets, hence forming homeostats of second and higher order [4]. The main relations of interconnection may be interallied, partner, competitive, neutral, and combined relations. In case of pathologies, conflict relations may take place in homeostats.

Homeostatic nets are hierarchical and possess specific properties—for example, the above-mentioned property of "self-sacrifice" to retain homeostasis in case of emergency; the property of adaptation to the environment (the latter, in case of deficiency of resources in the system, could be explained as the passage from competitive to interallied relations in the net). Investigations on the simulation model for fragments of such a net corroborated many of its properties [4], and experimentals carried out on living organisms have demonstrated homeostatic relations between the cardiovascular and respiratory systems [8], and also between the nervous and hormonal control systems and between central and vegetative nervous mechanisms in the digestive secretory system [9].

The above-mentioned property of impulse homeostats (viz., control of impulse signal parameters is executed by varying constant levels of input jobs) makes it possible to include impulse homeostats into the homeostatic net by the same principles used in case of single-parameter homeostats.

F.   Principal Pathologies in Homeostatic Control Structures

Homeostatic structures have their weak points and critical connections. Hence, by breaking direct, inverse, and cross-connections in the simulation model, one can cause effects that could be classified as paralysis, shock, and collapse in the homeostat. Other pathologies (e.g., "the virus effect," "the drug addict effect," "the allergy effect") can be simulated [4]. "The virus effect" is of particular interest because its investigation suggests general laws of degradation working in living, natural, and social systems. Viruses as a source of degradation can have a biological, software, social, or other nature.

On our simulation models [4] we carried out investigations demonstrating the conditions under which a virus is either activated or suppressed in a host homeostat [2,4]. The mechanism of neutralization of the viral effect as a result of its "sticking" to an antibody is also described [2,4], and the possibility that "the allergy effect" is caused by the pathological "sticking" of an antibody to a "host" is noted. Generally speaking, "the allergy effect" can take place also in a society, when the protective forces of a state ("antibodies") begin to suppress the "healthy" members of the society and, thus, destroy normal mechanisms of control in that society.

G.   The Prospects of Employment of Homeostatic Control Structures in Technical Problems

The requirements associated with survivability, adaptivity, and noise immunity of technical systems are becoming more and more rigorous. Known methods of synthesis of hierarchical controlling structures are neither optimal nor sufficiently general. Our preliminary investigations give us some grounds to believe that it will be possible to elaborate methods of optimal synthesis for hierarchical homeostatic structures. Optimality implies here coordination in attaining both global and local goals (homeostasis), as well as ensuring high degrees of stability and synchronism. We are sure that the more technical systems are supplied with technical controlling structures, the more they approach to the capabilities of living organisms in stability, adaptivity, and so on. Nevertheless, some pathologies characteristic of homeostatic control may be found in such systems.

One of practical applications of homeostatic control methods is bound up with our work in progress on the synthesis of a homeostatic system to control the initiation and operational rate in synchronous generators for autonomous energetic objects and for systems of adaptive control of manipulation robots [10].

H. Natural Language Investigations and Homeostatics

Ideas of homeostatics also have been applied in linguistics. In one of the applied works [10], natural language (NL) is considered as a homeostatic (i.e., self-correlated, self-conjugate, multilevel, hierarchical, etc.) system of NL components, relations (properties), characteristics, interconnections, etc.), meanings, senses, and accents. Structural elements that control the sequential order of text synthesis (or analysis), and also those controlling the directed attention of communicants in a dialogue, are identified in NL.

On the basis of postulated concepts of text A constructors and of logical–semantic sentence sequence, a unique system of logic analysis is constructed that employs the ideas of modal logic and nonmonotonous inference. The logic analysis is developed as a cooperative system of conceptual logic and structure–functional logic refined on account of the quantifier nature of NL (phrase and text) constructors.

NL is considered [10] as a multilevel, hierarchical, homeostatic system of structures and functions (logical, semantic, pragmatic, etc.). The first (structural) part includes variables (data) and constructors, the second, respectively, variables (generally, predicates) and control elements (operators, quantifiers). NL text structures from the viewpoint of structural sequential-order logic are considered as hierarchical superpositions of functions. Links between structural and conceptual logic are indicated. The semantic interpretation of some logic relations is given.

Application of a new analytical method elaborated on the basis of this approach (with the enriched version of NL logic) may constitute an important part of semantic analysis and synthesis of NL texts.

IV. HOMEOSTATIC MODELS OF COLLECTIVES

A. On the Models of Self-Organization of Collectives

Wide applications of homeostatics to sociology and psychology are possible. Here we consider one such application concerning models of expedient collective behavior. Investigations of such models were started in late 1950s by the well-known Soviet cybernetist M. L. Tsetlin.

Consider one of the models of expedient collective behavior. Suppose that we have a collective of N members, each member having his own goal of activity Z_i. All the members are active simultaneously in some common (for them) environment W. To achieve their goals Z_i, the members must perform some definite actions D_i, actions of some ith member being the factors that affect somehow the behavior of other members (e.g., breaking one's intention to attain his goal). Furthermore, there is a "host" for whom the environment and the collective operating in this environment is the means to achieve his own goal Z_h.

Consider the following problem. What possible goals could Z_i and Z_h have, and what possible form could interaction between the members of the collective take to ensure that the collective could operate with high stability and that the "host" could achieve its goal Z_h?

It is readily seen that this problem is of the type that necessitates achievement of homeostasis. Interaction of members may be cooperative, competitive, or antagonistic, hence may be interpreted as homeostatic control relations.

In the theory of collective behavior [12] one often considers a problem in which Nature plays the role of the "host." Since we cannot say that Nature has any goal Z_h, for this situation, it is interesting to consider the case in which the members of the collective have no information about existence of one another. This situation may be analyzed as the problem of the possibility of spontaneous self-organization of the collective. Spontaneous self-organization here means that if this property holds, then in a given environment, characteristics of which (a priori unknown for the members) are stationary, operation of this collective is stable. This concept of stability may be refined by generalization of the Nash stability principle known from the theory of games for N persons [13]. The definition of a Nash-stable point may be formulated as follows: if D_i ($i = 1, 2, \ldots, N$) are the actions chosen by the players on a given step of a game, then the point $(D_1, D_2, \ldots, D_N)$ is the Nash point such that there is no reason (no gain) for any player to vary his actions (form of behavior) on account of the failure of other players to vary their actions.

Consequently, the classical Nash point defines a stable state of the collective. This concept could be generalized by introducing the idea of Nash point rank. The Nash point has stability rank k if there is no gain for any k players in varying their actions when the rest of $N - k$ players do not vary their actions.

Other points, wherein the behavior of a collective is stable—for example, the Antos point or the Moore point—are known in the theory of collective behavior [12]. From the viewpoint of homeostatics, techniques of bringing a collective to equilibrium that assume the "host" effect on the members are of special interest. The "common cash principle" formulated by Tsetlin [12] is an example of such an effect. If this principle is realized, the gains of all the players, which they could have at the point $(D_1, D_2, \ldots, D_N)$, are added and divided into equal parts. Investigations of collective behavior show that the "common cash principle" allows one to keep a collective at the points wherein the goals Z_i are not correlated.

In more complex models of collective behavior, the members can form coalitions, compete with one another, and use a definite depth of reflexion and reflexive control [14]. Note that a stable (homeostatic) state for a collective is attained when reflexion ranks in the collective are distributed in a definite way. Other models of bringing a collective to a stable point are also discussed in reference 12.

Investigation of the behavior of such models allows us to explain different aspects of interaction within small human collectives.

B.   On Synthesis of Homeostatic Structures

Let us consider the combinations of relations within an elementary homeostatic control structure represented in the form of a small human collective (Fig. 4a). There are three levels of relations in such a structure: between the actuators and the controlled object (R_1), between the actuators (R_2), and between the leader and the actuators (R_3). On the R_1 level, the following types of relation are possible: interallied, competitive, partner, and neutral (Fig. 4b demonstrates the difference between the output characteristics of the homeostat under competitive and interallied types of actuators and object). On the R_2 level, interallied, partner, neutral, competitive, and conflict relations are possible. On the R_3 level, the relations are neutral, stabilizing with active and passive effects, and destabilizing with active and passive effects.

Consequently, it is possible to construct 100 types of organizing structure of a small collective with different combinations of internal relations. Some of these collectives will be necessarily unstable or insufficiently stable. Hence, likewise in the periodic table of chemical elements, we could construct a table of all possible combinations of organization structures for homeostatic-type small collectives, giving the properties (stability, possibilities of control under definite disturbances) of such structures.

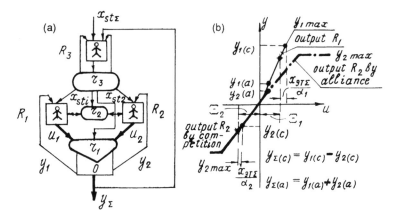

Figure 4   (a) Block diagram of a small team organized on homeostatic principles. (b) The output characteristic of the team under asymmetry of R_1 and R_2 and two types of relation on the level: $y\Sigma_{(c)}$, competition; $y\Sigma_{(a)}$, interallied relations.

Small collectives organized by the homeostatic principle can be "stuck" into hierarchical homeostatic nets. In this case, the collectives must satisfy all the requirements for hierarchical homeostatic nets (the principal restricting factor for operation of both a single person and the whole collective being the restriction due to stress as a result of physiological or psychological overload [3].

V. HOMEOSTATICS AND ARTIFICIAL INTELLIGENCE: SOME INTERCONNECTIONS

Ideas of homeostatics may be useful for progress in artificial intelligence (AI). Let us note some possibilities of application of homeostatics models in AI.

In knowledge bases of intellectual systems, contradictions in the knowledge are inevitable if these systems take information from the environment in the process of operating in it (as in case of intellectual robots). These contradictions can be circumvented only for a trivial environment, for which there is a complete model describing regularities. But in real environments, the knowledge introduced into a system a priori is always incomplete, insufficiently precise, or incorrect.

Resolution of contradictions in knowledge bases is the central problem of knowledge engineering. But present-day statements of this problem do not take account of possibilities of using contradictory information to organize the behavior. Homeostatic models will allow us to overcome this shortcoming. Because knowledge sources have as a goal the distribution of information, contradictory information can be employed to ascertain the true situation. Taking account of this information is characteristic of humans. Employment of this property in artificial systems is very promising. Knowledge in the knowledge base generally forms a hierarchical structure that is in many respects similar to hierarchical homeostatic nets. The tendency to activate the stored structures (the paradigm of active knowledge) makes the homeostatics approach very suitable for enhancing the operation of knowledge bases.

Neural net structures constitute one more area of applications of methods and models of homeostatics. In such nets, the character of interaction between the elements can be either interallied or competitive. The nets can form hierarchical structures, coordinating elements ("hosts") can be distinguished, and so on. If some achievements of homeostatics are employed, the theory of generalized neural nets will no doubt be enriched. The problem of control of a circuit on a neural structure under external perturbations is an example of the successful application of homeostatics ideas.

AI systems problems concerning investigations of behavior (especially those entailing the preservation of some internal comfort in an artificial system) necessitate the use of homeostatic models. This is especially obvious if one considered that technical implementations of some intellectual systems (e.g., robots) are based on the elements whose operation in many cases may be simulated by a homeostat circuit of the form shown in Figure 1.

VI. CONSTRUCTION OF SIMPLE HOMEOSTATS BY "STICKING" TWO ANTAGONISTS

"Sticking" of a "virus" with an "antibody," which leads under some conditions to formation of a neutral (compensatory) homeostat, offers evidence of the expediency of large-scale investigations to determine the conditions of "sticking" various antagonists into stable systems.

Our experiments with simulation modeling have shown that there are different principles of "sticking" two antagonists together, and antagonists themselves can be either autostable or nonautostable. We hope later to formulate the postulates defining the conditions of stability for the compensatory homeostat and to construct a table of all principal combinations of a stable compensatory homeostat.

If one "splits" the compensatory homeostat, the process of progressive violation of stability (degradation) of the decomposed antagonists will go more quickly, the greater is the degree of the internal (stored) contradiction (Ξ_{12}) (other conditions being similar) of the compensatory homeostat. Hence, we may speak about "degradation energy."

Figure 5 demonstrates a computer oscillogram of degradation development for two antagonists in case of decomposition of the compensatory homeostat: curves 1 ($\Xi_{12} = 0$) and 2 ($\Xi_{12} = 10$). We hope that the model of such a homeostat will help to explain the mechanisms of maintaining symmetry and asymmetry, and probably some other properties of matter.

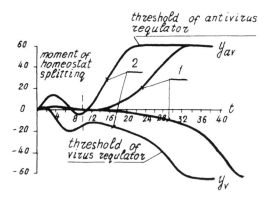

Figure 5   "Splitting" the compensatory homeostat (virus + antivirus) for different job settings: Curve 1, $\Xi_{12} = 0$; Curve 2, $\Xi_{12} = 10$.

VII. CONCLUDING NOTES

Homeostatic control is a specific type of organization of operation of interconnected systems (both living and technical), which for a long time was out of the
realm of specialists in control and cybernetists. We have tried to demonstrate the
significance of homeostatic control, which is characteristic of biological processes. In our opinion, self-organization processes observed also in artificial (technical and social) systems are homeostatic in nature.

These observations give us hope that homeostatics will survive as a direction of
control science employing the principle of contradiction. Present-day homeostatics is ready to solve such problems as identification of homeostatic systems,
operational analysis, and optimal synthesis. Homeostatic systems can provide
high levels of stability, coordination and self-organization.

REFERENCES

1. V. I. Astafyev, Y. M. Gorsky, and D. A. Pospelov, *Comput. Artif. Intell.,* 5(2): 89-102
    (1986).
2. Y. M. Gorsky and O. M. Popova, "Simulation Modelling of Homeostatic Nets," in
    Proceedings of the Second Symposium of Socialist Countries on Simulation Systems,
    Ostrava, Czechoslovakia, pp. 197-201, 1989.
3. Y. M. Gorsky, *System-Informational Analysis of Control Processes* (in Russian),
    Nauka, Novosibirsk, 1988 (326 pp.).
4. Y. M. Gorsky, "Homeostatics: Models, Properties, Pathologies," in *Homeostatics of
    Living, Technical, Social and Ecological Systems* (in Russian), Nauka, Novosibirsk,
    1990, pp. 37-82.
5. Y. M. Gorsky and N. I. Kulish, "A Draft Glossary of Homeostatic Terms," in
    Homeostatics of Living, Technical, Social, and Ecological Systems (in Russian),
    Nauka, Novosibirsk, pp. 343-368, 1990.
6. D. A. Pospelov, "Normative Behavior Models for Robots," in *Systems for Processing
    Knowledge and Images,* Vol. 2, Smolenitsy, Czechoslovakia, pp. 43-49, 1986.
7. A. M. Stepanov, Y. M. Gorsky, and V. V. Maslennikov, "Homeostatic Mechanisms
    and Frequency Characteristics of Acustatic Terms," in *Homeostatics of Living, Tech-
    nical, Social and Ecological Systems* (in Russian), Nauka, Novosibirsk, pp. 121-145,
    1990.
8. N. I. Moisseyeva, "Mechanisms of Homeostatic Regulation in Living Systems," in
    Homeostatics of Living, Technical, Social and Ecological Systems (in Russian),
    Nauka, Novosibirsk, pp. 99-120, 1990.
9. M. Y. Chernyshov, "The system of Homeostatic Control Mechanisms of Main Diges-
    tive Glands," in *Homeostatics of Living, Technical, Social and Ecological Systems* (in
    Russian), Nauka, Novosibirsk, pp. 371-389, 1990.
10. L. N. Volkov, "Robot Manipulators and Controlled Mechanisms: Homeostatic Ap-
    proach," in *Homeostatics of Living, Technical, Social and Ecological Systems* (in
    Russian), Nauka, Novosibirsk, pp. 223-235, 1990.

11. M. Y. Chernyshov, "A Tool for Linguistic Analysis and Synthesis," in *Homeostatics of Living and Technical Systems* (in Russian), Med. Publ., Irkutsk, pp. 61–66, 1990.
12. V. I. Varshavsky and D. A. Pospelov, *Puppets Without Strings. Reflection of the Evolution and Control of Some Man-Made Systems*, Mir, Moscow, 1984.
13. J. F. Nash, *Proc. Natl. Acad. Sci. USA, 36*: 48–49 (1950).
14. V. A. Lefebvre, *Algebra of Conscience*, Reidel, Dordrecht, 1982.

3
Systems Everywhere

Mario Bunge   McGill University, Montreal, Quebec, Canada

I. INTRODUCTION

Everything is a system or a component of a system. This principle is as true of concrete things as of ideas. It holds for atoms, people, societies and their components, and the things they compose. And it holds for ideas too: there are no stray ideas, whether in ordinary knowledge, science, technology, mathematics, or the humanities. It is hard to understand how an idea could be grasped, worked out, or applied except in relation to other ideas. As for concrete things, they too are interconnected in various ways. Only the universe as a whole is not connected to anything else—but it is a system rather than a mere aggregate. Indeed, any component of the universe interacts with at least one other component, whether directly (as in face-to-face social interactions) or indirectly (e.g., via physical fields).

The idea that everything is a system or a part of one is distinctive of the *systemic approach.* This is an alternative to both individualism (or atomism) and holism. The former sees the trees but not the forest, whereas the latter sees the forest but misses the trees. In contrast, the systemic approach facilitates our seeing both the trees (and their components) and the forest (and its larger environment). What holds for trees and forests applies, *mutatis mutandis*, to everything else as well.

The systemic approach was adopted only occasionally before our time, and when this occurred, it was tacitly rather than explicitly. For example, astronomers did not talk about the solar *system* before the seventeenth century; the cardiovascular *system* was not recognized as such before William Harvey, nearly four centuries ago; and talk about the nervous, endocrine, immune, and other *systems* is even more recent. Most of us have specialized to such an extent that we often find it unnecessary to admit that we handle systems, and bothersome to analyze them in any detail, or we are too near-sighted or lazy to place them in their larger contexts. In other words, most of us fail to take advantage of the systemic approach.

However, the explicit systemic approach is quickly gaining ground. It is becoming ever clearer that most of the items we deal with are systems and therefore many-sided and, as such, beyond the competence of narrow specialists. We are slowly learning that the best expert is the multidisciplinarian: we no longer feel contempt for the jack of all trades—unless of course he is an amateur in all. We are also learning that black box models, however handy, are shallow: that, if we wish to understand how a system works, or if we wish to improve on its design, or repair it, we must open it up and exhibit its composition and structure, and must identify the environment with which it interacts.

II. CONCEPTUAL SYSTEMS AND CONCRETE SYSTEMS

Modern mathematics is of course the systemic science par excellence. The contemporary mathematician does not handle stray items but systems or system components. For example, one speaks of the real number *system*, and of the Euclidean and Cartesian planes, as well as of Boolean algebras and Hilbert spaces, as *systems*. In all these cases what turns an aggregate or set into a system is a structure, that is, a set of relations among, or operations on, system components. (Mathematical systems are sometimes called "structures," but this is a misnomer, because structures are properties, and every property is the property of something. For example, a set has the group property if its elements are organized by the operations of concatenation and inversion.)

Actually mathematicians tackle systems of two kinds: mathematical objects proper, such as rings, topological spaces, and manifolds, and theories about such objects. A theory is of course a hypotheticodeductive system, a system composed by formulas linked by the implication relation. But a theory may also be viewed as a mathematical object—the object of a metatheory, such as the algebra of logic. Finally, the whole of contemporary mathematics may be regarded as a system composed of theories, every one of which refers to mathematical systems of some kind. All this is well known by mathematicians. Those of us who use mathematics and admire its rigor and deductive power (which derives from its systemicity) can learn from it how to organize our own nonmathematical research fields.

In what follows we shall consider only concrete systems (i.e., complex changeable things): we shall not deal with conceptual systems such as theories. We define a *concrete* system as a composite thing such that every one of its components is changeable and acts on, or is acted on by, other components of itself.

(Incidentally, the popular definition of a system as a set is mistaken because sets are concepts, not concrete things. Sets are immutable, i.e., they have fixed memberships and fixed relations if at all, whereas every concrete thing is in a state of flux. Not even mathematical systems are sets: at most some of them are structured sets. Others, namely categories, are complex systems not reducible to sets. Rather, on the contrary, set theory is reducible to category theory.)

In addition to being changeable, every concrete system—except for the universe as a whole—interacts with its environment. However, such system-environment interactions are weaker than the intercomponent interactions. If this condition were unrealistic, there would be no system other than the universe, which would be a single block.

Let us proceed to give a somewhat more precise characterization of the notion of a concrete system.

III. THE CES MODEL OF A CONCRETE SYSTEM

Consider a system s at a given instant t. Call $C(s,t)$ the set of all the parts, or *composition*, of s at t. Next, call $E(s,t)$ the *environment* of s at t, that is, the set of things, other than the components of s, with which s interacts. Because the system components act on one another, s has an *endostructure*, which is the set of all the relations—in particular the bonds or links—among the said components. (A bond or link between two things is defined as a relation that makes a difference to them. Chemical bonds and economic relations are bonds, whereas spatiotemporal relations are not.) And, because the system is embedded in its environment, it also interacts with some environmental items and so has an *exostructure*. This is the set of all the relations—in the particular bonds or links—among the system's components and things in its environment. (Obviously, the inputs and outputs of a system are included in its external structure.) $S(s,t)$ deserves then to be called the *total structure* of s at t.

We now have all the ingredients we need to build the simplest of all the realistic models of a concrete system. This, to be called the *CES model*, is the ordered triple of the three sets defined previously, that is:

$$M(s,t) = \langle\ C(s,t),\ E(s,t),\ S(s,t)\ \rangle$$

The input–output or black box models are special cases of the *CES* model. Indeed, the box with input and output terminals is a *CES* model in which $C(s,t)$ is a singleton, $E(s,t)$ is poorly specified, and $S(s,t)$ is the set of inputs and outputs.

Simple as it is, a *CES* model is unwieldy in practice for requiring the knowledge of all the parts of the system and of all their interactions, as well as their links with the rest of the world. In practice we use the notions of composition, environment, and structure *at a given level*. For example, we speak of the atomic composition of a molecule, or the cellular composition of an organ, or the individual composition of a society. Except in particle physics, we never handle the ultimate components of anything. And even in particle physics one usually neglects a number of interactions, particularly with environmental items.

More precisely, instead of taking the set $C(s,t)$ of all the parts of s at t, in practice we only take the set $C_a(s,t)$ of parts of kind a, that is, we form the intersection $C(s,t) \bigcap a = C_a(s,t)$. We proceed similarly with the other two coordinates of the triple $M(s,t)$; that is, we take $E_b(s,t)$, or the environment of s at t at level b, and $S_c(s,t)$ or the structure of s at t at level c. In short, we form what may be called the *reduced CES model*:

$$M_{abc}(s,t) = \langle \, C_a(s,t), \; E_b(s,t), \; S_c(s,t) \, \rangle$$

For example, when forming a model of a social system we usually take it to be composed of whole persons; consequently we limit the internal structure of the system to interpersonal relations. However, nothing prevents us from constructing a whole sheaf of models of the same society, by changing the meanings of "a," "b," and "c." We do this when we take certain subsystems of the given social system (e.g., families or formal organizations) to be our units of analysis. Similar sheaves of models can be constructed, of course, in all fields of knowledge.

In the light of the above, systemism is seen to subsume four general but one-sided approaches.

1. *Holism*, which tackles systems as wholes and refuses both to analyze them and to explain the formation and breakdown of totalities in terms of their components and the interactions among them; this approach is characteristic of the layperson and of philosophical intuitionism and irrationalism, as well as of the Gestalt school and of much that passes for "systems philosophy."

2. *Individualism*, which focuses on the composition of systems and refuses to admit any supraindividual entities or properties thereof; this approach is often proposed as a reaction against the excesses of holism, particularly in the social sciences and in moral philosophy.

3. *Environmentalism*, which emphasizes external factors to the point of overlooking the composition and internal structure of the system; this is the view of behaviorism.

4. *Structuralism*, which treats structures as if they preexisted things or even as if things were structures; this is a characteristically idealistic view.

Each of these views holds a grain of truth. The systemic approach puts them together and thus steers us to richer truths.

IV. THE STATE SPACE REPRESENTATION

If a quantitative model of a system is needed, it may be built in various ways. One of them is to set up a system of differential equations, one for each basic property of the system. A more powerful method is to start from a single variational principle involving those same variables and entailing the corresponding differential equations. A third method is even more general than the preceding ones, though it combines naturally with either of them: this is the state space approach. This representation was born with thermodynamics and statistical mechanics and is used in all advanced sciences and technologies. Only rather recently, however, have its power and generality been explicitly recognized.

The gist of the state (or phase) space approach is this. One starts by identifying all the n relevant properties of a system, representing each one by a function, for example, a real valued, time-dependent function. (Time is not one of them because it is not a property of a thing.) Every one of these functions is called a *state variable*. (This is only a special case. In other cases, particularly in the quantum theory, some properties are represented by operators and others by elements of an algebra. Moreover, in this case the state function Ψ has a single component and it is the source of other state variables.) Then one collects all such functions into an n-tuple, the *state function* of the system. This function spans an n-dimensional abstract space.

The next step is to study the changes of the state function over space and time. The outcome will be a system of equations representing the laws of the system. (If the equations are differential, the conceptual system they constitute is usually called a *dynamical system*. This is a somewhat unfortunate name because it obscures the difference between a real system and its mathematical model. Only real systems have dynamics.)

The equations satisfied by the state variables constrain the possible values of the state function to a certain space that shall be called the *lawful state space* of the system. This space may be pictured as an n-dimensional box in the space formed by the ranges of the n state variables. This box characterizes the entire class of systems under consideration. However, the box will shrink every time extra conditions, such as constraints or boundary conditions, are imposed.

Every point (or possibly region) inside the box represents a *really possible (i.e., lawful) state* of the system; the points outside the box are only *logically* possible states of the system. (These physically impossible states are of interest only to those who indulge in the philosophical pastimes called "possible worlds metaphysics" and "possible worlds semantics.")

As time goes by—pardon the metaphor—the system, being concrete, changes in some respect. (Only conceptual objects do not change by themselves.) Correspondingly the point (or region) representing the instantaneous state of the system describes a trajectory in the state space or, rather, in the lawful subspace of it. This trajectory, over a certain period of time, represents the *history* of the system over that period. If the model is sufficiently true, it will represent the changes in the composition, environment, and structure of the system over the given period. (Recall Section III.)

The state space method, like the CES model discussed earlier, can be used everywhere, from physics to sociology to the humanities. This does not mean that either will spare us a detailed investigation of the system of interest. The systemic approach is no substitute for research: it is a heuristic tool. It is not a ready-to-wear theory fitting all, but an enlightening approach or framework useful for *posing problems* concerning concrete systems of all kinds. Thus, provided the systemic approach be taken together with specific biological assumptions, it will guide us in modeling biosystems. Likewise the construction of theoretical models of sociosystems may be facilitated by adopting the systemic approach—but of course it will yield nothing specific unless enriched with specific sociological assumptions. This had to be said in view of the many attempts to solve specific problems with the sole help of a general systems theory. Such attempts clog the "general systems theory" literature and give the systemic approach a bad name.

What the systemic approach does in every case is to remind us that any adequate model of a concrete system must take into account its composition, environment, and structure. This may sound trivial but actually it is not. Consider, for instance, the problem of modeling an economy or a subsystem of an economy, such as a business firm. What are its components: people, capital goods, raw materials, capital, or all four and perhaps more? What is the environment of the economic system: nature, a social group, or perhaps the entire world? And what constitutes its structure: the relations of production, the trade relations, the links with governmental departments, or all three? The model and its adequacy will depend critically on the choice of variables as well as on the conjectured relations among them. Moreover we can predict that, since the economy is just one of the subsystems of any society, any model that ignores the links between the economy and the other subsystems of the society, in particular its polity, is bound to fail. Beware then the purely economic models of the economy: being largely false, they are likely to have disastrous practical consequences—consequences of ignoring the systemic approach and adopting some sectoral approach instead.

Let us now take a quick look at a handful of applications of the systemic approach in five different fields of scientific inquiry.

A. The Systemic Approach to Chemical Reactions

Consider, to begin with, the concept of a chemical system. A system of this kind may be characterized as a system whose components are chemicals (atoms or molecules) varying in numbers (or in concentrations) for being engaged in reactions with one another. Hence before the reactions set in, and after they are completed, the system is physical, not chemical. For example, a battery is a chemical system only while it is operating.

The state of a chemosystem at each instant and each point in space may be represented by a state function $F = \langle F_1, F_2, \ldots, F_n \rangle$. Whereas some components of this n-tuple represent the composition of the system, the others represent its remaining properties, such as pressure, temperature, and entropy. Since all changes in composition are caused by interactions among the components, or among the latter and the environment, the model incorporates not only the composition of the system but also its environment and structure: it is then a specification of our elementary CES model. If the causes of the chemical reactions are either ignored or held constant, we may focus on the part of the list F that represents the composition of the system at an arbitrary instant. Let us suppose that the first m coordinates of F do this job and call $F_c = \langle F_1, F_2, \ldots, F_m \rangle$ the *composition state function* of the system.

For example, the composition state function of a system in which water is formed out of hydrogen and oxygen according to the reaction "$2H_2 + O_2 \rightarrow 2H_2O$" is $F_c = \langle C_{H_2}, C_{O_2}, C_{H_2O} \rangle$, *where the C's* are the relative instantaneous concentrations. The initial and final values of F_c are

$$F_c(t_i) = \langle 2, 1, 0 \rangle \qquad \text{and} \qquad F_c(t_f) = \langle 0, 0, 2 \rangle .$$

Therefore the overall reaction can be represented as the net change

$$r = F_c(t_i) - F_c(t_f)$$

The converse reaction, of dissociation of water, is of course representable by

$$-r = F_c(t_f) - F_c(t_i)$$

Hence $r - r = \langle 0, 0, 0 \rangle = \mathbf{0}$, or the null reaction—a useful fiction, as we shall see in a moment.

In general, the positive components of r represent the reactants, while its negative components represent the reaction products. Furthermore, reactions and their conceptual counterparts can be added to form further reactions. Thus, let the m-tuples

$$r_1 = \langle a_1, b_1, \ldots, m_1 \rangle \qquad \text{and} \qquad r_2 = \langle a_2, b_2, \ldots, m_2 \rangle$$

represent each one reaction in a given chemical system. (Caution: some of the coordinates of r_1 and r_2 may be null.) Then the sum of the two reactions is the third reaction represented by

$$r_3 = \langle a_1 + a_2, b_1 + b_2, \ldots, m_1 + m_2 \rangle$$

Since in principle every reaction has an inverse, any two reactions in a chemical system can add up to form a third reaction, and the null reaction adds to any reaction, leaving it unaltered, we have Aris's theorem: "Let R be the set of all chemical reactions that may occur in a given chemical system, + the binary operation of reaction addition, – the unary operation of reaction inversion, and $\mathbf{0}$ the null reaction. The structure $\mathbf{R} = \langle R, +, -, \mathbf{0} \rangle$ is a group." Simpler: the set of reactions in a chemical system has the algebraic group structure. This theorem is part of the algebra of chemical reactions—which, though important, has yet to find its way into textbooks.

There are of course alternative ways of representing chemical systems and reactions, but the systemic model has certain advantages. For one thing some of the alternative models isolate the reactions from the total system in which they occur; in our model, on the other hand, the system and its environment are present all the time, because the basic concept is that of state function of the system.

So much for chemosystems. Let us move on to biosystems.

B. The Systemic Approach to Life

A perennial problem in biology and its philosophy has been the general characterization of its objects, that is, the definition of the concept of life. The systems approach should help here if only because it avoids the extremes of mechanism (and the attendant radical reductionism) and vitalism (a variety of holism often coupled with spiritualism), as well as machinism, or the artificial life fad. The mechanist mistakes the living cell for its composition; the vitalist overlooks the latter as well as the structure and the environment, and focuses instead on the emergent (supraphysical) properties of organisms; and the machinist ignores the composition and remains content with computer mockups of morphological features. All three perversions are avoided by granting that the components of a cell are not alive and asserting that they are organized in peculiar ways unknown to physics, chemistry, and computer science.

There are two traditional approaches to the definition of the concept of life. One is to postulate a single peculiar entity contained in every organism (e.g., the ancient immaterial entelechy); the second is to postulate a single peculiar property (e.g., the equally ancient purposefulness or teleology, nowadays rechristened "teleonomy"). Neither of these strategies has worked: entelechies are inscrutable, and only highly evolved organisms behave (sometimes) in a purposive way. We must look for an alternative. The systemic approach suggests one.

From a systemic point of view, an organism is an extremely complex system characterized by the conjunction of properties, every one of which can be possessed by some nonliving system. These properties of a biosystem are as follows:

1. It is composed of chemical and biochemical (hence metabolizing) subsystems, such as nucleic acids.
2. It incorporates some of the molecules it synthesizes (rather than releasing them immediately to its environment).
3. Its possible activities include the rearrangement, self-assembly, and dismantling of components; the replacement of nonfunctional components and the removal or neutralization of some chemicals; and the capture and storage of free energy (in ATP molecules, glycogen, and fat) for future consumption.

4. It can adjust to some environmental changes without jeopardizing its continued existence.
5. It is a component of some supersystem or else of some population of systems of the same kind.
6. Some of its subsystems are capable of reproducing parts of the whole system.
7. Some of its subsystems control some of the processes occurring in it, in such a way that a fairly constant inner environment is maintained in the system.
8. All the control systems in it are interconnected by signals (diffusion of chemicals, propagating chemical reactions, electrical signals, etc.) and so constitute a signals ("information") network.
9. One of its control systems, namely its genome, is composed of nucleic acid molecules, is unique to it, and controls its development and eventual reproduction.
10. Its descendants, if any, belong in the same species but may possess some traits of their own (by mutation or gene recombination).
11. It competes in some respects with other systems of the same species, as well as of other species, and cooperates with the same or others in further respects.
12. It descends proximately or remotely from biochemical systems devoid of some of the properties listed above, and its nucleic acid molecules keep traces (hence some record) of its ancestry.
13. It lasts for a limited time lapse.

According to this definition, chromosomes are not alive because they do not metabolize or reproduce. Likewise viruses are not alive because they do not function at all outside some host cell. (Only the host-virus system is alive though, alas, often sick.) Nor do robots, however sophisticated, qualify as biosystems, if only because they are made of mechanical and electrical components instead of biochemical ones, and because, far from having evolved spontaneously from lower level things, they have been designed and assembled by people.

C. The Systemic Approach to the Concepts of Species and Function

Our definition of the concept of a biosystem will help us give a precise definition of a much-discussed concept: that of a biospecies. We stipulate that a species of concrete things is a *biospecies* if, and only if (1) it is a natural kind (rather than either an arbitrary collection or a mathematical set), (2) all its members are organisms (present, past, or future), and (3) its members descend mediately from members of some other natural kind (biotic or prebiotic).

According to the preceding definition, a biospecies is not a thing but a collection of things; hence it is a concept, though of course not an idle one but one of the key blocks in any construction purporting to represent life. However, today many taxonomists prefer an alternative concept: they claim that a species is a concrete system extended over space and time. This view is mistaken for a number of reasons. First, the populations of many species are geographically dispersed, so that, although every one of them is a system, their totality is not. Second, the concept of a biospecies is necessary to build those of (monospecific) population and (polyspecific) community and ecosystem. Third, if one refuses to employ the concept of a class at the species level, it must be introduced at the next higher taxonomic level—otherwise it will be impossible to do systematics. One would presumably define a genus as a set of biosystems construed as systems. But then no individual organism would belong to any genus, for the members of a genus are species, not individuals. In particular, no person would be a member of the genus *Homo* and, a fortiori, no person would be a primate, a mammal, a vertebrate, or even an animal. To understand this, one needs to understand only that the part-whole, set membership, and set inclusion relations are different. Regrettably these elementary distinctions are not usually taught to biology students.

A consequence of the species muddle is that not all biologists are sure which are the so-called units of evolution: that is, they do not know exactly what it is that evolves. They know of course that individuals develop but do not evolve. Most of them believe that species evolve. But, although species are natural groupings, they cannot evolve by mutation and natural selection because they are concepts, not things. From a systemic viewpoint it is obvious that the units of evolution are biopopulations: these are systems, unlike species, and moreover they occupy the lowest supraindividual biolevel. However, if we remember that every biopopulation interacts with biopopulations of organisms belonging to different species, we realize that higher level systems, such as ecosystem and even the entire biosphere, evolve as well. This claim will become clearer upon elucidating the concepts involved in it.

We stipulate that a system is (1) a *biopopulation* if it is composed of individuals of the same biospecies, (2) an *ecosystem* if it is composed of several interacting populations of organisms belonging to different species, and (3) a *biosphere* if it is the smallest of all the supersystems containing all the biosystems in a given planet.

Another issue that can be clarified in the light of the systemic approach is that of biofunctions, often mistaken for purposes or goals—as, for example, when people say that the hand was "made" for the "purpose" of grasping. This is of course the core of teleology, or teleonomy as it is prudishly called nowadays. Thus, instead of saying that organ X *does* Y, or that X discharges the *function(s)* Y, many people, even some eminent evolutionary biologists, will say that Y is the *purpose* or *goal* of X. I submit that, although the notions or purpose and goal are indispensable in psychology and social science, biology can get along without them—nay, should get rid of them, for they are nothing but remnants of anthropomorphism and vitalism. I suggest moreover that the notions of purpose and goal be replaced, in biology and other disciplines, by that of specific function, which can be given the following exact definition.

Let b be an organism, and $a < b$ a subsystem of b, of kind $[a]$. Further, call $P(a, T)$ the totality of processes or activities involving subsystem a during period T. We stipulate that the *specific biological functions* of a during T are those functions performed by a and its likes (i.e., the other members of the equivalence class $[a]$), but not any other subsystems of b, during T. In obvious symbols,

$$Ps(a, T) = P(a, T) - \bigcup P(x, T), \qquad \text{with } a \neq x, x < b, x \notin [a]$$

In turn, the concept of a process occurring in a thing a is defined as the set of states of a during the period T of interest:

$$P(a, T) = \left\{ F_a(t) | t \in T \text{ and } \frac{dF_a}{dt} = 0 \text{ except at some points} \right\}$$

This definition turns out to be of particular importance in the science and philosophy of mind, to which we now turn.

D. The Systemic Approach to Brain and Mind

In psychology, as in every other scientific field, one should begin by identifying the object(s) of study or referents. If one were to believe the mainstream philosophical tradition, the object of study of psychology is the immaterial soul, spirit, or mind. In its most recent version, spiritualism holds the mind to be a collection of computerlike programs. Being immaterial, the mind could not be studied the way material things, such as brains, are investigated both experimentally and theoretically. Hence the science and philosophy of mind would have nothing to learn from brain research or from physiological and social psychology. By the same token it would be incapable of building and testing mathematical models of the kind that have been so successful in science. Consequently there would be a chasm between the study of mind and science.

Whoever takes seriously the recent findings of neurophysiology and biological psychology, as well as the systemic approach, will reject the foregoing view without necessarily rejecting the hypothesis that mental functions have special properties that set them apart from all other bodily functions. If we choose the scientific approach to mind, we shall single out the brain as our main (though not sole) system and shall endeavor to understand its specific properties and functions.

We already know some of these peculiar properties and functions. One is the unusual level of spontaneous activity of neurons. Another is lateral inhibition (which accompanies every excitation). A third specific property is the plasticity (as opposed to elasticity) of certain neurons, or rather interneuronal junctions. A fourth is the grouping of neurons into systems, such as minicolumns, columns, and larger systems, that have (emergent) properties of their own, act as wholes in certain respects, and often self-assemble in the course of individual development. A fifth is the functional differentiation and relative independence of some subsystems of the brain, which accounts for the parallel "processing" of, say, the shape, color, and motion of a visual stimulus.

The first two properties, spontaneity and lateral inhibition, suffice to relegate stimulus–response psychology to the dustbin of history. The third and fourth—plasticity and self-assembly—suggest building mathematical models of plastic neuronal systems. These systems are composed of neurons whose mutual (synaptic) connections can change in a lasting way. They are found in the phylogenetically more recent parts of the brain, and they are thought to be in charge of mental functions. In other words, the mind would be the collection of specific functions of the plastic regions of the brain. The animals lacking such plastic neural systems (i.e., those having rigid, or "wired-in," neural circuits, or no neuronal systems at all) would have no mental life. The fifth property, the comparative autonomy of certain subsystems of the brain, would explain why the loss of one subsystem impairs or erases some mental abilities but not others.

The key to the understanding of mind is neural plasticity, that is, the ability of interneuronal junctions to change and to retain such changes for a while, short or long. If the connectivity (or structure) of a neuronal system can change, then the system can acquire and lose certain functions in the course of its life; that is, it can learn and unlearn, it can perceive or conceive new items, and sometimes it can create wholly new ideas. On the other hand, a muscle, such as the heart, can only contract or relax from beginning to end. Likewise other organs, such as the lungs and the kidneys, have fixed specific functions. Only the brains of highly evolved animals can acquire new functions as they develop. Moreover, the acquisition of radically new abilities is assumed to be identical with the formation of new neural systems. People reconstruct ("rewire") their own brains as they learn and unlearn, and individuals with different experiences and different professions develop correspondingly different brains. This is of course speculation, but one worth being put to the test.

We hypothesize that an animal endowed with a nervous system undergoes a *mental process* (or performs a mental function) only if and while that system has a plastic subsystem engaged in a specific process. We call a *psychon* of kind K the smallest plastic neuronal system capable of discharging a mental function of kind K. Every state or stage in a mental process—or, equivalently, every state of a psychon or of a system of psychons—is called a *mental state* of the animal. For example, the formation of purposes and plans appears to be a specific activity of psychons in the frontal lobes. On the other hand, pain, hunger, thirst, fear, rage, sexual urge, and the control of circadian rhythms seem to be processes in subcortical neural systems, such as the hypothalamus, and the limbic system, which have little or no plasticity. (Yet, because these phylogenetically older systems are "wired" to the cognitive "centers," they can be influenced by them: there are neither purely cognitive nor purely affective processes. This is why, among other reasons, it is wrong to detach cognitive psychology from the rest of the science of mind and behavior.)

In sum, we can now propose an exact (though admittedly controversial) definition of the tricky concept of mind. We stipulate that the *mind* of an animal *b* during a period *T* is the union of all the specific functions (processes) occurring in the plastic part *p* of its nervous system. In obvious symbols,

$$M(b,T) = \cup_{x<p} P_s(x,T)$$

So far we have concentrated on the brain. Now it is time to recall that, far from being fully autonomous, the brain is intimately connected with the endocrine and the immune systems, not to speak of the muscles and the viscera. Therefore there are hardly any purely nervous processes. Hence an adequate understanding of mental functions and treatment of mental dysfunctions can be attained only by studying the neuroendocrinoimmune supersystem. In particular, the so-called psychosomatic phenomena, like blushing, premenstrual stress, and psychosomatic eczemas and ulcers, only began to be understood when psychoneuroendocrinoimmunology was born a few decades ago. Which is one more point for the systemic approach.

E. The Systemic Approach to Social Facts

Our last application of the systemic approach will bear on human society. Every structured human group, from the married couple to the world system, ought to be conceived of as a system composed of human beings and their artifacts, living in a partly natural and partly artificial environment, and held together by bonds of various kinds: biological (in particular psychological), economic, cultural, and political. (Such bonds coexist with competitive relations.)

No matter how primitive, every human society can be analyzed into four tightly interrelated subsystems: the biological system, characterized by kinship relations; the cultural system, revolving around cultural activities and relations, such as exchanging information; the economic system, centered on productive work and trade; and the political system, characterized by management and power links.

This systemic view of human society has a number of interesting consequences. First, the variety of types of interpersonal bond, and of the resulting subsystems, suffices to refute one-sided views of human society such as biologism (e.g., sociobiology), psychologism (e.g., symbolic interactionism), culturalism (or cultural idealism), economic determinism (e.g., Marxism), and political determinism. To be sure, the ultimate components of human society are organisms who have mental functions, hence both needs and wants. But society itself is a supra-organic and nonpsychological entity: it is not alive and it does not feel, perceive, think, or plan. Moreover, society has emergent (systemic or nondistributive) properties foreign to biology and psychology, such as division of labor, distribution of wealth, type of political regime, and level of cultural development. This does not entail that societies are spiritual entities and therefore objects of study of the so-called sciences of the spirit (*Geisteswissenschaften*). Societies and their subsystems are concrete or material systems for being composed by material entities; only, they are characterized by social properties and regularities. But, of course, these systemic properties and patterns are rooted in properties of individuals. For example, social plasticity may be traced back to behavioral plasticity, which in turn derives from neural plasticity. But, although individual actions have internal sources, they are conditioned by the natural and social environments. Such micro-macro links are beyond the reach of both individualism and holism.

Second, since the biological, cultural, economic, and political subsystems of a society are components of one and the same system, they are interconnected. An important methodological consequence of this platitude is that no subsystem can be adequately modeled unless the model contains some of the "exogenous" variables characterizing the remaining subsystems. For example, a realistic model of the political system will have to contain more than politological variables such as the level of popular participation in politics and the intensity of political repression. The model will also have to contain biological variables such as total population, age distribution, and birth and death rates; cultural variables, such as literacy and access to mass media; and economic variables, such as gross domestic product and its distribution among the various social classes.

Third, because every society has biological, cultural, economic, and political subsystems, it cannot possibly develop unless all four subsystems develop hand in hand. In particular, the purely biological (or cultural or economic or political) models of development are bound to fail. By the same token, the purely economic (or biological or cultural or political) development or aid programs are bound to miscarry. The sound development of a society, like that of an organism, is integral, not partial. Regrettably most development experts still adopt a sectoral approach: they still have to learn that systems must be tackled in a systemic way.

V. INDIVIDUAL–SYSTEM OR MICRO–MACRO RELATIONS

When adopting the individualist approach, the student of society starts by studying individuals—their preferences, choices, and actions. He hopes that, by some aggregation trick, he will succeed in explaining social facts or social systems, or even in explaining them away as mere constructs. In short, the individualist strategy is of the *bottom-up* type: the components are supposed to generate the system. In the holistic (or structuralist) perspective, one starts with social systems in the hope of accounting for individual behavior as an effect of social forces. The holistic strategy is of the *top–down* type: the system is supposed to determine its own composition.

But individualism and holism are philosophies no social scientist can live by. In fact, even the most radical individualists admit that individuals, though supposedly the origin and source of everything social, act differently in different situations or circumstances, and they do not even attempt to analyze such situations in terms of individual actions. Likewise even the most radical holist must acknowledge that individual actions, particularly when concerted, can generate, maintain, reform, or dismantle social systems. Consequently real-life social scientists combine the bottom-up and top-down strategies.

The point then is not to attempt an impossible *reduction* of systems to mere aggregates of individuals, or the converse *reduction* of individual beliefs and actions to systemic properties. Rather, the point is to *relate* the microsocial and the macrosocial levels, showing how individuals *combine* (in particular compete and cooperate) with one another and how, in turn, individual behavior is *determined* (inhibited or stimulated) by a person's social environment rather than being totally free. An example should serve to clarify this point.

Consider an ordinary young person faced with the problem of choosing a career. Obviously he or she is not totally free to choose. Even if the person has a definite preference for a given career, and feels competent to embark in it, he or she may lack family support, may not have access to a good school, or may be deterred by a current low demand for graduates in the favorite field. Hence the final choice will not be a faithful indicator of the person's preference, but rather of the latter jointly with the family circumstances and of the social situation. Something similar holds for all choice situations: it is not that we have no choice but that our choices are partly dependent on circumstances beyond our control. Hence all the "rational" choice theories, which are typically individualistic, are just as flawed as the theories that ignore individual attitudes, preferences, and actions altogether. Once again, the systemic approach is the ticket.

To go back to the predicament of our young person. Suppose he or she chooses a given profession only because there is presently much demand for it. Such an individual decision is then determined by a macrosocial factor. But if many other students of our friend's generation make the same choice, when graduating they will encounter a competition so stiff that many may not find employment. Shortage will have turned into glut. That is, a host of mutually independent parallel individual decisions will have a "perverse" macrosocial effect.

The logic of this loop is as follows:

Demand for P at t → popular choice of P at t macro-to-micro
Popular choice for P at t → glut of P at $t + n$ micro-to-macro
Therefore demand for P at t → glut of P at $t + n$ macro-to-macro

(Warning: "Popular choice" does not mean that "the people" makes the choice, but that many individuals make the same choice. "The people" of a society is just the composition of the latter. This collection is brainless and therefore it can make no choices.)

The moral of our story is that, because every individual belongs to some social system and behaves at least partly *qua* member of the system, it is mistaken to disregard the macrosocial level(s). Microsociological considerations must always intertwine with macrosociological ones and conversely, because there are no stray independent individuals, families, firms, or cultural or political organizations: every unit belongs to at least one social system, and nowadays we are all components of the world system. Consequently the task of social scientists is neither to study totally free persons nor to study social blocks as if they were opaque to analysis. Their task is to study the way individuals combine to produce social facts, how these in turn stimulate or inhibit individual agency, and how the various social systems interact.

VI. PHILOSOPHICAL DIVIDENDS

The systemic approach suggests elucidating a number of concepts and hypotheses that are philosophical for occurring in a large number of fields of inquiry. Let us only mention a few of them.

The very first philosophical concept that we come across is of course that of a concrete system, which involves the concepts of composition, environment, and structure. The concept of a system is so pervasive and suggestive that it deserves being treated as a philosophical category on a par with the concepts of matter, space, time, and law. A second philosophical category elucidated by the systemic approach is that of specific function. The *specific function* of a component *a* of a concrete system is the collection of processes that can occur only in *a* and its likes. This concept is necessary, as we saw in Section IV.B, to avoid attributing goal-directedness to things, such as business firms and governments, that cannot possibly be purposive because they lack frontal lobes.

Another philosophical category highlighted by the systemic approach is that of emergence. Emergence concerns both systems and their components. We say that a property of a system is *emergent* on level *A* if it is not possessed by any of the *A*-parts (or things belonging to level *A*) of the system. For example, mentation is a property of certain systems of neurons, not of individual neurons or of the entire nervous system. When two individuals (atoms, persons, or what have you) get together to form a system, each of them acquires a property it did not possess before. For example, when two people marry they behave to each other differently from the way they behaved before constituting their own microsocial system.

A fourth philosophical category we encounter when thinking about systems is that of level of organization, or integrative level, first used explicitly by biologists about half a century ago. We define a *level* as a collection of things characterized by a cluster of properties and relations among these. We distinguish five main levels: physical, chemical, biological, social, and technological. In turn, every level may be split into sublevels. (For example, the biological level may be subdivided into seven sublevels: cell, organ, organ system, organism, biopopulation, ecosystem, and biosphere.) And we stipulate that one level *precedes* another if all the things in the latter are composed of things in (some or all of) the former. For example, the cell level precedes the organ level because organs are composed by cells. (A popular misname for the level structure of a supersystem, and indeed of the world as a whole, is "hierarchy." This is a misnomer because there are no hierarchies proper without domination relations.)

Further philosophical categories that are elucidated in the course of studying systems of various types are those of bond or link, assembly (in particular self-assembly), breakdown, stability, selection, adaptation, evolution, life, mind, sociosystem, culture, history, and several others.

As for the philosophical hypotheses suggested by the systemic approach, let the following suffice. First, all systems but the universe receive inputs and are selective; that is, they react only to a subset of the totality of environmental actions impinging on them. Second, all systems but the universe react on their environment; that is, their output is never nil. Third, all systems but the universe originate by assembly, mostly spontaneously (self-assembly). Fourth, every assembly process is accompanied by the emergence of some properties and the loss of others (submergence). Fifth, all systems but the universe are bound to break down sooner or later. Sixth, all systems are subject to environmental selection. Seventh, every system belongs to some evolutionary lineage. Eight, all the systems belonging to levels above the physical one have resulted from processes of assembly or lower order things. Ninth, the world is a system of systems.

The upshot is an ontology or world view that endorses the following philosophical doctrines.

1. *Materialism*, for it countenances only material existence and discounts autonomous ideas, spirits, and the like; but not *physicalism*, which ignores all supraphysical levels.

2. *Systemism*, for it holds that every thing is either a system or a component of one; but not *holism*, which maintains that wholes are prior to their components and incomprehensible by analysis.

3. *Pluralism*, with regard to the variety of things and processes, hence the plurality of properties and laws; but not *dualism* with regard to the mind-body problem.

4. *Emergentism* with regard to novelty, for it holds that, while some bulk properties are resultant or aggregate, others are emergent; but not *irrationalism* with regard to the possibility of explaining and predicting emergence.

5. *Dynamicism*, for it assumes that every thing is in a state of flux in some

respect or other; but not *dialectics*, for it rejects the tenets that every thing is a unity of opposites and that every change consists in, or is caused by, some strife or ontic contradiction.

6. *Evolutionism* with regard to the formation and breakdown of systems, for it maintains that new systems emerge all the time and are selected by their environment; but neither *gradualism* nor *saltationism*, for it recognizes both smooth changes and leaps.

7. *Determinism* with regard to events and processes, for holding them to be lawful and denying that any of them may come out of the blue or disappear without leaving traces; but not *causalism*, for it recognizes randomness and goal-striving as types of process alongside causal ones.

8. *Biosystemism* with regard to life, for it looks on organisms as material systems that, though composed of chemicals, have properties that do not occur on other levels; but neither *vitalism* nor *mechanism* (or physicalism) nor *machinism* (or artificialism), for it maintains the ontological irreducibility of living systems.

9. *Psychosystemism* with regard to mind, for it holds that mental functions are emergent activities of systems of neurons; but neither *eliminative* nor *reductive* materialism, for it affirms that the mental, although explainable with the help of physical, chemical, biological, and social premises, is emergent relative to the physical and the chemical.

10. *Sociosystemism* with regard to society, for it claims that society is a system composed of subsystems and possessing properties (such as social stratification and a political power structure) that no individual has; hence neither *individualism* nor *collectivism*, and neither *spiritualism* nor *vulgar materialism*.

I will not apologize for combining ten ontological *isms*. A single *ism* is usually inadequate and it may even be dangerous for being one-sided, closed, and rigid. We achieve many-sidedness, openness, and flexibility only by building a *system of matching isms* in harmony with contemporary science and technology, and formulated in as exact a manner as possible—and by updating it as needed. Which is yet another systemist maxim.

BIBLIOGRAPHICAL NOTE

Details will be found in the following publications of the author: *The Furniture of the World* (Dordrecht/Boston: Reidel, 1977), *A World of Systems* (Dordrecht/Boston: Reidel, 1979), *Scientific Materialism* (Dordrecht/Boston: Reidel, 1981), "States and Events," in W. Hartnett, ed., *Systems: Approaches, Theories and Applications*, pp. 71-95 (Dordrecht/Boston: Reidel, 1977), "The GST Challenge to the Classical Philosophies of Science," *International Journal of General Systems*, 4:29-33 (1977), and "General Systems and Holism," *General Systems, 22*:87-90 (1977).

The problem of knowledge is approached in a systemic way in the author's *Exploring the World* (Dordrecht/Boston/Lancaster: Reidel, 1983), *Understanding the World* (Dordrecht/Boston/Lancaster: Reidel, 1983), and *Philosophy of Science and Technology*, two volumes (Dordrecht/Boston/Lancaster: Reidel, 1985). The author's philosophy of mind as the collection of specific functions of plastic neuronal systems is found in *The Mind–Body Problem* (Oxford/New York: Pergamon Press, 1980), and in his book with R. Ardila, *Philosophy of Psychology* (New York: Springer, 1987).

The problems of values and morals are approached systemically in *Ethics: The Good and the Right* (Dordrecht/Boston: Reidel, 1989). A sample of the reactions elicited by the above-mentioned works will be found in P. Weingartner and G. Dorn, eds., *Studies on Bunge's Treatise* (Amsterdam: Rodopi, 1990).

4

What is System-Science?
Definition One

Marc E. Carvallo State University of Groningen,
Groningen, The Netherlands

I. INTRODUCTION: SYSTEM-SCIENCE, OBSERVED SYSTEMS, AND OBSERVING SYSTEMS

In the course of proposing and founding a new field of knowledge, many individuals will formulate their own definitions. Indeed, since the terms *system theory, systems research, system analysis,* and *system science* first began to be bandied about in the early 1940s dozens of scientists have attempted to define the nature and scope of the field. These terms and definitions are often so polyinterpretable, broadly used, and occasionally misused, that outsiders often wonder what we really mean by them. It therefore becomes important for me at the outset to state some of my major premises.

First, I take *system science* as the generic term or generic concept for the whole complex of terms and concepts meant above. This is further explained in the sections that follow.

Second, in reducing this chaos or complexity, I do not follow the standard approach of semasiology or of the current scientometric analysis of the term "system," "system-science," or of terms related to these as has been done by a host of scientists since the beginning of this century (cf., e.g., Ritschl, 1906; Messer, 1907; von der Stein, 1968; Oeser, 1976; Klir and Rogers, 1977; Rescher, 1979; Troncale, 1978; 1985; 1988; Jain, 1981; Robins and Oliva, 1982; Lewicka-Strzalecka, 1986). Such an approach implicitly asserts that the *concept,* or *idea* of

43

"system," "system-science," etc. is identical to its *term, that is, to one of its semantic correlates*, which of course is completely erroneous. Mankind has always been dealing with systems, not only since the term "system" was used for the first time by Hippocrates in the sixth century B.C.! So my approach pretends to emphasize the recognition of "system," "system-science," etc. in other semantic correlates, namely, in "what is thought" or "what is meant" by a person or a sentence, a theory, etc., and not, or not primarily, in its perceivable, verbal, or formal representation through the sentence or the term; the latter is nothing but an (often) incomplete derivation of the former. My conclusions will then be somewhat different from those of the standard approach. To do some justice to this claim, I have tried elsewhere to find the thread of Ariadne in the labyrinth of systems-thinking using the history of the philosophy of nature as a metaphor (cf. Carvallo, 1991). In this chapter I confine myself to detecting systems-*ideas*, and to arranging them in a simple structure.

Third, in contradistinction to the classical problem of scientific inquiry of what I call the standard system-science (cf. Section VIII), which postulates first a description-invariant "system-science" as an objective system (as if there were such a system) and then attempts to write its description, I am now challenged to develop a description-invariant "system-science" as an subjective system, that is, a system that includes the observer. In other words, a definition of system-science implies those who make it, and accordingly in defining system-science we are challenged to develop a theory of system-scientists. A discussion of system-science unavoidably implies one of the system-scientists, just as a discussion of the "observed system" and one of the "observing system" are indissolubly bound up with each other. Only for the sake of the formal distinction is the definition of system-science from the viewpoint of the "observing system" or system-scientist, respectively, called here "definition one" of system-science, and "definition two" (of system-science) from the other view point. The attentive reader might have noticed that my third premise heavily draws on von Foerster's "Notes on an epistemology for living things" (von Foerster, 1984: 258–271). However, there are some differences between us, I presume. First, in von Foerster's description of the "objective world" (which in my case would be carried out by "definition two"), the description of the "subjective world" (which in this chapter is carried out by "definition one") is (necessarily) implied. The sequence in this chapter is just the other way round: in describing "definition one" the description of "definition two" is "necessarily" implied. But although our procedures are slightly different, I arrive at the same conclusion in that this sequence cannot always be kept consistently in the whole course of the description, probably because of its self-referential nature, so that it may be wiser to leave it to the readers to decide for themselves whether these (sub)definitions, or some of them, are about "system-science" as a subjective system or as an objective system. Second, I am not in complete agreement on, for instance, von Foerster's description of the "environment." His definition is bluntly "classical," if not atomistic, whereas my definition is nonclassical in that I take it to also belong to the system of the observers and in that I even seriously take for possible the observation without (subjective) observers (see Section IV). In addition, what I am going to do here is nothing but make an initial acquaintance with the development of a theory of system-scientists rather than with the development of a theory of *how* system-scientists observe, perceive, or know. A fully fledged development of the former (e.g., in the sense of a postpositivistic philosophy of system-science) still remains to be done.

Fourth, I am fully aware of the difficulties and traps of paradoxes inherent in the organization of knowledge of the above self-referential states of affairs. The definitions to follow might give nothing but the slightest impression of what has been or is being undertaken within the circles of nonstandard system-science such as that of the foregoing work of von Foerster, or of Atlan (1983), Hofstadter (1980), and Glanville (1988), just to mention a few.

Fifth, somewhat different, however, from the above nonstandard system-scientists whose subject matter of investigation is confined primarily, if not exclusively, to the universe of the measurable, I am trying, besides, to structurally couple the main ideas of that universe and those of the universe of the (presumed) immeasurable as might appear, for example, from Sections II. A, IV, or V, just to mention a few. This (unusual) trial-and-error attempt is more or less congenial to those of the nonstandard system-scientists discussed briefly in Section VIII. B.

Sixth, for a precise statement of the concepts in question, I will make use to some extent of "concept explication" as has been proposed by Carnap and others (see, e.g., Carnap, 1959; Wohlgenannt, 1969), where, in addition, the requirements of rigorous operationalism are avoided, in that it should be sufficient for the interpretability of the concepts to be (only) "partially empirical" (Hempel, 1972: 42 ff.). I hasten to add that behind this explication attempt there is no hidden essentialistic assumption of analytical philosophy, that is, the irrelevant assumption that the sense and meaning of the statements are a priori already there hidden beneath the surface of words, terms, or statements, and that by analysis one may be able to discover them. Contrarily, if there is any analysis in the following sections; it will pretend to act as nothing but a therapeutic method (Wittgenstein, 1953), namely as an attempt to smooth the misunderstandings concerning the use of words, primarily concerning "what is thought" or "what is meant" by a person, a statement, or a theory which could be characterized as systemic.

II. DEFINITION ONE: GENERAL OVERVIEW

Let us begin with the first definition. This definition will deal with the category of the *observing systems*. I will confine myself to the human observing systems. By "observation" I mean the more comprehensive genus of action, namely perception, or cognition. The more adequate term would then be the cognizing or the *perceiving systems.* The latter term is actually used by others—for example, Popper (1974) or Lorenz (1975) in their attempts to reinterpret Kant's theory of knowledge. For the sake of the terminological recognition of insiders however, and accordingly following von Foerster (1984), whose work is quite rightly characterized by Varela (1984a) as a framework for understanding cognition, the verb "to observe" is meant here to denote the above more comprehensive *genus* of human action.

Definition one runs as follows: "System-science is science of the system" (*genitivus subjectivus*); that is, the system has a science, the system theorizes about reality which is assumed to be a system), and it does that either on the basis of the system-paradigm or on the basis of a particular system-paradigm. Let us formally represent this general definition as **Def.1**. Let us further make explicit this definition successively. Further specification of the constitution[1] of **Def.1** in the form of statements might appear thus:

> "System-science is science of the system: the system has a science, the system theorizes about reality," let us formally call this first specification **Def.1^0'**
> "and it does that on the basis of the system-paradigm", let us formally call this second specification **Def.1^1'**
> "or on the basis of a particular system-paradigm." Let us formally call this third specification **Def.1^2**.

So, **Def.1** is constituted by

$$\left\{ \begin{array}{l} \textbf{Def.1}^0 \\ \textbf{Def.1}^1 \\ \textbf{Def.1}^2 \end{array} \right. \quad \text{or formally: } \textbf{Def.1} = \{\textbf{Def.1}^0; \textbf{Def.1}^1; \textbf{Def.1}^2\}$$

Def.1 is constituted by two complementary opposites: the invariant (i.e., **Def.1^0**) and the variant (i.e., **Def.1^2**) one. Somewhere between **Def.1^0** and **Def.1^2**, **Def.1^1** oscillates as the invariant constituent that tries to be variant or the variant constituent that pretends to be invariant. Note that this characterization of **Def.1^1** runs partially parallel to, among others, the general characterization of general systems theory (GST) by Boulding (1956). Boulding's characterization, however, appertains primarily to **Def.2**.

A. Def.1^0

Def.1^0 is the most general statement. It has the smallest intension and accordingly the greatest extension. Of the three constituents named above it is the weakest statement; that is, there are very many, if not all, states of affairs that fall under Def.1^0. Thus it constitutes more or less the "matter"[2] of Def.1. A provisional close examination of the intension of this constituent of Def.1 assures us that the "matter" of Def.1 is double-sided, it has a far and a near side.

The *far side* of the "matter" comprises (or maybe: is constituted by) both its actual (or, according to some philosophers, principal) inaccessibility to our knowledge and its most intimate immediacy to the near side of the "matter." Consequently the far side of the "matter" of Def.1 is primarily invisible. These two components or constituents of the far side of the "matter" might be viewed as, respectively, the *greatest lower bound* (glb) and the *least upper bound* (lub) of the near side of the "matter," if this near side of the "matter" as a system, imaginarily and for the sake of clear simplification, could be represented as a lattice. In other words, the far side of the "matter" as a whole is viewed here as the boundary of the near side of the "matter." This is the first possibility to describe the far side of the "matter" of Def.1. For the sake of clear formal distinction and accordingly to avoid any confusion, let me summarize the descriptions of the further specifications of this component of Def.1 as follows:

The "matter" of Def.1 is coined as Def.1^0.
The far side of the "matter" of Def.1 is coined as def.$(1^0)0$.
Consequently Def.$(1^0)0$ is the far side of Def.1^0.
If within the system of the further specification(s) of Def.1^0 its far side fractally might be viewed as "matter," then Def.$(1^0)0$ is tantamount to the "matter" of the "matter" of Def.1.

The *near side* of the "matter" of Def.1 comprises (or maybe: is constituted by) its macroscopic levels and dimensions and will be coined as Def.$(1^0)2$. Consequently the near side of the "matter" of Def.1 is primarily visible. For the sake of clear formal distinction and accordingly to avoid any confusion, let me summarize the descriptions of the further specification(s) of this component of Def.1 as follows:

The "matter" of Def.1 is coined as Def.1^0.
The near side of the "matter" of Def.1 is coined as Def.$(1^0)2$.
Consequently Def.$(1^0)2$ is the near side of Def.1^0.
If within the system of the further specification(s) of Def.1^0 its near side fractally might be viewed as "form," then Def.$(1^0)2$ is tantamount to the "form" of the "matter" of Def.1.

Note in passing that in this description the "form" of Def.1 (viz. Def.1^2, cf. below) is enfolded in the above near side of Def.1^0. Note further that in this description the ontic and/or ontological complementarity between "matter" and "form" repeats itself over and over again through this double-sidedness in ever-new manifestations (or fractals) of Def.1, which implies that this pattern-reiteration holds likewise for the "content" and "form" of Def.1, as one would notice throughout this chapter.

Let me return for a moment to my representation of the near side of the "matter" as a lattice, and accordingly to the first possible representation of the far side of the "matter" of Def.1 (viz, as the boundary of the near side of the "matter" of Def.1). At a closer look, this lattice would most probably be a semilattice, because the near side of the "matter" as a system is usually taken to be referentially and/or self-referentially closed, in short, explicately ordered (as is meant by Bohm, 1982), while its greatest lower bound and least upper bound, which in this connection are the very constituents of the far side of the "matter" of Def.1, tend (paradoxically) to be referentially and/or self-referentially open, in brief, implicately ordered. It (viz., the near side of the "matter" of Def.1) is referentially closed—for example, in the sense of the closure of the artificial systems as interpreted by the physical symbol systems hypothesis (see, e.g., Newell and Simon, 1976), or in the sense of the (at least actual) impossibility for any data processing system, whether artificial or living, to exceed Bremermann's limit (cf. Bremermann, 1962; Ashby, 1968; Klir, 1985). It is self-referentially closed—for example, in the way physical autopoietic machines endowed with circular and self-referential loops within their own boundaries are closed (cf. Maturana and Varela, 1980). It is explicately ordered, in the sense of the orderedness of the visible and definable relative invariant structures (cf. Bohm, 1979; 1982; Piaget, 1970), or in the sense of the White-headean temporal atomicity (Whitehead, 1926), or of the dissipative structures (Prigogine and Stengers, 1984). As an observing system, this near side of the "matter" of Def.1 appears to be identical to *S3 as paradigm*, as has been discussed elsewhere (Carvallo, 1986b).

Its boundary however (viz; its glb and lub, constituting the very far side of the "matter" of Def.1) is referentially open in the sense that it is or tends to be able to exceed Bremermann's limit and accordingly to turn out to be a transcomputational problem, which is tantamount to this: that this system does not belong (any more) to the universe of simplicity, nor even to that of complicatedness, but to that of complexity (see, e.g., Atlan, 1983; Carvallo, 1986a). It is partially self-referentially open in that it tends to transcend the boundaries of computability and to enter the domain of linguisticity (Löfgren, 1988; 1991). It is referentially and self-referentially open—for example, in the sense that its conversation with the "other" is not triggered by mediating relations but by a kind of unmediated coherence (see, e.g., Buber, 1937; M. C. Bateson, 1975; 1984; Bråten, 1988; Pask, 1991). It is implicately ordered in the sense that, as a multidimensionally ordered system, the dimensionality of which is effectively infinite, it is "enfolded" in the relative invariant structures (viz., it is enfolded in the "form," or the "forms" of Def.1[0]).

The boundary of the near side of the "matter" of Def.1 might then summarily be imagined as follows. First, as that regime where the near side of the "matter" of Def.1 (i.e., S3 as paradigm) gradually disappears. Second, as the perceiving apparatus, the senses, which means perception as structure, or even the perception itself (i.e., perception as function) of the near side of the "matter" of Def.1. This implies that this boundary is not an object (like, e.g., an apple) that is distinguishable from or perceivable by the near side of the "matter" of Def.1, but is part and parcel of the near side of the "matter" of Def.1, or is enfolded in the near side of the "matter" of Def.1, if this near side is viewed as a bounded portion of the total unbroken wholeness. It is the (event of) perceiving an object by the near side of the "matter" of Def.1 which (viz., this event of perceiving) itself is not perceivable (viz., by itself).

The next further step would bring us to the second possibility to view the far side of the "matter" of Def.1 as a system (or lattice) in its own right. It is a strict abstract system, constituted by boundaries being the glb and lub of the near side of the "matter." This observational state of affairs finds itself on the pyschometaphysical sphere. Or to be more precise, scientists and philosophers put it in this sphere because of their weakness of insight and the deficiencies of language inexorably standing in the way. And however metaphysical and psychological elements of language be stabilized as technicalities (viz., to describe this state of affairs), "they remain metaphors mutely appealing for an imaginative leap" (Whitehead, 1978: 4).

In this case Def.$(1^0)0$ and Def.$(1^0)2$ have a common boundary. This common boundary is then constituted by the common glb and lub of both, namely of Def.$(1^0)0$ and Def.$(1^0)2$. This common boundary might appropriately be viewed as a *transistional space* (Winnicott, 1953) where the more or less exactly demarcated lines of Def.$(1^0)2$ fractally and (consequently) naturally shade off into the dizzy heights and the abysmal depths of Def.$(1^0)0$ and vice versa. Or to put it differently, consider the boundary where the above closure of the near side of the "matter" of Def.1 (represented as a lattice) is bound to turn to its openness and vice versa, where the openness of the far side of the "matter" of Def.1 (represented likewise as a system or a lattice) is bound as well to turn to its closure. This common boundary is then constituted by the very actions of turning to its openness and to its closure of the near side and the far side of the "matter" of Def.1, respectively. Or represented differently (once again), this common boundary is the very hinge around which the near side and the far side of the "matter" of Def.1 converse with each other. This conversation regards the very subject of perception (in our context: observation), if not perception (i.e., observation) itself. It would accordingly appear that this common boundary is neither permanent nor preestablished but metastable or dissipative. This means, among other things, that *S3* (at least) *as the transcending system* by its nature is a self-amplifying system.

It may appear obvious that the above idea of transitional space is one of the many variants of the preconceptional view of the "continuous," which might be appropriately characteristic for natural or living systems, in short complex systems. To capture this complexity, one may come across a host of models ranging from the geometric to the human. A good illustration for its geometric modeling is provided by Escher's famous engraving *Sky and Water* (Erst, 1985; Johnson, 1985). Here we see a collection of what appear to be geese gradually being transformed into fish as the picture is scanned from top to bottom. At the same time, we also see a smooth transition from figure to ground as the shapes constituting the geese become the background for the swimming fish. A bit of reflection may soon lead to the view that the picture is really a statement about the relationship between various geometrical shapes (birds, fishes, and their intermediate forms) and features that pertain to the identification of the shapes as being birdlike, fishlike, or something in between. Here one recognizes a smooth passage from one type of figure to another, accompanied by a transition from figure to ground. Or consider, for instance, the complex structure in Mondrian's famous cubist painting *Checkerboard, Bright Colors?* which involves a seemingly random scattering of eight colors on a rectangular grid of 256 cells but at closer analysis turns out to be triggered by a hidden connective structure (cf. Atkin, 1974). Other mathematical models to characterize a change of state or the emergence of the (in principle) unlimited growth of the number and type of life patterns are provided by the research on the system of "cellular automata" or on the "geometry of . . . flesh," for a detailed account of which one should consult, for example, Gardner (1983), Wolfram (1986), and Poundstone (1987), or Mandelbrot (1983), Falconer (1985), and Barnsley (1988). Another way of representing the "transitional space" is to conceive it as a vortex where many (or all) levels and dimensions cross. Hofstadter (1980) has described three such vortices. Let us take (again) the Escher vortex referring to the latter's *Print Gallery.* What we see is first, the many kinds of "inness" different hierarchies are tangled in, and second, that the center of the whorl is—and must be—incomplete. Translated into our idea of "transitional space," we may describe it as a space where different levels and dimensions of different systems are paradoxically tangled, and say further that this strange loopy whirling both to the center and the periphery is damned to be incomplete.

Other ideas one might encounter in biological research. How biological species can be transformed into one another by smooth coordinate change is discussed, for example, by Thompson (1942) and Rosen (1978). The interactive concept of Winnicott, originating within psychoanalytic developmental psychology, refers to a boundary region that mediates and integrates two configurations of objects: initially mother and infant, then fantasy and reality. The "transitional space" is at once subjective and objective, in the mind and in objective reality. The space, initially formed through the infant's anticipation followed by the actualization of the maternal object, is expanded via the transitional object and culminates developmentally in play and cultural sublimations. Characteristic for this space is thus its mediation and integration of (or its "natural" tendency to coordinate) not only two geometric systems (as, e.g., the beach is the transitional space between land and sea) but also of the inside and the outside of both systems, and finally that it is the "natural niche" for growth, change, briefly evolution. An analogous idea, focused on sociocultural systems, one might find in Bohm's interpretation of "metaphor" (Bohm and Peat, 1987). From a different point of view—namely, from that of "double-aspectism" as further discussed in his theory of "implicate order" and of "soma-significance" (Bohm, 1982, 1987)—our "transitional space" plays the role of the magnetic field, and the two interacting systems that of the north and south poles (i.e., of the two aspects) of this field. Translating the latter theory into our context would yield the far-reaching conclusion that the "transitional space" is essential; it is the (ultimate) moving ground, of which the interacting systems are nothing but its conditioned unfoldings.

Let us call the above "transitional space" the "content" of the "matter" of Def.1, and let us coin it as Def.(1^0)1. For the sake of clear formal distinction and accordingly to avoid any confusion, let me summarize the descriptions of the further specification(s) of the constituent of Def.1 as follows:

The "transitional space" constituted by the (imaginary) glb and lub of both the far side and the near side of the "matter" of Def.1 is viewed as the "content" of Def.1^0.

This "content" of Def.1^0 is coined as Def.(1^0)1.

Consequently Def.(1^0)1 is the "content" of Def.1.

B. Def.1^2

Def.1^2, on the other hand, is the particular statement. It has a greater intension and accordingly a lesser extension. It is a strong statement; that is, the area of the states of affairs that comply with Def.1^2 is rather limited and more easily distinguishable. It constitutes more or less the "form" or the "forms" of Def.1. Being the "form" itself of Def.1, it consequently is (or more carefully: it might be) the *analogon* of the other "forms" occurring in all the near sides of Def.1. Def.1^2 might also be further specified in: Def.(1^2)0, Def.(1^2)1, and Def.(1^2)2.

Def.(1^2)0 refers to every particular science that "materially" is a system-science, or to every individual scientist who (at least implicitly) is a system-scientist, or more generally to every perceiver or observing system who (at least implicitly) is a system-observer. So Def.(1^2)0 is that constituent in the "form" of Def.1, or more simply: that constituent of Def.1^2, which concerns the question of the "matter" and consequently of the far side. For the sake of clear formal distinction and accordingly to avoid any possible confusion, let me summarize the descriptions of the further specification(s) of this constituent of Def.1 as follows:

The "form" of Def.1 is coined as Def.1^2.

The far side of the "form" of Def.1 is coined as Def.(1^2)0.

Consequently Def.(1^2)0 is the far side of Def.1^2.

If within the system of the further specification(s) of Def.1^2 its far side fractally might be viewed as "matter," then Def.(1^2)0 is tantamount to the "matter" of Def.1^2 and is identical to the "matter" of the "form" of Def.1.

Def.(1^2)2 refers to those particular system-sciences predicated on their appropriate (i.e., particular or explicit) system-paradigms. It refers likewise to those particular system-scientists, or to those particular system-scientists or system-observers within the category of S3, whose theorizing about reality is predicated on their appropriate (i.e., particular) system-paradigms or on particular paradigms that are explicitly spelled out (by these system-scientists or system-observers) as system-paradigms. So Def.(12)2 is that constituent in the "form" of Def.1 that regards the near side of the "form" of Def.1 and consequently the near side of Def.1^2. For the sake of clear formal distinction and accordingly to avoid any possible confusion, let me summarize the descriptions of the further specification(s) of this constituent of Def.1 as follows:

The "form" of Def.1 is coined as Def.1^2.
The near side of the "form" of Def.1 is coined as Def.(12)2.
Consequently Def.(12)2 is the near side of Def.1^2.
If within the system of the further specification(s) of Def.1^2 its near side fractally
   might be viewed as "form," then Def.(12)2 is identical to the "form" of Def.1^2
   and is tantamount to the "form" of the "form" of Def.1.

Def.(12)1 might be viewed as the "transitional space" constituted by the boundaries of the far and the near side of the "form" of Def.1, and as such Def.(12)1 forms the "content" of Def.1^2. It refers to every particular science that is predicated on the (general, implicit) system-paradigm. It refers to every individual scientist or observer whose scientific activity or observation is triggered by the (general, implicit) system-thinking: in other words to every particular science whose subject matter is implicitly or generally defined (by this particular science) as the "system" or to every individual scientist or observer whose subject of perception is implicitly or generally identified (by this individual scientist or observer) as the "system." For the sake of clear formal distinction and accordingly to avoid any possible confusion, let me summarize the descriptions of the further specification(s) of this constituent of Def.1 as follows:

The "form" of Def.1 is coined as Def.1^2.
The boundaries of the far and the near side of the "form" of Def.1 constitute a
   common "transitional space" of both sides.
If within the system of the further specification(s) of Def.1^2 its "transitional
   space" fractally might be viewed as "content," then Def.(12)1 is identical to the
   "content" of Def.1^2 and is accordingly tantamount to the "content" of the
   "form" of Def.1.

C. Def.1^1

Def.1^1 forms the synthesis of or attempts to synthesize Def.1^0 and Def.1^2. It pretends more or less to be both the materialized "form" and the formalized "matter" of Def.1. As such it might be interpreted both as the first fuzzy specification of

Def.1^0 and also as the first tentative generalization of Def.1^2. Being preeminently the synthesis between the most indefinite and the most definite and conditioned dimensions of Def.1 it forms the "content" of Def.1. It is consequently the *analogon* of all other "contents" and of "transitional spaces" occurring in Def.1. Def.1^1 might also be further specified in: Def.(1^1)0, Def.(1^1)1, and Def.(1^1)2.

Def.(1^1)0 is described here as the far side of the "content" of Def.1. As such it could be interpreted in the following two ways. First, as that regime of Def.1 that coincides with the near side of the "matter" of Def.1. This would mean that the "matter" of Def.1^1 is in fact identical to the "form" of Def.1^0, for practically the same state of affairs is found in both further specifications of Def.1, as might appear hereafter. Second, as the "transitional space" constituted by the boundaries of both the near side of the "matter" of Def.1 and of the "content" of Def.1^1. For the sake of clear formal distinction and to avoid any possible confusion, let me summarize the descriptions of the further specification(s) of this constituent of Def.1 as follows:

The "content" of Def.1 is coined as Def.1^1.
The far side of the "content" of Def.1 is coined as Def(1^1)0.
If within the system of the further specification(s) of Def.1^1 its far side fractally might be viewed as "matter," then Def.(1^1)0 is identical to the "matter" of Def.1^1 and is tantamount to the "matter," of the "content" of Def.1.

Def.(1^1)1 is described here as the "transitional space" constituted by the boundaries of both the far and the near side of the "content" of Def.1. As might be inferred from the description of Def.(1^1)0 (cf. above) and of Def.(1^1)2 (cf. below), Def.(1^1)1 is (also) identical to the "transitional space" constituted by the boundaries of both the near side of the "matter" of Def.1 (viz., Def.(1^0)2) and the far side of the "form" of Def.1 (viz., Def.(1^2)0). For the sake of clear formal distinction and to avoid any possible confusion, let me summarize the descriptions of the further specification(s) of this constituent of Def.1 as follows:

The "content" of Def.1 is coined as Def.1^1.
The "transitional space" is constituted by the boundaries of both the far and the near side of the "content" of Def.1.
If within the system of the further specification(s) of Def.1^1 its "transitional space" fractally might be viewed as "content," then Def.(1^1)1 is identical to the "content" of Def.1^1 and is tantamount to the "content" of the "content" of Def.1.

Def.(1^1)2 is described here as the near side of the "content" of Def.1. Analogous to Def.(1^1)0, it might be interpreted in two ways. First, as identical to the far side of the "form" of Def.1. Second, as the "transitional space" constituted by the boundaries of both Def.(1^1)1 (i.e., the "content" of the "content" of Def.1) and Def.(1^2)0 (i.e., the far side of the "form" of Def.1). For the sake of clear formal distinction and to avoid any possible confusion, let me summarize the descriptions of the further specification(s) of this constituent of Def.1 as follows:

The "content" of Def.1 is coined as Def.1^1.
The near side of the "content" of Def.1 is coined as the near side of Def.1^1.
If within the system of the further specification(s) of Def.1^1 its near side fractally might be viewed as "form," then Def.$(1^1)2$ is identical to the "form" of Def.1^1 and is consequently tantamount to the "form" of the "content" of Def.1.

The constitution of Def.1 according to these last specifications therefore appears schematically as follows:

$$
\text{Def.1} \left\{
\begin{array}{l}
\text{Def.}1^0 \left\{
\begin{array}{l}
\text{Def.}(1^0)0 \\
\text{Def.}(1^0)1 \\
\text{Def.}(1^0)2
\end{array}
\right. \\[2em]
\text{Def.}1^1 \left\{
\begin{array}{l}
\text{Def.}(1^1)0 \\
\text{Def.}(1^1)1 \\
\text{Def.}(1^1)2
\end{array}
\right. \\[2em]
\text{Def.}1^2 \left\{
\begin{array}{l}
\text{Def.}(1^2)0 \\
\text{Def.}(1^2)1 \\
\text{Def.}(1^2)2
\end{array}
\right.
\end{array}
\right.
$$

Because of the limited scope of this chapter, which moreover is written primarily for insiders, I shall in the further treatment of these constituent parts confine myself to the most necessary explanations and to a few fundamental but possibly forgotten or suppressed problems thereof.

III. FURTHER EXPLICATION OF DEF.$(1^0)2$: THE "FORM" OF THE "MATTER" OF DEF.1

For didactic considerations we shall first treat the near side of the "matter." This source constituent of Def.1 is found primarily on p^1-level (i.e., the level of the chief styles of thought) and in the sociocultural context. With regard to this very general aspect of Def.1, the further explications will focus on the concepts "system" and the connected concept "frame" or "groundplan" (cf. Radnitzky, 1970: 11–14) of the system-paradigm.

A. The "System"

"System" (in the *genitivus subjectivus* sense) is meant here as a whole that is constituted by the following two complementary opposites and by their mutual relations:

1. The (scientific) tradition whose frame or groundplan is the systemic one. Stated another way, "system" is here the systemic scientific culture, the systemic scientific society, or paradoxically (i.e., when system and environment are viewed as each other's opposite): the systemic scientific environment.

2. The members of the systemic scientific culture—that is, those who are more or less encultured into this environment and who are, or are supposed to be, the bearers of this culture. Stated another way, this membership can range from those who because of their tacit knowledge may "gravitate" toward a systemic (scientific) culture (regardless of what is meant by this) to those who actually are professing members of certain system (scientific) societies (which may indeed be intrinsically transformed, although this does not per se guarantee their prerogative rights in the one authentic interpretation of what systemic scientific culture is).

So the first constituent (i.e., the systemic scientific culture) refers here to the whole, whereas the second constituent (viz., the members of this systemic-scientific culture) refers to the parts. Or: the first constituent refers to the environment or the frame, and the second to the system or the reference. Or more explicitly (but at the same time befuddlingly): the first constituent refers to the environment or the frame, which—taking it that system (or reference) and environment (or frame) are, at least according to the standard assumption, each other's opposite—paradoxically is the "system"; and the second constituent refers to the "system" (that is embedded in the culture or enframed by the culture), which paradoxically is the environment (that bears and develops the culture, i.e. wherein the culture is framed).

The relations between system and environment (or part and whole, or reference and frame) in the sense as interpreted above, which help to constitute the "system" of Def.1, are actually (and possibly) manifold, when one considers that following from the above, the general whole of the relations or even of the structural couplings may appear as follows:

{system : environment} = {a) scientific culture: its members; b) its members: scientific culture}

If one translates the whole set of the relations or even of the structural couplings as:

{system : environment} = {{1. variety : constraint} = {{a) ; b)}}; {2, constraint : variety} = {a) ; b)}}}

one obtains an even more subtle and oscillating image of the "system" that "plays" in the sense of gestalt witches, or of the Borgesian garden of the forking paths, or of the strange-loopiness etc., etc. This dynamic (and almost elusive) fine-structure flavoring of some complexity, and constituting the basic and prime themes of the social sciences, the humanities, and the contemporary philosophy of science, will not be discussed in detail in the present restricted frame.

B. The Frame or the Groundplan

The above-mentioned many-faced states of affairs, namely, of the scientific sys-temic culture (= environment and system) and the members of this culture (= system and environment), one sees reflected again in the frame or the groundplan of the system-paradigm: it is the frame and simultaneously the reference, the mat-ter of the heart and simultaneously the heart of the matter. It is the paradigmatic gravitation that acts extrinsically on its members and triggers motion, and simul-taneously the paradigmatic heat that transforms its members, determines changes of state, and leads to a modification of intrinsic properties, just to use the two an-tagonistic universals in physics as metaphors (for more details, see e.g., Serres, 1977). Let us have a closer look at it using the Popperian worlds. I shall follow the reverse sequence, as I think that this gives a better representation of the increasing grade of complexity of this subject matter.

First, the frame or the groundplan can be viewed as world3 or part of it. This means that "noëtic structure" (cf. Carvallo, 1982) or part of it, interpreted as the Popperian "objective knowledge," is able to function as a set of science-as-(finalizable) product, which recursively exercises an influence on the individual or the community in his or its conversation with the outer reality (i.e., world1).

Second, the frame or the groundplan can be viewed as world2. The following types hereof could be distinguished:

1. The frame of every actual individual member—let us call it the *actual frame*—that may differ from both of the following types of frame.
2. The type of frame that is most encouraged and most rewarded in a particular system-scientific community, let us call it the *preferred frame*, which might be internalized by the individual either voluntarily or not.
3   The articulate cultural myth about the *desirable frame*, which:
    (a) if viewed in its h2-dimension (i.e., as a historically given scientific tradi-tion in a historiographic–cultural study), is constituted by the systemic world-picture–hypothese and ideals of science one has acquired as the result of the intentional socialization (or more correctly: intentional enculturation);
    (b) if viewed in its h1/v2 dimension (i.e., in the dimension of breadth referring to subject matters on object-level and operating mainly with statis-tic–inductive methods/in the dimension of depth referring to the eidetic and the existential–phenomenological and operating with purely qualitative meth-ods), is constituted by the systemic worldpicture–hypotheses and ideals of science one has as a result of the spontaneous mimesis with the life-world, whereby a system is stabilized of implicit, tacit, or sedimented elements rooted in bodily or instrumental expertise, in subjective habitualities, or in that limit mode of sedimented consciousness, which Husserl (1969: 319) calls "the unconscious."

These three types of frame may overlap or diverge in any given scientific community. For example, the frame of most individual scientists may differ both from the preferred and the desirable frame, and on the other hand may converge with the desirable frame if viewed in its h1–v2 dimension.

Furthermore, the cultural myth about what is desirable may not correspond to the actual handling out of rewards and sanctions by the society. Following the interpretation of some sociologists (see, e.g., Merton, 1968), these discrepancies form the natural niche for the mutual alienation between the systemic culture and its members. These discrepancies might however be viewed either as a source of disorder and of decline of the established culture, as is suggested by order–sociology, or as a source of order and of the rise of a new culture, as is suggested by conflict–sociology.

The category of the observing systems constituting Def.$(1^0)1$ refers to or (at least partially) belongs to *S3 as paradigm*.

IV. FURTHER EXPLICATION OF DEF.$(1^0)0$: THE "MATTER" OF THE "MATTER" OF DEF.1

This primodial constituent of Def.1 is found primarily on or even beyond the p^0-level (i.e., the level of ontological, axiological, epistemological, and praxiological preconceptions) and in the psychometaphysical sphere. It is the most general and consequently the most fuzzy and elusive aspect of Def.1. To have any idea about it, I have suggested two possible ways of viewing it, namely, as the boundary of Def.$(1^0)1$ and as a system (or lattice) in its own right. Let us however try again to catch a glimpse of it.

1. Viewed as the boundary (viz. of Def.$(1^0)1$), it itself necessarily cannot have any boundary, not only in that it has nothing outside it—compare Russel's interpretation of Wittgenstein's "boundary" (Russel, 1961)—but also in that *being* the boundary itself, it necessarily excludes *having* the boundary—compare, for example, Marcel's distinction between "being" and "having" (Marcel, 1935).

2. Viewed as that fuzzy regime where Def.$(1^0)1$ gradually disappears, it alludes more to the gradual entry of the absence or of the breakdown or our knowledge, than to its nonexistence. Compare what will be said below (Section IX.A) about the symmetry break in its pejorative sense.

3. Viewed as the perception (itself) of Def.$(1^0)1$ (cf. Smullyan, 1977), it refers to the objectlessness, or more precisely the nonobjectness, of Def.$(1^0)0$. It also alludes to the (possible) fact that Def.$(1^0)0$ is cognition itself, if perception and cognition are convertible, as is implicitly suggested by von Foerster (1984), Bohm (1979, 1982), and others. It likewise alludes to the (possible) fact that Def.$(1^0)0$ is life itself, if cognition and life are convertible, as is suggested implicitly by Maturana (1980). It further alludes to the strange fact that Def.$(1^0)0$ is both

part and parcel and Def.(10)1, namely, being the structure and function of perception of Def.(10)1, and the whole, namely, as perception itself, of which Def.(10)1 is only a bounded portion. Finally it alludes to the paradoxical fact that such a concrete, empirical fact, (viz., perception) escapes any perceivability by itself!

4.   Viewed as a system (or lattice) in its own right, it should then be a system that spatially is infinite and all-encompassing, temporally is eternal, and informationally is all-permeating. Just by way of illustration and as a metaphor, let us first briefly follow the main lines of ancient Greek atomic theory, (see, e.g., Sambursky, 1987), which primarily touches the spatial and indirectly the informational aspect of it, and those of Wittgenstein's notion of the "world as a whole."

The second axiom of the atomic theory concerns the postulate of a "vacuum": given that matter is composed of *atoms* (i.e., ultimate unchanging particles), then all changes must be the result of their movements, and the prerequisite of movement is a *vacuum*, a space entirely devoid of matter in which a particle can pass from place to place. This postulation of the vacuum as a prerequisite for the movement of the atoms unavoidably leads to the postulation of the absolute solidity of both the atom itself and the void. As for the absolute solidity of the former: there should be no possibly of a vacuum inside the atom itself; that is, the atom should not have an "inner environment," to express it in Simon's term (Simon, 1975), no own "inside," to express it in the second-order cybernetics parlance, no own identity, to express it in the terminology of modern philosophy of nature (cf. e.g., Leclerc, 1986), no own information or internal information processing mechanism: it is simply *res extensa*. The absolute solidity of the latter should be understood as a negative state of affairs; that is, it refers to the absolute solidity of this emptiness in that this emptiness should be absolute (which, in my opinion is impossible, for the absolute solidity of the infinite number of atoms has broken the solidity of the void and has rendered it infinitely distinguishable, albeit randomly corresponding to the randomness of the positions and motions of these atoms.[3] "The void, in so far it is void, admits no difference," Aristotle says in one of his many reasons advanced against the existence of a vacuum (*Physics*, 214b); it should not contain any matter even in its most rarefied form, such as air or ether. The void is a "not-being," and no part of "what is" is a "not-being," for "what is" in the strict sense of the term is an absolute plenum. So matter and vacuum entirely exclude each other empirically and logically. On the other hand, the void is necessarily interrelated to the atoms in that it should be infinite because the number of atoms is infinite. The universe of the atomic school thus consisted of a vacuum of infinite size filled with solid particles of infinite number. So we can distinguish here three kinds of totality: that of "full" physical units, that of the "void," and that constituted by the former totalities. Returning now to our system of interest, we could ask ourselves: (1) whether our system should be interpreted in the sense of the infinite agglomeration of solid particles, since it is (according to the atomic theory) the totality of "what is," the totality of "beings," the totality of "everything." The answer is bound to be negative for the following reasons. First, the system (which is supposed to be the subject matter of the system-science) according to Def.(1^0)0 should then be constituted by a totality of systems (which are supposed to be the subject matters of system-science) according to Def.1, whose index or indexes are essentially different from that of Def.(1^0)0 itself. For solid particles are appropriately the subject matters of (system-science according to) Def.(1^0)1, or of the higher indexed ones (cf. Section V and throughout). Second, since this totality (of solid particles) needs the infinite field of "nonbeing" for its very existence, and accordingly cannot be defined completely without defining the latter; (2) whether our system should be interpreted in the sense of the infinite void [i.e. the infinite system of "nonbeing," the absolutely empty system of infinite size, the absolutely $S\phi$ (for short) of infinite size, which tantamounts to the absolutely nonsystem, the absolutely $\sim S$ (for short) of infinite size]. But this system, the existence of which was postulated by the atomists for their explanation of the position and motion of the atoms, "is" there then by the grace of a straight *contradictio in terminis*; (3) whether our system should be interpreted in the sense of the universe constituted by both the system of "full beings" of infinite number and the system of absolute "nonbeing" of infinite size. What the hell then is this complementary system?

An analogous ambiguity may be found in Wittgenstein's notion of the "world as a whole," about which nothing can be said because whatever can be said has to be said about bounded portions of the world. In partial disagreement with Russel's critical observations on this suggestion in his introduction to the *Tractatus* (Wittgenstein, 1961), let us investigate what this world exactly is. Wittgenstein's first answer would read as follows. The world as a whole is the totality constituted by bounded portions of the world actually (and possibly) spoken about (cf., e.g., propositions 1–2, or 6.341) clearly demarcated from the vacuum, that is, the totality of nonexistent entities not spoken about (meaningfully). Obviously, this answer contradicts Wittgenstein's notion of the world about which nothing can be said. His second answer would run as follows. The world as a whole is the logical space constituted by the totality of both the positive and the negative states of affairs (cf., e.g., propositions 2.04, 2.06). It is a system constituted by both the totality of solid particles and the vacuum, to use the atomic vocabulary. His third answer, partially contrary to the second one (which implies the infinite number of bounded portions of the world actually and possibly spoken about, and accordingly the infinite size of what is, actually and prescriptively, passed over in silence), reads as follows. The world as a whole, as is meant by the first and second answer, is a limited whole (cf., e.g., propositions 5.6, 5.61, 6.45).

Contradicting the preceding responses, Wittgenstein's fourth answer does not exclude the infinity of this world (cf., e.g., proposition 4.2211); this may remind us of the atomist's view of the infinite number of particles and the void of infinite size. His fifth answer consists of two incompatible parts. On the one hand, the feeling of the world as a limited whole (so the world according to his first, second, and third answer) is the mystical (cf. proposition 6.45). On the other hand, the mystical is the unspeakable (cf. proposition 6.522), which then alludes to its unlimitedness. His sixth answer reads as follows. It is the system one perceives after ascending and transcending the system of the bounded portions (actually and possibly) spoken about (cf. propositions 6.54, 7). It is not unambiguously clear what system he sees after ascending and transcending the system of bounded portions of the world actually and possibly spoken about. Is it the totality of the system of bounded portions of the world actually and possibly spoken about? His first, second, third, and the first part of the fifth answer seem misleadingly to allude to this. Misleadingly, since to be able to see this totality he has to transcend even the boundary of this totality, which would be impossible since there are no longer any bounded portions of actual and possible descriptions for Wittgenstein to use as scaffoldings. But maybe he could or has to use the bounded portions of silence (comparable to the distinguishable parts of the void I noted above) as scaffoldings in order to be able to perceive it. Here one comes across the knotty problem of the "self-consistency." ~S may appear to be self-consistent in that the content of ~ S is ~S itself. This of course touches on the issue of the describability of ~S. Analogous to Russel's insightful conjecture in his introduction to Wittgenstein's *Tractatus*, one might assert that every content of thought has a structure concerning which, in that content of thought, nothing can be said, but that there may be another content of thought dealing with the structure of the first content of thought, and having itself a new structure, and that to this hierarchy of contents there may be no limit. In contradistinction to Russel, who inclines to deny such a limitless hierarchy, it might be preferable to say that its existence cannot be completely described. Elaborating Gödel's and Tarski's understanding of undecidability and nondescribability and Bohr's "complementarity" Löfgren proposed an elegant solution for this called the "linguistic complementarity" (Löfgren, 1988, 1991). One kind of this complementarity, (viz., the transcendable one), reads as follows: there is a possibility or need of a metalanguage with, on the one hand, a describability higher than that of ~S, allowing a complete description of ~S, and, on the other hand, autological properties that can partially describe themselves. But even this solution is nothing but a metaphor. For, ~S seems to be an infinite set, and Löfgren's "language" regards (only) the levels and dimensions ranging from the microscopic aspect of Def.$(1^0)1$ to those of Def.$(1^2)2$ (cf. note 6, in Section IX.B). All the above explication is just meant to give a scanty idea of how clumsy our description of this type of system could be. Whitehead rightly notes that discussing it ". . . is a paradox. Indulging in a species of false modesty 'cautious' philosophers undertake its definition" (Whitehead, 1978: 4). As I have argued elsewhere (cf. Carvallo, 1991) some, if not many, nonstandard system-scientists happen to belong to these "cautious" philosophers. Conversely, the discussion of the unknown or unknowable as the observed or observable system has never been the primary concern of classical science, not even of standard system-science, let alone the discussion of the unknown or unknowable as the observing system.

5.   From the classical-scientific, or even from the standard system-scientific point of view, the atomic system as a whole, or Wittgenstein's "world as a whole," is an impossible system, or as a system it exists by the grace of a straight *contradictio in terminis*, or a notoriously fuzzy system. Note however that every non-system in the universe of actual entities (i.e., every environment as understood commonsensically or even system-scientifically) is (only) a metaphor for this ~S. Note further that in science, "system" is usually identified as the observed system, and "nonsystem" stands for the nonobserved system, including the observing system. Consequently every observing system might be also a metaphor for this ~S. Compare the description of this ~S as observation (as such) (cf. item 3, above). Subscribing to the nonclassical scientific view, which rejects the term "observer" of classical theory, the man who stands safely behind the thick glass wall and watches what goes on without taking part, the observing system in our context, including ~S, is part and parcel of the same whole constituted by both the observed and the observing system itself. That is why we call ~S as the far side of the (one and same) "matter."

V.   FURTHER EXPLICATION OF DEF.(1^0)1: THE "CONTENT" OF THE "MATTER" OF DEF.1

As has been suggested earlier, the "content" of the "matter" should display the features of both the far and the near side of the "matter". It comprises (or maybe: is constituted by) the microscopic and the megascopic levels and dimensions of S3 as observing systems. Let us try to have a look at these levels and dimensions as process and as (metastable) product.

1.   As process, it is the gradual disappearance of the near side of the "matter" into the indescribable realm of the far side of the "matter," and the gradual appearance of the near side of the "matter" out of the indescribable realm of the far side of the "matter." Or, to give the impression of their belonging to the same system, the gradual appearance or disappearance of the "matter" out of its far side into its near side and *vice versa*. Confining ourselves to its positively valued aspect (i.e., the appearance out of, etc. . .), it could be characterized as the passing of pure possibility into real possibility, and the passing of real possibility in its turn into actuality. It is ". . . a real incoming of forms into real potentiality, issuing into that real togetherness which is an actual thing" (Whitehead, 1978: 96). It refers to the congression of the "first matter" and the "substantial form" of Aristotle and the scholastics. It is the coming into existence of the "second matter," or the "second matter" itself as the outcome of this congression. It is the coming into existence of Whitehead's categories of existence, or these categories of existence themselves as the (metastable) outcomes of this becoming. It is the "contraction" both in the

natural philosophical and metaphysical sense. In the natural philosophical sense it refers to the self-limitation of ~S as it was represented, for example, in the first century A.D. by the Jewish gnosis (cf. Scholem, 1967), and touched on in passing by Thomas Aquinas (cf. *Summa Theologiae,* III q. 14 a. 3) and later on explicitly represented by some fifteenth century philosophers of nature for example, Isaac Luria (cf. Scholem, 1977) or Nicholas of Cusa (1932; Blumenberg, 1976), and later by some seventeenth and eighteenth century philosophers of nature for example, Jacob Böhme, Henry More, or Goethe (cf., e.g., Miller-Guinsburg, 1980; Steiner, 1926; Gray, 1952). Note by the way that Newton's concept of space was, to a considerable extent, influenced by these ideas, particularly those of Böhme and More (cf. Dobbs, 1983; Figala, 1977; Gasztonyi, 1976).

In the metaphysical sense it refers, according to Aristotelians (cf., e.g., Gredt, 1921), to the descent of a superior concept to the inferior ones, or the other way round, to the logical procedure by which the inferior concepts that are "implicately" enfolded in the superior ones are unfolded. A superior concept, such as that of "being," is characterized as "transcendental" if it is encountered in its inferiors in such a way that it has all their essential and accidental, absolute and relative, partial and total determinations which are *formally identical* to itself. Well, this is the very characterization of our concept of ~S. Accordingly, ~S, by the way, is a "transcendental" concept. Referring to the major ideas of some nonstandard system-scientists we suggest the combination of both senses of "contraction" and the interpretation of the "content" of the "matter" of Def.1 as the "contraction" of ~S to S0 (if the Aristotelian "second matter" in general may be called formally as such), and subsequently of S0 to S1 (the category of nonliving systems), S2 (the category of living systems), S3 (the category of human systems), *et ita porro in infinitum.* It is the break or rupture in the indescribability of ~S, so that the incompleteness of ~S might be understood in the following twofold sense. First, in that by definition it (i.e., ~S) does not have any boundary. Second, in that its indescribability is not complete any more. It is the refraction of the indistinctness and indistinguishability of ~S. It is the interruption of the silence-and the sameness-*an sich* called ~S. It is the "clinamen" of ~S. Viewed positively, this "contraction," (or break, etc.) regards the first morphogenesis and subsequently the limitless complexification of morphogenetic processes.

Note by the way that some scientists among the above "cautious" philosophers, or "cautious philosophers" among scientists, are not always unambiguous with respect to this. They often overlook the (admittedly) knotty distinction between ~S and S0. For instance, the "apeiron" ("the unlimited") of Anaximander seems to allude to our ~S but most probably it finds itself in the universe of S0. The "clinamen" of Lucretius (1986) and of Serres (1983) refers to the break in the universe of S0, not in that of ~S. Similarly "symmetrybreak" both as process and as product—the latter is called "(dissipative) structure" in Prigogine's theory, which in principle is tantamount to the "conjunctum" of Lucretius—refers to the contraction of S0 to S1, etc. Bell's theory of "beables" (Bell, 1987), irrespective of his implicit classical theistic assumption, and similarly Chew's "gentle quantum events" (Chew, 1987), refer to the contraction of S0 to S1, etc. "Symbolein" as introduced by von Domarus (1934) and "contraction" or "symbole" as discussed by Kallikourdis (1988) refer to the contraction of 0-level to 1-level within the internal space of S3. As might appear from this, practically none of them discusses the contraction of ~S to S0. Taking our cue from the concepts of "symbolein" and "symbole" of von Domarus and Kallikourdis, respectively (i.e., confining ourselves to human observing systems), let us pursue our discussion by touching on some microscopic aspects of S3, that is, by looking at some of its intrapersonal aspects.

2.   The frame or the groundplan as world2 can further be interpreted as the innate program of the individual members to see reality as a system. It is one of the subcriteria of the teleonomic criterion (which is one of the invariant criteria of human being). This subcriterion, which in fact is one of the latest results of the evolution of the "triune brain" (cf. MacLean, 1973) and might be localized primarily on the neomammalian level, is one of the guiding forces in the human being in his self-realization. This self-realization might be viewed as a never-ending endeavor to systemize the humanization of nature and the naturalization of the human. In this complex sequence of efforts one might roughly discern three major stages: first the very general abstract or assumptive and primordial interactions between human being and outer nature, second between human beings as concrete individuals and the second outer nature (i.e., the societal structure), and finally between human beings and the third outer nature (i.e., the scientific or cyberspatial structure).

Putting the discussion about the second and the third stage provisionally in parentheses, let us catch a glimpse of the first stage. The primordial environmentalization of the human being by outer nature and the primordial emergence of the human being as an act of consciousness might be located in the following structure of time as their environment. First a period when there was not yet any data-environment, a period when the data had not yet gathered together in some way to form a distinguishable domain, a period when there was not even any lowest level of gestalt, the time when there were neither "ducks" nor "antelopes" (for details about patterns of theory-formation alluded to by these metaphors, see, e.g., the exciting book of Hanson, 1972). Second a (subsequent) period when the data had come to a rudimentary equilibrium, a primitive gestalt, and when the perceiver of the gestalt was himself a part of the gestalt, a period when the individual was not yet a complete and distinguishable unit, and when the unit was an environment–individual setup. (Admittedly I am giving here a sketchy picture of a possible world that is searched for industriously by paleontologists, developmental psychologists, and genetic epistemologists.) And finally the period when the prime ancestor of mankind discovered himself as the metaphysical Columbus in the midst of a world as a system of successions of events and where certain "ducks" and "antelopes" were already there to be affirmed as such, while others were still waiting to be reconstructed by him. This sounds like a simple compromise in the age-old controversy about the problem of which has priority (logically or onto-logically): the human being or outer nature; systemization by the human being as an ontological statement or as epistemological action; whether in the human being the mind (or in our case: the innate program) is dependent on the senses (as defended by Aristotle up to and including the present-day positivists) or the senses on the mind, or the innate program (as defended by Plato up to and including the present-day postpositivists), a problem that in the final instance rests on the question of whether the senses as the common transitional space are conditioned by the human mind or by outer nature. [Note for the record that in touching on the subject matter of "innate program" my (possible) commitment to any of the major currents in the psychological theories of perception is explicitly suspended here.] Remarkably enough, the frame or the groundplan as the innate program appears to be one of the central themes of cybernetics and of the recently emerging computational paradigm. It seems then as if (some) aspects of the near side of the "form" of system-science are already immanent (as hidden variables?) in the far side of the "matter" of this science. For further discussion of these issues, see my planned article on definition two.

There are, in my opinion, two possible implications for our present theme, which are sideshoots of the age-old controversy between Aristotelians and Platonists. First, that the outer world (i.e., world1) might play a role as codeterminant and part of the frame, in the sense that systemization is a two-partner game between man (or: mind, or world2, or innate program) as reality-structurer and outer reality (or: world1) as the (co)structurer of man's (world2's, innate program's) image about itself (i.e., about outer nature). For an elegant discussion of this two-partner game brought about by modern science, see, for example, Koyre (1978), Prigogine and Stengers (1984), or von Foerster (1984). Second, that there is an even convergence between man (world2 etc.) as reality-structurer and outer reality (world1) as structurer of man. This means that the frames as world2 and as world1 converge. This scientifically rather exotic view is proposed by the holographic paradigm.

3.   System-science in this primordial sense has a very large extension, for it concerns the science of every human subject. It concerns the science whose origin coincides with the emergence of human nature–that is it concerns science since the emergence of *Homo sapiens*—and, provided the innate program remains unchanged and this human species continues to exist, it will extend beyond the boundaries of the contemporary *homo* of Silicon Valley. The only determining element in this extension seems to be the innate program. This has however the following implications that seem to interfere with the consistency of the already so fuzzy concept "system" of Def.$(1^0)0$. These are: (a) that it is conceivable that

another human race exists which is equipped with a different innate program [this suggests the contingency of the system: the system (both as subject and as object) need not necessarily be identical with the system that we know de facto and/or that we are]; (b) that even in our own human species exceptions are conceivable (and perhaps even exist de facto), in the sense that the innate program can function otherwise than normally so that one can have a concept of system different from the normal one; studies and researches about human "alienation" might be very relevant for understanding this possibility; (c) that it is, finally, conceivable that the innate program to imagine the system in the normal sense harbors within itself its own negation, in that the innate program incorporates a possibility of not seeing the system as a gestalt, or not only so.

Implication (a) offers less difficulty. It is even the only implication that at least indirectly says that the "system" in Def.$(1^0)0$ is *de dictu*, or modal–logically, distinguishable. We accept it as science-fiction or, more philosophically expressed, as a "possible world." It hangs on the walls of our mind as an epistemological surrealistic painting. Implications (b) and (c) seem to refer to a few central issues of some contemporary studies in the quality of mind, ranging from quantum physics to transpersonal psychology. These two implications seem to trouble us more, for they touch on the very heart of science as until the present we have (normally) known it: it seems to be essential that a system (either as subject or as object of science) should be a gestalt (i.e., have boundaries); a totally open system reaches an equilibrium with its environment, becomes indistinguishable from it, and disappears, and a science whose subject and/or object were such a system would fall to pieces. . . Or would the innate program after all be, at least partially, a human construction? That is, in the sense that certain kinds of thinking (in our present connection: thinking exclusively in terms of discrete systems) may in the long run affect the structure of the brain in a permanent way. (Some experiments seem to confirm this hypothesis.) Or to put it differently: some phenomena (e.g., on the subquantum level) that are being studied according to scientifically respectable modes of research contradict these methods. The embarrassed scientist is then like the guy who invented the universal solvent but found soon enough that there was no bottle to put it in. For heaven's sake, what is he to do with the solvent (which is there), or with the bottle (which is not there)? We shall not go here into these perennial problems of system-science.

4. Viewed from the megascopic point of Def.$(1^0)1$, S3 as a transpersonal transcending system is part and parcel of the dissipative structure of genetic, genealogical, and cultural perception. This refers to the learning of mankind at large: S3's evolution is thus the rediscovery of the genetically, genealogically, and culturally transmitted dynamic rules. S3's evolution is likewise the imposing of these rules upon itself, which generates a variety of ordered morphological, behavioral, and cultural patterns (cf. Carvallo, 1988).

5. An alternative for the above view is that of S3 as transcending system,

which as it were is condemned to travel along every path to find out the boundaries of the transcendental space, that is, to find out the boundaries of ~S. For this wandering there are of course many possible guiding ideas. One of these is the idea of the furling back of S3 on its origin. The following conclusion drawn by Varela might be illustrative for this idea: " . . . In fact, whenever we do try and find the source of, say, a perception or an idea, we find ourselves in an ever-receding fractal, and wherever we choose to delve we find it equally full of details and interdependencies. It is always the perception of a perception of a perception. . . . Or the description of a description of a description . . . There is nowhere we can drop anchor and say, "This is where this perception started; this is how it was done" (Varela, 1984b; cf. also Maturana and Varela, 1987). The reverse idea is that of the incessant unfurling of S3 toward the last symmetrybreak in its (i.e., S3's) endeavor to encounter the first symmetry and finally the boundaries of this symmetry. According to the "evolutionary vision" as propounded by Jantsch, there is " . . . no end in sight, no permanency, no telos" in this wandering. We (i.e., S3) are the stream, the sheer-going-on-ness (cf. Jantsch, 1980a: 255, 267). Or, to describe it somewhat concretely and down to earth, this state of affairs refers, among other things, to the key-phenomenon of "learning" as is diversely interpreted, for example, by G. Bateson (1978, 1980) and Jantsch (1976) or by Wiener (1980) and Turing (1950), the development of metamathematical insights into which is currently sorely needed (Löfgren, 1988).

VI. FURTHER EXPLICATION OF DEF.(1^1)0: THE "MATTER" OF THE "CONTENT" OF DEF.1

This (assumed) first deduction of Def.1^0 (which at the same time helps to constitute the "content" of Def.1) oscillates between the p^0- and p^1-level. It is characterized here as the far side (of the "content") to hint at the hidden deep-structural and historically not-new aspects of system-science. With regard to this first fuzzy specification of Def.1^0 I shall confine myself to the further explication of the concept of system-paradigm. The systemic scientific culture is and can be interpreted diversely by diverse people, as was alluded to above. This might bear the following implications.

1.   That it is not only difficult to find any set of doctrines that system-scientists (as diverse as the system itself) hold in common other than the belief that the essential systemic structure of reality is true.

2.   Nor only that it is hard to find any common elements in the system-paradigm (paradigm meaning here the Kuhnian paradigm in the sense of disciplinary matrix) that they all subscribe to as "normal" system-scientists. In other words, that to ascribe a rigid monolithic character to the system-paradigm—as Kuhn, according to a number of critics (e.g., Laudan, 1977: 75; Frankel, 1978: 209; Bohm and Peat, 1987) attributes to paradigms (somewhat similar to the Lakatosian con-

cept of the "hard core" of research program)—would be in conflict with the empirical findings that suggest that even the most basic assumptions of system-research traditions change with time, and that system-paradigms need not dominate a system-research community to the exclusion of rivals: many system-scientists borrow bits and pieces from their extra-scientific-community paradigms without endorsing them as a whole. Or to put it differently using Pask's vocabulary: no precise correspondence could be made between M-individual and P-individuals. It would not be impossible for one M-individual to correspond to several, sometimes conflicting, P-individuals (cf. Pangaro, 1985; Pask, 1991);

3. But that system-paradigm should consist of an oppositional system constituted by diversity and unity. This implies that:

(a) It is precisely the polarity, or in one of its contemporary versions, the incommensurability, between rival system-paradigms—this in contrast then with the Kuhnian view of paradigm and perhaps even beyond the surmise of his critics—that constitutes (or more correctly: ought to constitute) the system-paradigm. Being constituted by the opposite poles belongs to the invariant criterion of the system-paradigm. (Besides many other implications, this criterion, curiously enough, also means that system-science in this sense can also signify the system of sciences, the unification of sciences.) The present hypothesis is only in the state of a preliminary exploration (cf., e.g., Bråten, 1981, 1988; Zwick, 1984; Locker, 1991): most of the work on this subject remains to be done.

(b) Being constituted by the opposite poles is one of the basic criteria of the particular system-paradigms and of those system-paradigms that claim to be embodiments of the invariant system-paradigm, or generalizations of the particular system-paradigms.

(c) Being constituted by the opposite poles brings about system-amplification: system-paradigm then becomes extensionally and intensionally larger and fuller than the "normal" paradigm of Kuhn or even of his critics.

VII. FURTHER EXPLICATION OF DEF(1¹)1: THE "CONTENT" OF THE "CONTENT" OF DEF.1

A. Synthesis I

System-science that is predicated on the system-paradigm interpreted as such is generated by the primary assumption about the system. This universe of system-thinking is constituted by two primordial opposite preconceptions about reality, namely, the preconception on the one pole that reality is discrete and on the other pole that reality is continuous. So system-science in this sense concerns thinking (or: thought-culture) in its diversity of contents and forms, located or oscillating within the continuum of this preconceptional polarity.

Confining ourselves to one of the constituents of Western culture or philosophy, as far as it is recorded, we might say that system-science in this sense already dates from the pre-Socratic period or, referring to the (Western) "hermetic" tradition (see., e.g., Ficino, 1962; Walker, 1954), even before it. The general characterization of the European philosophical tradition as consisting of a series of footnotes to Plato, as remarked by Whitehead (1978: 39), is in my opinion, no longer safe in our times and that for the following two reasons. First, considering the characteristics and developments of many contemporary scientific disciplines (e.g., the new physics, the new biology, the new psychology, and their environing metaphysics), one discerns a rather clear tendency to bypass classical Greek philosophy and to go further back into the past and particularly to the pre-Socratic philosophers in their attempts to reconcile the aforementioned ideal opposites and to explain the unity and dynamics of things. For details on this, compare, for example, Chew's monadology, Bohm's holistic quantum theory, Prigogine's Lucretian physics, Bunge's remarks on the three contemporary misconceptions about "panta rhei" (Bunge, 1977: 271–275), or Popper's plea for a return to the simple, straightforward rationality of the pre-Socratics (Popper, 1974: 136–165). Second, if it were true that the train of European thought is that of classical Greek philosophy—Whitehead even explicitly names Plato and Aristotle as the two founders of all Western thought (Whitehead, 1978: xi) and with regard to system-philosophy, Laszlo maintains more or less the same (Laszlo, 1973: 12)—then it would be necessary in the interest of its own self-organization for contemporary Western science and philosophy, where system and process-thought are being rediscovered, to furl back on itself and to submit the supposed unshakability of its foundations to a critical reflection. There may be good reasons for some doubt about this! (For Plato's misleading "panta-rhei" interpretation, see, e.g., Kirk, 1978: 366–384. For Aristotle's historical perversions and deficiencies as a historian of ideas, see, e.g., Cherniss, 1971.)

There are further many synthesis-attempts in the course of Western history (cf., e.g., Sambusky, 1975; Prigogine and Stengers, 1984) which, due to limitations of space, have to be left undiscussed here.

VIII. FURTHER EXPLICATION OF DEF.$(1^1)2$: THE "FORM" OF THE "CONTENT" OF DEF.1

The near side of the "content" of the system-science is used here to indicate that aspect of system-science which by most people (including its "founders" and its "critics") is actually perceived and conceived or identified as system-science itself. This aspect consists partly of the supposed new aspects of system-science (i.e., aspects of the Def.$(1^1)0$ constituent) and partly of the actually new aspects of system-science (i.e., aspects of the Def.$(1^2)1$ and of the Def.$(1^2)2$ constituents). Thus the near side of the "content" of system-science has reference to contemporary system-science.

This is claimed by its founders and propounders to be either a major reorientation in scientific thought of the type of the Kuhnian scientific revolution (cf. von Bertalanffy, 1973: xv–xxii) or a reformation of the content of a lost paradigm (cf. Zeleny, 1980: 3–43). This assumed first generalization of the many and fragmented sciences (and which simultaneously helps to constitute the "content" of Def.1) oscillated between p^1- and p^2-level (i.e., the level of styles of thinking and that of modes of research, respectively). Temporarily conforming in part to Zeleny (1980; 1981), I shall make a very general division in this contemporary system-science into two streams, or two cultures: the mainstream of the current versions of well-established theories of general systems and (first-order) cybernetics on the one hand, let us call it the *standard stream*, and on the other hand the alternative stream, which is either more or less outside the standard stream or can be viewed as an anomalous current within the *standard stream*, let us call it the *nonstandard stream*. This classification, however, is by no means intended to suggest that these streams are quite distinct from each other, for in fact they are related at many points, and in some cases they are even concrescent, so that there is more reason to speak of fuzziness than of distinction. A relevant example of this is the question about the precursors and founders of system-science in the sense of Def.(1^1)2.

A. The Precursors and Founders

A few snatches from the system-literature, more or less arbitrarily chosen, might suffice to give an impression of this fuzziness that could lead to controversies:

1. Von Bertalanffy explicitly claims that it was he who introduced the idea of a "general system theory" (cf. von Bertalanffy, 1973: 9, 96). As precursors of the systems concept he mentions many illustrious names such as Leibniz, Nicholas of Cusa, Paracelsus, Vico, Ibn Khaldun, Hegel, Marx, Hesse, Köhler, and Lotka. Also mentioned are Whitehead, Canon, and Claude Bernard (cf. id. p. 9, 10).

2. Mattessich poses the question of who is the father of system-theory: Bogdanov or von Bertalanffy (Mattessich, 1978: 283–286). According to him it would be far more fair to assign this honor to Bogdanov, and that on historical grounds and arguments of substance. Historical, because Bogdanov's work appeared many years (viz., about 16 years) before von Bertalanffy's first system-theoretic notions. Regarding substance, because many general theoretical problems of the systems approach are elaborated by Bogdanov more fully and rigorously than is the case in the contemporary theory of systems and cybernetics. The question regarding von Bertalanffy's persistent silence about Bogdanov for the present still remains an interesting puzzle for historians of science.

3. Zeleny in his prize-winning article does explicitly name Wiener as the founder of the science of cybernetics, but not explicitly von Bertalanffy as the founder of system-theory, though he does quote von Bertalanffy, from which it

may be concluded that von Bertalanffy is the postulator of a new discipline called GST, whose direct precursor is Bogdanov (cf. Zeleny, 1979). In any case Zeleny also exerted himself to acquit Bogdanov of his Bertalanffyan *damnatio memoriae*. In the same article he names two other leading figures besides Bogdanov as precursors of contemporary system-science: Trentowsky and Smuts.

4.   Beer speaks very generally of the many founders of cybernetics, specially mentioning three of them: Wiener, McCulloch, and Ashby (cf. Beer, 1983).

5.   Of the early precursors of the autopoiesis paradigm, Zeleny, in later publications, names the following: Claude Bernard, Vico, Trentowsky, Menger, Bogdanov, Leduc, Smuts, von Hayek, and Weiss (cf. Zeleny, 1980, 1985, 1987, 1988a,b).

6.   The touchy controversy about the precursorship is even still of current interest as witness the correspondence conducted between Smith and Powers and their respective groups with regard to the feedback control behavior theory (cf., e.g., Smith and Smith, 1988, 1989, Glaserfeld, 1989; Powers, 1989).

So far the examples by way of illustration. The fuzzy and controversial state of the matter may perhaps in part be due to the fact that the question of precursorship and foundation is historically situated in the *transitional space* of Def.$(1^1)0$ and Def.$(1^1)2$ and conceptually in the transition space of GST and (first-order) cybernetics (thus of the two main constituents of the standard stream) on the one hand, and in the transitional space of the standard stream and the nonstandard stream on the other. Furthermore one might see in the illustration given above a standard example of the entanglement of environment and system, that is, if one may regard the relation {precursorship: foundation} as {environment: system}. Or, to put the problematic aspect of this in one single essential question: To which does the transitional space itself belong: to the system or to the environment?

Finally and in passing I would like to object to the one-sided active view with respect to the emergence of a theory (cf. fathership, foundation): Is it not more often so that people are gripped by an idea? (Compare the metaphors of gravitation and heat, mentioned earlier.) Here we might then interpret the aforesaid controversial states of affairs as states of affairs that may arise when the "system" as frame and in the state of world3 is in the process of becoming the "system" as frame and that as world2. In short, when the "system" as frame is about to become the "system" as reference. Or, when the referential and/or self-referential openness of the system is bound to represent itself as the referential and/or self-referential closure of the system. In the history of science this process very often takes place simultaneously and dissipatively in different places, in many mutually practically closed cultural circles, in various mutually unacquainted or mutually independent scientific disciplines, or in various mutually unacquainted or mutually independent human minds. One of the archetypes of this phenomenon is perhaps the period that Jaspers (1953) called the "axial era," the period between 500 B.C.

and about A.D. 500, the period when the philosophy of antiquity simultaneously budded forth in different parts of the world from its mythological garb.

B.   Synthesis II: The Standard Stream

The same phenomenon is seen with regard to the standard stream. System-theory and cybernetics seemed to respond to a secret trend in various disciplines: they put into words and explicate that which is tacitly alive in the minds of many people in the post–world war era. For this secret trend emerges in a paradoxical niche that is structured by two opposite developments: on the one hand, the extreme classical position with respect to the "objectivity" of scientific knowledge and to the detachment of the observed had created what appeared to be insurmountable dificulties in developing "scientific" sciences other than the classical ones. This seems to be the general (and tacit) discontent (e.g., against logical positivism, which has dominated the scientific scene for almost half a century). On the other hand, the sophisticated emphasis on and study of machines and machine constructability (which is partially based on the classical attitude) has significantly contributed to the awareness necessary to free scientists from the religious quest for immutable observer-independent laws. (For further details about the motives leading to the postulate or a general theory of systems, see, e.g., von Bertalanffy, 1973: 97–100).

This sketch is intended only as a passing allusion to the indistinctness and controversies concerning the status of system-theory on the one hand and to the recent attempts to focus system-theory as one single theory on the other. The indistinctness is apparent, among other things, with regard to:

1.   The interpretation of system-theory as having sprung from the last war effort and being rooted in military hardware and related technological developments such as systems analysis and systems engineering.

2.   The interpretation of system-theory as being identical with (first-order) cybernetics. Von Bertalanffy has explicitly drawn our attention to these misinterpretations (cf. von Bertalanffy, 1973: 15). Yet there are still perhaps reasons enough for many misinterpretations, which are precisely due to vagueness and inconsistencies in von Bertalanffy's formulations (cf. Blauberg et al., 1977: 56–68);

3.   The distinction between system-theory and system-research as proposed by Ackoff (cf. Ackoff, 1963; Ackoff and Emery, 1972). It lies beyond the scope of Def.1 to go into details in this, or into the current attempts to synthesize the oppositional points referred to as undertaken, for example, by Klir (1970) or Zeleny, already referred to, and others in *Kybernetes* of 1979. This sketch of obscurities is chiefly intended to convey some impression of the not-unusual fact that a theory at its earliest and muddled stage of development can still be full of all kinds of "weak" elements (in our context, consisting of fuzziness, inconsistencies, and perhaps even contradictions). In these fluctuations, however, we should like to recog-

nize some (presumable) structure: against the background of the paradoxical niche sketched above, one could probably say that the emergence of the research-guiding interest of system-theory is primarily conditioned by the first and that of (first-order) cybernetics by the second opposite development. In this sense one might regard system-theory and (first-order) cybernetics as two complementary currents in the standard stream. Anticipating the constituents of Def.1 to be discussed below, one might perhaps also represent this state of affairs as follows. System-theory is primarily occupied with the synthesis within the universe of Def.(12)1, and (first-order) cybernetics with the synthesis within the universe of Def.(12)2. The pretense then of GST (and afterwards of general systems research and now of the International Society for Systems-Sciences) is the synthesis of system-theory and cybernetics. As this latter synthesis has not yet fully evolved into a complete theory, it should for the present be regarded as a framework of thought rather than as a theory guided by specific assumptions and derived testable predictions, as some (e.g., Rapoport, 1981; Capra, 1983: 285–466; Laszlo, 1983: ix) have argued.

In spite of its rather entangled initial stage, the standard stream should not be regarded as a neutral common platform for the Mannheimian free-floating intelligentsia. The systemic-scientific culture as it constantly organizes itself and stabilizes itself in the form of the standard stream does have an identifiable profile. Explicitly stated (e.g., in terms of the theory of collective behavior), this culture would even have beliefs that can be ranged between the pole of "value-oriented beliefs" and that of the "norm-oriented beliefs" (for details about these beliefs, see Smelser, 1962). It is even a movement either value-oriented or norm-oriented (cf. especially the history of the system-theory, e.g., von Bertalanffy, 1972: 21–41, 1973: 1–28; Laszlo, 1973: chap. 1; Cavallo even bluntly speaks of "system research movement," cf. Cavallo, 1979). It even had its own enemies (cf. Churchman, 1979), it gives concrete form to the "great refusal" toward the established absurdities of classical science and, *sit venia verbo*, the classical conscience. By projecting and pleading for the systemic world-picture–hypothesis it tries to realize an ideal science, and implicitly an ideal human life (cf. topics ranging from "world-order models" to Churchman's conversations; see Churchman, 1984). Naturally it would not be right to identify the aforesaid forms of collective behavior with tendencies toward rigid monolithicity. For it is precisely openness (at least tacitly or prescriptively) toward many kinds of science, including those forms incommensurable with it, that constitutes the great appeal of and at the same time the great challenge for this culture itself, which in origin presented itself not only as the "great refusal" already referred to, but also as a self-organizing embodiment of new admirations, new scepsis, and new interests, requiring us to enter into new dialogues and to look for new coherence. Listen to Stafford Beer's eulogium on the three great founders of contemporary cybernetics: "They scorned the protection of specialism within the strong walls of which each was vulnerable.

Their minds ranged without limit and without fear in the search for the invariance in regulatory systems." (Beer, 1983).

C. Synthesis III: The Nonstandard Stream

The alternative stream harbors various subparadigms or currents that seem to be capable of merging into one paradigm, which Jantsch (1980b: 86) calls the *paradigm of dissipative self-organization*, and Zeleny (1980, 1981) the *paradigm of autopoiesis*.

This already indirectly suggests that by some the theory of dissipative structures of the Brussels school, and by others the autopoiesis theory of the Chilean group, is (tacitly) regarded as the respective standard image of this new unifying system-paradigm. Passing over possible differences of nuance, this newly emerging paradigm might be regarded as the contemporary effort to structurize our perplexity when confronted with one of the great puzzles of the universe as far as we now know it, which is that it (this universe) seems to contain two time-arrows: one is the famous second law of thermodynamics, which refers to entropy-increase and potential decay, and the other is that of evolution, which segregates entropy and builds up increasingly complex structures of order, no doubt at the cost of creating more disorder elsewhere (cf. e.g., Boulding, 1981a: xi; Prigogine and Stengers, 1984). Synthesizing these two opposite time-arrows thus seems to be the common denominator of this system-scientific (sub)culture, which includes a large variety of disciplines—for example, biology, economy, philosophy, cybernetics, biophysics, logic, system and computer analysis, engineering, operations research, and linguistics (cf. Zeleny, 1981).

D. Stream Within Stream

Though it is nowhere explicitly stated, I presume from the scanty literature available to me that the system of this perplexity is greater than many of the propounders of this newly emerging system-paradigm suppose. By this I mean that some (presumed) constituents of this perplexity are already dimensionally "different" and that these undercurrent constituents might conflue sometime in the near future into a "different" stream, which in its turn would become an alien stream within the not yet established paradigm of autopoiesis or of dissipative self-organization. This seems to become apparent in the fact that many people within the dissipatively emerging system-scientific community of autopoieticians and of the dissipative self-organization are very much out of their depths (at least tacitly) when reading some ideas, approaches, or efforts to structurize the above-mentioned perplexity (cf. Boulding, 1981b: xvi).

The reference here is to the ideas etc. of the new physics, at least those parts of it which take seriously, the consequences of the third scientific revolution in wave mechanics, so that they "happen" to be on the same wavelength as a few types of the new psychology (where the system of consciousness is radically amplified) and of the new biology (where mind is interpreted as a part of nature and not as a supernatural entity). These concepts have been admitted into the literature of the newly emerging paradigm. With regard to this possible alien stream within the newly emerging paradigm, there seems to exist a tacit ambivalence among the propounders of the autopoiesis and of the dissipative self-organization paradigm. Jantsch and some others such as Pankow, Abraham, Markley, and Gunther seem to sympathize with and even to promote these ideas without regarding them as belonging to a (possible) different stream. They subsume these ideas under the paradigm of evolution, whereby the system of evolution is richly amplified. Or rather: self-transcendence is according to them incorporated as a principle in self-organization (cf. e.g., Jantsch, 1976, 1980a, 1981). This hypothesis certainly does not sound classical (but that does not necessarily make it nonscientific), since here a characteristic that according to the classical assumption belongs only to human beings is assigned to all the rest of evolution! The tendency here is very plain: to overcome the basic dualistic attitude of Western culture! There is only one evolution that is constituted by us, we are evolution (Jantsch, 1980a: 8, 1981, : 4). Jantsch even expressly mentions that "there is a link here to the recent 'holographic' image of our relations to reality" (cf. Jantsch, 1981: 3).

If so, then the universe of discourse of Jantsch's extended evolution does indeed have points of contact with the universe of discourse of system-science in the sense of Def.$(1^0)0$. Or more explicitly, Jantsch and colleagues have (re)introduced the themes of Def.$(1^0)0$ into the universe of discourse of Def.$(1^1)2$ and by doing so have made a valuable attempt to synthesize the "matter" and the "form" of system-science in the sense of Def.1. (Note in passing that Jantsch also belongs to those earlier mentioned "cautious philosophers" who do not make a clear distinction between ~S and S0). For contemporary system-scientific culture, or at least for this alien current within the nonstandard stream, this may engender a double effect. On the one hand it may be rewarded by being labeled unscientific by a certain established scientific culture; on the other hand it has thereby unmasked the age-old established demarcation between science and religion as an ideology. The bold (re)synthesis of these two universes—for this is not a novel, but a lost synthesis—seems to answer to the secret trend in the mind of many contemporary scientists (see, e.g., Wilber, 1982).

Other authors, such as Prigogine, do indeed plainly show an ambivalent attitude toward this category of ideas. On the one hand he (Prigogine) characterizes the "revelations" of relativity and quantum mechanisms as irrational and antiscientific (cf. Prigogine, 1984: 34); on the other hand he attributes to matter in far-from-equilibrium-conditions mindlike properties such as the ability to perceive and to communicate, an attribution that means no more to him than an anthropomorphism (cf. Prigogine and Stengers, 1984: 14, 148, 165), whereas in circles of quantum physicists this is surely a highly serious scientific issue! (cf. Bohm and

Hiley, 1975, 1987.4) In much the same tone as Prigogine, Zeleny considers that " . . . these anthropomorphic analogies are being invoked in order to close conveniently in the gap between the isolated components and their behavior as a whole. Yet, all the 'function' are observer dependent anthropomorphisms, convenient descriptors of how things *appear* to us, not necessarily reflecting how things *actually are*" (Zeleny, 1980: 21). Leaving aside further reactions to this suggestion that anthropic analogies can merely serve to take place of the Laplacian or Maxwellian demon, the fundamental problem arises here of whether science can make any statement at all as to how things actually are. The anthropic bias is not new in the biological sciences. The Aristotelian telos and/or entelecheia, the medieval "imponderabilia," the vitalism of the eighteenth and nineteenth century, and contemporary controversial issues with regard to concepts such as purpose, cognition, information, and communication are, I think, items whose natural niche is the transitional space constituted by three—and not two, as suggested indirectly by Varela (1979: 3–7)—major paradigms: the mechanistic, the organicistic, and what one might call the anthropic. This anthropic bias is not only not new in the biological sciences, it even seems to be one of the items that help to constitute the crucial hinge around which the contemporary organicistic paradigm interacts both with the mechanicistic paradigm (see, e.g., the case of molecular biology or Monod's synthesis of chance and necessity) and with the anthropic paradigm (see, e.g., the argument advanced by Jantsch c.s.). As we already remarked, the anthropic paradigm implied in the evolutionary vision of Jantsch c.s. seems, at closer inspection, (even) to be one of the nonclassical variants of the anthropic paradigm (for more details about this, see Carvallo, 1991).

IX. FURTHER EXPLICATION OF DEF.(1^2)0: THE "MATTER" OF THE "FORM" OF DEF.1

Def.(1^2)0 might be regarded as the matter of the form of Def.1. This matter of the form of Def.1 refers, as already shown, first to every particular science that is "materially" a system-science—that is, that Def.(1^0)0 translates itself at p^2-level in the shape of Def.(1^2)0; second to every particular sciences whose subject is the "system," and this conveys that Def.(1^0)1 translates itself as p^2-level in the form of Def.(1^2)1. With this representation it is not only suggested (as, e.g., by Arbib, 1984: 362) that there are no firm boundaries that distinguish cybernetics or systems-research from other scientific disciplines. It is even further hypothesized here that every (particular) science is "materially" a system-science and that every (particular) science has the "system" as its subject matter. In other words, if every science that is of the system (in the *genitivus subjectivus* sense) necessarily must have a system to be investigated (viz., a "system of interest," in the usual GST term, or an "observed system," in second-order cybernetics parlance), and if every "system of interest" is by definition a system (see the usual GST definition), then every science is in principle system-science! Viewed as such, contemporary system-science is the "conscientization" (Freire, 1973) of science of its systemic nature. This has been done and is still being done by the aforementioned systems-research movement, admittedly within the restricted framework of Def.(1¹)2.

In the further explication of this definitional state of affairs, I shall confine myself to setting forth conditions for discussing the origin and the development of the many separate sciences. This development is triggered by one of the criteria of the frame, namely its teleonomic criterion.

A.   The Telenomic Criterion[5]

The frame—metaphorically an autopoietic unity—has a teleonomic criterion: it is constituted by two mutually, complementary subcriteria, the cognitive subcriterion and the evaluative-volitional subcriterion. These subcriteria function at that instant when the abstract, fuzzy, implicit, potential, and general frame (i.e., the frame as "matter") becomes manifest in concreto, that is, when the frame ignores its abstractness, etc., when the frame appears out of its abstractness, etc., or when the frame as "matter" "exists" via its dimensions and levels. Or to put it the other way round: when the telenomic criterion comes into action, it triggers the "existence" of the frame. Historically, that is, in fact, the frame as "Bestimmung" (destination) continually manifests itself more concretely in frames as "Beschaffenheit" (talification), to represent this state of affairs from the Hegelian point of view (cf. Hegel, 1929). Actually, the development of Western science up to the present proceeds via this mechanism. And perhaps this is even one of the laws governing the development of science in general, cutting both ways. On the one hand science has proved to owe its actual development largely to reductionism, both in its classical (mechanistic) form (which is predicated on the idea that all reality is governed by a few simple physical laws, which can at least in principle explain every phenomenon), and in its nonclassical form, as it is proposed, among others, by the GST (cf. Def.2). On the other hand the mutual estrangement between the frame as destination and the emerging frames as talification seems to be the price that must be paid by this mechanism of development: the frames as talification are continually less identical to the frame as destination, they are the continually smaller and independent severances and diminutions of the frame as destination. They embody the brokenness of the frame in general. This is the negative aspect of scientific enlightenment; there is something about it that makes us think of the myth of the Fall. By some, indeed, this state of affairs refers to the symmetrybreak in its perjorative sense, namely as deterioration or diminution or limitation either in the philosophical sense as breaks in our understanding of the a priori symmetry (i.e., the Platonic symmetry), or scientifically as symmetry-breakdown (see, e.g., Prigogine, 1967: 120, 132, 134; Turing, 1952). The many controversies within the modern sciences are in principal generated by this state of affairs. The tacit tension between philosophy (including system-philosophy) and the many branches of science stem from this mutual alienation. Modern system-science, especially system-science in the sense of Def.$(1^1)2$, did indeed originate from the unhappy consciousness of confrontation with this broken frame. But symmetrybreak also (and simultaneously) concerns positive states of affairs, namely the increase of perfection either in the philosophical sense as the coming into real existence of the a priori, or scientifically as the transformation to higher levels of complexity. (Compare also the above characterization of the "content" of the "matter" of Def.1.) The nonstandard stream is characterized by its bold attempts to synthesize both meanings of symmetrybreak.

B. The Cognitive Subcriterion

The cognitive subcriterion of the frame includes the selection from the available products of the aforementioned metaphysics (viz., the system constituted by ontology, axiology, epistemology, and praxiology, as products). In this selection it is guided by the systemic image of the reality to be studied and the systemic image of that particular science. Ideally these two items should be in close interaction; that is, there should be a strong interaction between the issues proper to the systemic culture as a whole and the internal conceptual problems of a particular (system-) science. Yet in actual fact the mutual alienation referred to above may appear here, this time in the shape of mutual alienation between the language-axis and the experience-axis of the same frame.

Ideally language and experience ought to constitute one system. Language includes experience and vice versa. There are strong philosophical arguments for the position that the qualitative content of our conscious experience is intelligible in publicly communicable terms (see, e.g., Locke, 1690; Harrison, 1979), without being fully describable[6]. Language and experience in this (ideal) sense seem to be convertible. Referring to our aforementioned distinctions of system-science, language (and/or experience) might be distinguished in an analogous hierarchy of levels and dimensions, namely, language according Def.$(1^0)0$, language according to Def.$(1^0)1$, language according to Def.$(1^0)2$, language according to Def.$(1^1)0$, language according to Def.$(1^1)1$, language according to to Def.$(1^1)2$, language according to Def.$(1^2)0$, language according to Def.$(1^2)1$, and language according to Def.$(1^2)2$. Because of the restricted scope of this chapter, I will not enter into the further specifications of these levels and dimensions of language, which paradigmatically might be the same as those of the above system-science. In the following context I will confine myself primarily to language (and/or experience) according to Def.$(1^2)0$, $(1^2)1$, and $(1^2)2$, where its symmetry (i.e., its primordial wholeness with experience) happens to be broken.

Let us look at the two major variants of this mutual alienation that can appear within the cognitive subcriterion. [Note the following nuances: the first major variant primarily refers to the interaction between the systemic culture (as a whole) and the particular system-sciences (as parts). The second major variant has reference primarily to the internal interaction of the particular (system)sciences with one another, where the relationship within the first major variant (i.e., whole: parts) is analogously repeated within the smaller space of the (system)scientific community. Obviously the concrete state of affairs in these two major variants may overlap.]

In the first place, there may be a discrepancy between the systemic image of that slice of reality to be studied (i.e., the p^0- and p^1-components of the science) and the systemic image of a particular science concerning the modes of procedure to be applied (i.e., the p^2-component of the science) in the mind of an individual system-scientist or within a system-scientific research group. For instance, the question might be raised here in: How far can quantitative sociology be justified system-scientifically in confining the social system to its macroscopic level only? Admittedly, it makes possible the measurement (at present available) but does it also render the true state of human affairs? Must not the "language" (here = the modes of procedure) of that particular (system)science be constantly changed, even qualitatively if necessary, to render adequately that particular system of interest? May a system that in substance (thus in its p^0-dimension) belongs to the anthropic paradigm be sufficiently, if not necessarily, "explained" by means of the mechanicistic modes of procedure (thus on the p^2-dimension/level), which at the moment are indeed more advanced system-scientifically? Can the language appropriate for the discrete universe also be simply applied to the continuous one? And so on. In short: Should not the modes of procedure of the particular (system)sciences each time be adequately receptive to the cultural content of the system? Should they not develop by freeing themselves each time from outmoded or inadequate forms of understanding reality? These questions, which are raised every now and again, are also indications of the internal discontent of the systemic culture in general at this moment. For instance, in the 1980s and 1990s courses in system-science are given (to the new generation) in many universities across the world, but there are but few who address themselves fully to the problems of applying systemic concepts to their particular sciences. (For management science, see, e.g., Muster and Weekes, 1984.) It seems as if many scientists (teachers, not all of whom belong to the older generation) still suffer from the reductionism syndrome. To those who study the history of science, this is no surprise. For several centuries the scientific scene was dominated by the paradigm of "classical science" and for about half a century by its contemporary variant, logical positivism. Well now, when a simple research tradition is allowed to dominate the scientific field for much too long a period, the cost in terms of lost opportunities is bound to be high.

Second, the discrepancy between the speed rate of the self-organizing process of the *thought-content* (which thus refers to insights and "experience") and that of the *form of thought* (which thus refers to the modes of procedure, in other words to "language"). More closely specified, this second major variant of the mutual alienation might appear in the following states of affairs:

1.   The thought formal self-organization process, at least part of it, is more rapid than that of the thought-content. Or, formal knowing—that is, knowledge that is primarily based on the generated by hypothetical–deductive reasoning, or even more generally, knowledge that is located in the v1-dimension (i.e., the dimension of subject matters on the metalevel where one normally operates both with theoretical constructs and empirical methods), is ahead of material knowledge or of thought-content (or factual, experimental, and experimental knowledge). In illustration of this, let us take two illustrious examples from history. The conic sections in Euclid's Elements (300 B.C.) are purely hypothetical–deductive constructions. No one, in Greek times, supposed them to have any utility; at last, in the seventeenth century, Galileo discovered that projectiles move in parabolas, and Keppler discovered that planets move in ellipses! Thus only after 20 centuries (!) did the development in the axis of experience (at least the experimental pole of this axis) catch up with that on the axis of language. The second example is Einstein's general theory of relativity, which for a time was regarded as no more than a fantastically constructed possible world. Later on (i.e., ranging from a couple of years to more than 70 years), this theory was vindicated in four ways: the first way in connection with the problem of the perihelion of Mercury; the second way concerning the fulfillment of a prediction made by Einstein that lightbeams are bent twice the deflection that Newton's law predicted; the third way with regard to the gravitational redshift, and fourth way with regard to the phenomenon of the black hole. (For more detail on this, see, e.g., Einstein and Infeld 1961; Finkelstein, 1958; Will, 1990.)

2.   The self-organization process of the thought-content is faster than that of the thought-form. Or, material or experimental knowledge-content, either in the sense of knowing through scientific experiments, or in the sense of existential experience, is faster than formal knowledge. For instance, in thought-content we are already aware of the peculiar state of the sub-quantum-level affairs, but in formal thought we still have no adequate language for this matter. This example is less simple than it may seem, for what actually happens is this: via symbols (which therefore belong to the language-axis) the observing system meets with the self-presentation of the observed system, which it (viz, the observing system) cannot (yet) adequately describe. In modern quantum theory, for instance, one is thus for the present hopelessly dependent on the language of classical physics. In the recent developments of system-science an analogous phenomenon is to be observed (cf. Cavallo, 1979). Nevertheless modern quantum theoreticians—ignoring the Wittgensteinian prohibition (Wittgenstein, 1961: 7th proposition)—constantly keep on trying to communicate with those around them, even if this must sometimes be in a language that seems to us more like hermeneutics in its very original

sense. (For fascinating conversations among the early quantum theoreticians, see, e.g., Heisenberg, 1969, or Casimir, 1984.) The example mentioned above also suggests by the way that through the continued development of the "language" (in our context: technics or technology, on the understanding that in modern times these are indissolubly connected with the v1-dimension) this (i.e., the "language") comes to stand before the second perplexity—note for the record that the first perplexity is that of the prelinguistic period—and introduces modern man into the second lifeworld or, to follow Merleau-Ponty's discourse, into the "second visibility" (cf. Merleau-Ponty, 1980).

Curiously enough, the variants mentioned above display a striking isomorphy with the variants of the "structural anomy" in the sociocultural sphere as these are elegantly analyzed by, among others, Durkheim, Merton, Marcuse, or Habermas, which will not be discussed within this limited scope.

C. The Evaluative–Volitional Subcriterion of the Frame

The evaluative–volitional subcriterion includes an ideal of system-knowledge in general from which an ideal of system-science is derived. This ideal of system-science is applied to that particular system-science: it articulates what the system-scientific community or a particular system-research group would want that particular system-science to become. This evaluative–volitional aspect returns upon the p^3-level—that is, the level of science as (finalizable) product, which recursively exercises as influence on the scientist of the scientific community (this in connection with the further internal development of that particular system-science and indirectly with the further internal development of system-science in general), and on the p^4-level—that is, the level of social norms and technical rules orienting action generated by the previous paradigmatic components (in connection with the interaction between system-science, or a particular system-science and its environing reality or, least we forget the earlier mentioned befuddling state of affairs, between system-science or a particular system-science and the reality environed by it). There ought to be many feedback relations between the said items of the two constituting parts of the teleonomic criterion of the frame, both within each particular system-science and within (the supposedly general) system-science as a whole. For these two subcriteria are the two faces of one and the same "information" [in the Aristotelian sense (cf. de Beauregard, 1979)] of the frame.

Alas, it is not rare for the facts to contradict this. There ought also to be many feedback relations between system-science as a whole or a particular system-science with its (environing and environed) reality. In how far system-science or a particular system-science offers a (substantial) contribution toward the solution of the internalism–externalism controversy that modern philosophers of science are assiduously searching for, and which at closer investigation is the very "matter" of system-science, is a question many particular system-scientists, apparently still laden with the traditional Kantian cleavage between what is "true" and what is scientifically most fruitful, will answer in a skeptical manner. On the other hand the paradoxical mechanism that helped to trigger the emergence of the standard stream of system-science seems again (unexpectedly) to be at work here. Think for instance of the many possibilities opened up by technological development and of the innumerable areas for the theoretical and practical application of cybernetics and system-research (cf. Trappl, 1984)! But how these 1001 pragmatic and more or less ad hoc relevances are to be structurally fitted into a more comprehensive scientific whole—in other words, how to transform this complexity into an intelligible world—is a challenge for system-science itself.

X. FURTHER EXPLICATION OF DEF.$(1^2)1$: THE "CONTENT" OF THE "FORM" OF DEF.1

By analogy with the three levels of communication theory, as distinguished by Weaver (cf. Shannon and Weaver, 1963) but reducing them to two (viz., the semantic or the conceptual and the technical), I propose to regard the semantic level as the far side of the form of Def.1 (and for the moment the technical level as the near side of the form of Def.1). This definitional state of affairs is still situated on the p^2-level. More explicitly, the far side of the form of Def.1 refers to the first further specifications of the near side of the content of Def.1., that is, to the first further specifications of the standard and the nonstandard stream of modern system-science. These first specifications regard primarily that which Blauberg et al. (1977: 88) described as the construction of conceptual means (i.e., systems of concepts, conceptual models of a special type, etc.) for the expression (representation) of the systems nature of corresponding objects.

Analysis I

1.   Von Bertalanffy enumerates a number of novel developments that in our context might be regarded as these first further specifications of the standard stream. They are cybernetics, information theory, game theory, decision theory, topology or relational mathematics (including nonmetrical fields such as network and graph theory), factor analysis, and general system theory in the narrower sense (cf. von Bertalanffy, 1973: 96).

2.   At the nonstandard end Jantsch enumerates a number of recent system concepts focusing on self-organization and evolution, which may be understood as particular views taken of the phenomenon of dissipative self-organization (Jantsch, 1980b: 81–87). In the light of such a unifying paradigm, they are interpreted by him as hierarchically ordered levels of description. In our context they might be regarded as the first further specifications of the nonstandard stream. On

the first level the discourse has reference to the relations of the system with its environment. The notion of an open system is central here. On the second level the reference is to the macroscopic internal system state. The contemporary distinction between equilibrium and nonequilibrium systems is of crucial importance here. On the third level we find the (logical) organization of a system that refers to the characteristic pattern in which processes are linked in the system. On the fourth level we find the function of a system. It embraces the total characteristics of its processes, including the relations with the environment and the system organization, but beyond that the kinetics of the individual processes and their interaction as well. On the fifth level we have to do with the space–time unity; the notion of a space–time structure is in focus. On the sixth level a time sequence of space–time structures yields the total system dynamics. And the seventh level of description concerns the interaction among systems. The unifying paradigm behind all the new concepts that have reference to the levels of description enumerated above is according to Jantsch the paradigm of dissipative self-organization.

XI. FURTHER EXPLICATION OF DEF.(1^2)2: THE "FORM" OF THE "FORM" OF DEF.1

Analysis II

In further explication, the near side of the form has reference to the second further specification of the near side of the content of Def.1, that is, to the many further specifications of the theories and levels of description by von Bertalanffy and Jantsch mentioned above. This universe of complex further specifications includes items and matters ranging from specific methods (e.g., the specific calculus for self-reference, continuous lattices, etc.), which might well be ranged in the general category of the computing sciences, to the most technical and instrumental aspects of system-science (e.g., the tesselation model, computer architecture, etc., and even brute technical hardware), which might well fall under the heading of computer science.

   1.   System-science, within this dimension (i.e., of Def(1^2)2) viewed as process consists of scientific actions ranging from the construction of formalized systems for the description of systems, including the formalization of specific rules of inference for such systems, to the development of apparatus for the description of the most important characteristics of systems, as described (and perhaps also intended) by Blauberg et al. (1977: 88). In substance, this universe of actions therefore covers the area lying between the $h1$- and the $v1$-pole. Its state of affairs is still at the $p2$-level.

   2.   System-science, within this dimension (i.e., of Def.(1^2)2), viewed as product consists both of the knowledge-systems about specific cases or specific slices

of reality and of the technologies based on these knowledge-systems, and also of artifacts and instruments. As a component localized on the p^3-level it recursively exercises (or ought to exercise) influence on the system-scientific culture, while it constantly oscillates between the p^2- and the p^4-level, either as one of the constituents of the context of implementation, or as one of the constituents of the context of discovery. In this capacity as "cyberspace" it also indirectly reveals one of the specific characteristics of system-science, which is that system-science also tries to be a synthesis of the two poles of the scientific world, which in the history of ideas were not infrequently on bad terms, namely the experimental and the conceptual pole. As a paradigmatic component it would indeed literally be classified under what Masterman (1976) coins as the construct or artifact-paradigms. Another unsuspected feature, burgeoning forth from the branch of computer science, is that at this moment these artifacts (i.e., computers) enable us to interact, not with the computer itself as many people tend to believe, but with our own thoughts and thought processes! For, we are forever at the "keyboard" of our senses, continually extracting, interpreting, and acting on *information* (cf. Pope, 1989). To a certain extent the computer as artifact has externalized some regions of our "internal self," which up to now was invisible and wordless. And, who knows, some day it might enhance this "second visibility" by rendering visible also our "internal non-self," which seems to be continuous with our "internal self." (For details about the "internal self" and the "internal non-self," cf. Kallikourdis, 1988, or Carvallo, 1986b, 1991). Besides, through the performance of complicated equations, this electronic artifact is able equally well to help us discover the overwhelming field of our "external space" whereby our insight into the nature of the macro- and microcosmos will be improved over and over again. In the light of these developments one might imagine here the furling back of the near side of the "form" of system-science on the far side of the "matter" of this same system-science.

Both universes (i.e., those referred to in the above points 1 and 2) take part in determining the identity of contemporary system-science, which therefore—this in contrast with the mistaken view and prejudice of the anti-system-scientific community—is not identical with them. Both are in principle not new, any more than science and system-science are new in principle: the emergence of man coincides with and is identical with the emergence of the text called "activity," which is posterior to and simultaneously determinant of its antecedent texts called "being" and "becoming" (cf. Carvallo, 1986b). The necessity to "act" seems to be the specific trace the course of evolution has left in us. This "activity," which, for human systems, ought to be understood in terms of a synthesis of such key concepts as "ergon," "energeia," "praxis," and "poiesis," is constituted by question-raising and tool-making. System-science within the dimension of Def.(12)2 ought therefore not to refer exclusively to the system of *actions of man*, but also, if not primarily, to that of *human activities* themselves.

XII. CONCLUDING REMARKS

1. In analyzing the constituents of Def.1 and in forging them together again into a relatively intelligible whole, I have in the course of writing this chapter found myself unconsciously constructing a far-side–near-side curvature, which is somewhat isomorphic with the spacetime curvature in modern physics. If you read on the one hand *time* in the index^0 (its extreme pole in this definition is Def.(1^0)0) and the *far side* in time, and on the other hand *space* in the index^2 (its extreme pole in this definition is Def.(1^2)2) and the *near side* in space, maybe this isomorphic image will present itself to you. The sequence from index^0 to index^2 should in the first place be read as a logical sequence and not as a historical sequence. Sometimes the logical sequence and the historical sequence do converge, as for instance the sequence Def(1^0)2 $\rightarrow$ Def.(1^1)0. Whereas the sequence Def.(1^1)2 $\rightarrow$ Def.(1^2) . . . n is correct in logic and at least meets with no objection in principle, it is not correct historically, for there the reversed sequence is in force. Attention is drawn to this here and there in the text. The sequence Def.(1^0)2 $\rightarrow$ Def.(1^0)0 is a didactic sequence, as we stated when it was first mentioned.

2. Concluding from the present chapter and anticipating a forthcoming article about Def.2, I might fairly safely propound that discussion of Def.1 is in principle indissolubly bound up with discussion of Def.2, or that discussing Def.1 unavoidably also implies discussing Def.2. It seems as if these two have very much in common, or as if they are as like two drops of water, are twin sisters, or—who knows—two aspects of the same reality, the system as subject and as object. Are they not?

3. After all it is striking that modern system-science, especially the standard stream and its further specifications, is primarily, if not exclusively, occupied with Def.2, or with Def.(1^2) within Def.1. That is, the standard stream flows primarily within the region of space. Or more sharply defined, modern system-science, especially the standard stream, does indeed neglect Def.1. In practically all introductory literature about system-theory the beginning until now is usually a very short introduction regarding the history of system-science (referring then to Def.1), after which the writers proceed with the "real" theme, that is, treating systems (according to Def.2), and this then is practically the whole extent and content of an introductory book, to end with the conclusion, which in content and extent more or less links up with the introduction. The treatment of Def.1 here represents the opposite picture: the system that storms through the chapter is called Def.1, its Doppler effect is called Def.2.

ACKNOWLEDGMENTS

Thanks are due to the late Prof. Dr. H. G. Hubbeling (State University of Groningen, the Netherlands), to Prof. Dr. Milan Zeleny (Fordham University, New

York), and to Prof. Dr. Lars Löfgren (University of Lund, Sweden) for having alerted me to some substantial points after reading the first draft. The possibly remaining errors or flaws of logic are mine.

NOTES

1. To avoid the (classical) mechanistic bias, the terms constitution, to constitute, constituents, etc. are used here consciously and are preferred to the usual (summative) ones (composition, to compose, components, etc.). For further argumentation, see, for example, von Bertalanffy (1973: 54).

2. The term or concept "matter" used here is analogous to the term or concept "(prime) matter" in Aristotelian metaphysics: both are "formless." The term or concept "content" as discussed here (see, e.g., Def.1¹) is analogous to the primordial "second matter" in Aristotelian metaphysics: both are "formed (primely)." It is analogous also to Leisegang's "thought-content" (Leisegang, 1951), which is explicitly used in Section IX.B. The distinction between "matter" and "content" is often overlooked by many contemporary (system-)scientists. The term or concept "form" as discussed here (see, e.g., Def.1²) is analogous to the Aristotelian term or concept "form" as the subsequent complification of the above "content." The three main frames of Def.1 ("matter", "content", and "form") telescope into each other. The far sides and the near sides of each main frame might be viewed as the "transitional spaces" connecting them into one continuum. Toward the end of the "form" there is a coincidence of an increase of "formation" and a decrease of "formlessness." Toward the end of the "matter" there is a coincidence of an increase of "formlessness" and a decrease of "formation".

3. Analogously, others (e.g., Kallikourdis, 1976; Glanville, 1979; Glanville and Varela, 1980), discussing Spencer-Brown's laws of form, have raised the question of the distinction of the space in which a distinction is drawn, etc. For a different reason and from a different point of view, space in Aristotle's theory is conceived of as a kind of communion of the body and its surroundings: it is the body that determines the geometry of its environment, and this geometry cannot be artificially separated from the body itself (Samburshy, 1987: 96).

4. Even Marx saw subjectivity in the atom as if it were a question of a Leibnizian monad and saw the orbiter in the (Lucretian) clinamen as if he were rewriting the theodicy (Marx, 1970: 171). And also for contemporary Lucretians, like Prigogine or Serres, this is surely a highly serious scientific issue. Serres even points out that in every system with integration levels there are as many (Freudianlike) unconsciousnesses as there are integration levels (Serres, 1983: 71–83). Consequently, nothing distinguishes the human system ontologically from a crystal, a plant, an animal, or the order of the world. So anthropomorphism of world1, (i.e., the nonhuman world) seems to be a serious scientific issue. There is even a kind of anthropomorphism attributed to the Popperian world3. In a somewhat different sense, Platonists among mathematicians and physicists, for example, the nineteenth century German physicist Heinrich Hertz, ". . . cannot escape the feeling that (these) mathematical formulae have an independent existence and an intelligence of their own . . . " And Weinberg, echoing the thoughts of Hertz, wrote: "This is often the way it is in physics—our mistake is not that we take our theo-

ries too seriously, but that we do not take them seriously enough. It is always hard to realize that these numbers and equations we play with at our desks have something to do with the real world" (cf. Pagels, 1985: 167). And Kurt Gödel seriously believes that "... we do have something like a perception also of objects of set theory, as is seen from the fact that the axioms force themselves upon us as being true. I don't see any reason why we should have less confidence in this kind of perception, i.e., in mathematical intuition, than in sense perception . . . . They, too, may represent an aspect of objective reality." (cf. Davis and Hersch, 1981: 319.)

5. For further details about the teleonomic criterion as one of the invariant categories of human systems, cf. Carvallo (1986b).

6. The interaction, or more precisely the structural coupling, between these two axes could be represented in terms of both the nontranscendable and the transcendable complementarity as is meant by Löfgren (1988). Note however that by representing language and experience as one single system, I feel obliged to extend Löfgren's concept of linguistic complementarity, in that the complementarity between language and experience in this chapter might be analogous to both the nontranscendable and the transcendable linguistic complementarity of Löfgren. As far as I have not misunderstood him, the extension and intension of his concept of language encompasses the levels and dimensions ranging from the microscopic aspect of Def.$(1^0)1$ to those of Def.$(1^2)2$ according to my denotation. He correctly suggested looking for another term for this concept of language, to avoid any confusion with the concept of language as is tacitly meant in commonsensical conversation (Löfgren, 1989). Other, more befuddling representations of this complicated complementarity (e.g., in terms of "viral sentences" are suggested by Quine, Hofstadter, and many others (cf. Hofstadter, 1985). I am fully aware that these fascinating ideas are not yet fully processed in the present section.

REFERENCES

Ackoff, R. L. (1963). "General System Theory and Systems Research, Contrasting Conceptions of Systems Science," *General Syst.*, 8: 117-124.

Ackoff, R. L., and Emery F. E. (1972). *On Purposeful Systems*. Chicago: Aldine.

Arbib, M. A. (1984). "Cooperative Computation and the Cybernetic Society," in Trappl, R. (ed.), *Cybernetics*. New York: Springer, pp. 361-372.

Ashby, W. R. (1968). "Some Consequences of Bremermann's Limit for Information-Processing Systems," in Oestreicher, H., and Moore, D. (eds.), *Cybernetic Problems in Bionics*. New York: Gordon and Breach, pp. 69-76.

Atkin, R. H. (1974). *Mathematical Structure in Human Affair.* London. Heinemann.

Atlan, H. (1983). "Information Theory," in Trappl, R. (ed.), *Cybernetic: Theory and Applications*. Washington, D.C.: Hemisphere, pp. 9-41.

Barnsley, M. (1988). *Fractals Everywhere*. San Diego: Academic Press.

Bateson, G. (1978). *Steps to an Ecology of Mind*. London/New York: Paladin.

Bateson, G. (1980). *Mind and Nature*. New York/London: Bantam.

Bateson, M. C. (1975). "Mother–Infant Exchanges: The Epigenesis of Conversational Interaction," in Aaronson, D. and Rieber, R. (eds.), *Developmental Psycholinguistics and*

Communication Disorders. Annals of the New York Academy of Sciences, Vol. 263, pp. 101–113.

Bateson, M. C. (1984). *With a Daughter's Eye: A Memoir of Margaret Mead and Gregory Bateson.* New York: Morrow.

Beauregard, de O. C. (1979). "Quantum Paradoxes and Aristotle's Twofold Information Concept," in Tart, C. T. *et al.* (eds.), *Mind at Large.* New York: Praeger, pp. 177–187.

Beer, S. (1983). "Introduction: Questions of Quest," in Trappl, R. (ed.), *Cybernetics.* New York: Springer, pp. 1–6.

Bell, J. S. (1987). "Beables for Quantum Field Theory," in Hiley, B. J., and Peat, F. D. (eds.), *Quantum Implications.* London/New York: Routledge & Kegan Paul, pp. 227–234.

Bertalanffy, von, L. (1972). "The History and Status of General Systems Theory," in Klir, G. J. (ed.), *Trends in General Systems Theory.* New York: Wiley, pp. 21–41.

Bertalanffy; von, L. (1973). *General System Theory.* Harmondsworth: Penguin.

Blauberg, I. V., *et al.* (1977). *System Theory.* Moscow: Progress.

Blumenberg, H. (1976). *Aspekte der Epochenschwelle.* Frankfurt: Suhrkamp.

Bohm, D. (1979). *The Special Theory of Relativity.* London: Benjamin/Cummings.

Bohm, D. (1982). *Wholeness and the Implicate Order.* London: Routledge and Kegan Paul.

Bohm, D. (1987). *Unfolding Meaning.* London/New York: Ark Paperbacks.

Bohm, D. and Hiley, B. (1975). "On the Intuitive Understanding of Non-locality as Implied by Quantum Theory," *Found. Phys.,* 5: 93–109.

Bohm, D., and Hiley, B. (1987). *An Ontological Basis for the Quantum Theory.* Amsterdam: North Holland.

Bohm, D., and Peat, F. D. (1987). *Science, Order, and Creativity.* New York: Bantam.

Boulding, K. E. (1956). "General Systems Theory—The Skeleton of Science," *Manage. Sci.,* 2: 197–208.

Boulding, K. E. (1981a). "Foreword," in Zeleny, M. (ed.), *Autopoiesis.* New York: North Holland, pp. xi–xiii.

Boulding, K. E. (1981b). "Foreword," Jantsch, E. (ed.), *The Evolutionary Vision.* Boulder, CO: Westview, pp. xv–xvi.

Bråten, S. (1981). "Time and Dualities in Self-reflective Dialogical Systems," in Lasker, G. E. (ed.), *Applied Systems and Cybernectics.*

Bråten, S. (1988). "Dialogic Mind: The Infant and the Adult in Protoconversation," in Carvallo, M. E. (ed.), *Nature, Cognition, and System,* Vol. 1. Dordrecht/Boston/London: Kluwer, pp. 187–205.

Bremermann, H. J. (1962). "Optimization Through Evolution and Recombination," in Yovits, M. C., and Cameron, S. (eds.), *Self-organizing Systems.* Washington, DC: Spartan, pp. 93–106.

Buber, M. (1937). *Ich und Du.* Heidelberg: Lambert Schneider.

Bunge, M. (1977). *Treatise on Basic Philosophy,* Vol. 3. Dordrecht: Reidel.

Carnap, R. (1959). *Induktive Logik und Wahrsheinlichkeit.* Vienna: Springer Verlag.

Capra, F. (1983). *The Turning Point.* London: Fontana.

Carvallo, M. E. (1982). "In Search of the Noëtic Structure of Systems," in Trappl, R. (ed.), *Cybernectics and Systems Research,* Vol. 1. New York: North Holland, pp. 31–37.

Carvallo, M. E. (1986a). "Natural Systems According to Modern Systems Science: Three

Dualities," in Trappl, R. (ed.), *Cybernetics and Systems '86.* Dordrecht: Reidel, pp. 47–54.

Carvallo, M. E. (1986b). "Systemization as Human Action," in de Zeeuw, G., and Pedretti, A. (eds.), *Problems of Action and Actors.* London: Princelet, pp. 25–86.

Carvallo, M. E. (1988). "Selftranscendence and Symmetrybreak," in Carvallo, M. E. (ed.), *Nature, Cognition, and System,* Vol. 1. Dordrecht/Boston/London: Kluwer, pp. 253–277.

Carvallo, M. E. (1991). *Steps to the Anthropic Paradigm* (in preparation).

Casimir, H. B. G. (1984). *Haphazard Reality.* New York: Harper & Row.

Cavallo, R. E. (1979). *Systems Research Movement,* General Systems Bulletin, Special Issue, Vol. IX, No. 3.

Cherniss, H. (1971). *Aristotle's Criticism of Presocratic Philosophy.* New York: Octagon.

Chew, G. F. (1987). "Gentle Quantum Events as the Source of Explicate Order," in Hiley, B. J. and Peat, F. D. (eds.), *Quantum Implications.* London/New York: Routledge & Kegan Paul, pp. 249–254.

Churchman, C. W. (1979). *The Systems Approach and Its Enemies.* New York: Basic Books.

Churchman, C. W. (1984). "Churchman's Conversations," *Syste. Res., 1* (ff.).

Cioran, E. M. (1970). *The Fall into Time.* Chicago: Quadrangle.

Davis, P. J. and Hersch, R. (1981). *The Mathematical Experience.* London: Harvester.

Dobbs, B. J. T. (1983). *The Foundations of Newton's Alchemy or 'The Hunting of the Greene Lyon'.* Cambridge: Cambridge University Press.

Domarus, von E. (1934). *The Logical Structure of Mind.* Ph.D. thesis, Yale University, New Haven, CT.

Einstein, A., and Infeld, L. (1961). *The Evolution of Physics.* New York: Simon & Schuster.

Ernst, B. (1985). *The Magic Mirror of M. C. Escher.* Stradbroke: Tarquin Publications.

Falconer, K. (1985). *The Geometry of Fractal Sets.* Cambridge: Cambridge: University Press.

Ficino, M. (1962). *Opera Omnia.* Turin: Bottega d'Erasmo.

Figala, K. (1977). *Die Kompositionshierarchie der Materie—Newton's Quantitative Theorie und Interpretation der Qualitativen Alchemie.* Munich: Habilitationsschrift.

Finkelstein, D. (1958). "Past–Future Asymmetry of the Gravitational Field of a Point Particle," *Phys. Rev., 110:* 965.

Foerster, von H. (1984). *Observing Systems.* Seaside, CA: Intersystems.

Frankel, H. (1978). "The Non-Kuhnian Nature of the Recent Revolution in the Earth Sciences," PSA, 2: 197–214.

Freire, P. (1973). *Pedagogy of the Oppressed.* Hanmondsworth: Penguin.

Gardner, M. (1983). *Wheels, Life and Other Mathematical Amusements.* San Francisco: Freeman.

Gasztonyi, A. (1976). *Der Raum. Geschichte seiner Probleme in Philosophie und Wissenschaften,* 2 vols. Freiburg/Munich: Alber.

Glanville, R. (1979). "Beyond the Boundaries," in Ericson, R. F. (ed.), *Improving the Human Condition.* New York: Springer Verlag, pp. 70–75.

Glanville, R. (1988). *Objekte.* Berlin: Merve Verlag.

Glanville, R., and Varela, F. J. (1980). "Your Inside Is Out and Your Outside Is In," in Lasker, G. E. (ed.), *Proceedings of the International Congress on Applied Systems Research and Cybernetics.* London: Pergamon Press.

Glasersfeld, von E. (1989). "The Cybernetic Basis of Behavior," *Continuing the Conversation, 16:* 5-6.

Gray, R. D. (1952). *Goethe, the Alchemist.* Cambridge: Cambridge University Press.

Gredt, J. (1921). *Elementa Philosophiae Aristotelico-Thomisticae,* Vols. I and II. Freiburg im Breisgau: Herder.

Hanson, N. R. (1972). *Patterns of Discovery.* New York: Cambridge University Press.

Harrison, B. (1979). *Form and Content,* Oxford: Blackwell.

Hegel, G. W. F. (1929). *Science of Logic* (tr. W. H. Johnston and L. G. Struthers). New York: Macmillan.

Heisenberg, W. (1969). *Der Teil und das Ganze.* Munich: Piper.

Hempel, C. G. (1972). *Fundamentals of Concept Formation in Empirical Science.* Chicago/London; the University of Chicago Press.

Hofstadter, D. R. (1980). *Gödel, Escher, Bach.* New York: Vintage Books.

Hofstadter, D. R. (1985). *Metamagical Themas.* New York: Basic Books.

Husserl, E. (1969). *Formal and Transcendental Logic* (tr. D. Cairns). the Hague: Nijhoff.

Jain, V. (1981). "Structural Analyses of General Systems Theory," *Behav. Sci., 26:* 51-62.

Jantsch, E. (1976). "Evolution: Selfrealization through Selftranscendence," in Jantsch, E., and Waddington, C. H. (eds.), *Evolution and Consciousness.* London: Addison-Wesley, pp. 37-70.

Jantsch, E. (1980a). "The *Selforganizing Universe.* New York: Pergamon Press.

Jantsch, E. (1980b). "The Unifying Paradigm Behind Autopoiesis, Dissipative Structures, Hyper- and Ultracycles," in Zeleny, M. (ed.), *Autopoiesis, Dissipative Structures, and Spontaneous Social Orders.* Boulder, CO: Westview, pp. 81-87.

Jantsch, E. (1981). "Unifying Principles of Evolution," in Jantsch, E. (ed.), *the Evolutionary Vision.* Boulder, CO: Westview, pp. 83-115.

Jaspers, K. (1953). *The Origin and Goal of History* (tr. M. Bullock). New Haven, CT: Yale University Press.

Johnson, J. (1985). *Combinatorial Structure in Digital Pictures,* NERC Remote Sensing Project, Discussion Paper No. 1, Center for Configurational Studies, The Open University, Milton Keynes, UK, January 1985.

Kallikourdis, D. M. (1976). Seminar on Distinctions. Brunel University, U.K.

Kallikourdis, D. M. (1988). "The Genesis of Psychological Content," in Carvallo, M. E. (ed.), *Nature, Cognition, and System,* Vol. 1. Dordrecht/Boston/London: Kluwer, pp. 207-252.

Kirk, G. S. (1978). *Heraclitus, The Cosmic Fragments.* London: Cambridge University Press.

Klir, G. J. (1970). "On the Relation Between Cybernetics and General Systems Theory," in Rose, J. (ed.), *Progress in Cybernetics.* London: Gordon and Breach.

Klir, G. J. (1985). *Architecture of Systems Problem Solving.* New York: Plenum Press.

Klir, G. J., and Rogers, G. (1977). *Basic and Applied General Systems Research: A Bilbiography.* Binghamton, NY: State University Center.

Koyre, A. (1978). *Galileo Studies.* Hassocks: Harvester.

Laszlo, E. (1973). *Introduction to Systems Philosophy*. New York: Harper & Row.

Laszlo, E. (1983). *Systems Science & World Order*. Oxford/New York: Pergamon Press.

Laudan, L. (1977). *Progress and Its Problems*. Berkeley: University of California Press.

Leclerc, I. (1986). *The Philosophy of Nature*. Washington: The Catholic University of America Press.

Leisegang, H. (1951). *Denkformen*. Berlin: de Gruyter.

Lewicka-Strzalecka, A. (1986). "Is 'Cybernetics and Systems Research' A System? A Scientometric Analysis," in Trappl, R. (ed.), *Cybernetics and Systems '86*. Dordrecht /Boston/Lancaster/Tokyo: Reidel, pp. 1-8.

Locke, J. (1690). *An Essay Concerning Human Understanding*. London.

Locker, A. (1991). "Complementarity-Polarity-Dialectic-Autology," in Carvallo, M. E. (ed.), *Nature, Cognition, and System*, Vol. 2. Dordrecht/Boston/London: Kluwer.

Löfgren, L. (1988). "Towards System: From Computation to the Phenomenon of Language," in Carvallo, M. E. (ed.), *Nature, Cognition, and System*, Vol. 1. Dordrecht/Boston/London: Kluwer, pp. 129-155.

Löfgren, L. (1989). Personal communication.

Löfgren, L. (1991). "Complementarity in Language: Towards a General Understanding," in Carvallo, M. E. (ed.), *Nature, Cognition, and System*, Vol. 2. Dordrecht/Boston/London: Kluwer.

Lorenz, K. (1975). *Die Rückseite des Spiegels*. Münich: Piper.

Lucretius (Titus, Carus) (1986). *On the Nature of the Universe* (tr. and intr. by R. E. Latham). Harmondsworth: Penguin.

MacLean, P. D. (1973). "A Triune Concept of the Brian and Behavior," in Boag, T., and Campbell, D. (eds.), *The Hincks Memorial Lectures*. Toronto: University of Toronto Press.

Mandelbrot, B. (1983). *The Fractal Geometry of Nature*. New York: Freeman.

Marcel, G. (1935). *Etre et Avoir*. Paris.

Marx, K. (1970). *Différence de la philosophie de la nature chez Democrite et Epicure* (tr. J. Pommier). Paris: Ducros.

Masterman, M. (1976). "The Nature of a Paradigm," Lakatos, I., and Musgrave, A. (eds.), *Criticism and the Growth of Knowledge*. London: Cambridge University Press, pp. 59-89.

Mattessich, R. (1978). *Instrumental Reasoning and Systems Methodology*. Dordrecht: Reidel.

Maturana, H. R. (1980). "Biology of Cognition," in Maturana, H. R., and Varela, F. J., *Autopoiesis and Cognition*. Dordrecht: Reidel, pp. 2-58.

Maturana, H. R. and Varela, F. J. (1980). *Autopoiesis and Cognition*. Dordrecht: Reidel.

Maturana, H. R. and Varela, F. J. (1987). *The Tree of Knowledge*. Boston and London: Shambhala.

Merleau-Ponty, M. (1980). *The Visible and the Invisible*, (tr. A. Lingis). Evanston, IL: Northwestern University Press.

Merton, R. K. (1968). *Social Theory and Social Structure*. New York: Free Press.

Messer, A. (1907). "Otto Ritschl, System und systematische Methode in der Geschichte des wissenschaftlichen Sprachgebrauchs und der philosophischen Methodologie," *Göttinger gelehrte Anzeigen, 8*.

Miller-Guinsburg, A. (1980). *Henry More, Thomas Vaughan and the Late Renaissance Magical Tradition. Ambix*, vol. 27, Part I.

Muster, D., and Weekes, W. H. (1984). "Concepts and Design in Engineering and Management Education," in Smith, A. W. (ed.), *Systems Methodologies and Isomorphies*. Seaside, CA: Intersystems, pp. 71-83.

Newell, A., and Simon, H. (1976). "Computer Science as Empirical Inquiry: Symbols and Search," *Commun. ACM, 19*: 3.

Oeser, E. (1976). *Wissenschaft und Information*, Vol. 1-3. Vienna: Oldenbourg.

Pagels, H. R. (1985). *Perfect Symmetry*. New York: Simon & Schuster.

Pangaro, P. (1985). "An Introduction to the Many Gordon Pasks," *Cybernetic, 1*(1): 77-78.

Pask, G. (1991). "Complementarity in the Theory of Conversations and Lp," in Carvallo, M. E. (ed.), *Nature, Cognition, and System*, Vol.2. Dordrecht/Boston/London: Kluwer.

Piaget, J. (1970). *Genetic Epistemology*. New York: Columbia University Press.

Pope, N. V. (1989). "The New World Synthesis," *Phil. Math., 2/4*: 23-28.

Popper, K. R. (1974). *The Logic of Scientific Discovery*. London: Hutchinson.

Poundstone, W. (1987). *The Recursive Universe*. New York: Oxford University Press.

Powers, W. T. (1989) "Problems with the Smiths," *Continuing the Conversation, 16: 3-4.*

Prigogine, I. (1967). *Introduction to Thermodynamics of Irreversible Processes*. New York: Wiley-Interscience.

Prigogine, I., and Stengers, I. (1984). *Order Out of Chaos*. New York: Bantam.

Radnitzky, G. (1970). *Contemporary Schools of Metascience*. Göteborg: Scandinavian University Press.

Rapoport, A. (1981). "Two Approaches to General System Theory," paper presented at the Fifth International Congress of Cybernetics and Systems, Mexico City, Aug. 17-22, 1981.

Rescher, N. (1979). *Cognitive Systematization*. Oxford: Blackwell.

Ritschl, O. (1906). *System und systematische Methode in der Geschichte des wissenschafttlichen Sprachgebrauchs und der philosophischen Methodologie*. Bonn: Georgi.

Robbins, S., and Oliva, T. A. (1982) "An Empirical Classification of General Systems Theory Concepts," in Troncale, R. L. (ed.), *A General Survey of Systems Methodology*, Vol. I. Seaside, CA: Intersystems, pp. 3-14.

Rosen, R. (1978). "Dynamic Similarity and the Theory of Biological Transformations," *Bull. Math. Biol., 40*: 549-579.

Russel, B. (1961). "Introduction" to Wittgenstein's *Tractatus Logico-Philosophicus*" (cf. Wittgenstein).

Sambursky, S. (1975). *Physical Thought from the Presocratics to the Quantum Physicists*. New York: Pica.

Sambursky, S. (1987). *The Physical World of the Greek*.Princeton, NJ: Princeton University Press.

Scholem, G. (1967). *Jüdische Mystik in ihren Hauptströmungen*. Franfurt: Suhrkamp.

Scholem, G. (1977). *Zur Kabbala und ihrer Symbolik*. Frankfurt: Suhrkamp.

Serres, M. (1977). *Hermes*, Vol. IV: *La Distribution*. Paris: Minuit.

Serres, M. (1983). *Hermes: Literature, Science, Philosophy*. Baltimore/London: Johns Hopkins University Press.

Shannon, C. E., and Weaver, W. (1963). *The Mathematical Theory of Communication*. Chicago: University of Illinois Press.

Simon, H. A. (1975). *The Sciences of the Artificial*. Cambridge, Mass.: MIT Press.

Smelser, N. J. (1962). *Theory of Collective Behavior*. New York: Free Press.

Smith, T. J., and Smith, K. U. (1988). The Cybernetic Basis of Human Behavior and Performance," *Continuing the Conversation, 15*: 1-28.

Smith, T. J., and Smith, K. U. (1989). Rejoinder, *Continuing the Conservation, 16*: 15-25.

Smullyan, R. M. (1977). *The Tao Is Silent*. New York: Harper & Row.

Stein von der A. (1968). "Der Systembegriff in seiner geschictlichen Entwicklung," in Diemer, A. (ed.), *System und Klassifkation in Wissenschaft und Dokumenation*. Meisenheim am Glan: Anton Hain, pp. 1-13.

Steiner, R. (1926). *Goethe's Naturwissenschaftliche Schriften*. Dornach: Philosophisch-Anthroposophischer Verlag.

Thompson, d'Arcy (1942). *On Growth and Form*. Cambridge: Cambridge University Press.

Trappl, R. (1984). "Impacts of Artificial Intelligence," Trappl, R. (ed.), *Cybernetics and System Research*, Vol. 2. New York: North Holland, pp. 831-838.

Troncale, R. L. (1978). "Linkage Propositions Between Fifty Principal Systems Concepts," in Klir, G. J. (ed.), *Applied General Systems Research: Recent Development and Trends*. New York: Plenum. Press, pp. 29-52.

Troncale, R. L. (1985). "The Future of General Systems Research: Obstacles, Potentials, Case Studies," *Syst. Res., 2*/(1): 43-84.

Troncale, R. L. (1988). "The New Field of Systems Allometry: Discovery of Empirical Evidence for Invariant Proportions Across Diverse Systems," in Trappl, R. (ed.), *Cybernetics and Systems '88*. Dordrecht/Boston/London: Kluwer, pp. 123-130.

Turing, A. M. (1950). "Computing Machinery and Intelligence," *Mind, 59*: 433-460.

Turing, A. M. (1952). "The Chemical Basis of Morphogenesis," *Phil. Trans. R. Soc. London, 237*(37): 41-44.

Varela, F. J. (1979). *Principles of Biological Autonomy*. New York: North Holland.

Varela, F. J. (1984a). "Introduction: The Ages of Heinz von Foerster," in Foerster, von H., *Observing Systems*, Seaside, CA: Intersystems, pp. xiii-xviii.

Varela, F. J. (1984b). "The Creative Circle: Sketches on the Natural History of Circularity," in Watzlawick, P. (ed.), *The Invented Reality*. New York/London: Norton, pp. 309-323.

Walker, D. P. (1954). "The Prisca Theologia in France," *J. Warburg Courtauld Ins., 17*: 204-259.

Whitehead, A. N. (1926). *Science and the Modern World*. New York: Macmillan.

Whitehead, A. N. (1978). *Process and Reality*. New York: Free Press.

Wiener, N. (1980). *Cybernetics*. Cambridge, MA: MIT Press.

Wilber, K. (ed.) (1982). *The Holographic Paradigm and Other Paradoxes*. Boulder, CO: Shambala.

Will, C. M. (1990). "General Relativity at 75: How Right Was Einstein?" *Science, 250*: 770-776.

Winnicott, D. (1953). "Transitional Objects and Transitional Phenomena: A Study of the First Not-Me Possession, *Int. J. Psycho-Anal., 34*: 89-97.

Wittgenstein, L. (1953). *Philosophical Investigations.* London: Blackwell.

Wittgenstein, L. (1961). *Tractatus Logico-Philosophicus.* (tr. D. F. Pears and B. F. McGuiness, introduction by B., Russel, 2nd ed. London: Kegan Paul, Trench, Trubner.

Wohlgenannt, R. (1969). *Was ist Wissenschaft?* Braunschweig: Vieweg.

Wolfram, S. (ed.) (1986). *Theory and Applications of Cellular Automata.* Singapore: World Scientific.

Zeleny, M. (1979). "Cybernetics and General Systems—A Unitary Science?" *Kybernetes, 8:* 17–23.

Zeleny, M. (1980). "Autopoiesis: A Paradigm Lost?" in Zeleny, M. (ed.), *Autopoiesis, Dissipative Structures, and Spontaneous Social Orders.* Boulder, CO: Westview, pp. 3–43.

Zeleny, M. (1981). "Preface," in Zeleny, M. (ed.), *Autopoiesis.* New York: North Holland, pp. xv–xvii.

Zeleny, M. (1985). "Spontaneous Social Orders," *Inter. J. General Syst., 11:* 117–131.

Zeleny, M. (1987). "Cybernetika," *Inter. J. General Syst., 13:* 289–294.

Zeleny, M. (1988a). "La grande inversione. Corso e ricorso dei modi di vita umani," in Cerutti, M. and Laszlo, E. (eds.), *Physis: Abitare la terra.* Milan: Feltrinelli, pp. 413–441.

Zeleny, M. (1988b). "Tectology," *Inter. J. General Syst., 14:* 331–343.

Zwick, M. (1984). "Incompleteness, Negation, Hazard: On the Precariousness of Systems," *Nature and System, 6:* 3–42.

5

Sociocybernetics

R. Felix Geyer Netherlands Universities' Institute for Coordination of Research in Social Sciences (SISWO), Amsterdam, The Netherlands

Johannes van der Zouwen Vrije Universiteit, Amsterdam, The Netherlands

I. INTRODUCTION

Sociocybernetics can be defined as the application of concepts, methods, and ideas of the so-called new cybernetics or second-order cybernetics to the study of social and sociocultural systems, but also vice versa: second-order cybernetics is certainly enriched by the often unexpected results of social science studies in which concepts of second-order cybernetics are applied.

This chapter cannot give more than a rough impression of the wide variety of innovative theoretical and empirical research that is executed within the sociocybernetics paradigm, and an overview of the main trends and developments since the late 1970s. It is based on the work of what is conceivably the most important international forum devoted explicitly to sociocybernetics, and to a relatively sustained critical assessment of issues, priorities, and directions for further work in the field: the Sociocybernetics Sections at the triannual International Congresses of Cybernetics and Systems of the World Organization of General Systems and Cybernetics (WOGSC), co-organized by the authors.

After each of these congresses, the organizers coedited a volume with a selection of papers; for reasons of space, only some of these papers can be discussed in more detail. They are selected both to give the reader an impression of the widely divergent subject matter covered by sociocybernetics, and also to show the direction in which sociocybernetics is developing. The present contribution is an adapted version of a recent overview of the field (Geyer and van der Zouwen, 1990b).

II. SOCIOCYBERNETICS: AN OVERVIEW OF DEVELOPMENTS DURING THE LAST DECADE

Quite a lot has happened in the field of sociocybernetics since the first two volumes with that title appeared (Geyer and van der Zouwen, 1978). An effort is made to sketch these developments, and to show where we started and where the frontiers of the field are now.

Buckley, as one of the first pioneers to correctly apply systems concepts to the social sciences, reckoning with the specific nature of social systems, stressed already in the 1960s (Buckley, 1967) the as-such hardly surprising fact that social systems are essentially different from biological and technical ones, the most frequently studied systems up till then—and studied largely with the aid of classical first-order cybernetics. It took almost a decade for systems concepts to be applied to the social sciences.

In the introduction to the above volumes, the term "sociocybernetics" was chosen to refer to the interpenetration of general systems theory and the social sciences—not merely to the one-way traffic of applying concepts from general systems theory without further reflection to the social sciences. The authors then were, and still are, convinced that the emergence of the so-called second-order cybernetics was largely due to this increasing focus, within general systems theory, on the social sciences—a field where the inapplicability of first-order cybernetics soon became evident. These were intellectually exciting days, although the systems movement within the social sciences still had to gather steam, and pronouncements still had a defensive ring—toward the social science community, rather than toward the colleagues in systems theory.

Indeed, the themes in these 1978 volumes could still be described as refutations of the frequently voiced objections against the application of systems theory to the social sciences: for example, the reproach of implicit conservatism that was largely caused by the fact that the Parsonian systems approach, with its stress on homeostasis rather than morphogenesis, was virtually the only one known in social science (cf. Buckley, 1967). Other objections voiced against the systems approach were technocratic bias and unwarranted reductionism; in view of the prevalence of the rather mechanistic type of first-order cybernetics then in fashion, these perhaps somewhat stereotypical objections among social scientists only superficially acquainted with the systems approach were certainly understandable (Lilienfeld, 1978).

Less defensively and more positively, we tried to define the main themes of sociocybernetics as aspects of the emerging "new cybernetics," known in the meantime as second-order cybernetics:

1. Sociocybernetics stresses and gives an epistemological foundation for science as an observer-observed system. Feedback and feedforward loops are constructed not only between the objects that are observed, but also between them and the observer. The subjective and time-dependent character of knowledge is emphasized by this approach: information, in the broadest sense of the word, is neither seen as inherently "out there," waiting to be discovered by sharp analytical minds, nor is it entirely viewed as a figment of the observer's own imagination, or as an environment-independent automatic end-result of his own inner cognitive processes. Knowledge is constructed—and continually reconstructed—by the individual in open interaction with his environment.

2. The transition from classical, rather mechanistic, first-order cybernetics to modern, second-order cybernetics is characterized by a number of interrelated problem shifts:

(a) One shift is from the system that is being controlled to the actively steering system and consequently: to the nature and genesis of the norms on which steering decisions are based; to the information transformations, based on both observations and norms, that are necessary to arrive at steering decisions; and to the learning processes behind repeated decision-making.

(b) Especially when several systems try to steer one another, or an outside system, attention is focused on the nature of, and the possibilities for, communication or dialogue between these systems.

(c) When the behavior of a system has been explained in the classical way, through environmental influences and systemic structure, the problem is raised of the "why" of this structure itself, qua origin and development, and the "why" of its autonomy with regard to the environment. In systems terminology: the questions of morphogenesis and autopoiesis.

3. These problem shifts in cybernetics involve an extremely thorough reconceptualization of many all too easily accepted and taken for granted concepts— which yields new notions of stability, temporality, independence, structure versus behavior, and many other concepts.

4. The actor-oriented systems approach, promulgated in 1978 as part of sociocybernetics, makes it possible to bridge the "micro–macro" gap,—the gap in social science thinking between the individual and society, between freedom and determinism, between "anascopic" explanations of society that depart from the activities of individuals conceived as goal-seeking, self-regulating systems, and "katascopic" explanations that view society "from the top down" and see individuals as subservient to system-level criteria for system stability.

In 1982 a volume was published containing largely empirical work applying systems concepts to an integrated, cross-disciplinary study of the problems of underdeveloped countries (Geyer and van der Zouwen, 1982). A general theme here was: How can general systems theory and general systems methodology contribute toward an improved understanding of the problems of social systems in transition, particularly those of developing countries? Does the application of the systems approach in this area indeed lead to new insights, and especially to new solution alternatives, over and above those of the traditional disciplines?

However, we are concerned here with the conceptual-theoretical advances that were made. For example, the actor-oriented approach to dependency theory employed in this volume not only elucidated the individual versus society problem by concretely demonstrating the existing links between motivations and actions of individual actors and large-scale societal processes, thus explaining how a certain historical process has led to a certain result: present-day dependency of Third World nations. This approach also differentiates hierarchically between the game itself and the "metagame": that is, the capability of certain actors to determine the rules of the game, and therewith largely its contents (unequal exchange) and its outcome (perpetuation of inequality).

Another interesting theoretical development, demonstrated "empirically" by computer simulation (Gierer, 1982), lies in the explanation of inequality as resulting from the cumulative interaction over time of the autocatalytic, self-enhancing effects of certain initial advantages (e.g., generalized wealth, including education) with depletion of scarce resources. It then turns out that striking inequalities can be generated from nearly equal initial distributions, where slight initial advantages tend to be self-perpetuating within the boundary conditions of depleting resources; it is here that the concept of autopoiesis, developed in the mid-1970s in cellular biology by Maturana and Varela (1980), finds one of its first applications in social science.

It became increasingly clear around this time, the early 1980s, that it is precisely general systems theory, paradoxically, that does not recognize the existence of systems, at least not as immutable and objectively existing entities with fixed boundaries. Unlike many of the traditional disciplines, modern systems theory is in this sense explicitly opposed to reification: the tendency to ascribe a static "thing" character to what really are dynamic processes. Especially when trying to apply second-order cybernetics to the investigation of social systems—in this case, developing countries—the way in which one can analytically distinguish systems turns out to be problem-dependent (hence implies relativism), observer-dependent (hence ultimately subjective or intersubjective), and time-dependent (hence implying a dynamic rather than static character).

Already implicit in the themes of this 1982 volume were the main concerns of our third volume (Geyer and van der Zouwen, 1986): the sociocybernetic paradoxes inherent in the observation, control, and evolution of self-steering systems—especially the paradox important to policy makers worldwide: How can one steer systems that are basically autopoietic, hence self-referential as well as self-steering? The authors of a number of empirical studies in this volume were rather pessimistic about the possibilities of planning and steering a number of specific social systems, while a theoretical study by Masuch drew attention to the planning paradox, which can be expressed as follows.

Perfect planning would imply perfect knowledge of the future, which in turn would imply a totally deterministic universe in which planning would not make any difference. While recognizing the usefulness of efforts to steer societies, a cost-benefit analysis, especially in the case of intensive steering efforts, will often turn out to be negative: intensive steering implies intensive social change—that is, a long and uncertainty-increasing time period over which such change takes place, and also an increased chance for changing planning preferences and for conflicts between different emerging planning paradigms during such a period. Nevertheless, given a few human cognitive predispositions, there unfortunately seems to exist a bias for oversteering rather than understeering.

A historical overview of planning efforts concludes that —in spite of intensified theorizing and energetic attempts to create a thoroughly planned society during the past two centuries—the different answers given so far regarding the possibility of planning cancel each other out. There is even no consensus about a formal definition, though usually planning is seen as more comprehensive, detailed, direct, imperative, or expedient when compared with other steering activities that are not defined as planning. In our most recent volume (Geyer and van der Zouwen, 1990a) we have gone further into why increased knowledge about human (i.e., self-referential) systems often does not help us to improve our planning of such systems.

In our 1986 volume, apart from discussing the possibilities of planning, we tried to answer two other important questions:

Should one opt for the "katascopic" or "anascopic" view of society? In other words, should the behavior of individuals and groups be planned from the top down, in order for a society to survive in the long run, or should the insight of actors at every level, including the bottom one, be increased, and therewith the actors' competence to handle their environment more effectively and engage more successfully in goal-seeking behavior?

What should be the role of science, especially the social sciences, in view of the above choice? Should it try mainly to deliver useful knowledge for an improved steering of the behavior of social systems and individuals, or should it strive to improve the competence of actors at the grass-roots level, so that these actors can steer themselves and their own environment with better results?

To answer these questions, Aulin followed a cybernetic line of reasoning that argues for nonhierarchical forms of steering. Ashby's Law of Requisite Variety indeed implies a Law of Requisite Hierarchy in the case where only the survival of the system is considered (i.e., if the regulatory ability of the regulators is assumed to remain constant). However, the need for hierarchy decreases if this regulatory ability itself improves—which is indeed the case in advanced industrial societies, with their well-developed productive forces and correspondingly advanced distribution apparatus (the market mechanism). Since human societies are not simply self-regulating systems, but self-steering systems aiming at an enlargement of their domain of self-steering, there is a possibility nowadays, at least in sufficiently advanced industrial societies, for a coexistence of societal governability with ever *less* control, centralized planning, and concentration of power.

As the recent history of the Soviet Union demonstrates, this is not only a possibility, but even a necessity: when moving from a work-dominated society to an information-dominated one, less centralized planning is a prerequisite for the very simple reason that the intellectual processes dealing with information are self-steering—and not only self-regulating—and consequently cannot be steered from the outside by definition. Our answer to the above questions, in other words, was quite straightforward: there should be no excessive top-down planning, and science should help individuals in their self-steering efforts and certainly should not get involved in the maintenance of hierarchical power systems.

Of course, this is not to deny that there is a type of system within a society that can indeed be planned, governed, and steered, but this is mainly because such systems have been designed to be of this type in the first place, that is, to exemplify the concept of the control paradigm. Modern, complex multigroup society in its entirety, conceptualized as a matrix in which such systems grow and thrive, can never be of this type.

If one investigates a certain system with a research methodology based on the control paradigm, the results are necessarily of a conservative nature; changes of the system as such are almost prevented by definition. According to De Zeeuw (1986), a different methodological paradigm is needed if one wants to support social change of a fundamental nature and wants to prevent "postsolution" problems; such a paradigm is based on a multiple-actor design, does not strive toward isolation of the phenomena to be studied, and likewise does not demand a separation between a value-dependent and a value-independent part of the research outcomes.

Our 1986 volume also analyzed the emerging broader context of the steering problematique, and thus contributed to the development of a systems epistemology for the social sciences, the necessity of which we had argued as long ago as 1978. Two interesting "theory transfers" from other disciplines should be mentioned in this respect.

In a fascinating contribution by Laszlo, comparing the evolution of social systems with the wider context of the basic cybernetics of evolution per se, use was made of the theoretical framework of Prigogine and Stengers (1984). The thesis was defended here that, while evolution admittedly may follow widely divergent paths in different fields of inquiry, there are unitary principles underlying the concrete course of evolution in different domains—that is, basic invariances in dynamics rather than accidental similarities in morphology—and discovering them has a survival value in highly complex modern societies with their uncertain futures. Contradictory theories of evolution (e.g., classical thermodynamics based on particles in or near equilibrium vs. Darwin's theory of the origin of species) have uneasily coexisted for more than a century.

With the development by Prigogine and others of nonequilibrium thermodynamics—which also considers particles far from equilibrium and can therefore deal with cross-catalytical chemical oscillators—these contradictions turn out to be only apparent. Evolution occurs when *open* systems are exposed to massive and enduring energy flows. It now turns out that evolution—in physics, biology, and the social sciences—goes together with *increasing* size and complexity and *decreasing* bonding energy. Strongly bonded, but relatively simple particles—whether atomic nuclei, cells, or human individuals—act as building blocks for more weakly bonded, but larger and more complex entities.

Another interesting "theory transfer" was the reconceptualization of the autopoiesis concept developed by Maturana and Varela (1980) to make it applicable to the field of the social sciences. Luhmann (1986) defended the quite novel thesis here that, while social systems are self-organizing and self-reproducing systems, they do not consist of individuals or roles or even acts, as commonly conceptualized, but of *communications*. It should not be forgotten that the concept of autopoiesis was developed while studying living systems. When one tries to generalize the usages of this concept to make it also truly applicable to social systems, the biology-based theory of autopoiesis should therefore be expanded into a more general theory of self-referential autopoietic systems. It should be realized that social and psychic systems are based on a type of autopoietic organization other than living systems; namely on communication and consciousness, respectively, as modes of meaning-based reproduction.

While communications rather than actions are thus viewed as the elementary unit of social systems, the concept of action is admittedly necessary to ascribe certain communications to certain actors. The chain of communications can thus be viewed as a chain of actions—which enables social systems to communicate about their own communications and to choose their new communications, that is, to be active in an autopoietic way. Such a general theory of autopoiesis has important consequences for the epistemology of the social sciences: it draws a clear distinction between autopoiesis and observation but also acknowledges that observing systems are themselves autopoietic systems, subject to the same conditions of autopoietic self-reproduction as the systems they are studying.

The theory of autopoiesis thus belongs to the class of global theories, theories that point to a collection of objects to which they themselves belong. Classical logic cannot really deal with this problem, and it will therefore be the task of a new systems-oriented epistemology to develop and combine two fundamental distinctions: between autopoiesis and observation, and between external and internal (self-)observation. Classical epistemology searches for the conditions under which external observers arrive at the same results and does not deal with self-observation. Consequently, societies cannot be viewed, in this perspective, as either observing or observable. Within a society, all observations are by definition self-observations.

III. SELF-REFERENCING

It is in our most recent volume (Geyer and van der Zouwen, 1990a) that we have concentrated on this emerging problem area: the often unexpected consequences of the fact that all observations within a society are self-observations. One of the main characteristics of social systems, distinguishing them from many other systems, is their potential for self-referentiality. This means that the knowledge accumulated by the system itself about itself in turn affects the structure and operation of that system. This is the case because, in self-referential systems like social systems, feedback loops exist between parts of reality, on the one hand, and models and theories about these parts of reality, on the other hand.

Concretely, whenever social scientists systematically accumulate new knowledge about the structure and functions of their society, or about subgroups within that society, and when they subsequently make that knowledge known, through their publications or sometimes even through the mass media—in principle also to those to whom that knowledge pertains—the consequence often is that such knowledge will be invalidated because the research subjects may react to this knowledge in such a way that the analyses or forecasts made by the social scientists are falsified.

In this respect, social systems are different from many other systems, including biological ones. There is a clearly two-sided relationship between knowledge about the system on the one hand and the behavior and structure of the system on the other hand. Biological systems, like social systems, admittedly do show goal-oriented behavior of actors, self-organization, self-reproduction, adaptation, and learning. But it is only *social* systems that arrive systematically, by means of experiment and reflection, at knowledge about their own structure and operating procedures, with the obvious aim of improving these.

In our 1986 volume, we dealt in detail with several aspects of the specific character of social systems. The accent then, however, was rather on the degree of governability of those systems: our core area of interest there was the paradox of steering self-steering systems. Our 1990 volume, on the other hand, reflects a shift to the present preoccupations of sociocybernetics. The accent in this case lies on the consequences of self-referentiality, in the sense of self-observation, both for the functioning of social systems and for the methodology and epistemology used to study them. We do have a paradox here too: the accumulation of knowledge often leads to a utilization of that knowledge—both by the social scientists and the objects of their research—which may change the validity of that knowledge.

In Subsections A–H of Section III, italic type is used to identify, at first mention, contributors to our 1990 volume (Geyer and van der Zouwen, 1990a).

A. Self-Referencing and Prediction

This trend is illustrated for example by *Henshel*, who analyzes what he terms credibility and confidence loops in social prediction. Self-fulfilling prophecies have of course been studied before. Merton (1948) defined the self-fulfilling prophecy as "an unconditional prediction or expectation about a future situation such that, had it not been made, the future situation envisaged would not have occurred, but because it is made, alterations in behavior are produced which bring about that envisaged situation, or bring that envisaged situation to pass." The notion of a self-fulfilling prophecy was later supplemented by its mirror opposite: the self-defeating prophecy.

The novelty of Henshel's approach lies in the fact that he extends the notion of self-fulfilling prophecies to serial self-fulfilling prophecies, where the accuracy of the earlier predictions, themselves influenced by the self-fulfilling mechanism, has an impact on the accuracy of the subsequent predictions. He distinguishes credibility loops and confidence loops.

In credibility loops, source credibility (i.e., the credibility of the forecaster) becomes significant, because it is the same forecaster who is issuing repeated predictions. There is a deviation-amplifying positive feedback loop here between (1) a self-fulfilling mechanism, (2) the accuracy of the prediction, and (3) the credibility of the forecaster. Several examples are given, in widely varying fields (preelection polling, stock market predictions, intelligence testing, etc.).

Confidence loops have certain features in common with credibility loops; the critical difference between the two lies precisely in what is held constant, or uniform, across the repeated prediction iterations. In the case of the credibility loop it is the person of the predictor that must remain the same for the associated credibility to rise or fall. In the confidence loop, continuity across predictive iterations in the prediction itself is at issue. The prediction in the confidence loop must exhibit constancy in either rank-order or direction on successive pronouncements. Such uniformity in the direction of the prediction, together with the postulated self-fulfilling mechanism, produces increased accuracy, which in turn produces increased confidence in the prediction as iterations of the loop unfold. Examples are given here in fields like inflationary spirals, validation of criminality theories, and attribution theory.

Of course, feedback loops involving a self-defeating mechanism lower rather than increase predictive accuracy over several iterations. When a self-defeating dynamic is inserted in the system, an oscillating system is created in which the time paths of the key variables now oscillate instead of assuming a monotonic form. The so-called cobweb cycle is a good example here.

Henshel's analysis has fascinating implications in two different areas.

1. He demonstrates two "nested" differences between the natural world and the social world: self-fulfilling or self-defeating prophecies exist only within the social world, while moreover these self-fulfilling or self-defeating tendencies are magnified by the feedback loops in which they are embedded and impact directly on the accuracy of the predictions made.

2. He also demonstrates differences between prediction in the natural versus the social sciences: the existence of credibility loops and confidence loops suggests that, on certain occasions at least, the social sciences can pull themselves up by their own bootstraps, in terms of improving their predictive accuracy. Such a "bootstrap" enhancement of accuracy is not possible for prediction in the natural sciences. The social sciences appear to be aided especially with respect to the accuracy of directional and ordinal predictions, in ways that are impossible for natural phenomena. If a social scientist issues a directional or ordinal prediction, he *may* be *aided* by self-fulfilling dynamics. On the other hand, if the same social scientist issues a quantified prediction, he *may* be *damaged* in ways that do not apply to the natural science world. That is, for quantified prediction, his accuracy may be damaged by the same self-fulfilling dynamics.

Self-defeating tendencies necessarily reduce rather than increase the accuracy of directional and ordinal predictions, and again have equivocal but usually damaging effects on quantified accuracy. Considering both tendencies, self-fulfilling and self-defeating, we find that the weaker forms of prediction (directional and ordinal) are sometimes aided, sometimes damaged. Quantified predictions, long taken as the hallmark of mature science, are ordinarily damaged. In terms of obtaining precision and high accuracy in quantified forecasts, the social sciences are therefore uniquely disadvantaged as a result of the existence of self-fulfilling and self-defeating tendencies in the social world as opposed to the natural world.

B. Self-Referencing and Methodological Research

Van der Zouwen addresses a similar problematique, looking at the consequences of self-referentiality for research methodology in the social sciences. Methodological research is defined here as research aimed specifically at the evaluation and improvement of the performance of research methods. This contribution deals with the following questions, especially within the area of survey research.

1. Can a feedback loop be observed between the available, and presumably valid, knowledge about the quality of particular methods of data collection on the one hand, and the way in which these methods are used on the other hand?

2. To what degree do public opinion researchers anticipate on the outcomes of their research when choosing and implementing their research methods?

3.   What are the consequences of this anticipation for the possibilities to conduct methodological research? What are the consequences of the self-referentiality of the social system called "the survey industry" for methodological research aimed at improving the operation of that system?

To answer these questions, van der Zouwen deals with a subset of methodological research: methods research, or the development of particular types of justification for research methods, conceived as prescriptions and recommendations for the activities of researchers.

In experimental methods research, research efforts are focused on such problems as the effect of a personal versus a formal interviewing style on the accuracy and amount of information obtained from the interviewees, and the effects of question wording on responses obtained (e.g., open vs. closed questions; adding "don't know" as a separate category; the order in which response categories are presented). Usually, there is a "split ballot" design here, with respondents randomly assigned to the experimental conditions relating to either the questionnaire or the interviewers. This experimental design has optimal internal validity: differences on the dependent variables (i.e., the response distributions) can unequivocally be attributed to differences in the experimental conditions. However, the drawback of this type of research is that it excludes feedback from the dependent variables to the independent ones; in other words, self-referentiality cannot be observed with this type of research design. Moreover, the results are difficult to generalize: experiments with the wording of a specific question cannot be generalized to the wording of questions in general.

Nonexperimental methods research deals, ex post facto, with the statistical relationships in current opinion research between the ways in which questions are formulated and the characteristics of the response distributions obtained, or with the correlations between characteristics of the interview situation and the behavior of interviewers and respondents.

This type of research demonstrated, for example, that variance increases with the number of response categories, while the proportion of "don't know" responses increases when this response category is explicitly offered by the interviewer.

While such results sound rather obvious, there is a tricky problem here: this type of methods research has to assume that the designers of the questionnaires (i.e., the public opinion pollers) were not aware of these wording effects while formulating the questions, or at least did not reckon with them. In other words, they did not formulate their questions in such a way that the response distribution obtained would meet certain criteria, such as not being too skewed. If this assumption is invalid, then the causal interpretation of the correlations found becomes dubious: Is it the question wording that has produced this particular response distribution, or are feedback loops resulting from (previous) research results on the researcher involved? Is it rather, in other words, the researcher's need for a particular kind of response distribution that has led to a specific formulation of the question?

Van der Zouwen tried to find an answer to this question in a research project involving the analysis of verbatim transcripts of six quite different survey projects, making use of a cybernetic model of interviewer–respondent interaction. The hypotheses themselves are not at issue here. The interesting point is that, when these hypotheses were tested, a number of unexpected statistical relations between variables turned up, which can best be typified as consequences of anticipation: those researchers who expect problems regarding the task-related behavior of their interviewers, or regarding the quality of the information to be gained from the respondents, will understandably take countermeasures. They design the questionnaire more carefully and in more detail than usual, spend much time selecting and instructing their interviewers, decrease the "distance" between themselves and the interviewers by intensive monitoring of the fieldwork, and so on.

While such countercontrol measures look plausible and quite rational at first sight, their effect is that the correlations between the independent variables (the above points: complexity, distance, experience, and difficulty) and the dependent ones (interviewer behavior and response quality) can no longer be interpreted in terms of one-way causality. The sophisticated, anticipating researcher actually reduces the interpretability and thus the utility of nonexperimental methods research.

Similar results were obtained in an ex post facto meta-analysis of some 20 research projects regarding the effects of the mode of data collection (mail survey, telephone interview, face-to-face interview) on the information obtained.

Van der Zouwen's conclusion from all these different research projects not only is relevant for all social science research—as opposed to research in the exact sciences—but deals also with the core problematique of the 1990 volume: To what extent is the accumulation of valid knowledge about social systems possible, given that they are self-referential, for researchers who, either as individuals or as a group, are themselves self-referential systems?

Van der Zouwen stresses the paradox that it is precisely methods research that hampers its own further development, in two different ways: by an increasing *standardization* of research practice and by *anticipatory behavior* of survey researchers. Standardization reduces the variance in the data collection procedures used, which results in unreliable estimates of the effects of the methods on the research outcomes. And when there are differences with respect to the methods used, these are largely caused by the anticipation of the researchers on the effects of their methodological decisions. As these anticipations become more frequent and more adequate, the relations between the characteristics of the methods used and the data obtained increasingly become artifacts of these anticipations.

C. Self-Referencing and Political Systems

Anderson concentrates on political systems, and he stresses their intelligence rather than their self-referentiality. This enables him to draw parallels with developments in artificial intelligence (AI). He considers present theory about complex organizations and political structures to be rather weak, and feels this to be the case because it focuses on stasis rather than on change and dynamics. New intellectual tools need to be developed for theories of social processes, but they should be formal and should fit the substantive domains of application. Artificial intelligence, unlike other formal tools borrowed by sociology from other disciplines, has developed techniques specifically geared to the study of human action and human capacities.

Political systems or "polities" (i.e., subsystems of societies that specialize in solving certain kinds of problems), conceptualized as sets of roles rather than individuals, have goals, beliefs, and knowledge about themselves and their environment as well as inference rules. Roles are conceptualized, in AI terminology, as frames, that is, hierarchical structures in which objects at each lower level are related to objects at the next higher level by the transitive "is a (class inclusion)" relation. In frames, the objects are described through declarative rules, expressing their properties and rules for action. Roles have memories; the role-specific memories are abstracted events connected to present action options, including defaults, through so-called Minsky C-lines (Chomsky and Miller, 1963). Although each role implies a unique perspective on the system itself and its environments, roles are organized into role sets, within which one may expect to find shared subclasses of beliefs.

Political systems obviously need the relevant and correct facts to solve their specific problems. However, they perceive selectively and anyhow filter information—even apart from the possibility of distorting it. Their problem, also one of the central problems in AI, is how to select among large sets of possibly relevant facts that subset which can be used to reason about or solve the problem concerned, and do this in the limited amount of time available.

Three processes determine how a problem-relevant subset of facts is determined:

Insulation: the environments of political systems are stratified systems, where especially power and social distance are relevant variables.

Learning: generally not too fast, since politicians have a tendency to scan their environments for facts that fit with their repertoire of familiar issues and problems.

Self-reflection: political systems are self-referential and through self-reflection try to develop new insights.

While it is relatively arbitrary where one draws the boundaries of political systems, it seems useful to anyhow distinguish the decision-making inner political apparatus, those engaged in implementing the decision, and the clientele to whom the decisions pertain. Politics is obviously always competitive, and even within authoritarian political systems there is always internal competition for influence and power, which forces the actors to engage in self-referencing, by taking note of the different points of view of allies and adversaries alike. This capacity for self-referencing is what constitutes the intelligence of a polity. The necessity to learn to shift between multiple perspectives (Bråten, 1986) helps to explore the hidden potential of the system's goals, rules, beliefs, and capacities.

Anderson then analyzes the role concept and political goal structures, conceptualizing roles and goals in political systems as hierarchical structures of production rules. At the top of the hierarchy are rules that express the system's ideology or belief regime, and the elite's strategic rules for the reproduction and extension of its arena of power. The next level contains the rules of policy formation and communication, and the strategic rules followed by the incumbents of the different roles in the structure. At the bottom of the hierarchy we find rules for the selection of actions on the system's environments.

A frame can now be more clearly defined as a hierarchical structure that consists of rules, relations, and abstract objects. A national political system can be viewed as a frame, with a hierarchy going down from the nation state via sectors and sector-objects to agents and agencies. Properties defined by rules at the higher levels are inherited by the lower levels, and thus the "top rules" provide default assignments to the actions at the bottom level, although they can obviously be overridden by other instructions.

One of the problems with this type of modeling, as with all modeling, is that models of political systems require a high degree of resolution to be realistic—which makes them hard to comprehend and analyze. Moreover, frames were originally developed to model knowledge systems, where the rules at the different hierarchical levels are made to be consistent. However, it is typical for political systems that inconsistencies occur in the rule systems at all levels, while moreover these inconsistencies are strategically exploited by political actors. Also, rules in social science theory are context-dependent and undergo interpretation; they are not like the "if–then" statements in frame methodology, which carry precise and unambiguous instructions. An unsolved problem is therefore how the frame model should be modified to fit the contextuality of human social rule use.

One should not forget that it is only events that occur in the environment; these events give rise to a political problem through conceptualization. However, as Luhmann (1986) has also stressed, a political system can recognize only the problems it is "programmed" to recognize. Problems sometimes become important because the means for their solution exist. The way of defining the problem, the choice of alternative solutions, and the means to implement these may be different in different political systems, with the result that national styles of problem solving may develop.

The self-referentiality of the political system comes out clearly in the fact that a successful solution of a high-priority problem or the failure to solve such a problem will strengthen or weaken the relevant part of the political system. When a new problem makes itself felt, previous successes or failures will have caused a change in the system's state. Detailed case studies are necessary to demonstrate how precisely such successes and failures in problem solving affect the internal structure of politics. We see a variant here of the problem analyzed by van der Zouwen; the successes as well as the failures of previous efforts at solving specific political problems feed back on present-day efforts and tend to produce a *standardization* of the solutions deemed possible in certain cases, while political decision making obviously thrives on *anticipatory behavior*. If a politician has learned his lessons well, he knows what manipulative stimuli to give in order to elicit specific reactions from the public, not unlike the methodologist who more or less determines the answer distribution of his respondents by using certain methods.

D.   Self-Referencing and Participatory Democracy

Robinson reports an interesting experiment designed to improve the effective organization of participatory democracy in a cooperative organization. Especially during the past decade, participation problems have appeared—and have been documented—in socialist as well as capitalist economies. In general, these problems fall into two broad categories:

How can ordinary members exercise control *over* management?
How can ordinary members exercise control *with* management?

It turns out that concern with control over management leads to a concentration on cooperative structure, while concern with control with management leads to a concentration on means. While some structures and means (techniques) certainly have been successful in some instances, co-ops that fulfil democratic criteria, and are felt by their members to do so, are generally small, with fewer than 20 members. Larger cooperatives usually find such techniques as frequent general meetings and job rotation impracticable. Their formal structures may be sophisticated, but they fail to instill feelings of involvement on the part of their members.

Member participation in decision making at all levels of an enterprise—requiring both control *over* and control *with* management—is problematic. The effective managerial monopoly on information excludes the majority of cooperators from anything but token supervision of decision making. Control with management is likewise almost impossible; the co-op members are not immersed in the information and value flows, but have other jobs to do. This managerial information monopoly is a self-reproducing process; the more information and power is centralized already, the greater becomes the ability of management to monopolize information and power even more. The result is the reappearance of alienation, strikes, and management-labor conflict—even where ownership-labor conflict has been eliminated.

Robinson does see a way out of this dilemma. It is to recognize that agents, and especially collective agents, are constituted and reproduced only in relation to objects they influence and control. If "the membership" is to become an agent, it must do so in relation to specific issues or projects. The problem now, under a primary management-worker role division, is that workers are not in a control relationship. Consequently, they do not produce and reproduce themselves collectively as "an agent." "Agents" have to engage in *learning* if they want to be effective. Now, the advantage of Robinson's approach is that this is fully recognized; member participation and worker control can be exploratory, experimental, and partial. No one has the impossible task of knowing about everything; the objects of control can be changed. Yet, control is quite clearly there, and immediately so; this is not a partial or gradual process.

Basing himself on Bernstein's theory of economic return, and modifying its shortcomings—especially its demand that economic return be directly related to what the workers themselves have produced—on the basis of Ashby's Law of Requisite Variety, Robinson then first discusses a production problem in one of the departments of a cooperative. He comes to the conclusion that control is interesting only when it is partial. Strategies of the department concerned have to reckon with the strategies of (inputs from) the other departments. Thus, a nested set of choices and outcomes emerges that can give rise to "metastrategies": "if they do this, we'll do that"—and in this way an immersion in dialogue occurs that is characteristic for management. Clearly, the dialogue needs an object, or there would be nothing to discuss, and there also would be no basis on which an otherwise unstructured group, such as the membership at large of a cooperative, could form itself as an agent.

Robinson, recognizing the inherent limitations of general meetings in larger cooperatives, developed a computer model that can serve as the forum of discussion in cases where such meetings are not practical. He implemented Ashby's definition of control on a number of computers, removing some restrictive assumptions from Ashby's account of control: the actions that determine the outcome are now themselves determined in the course of the dialogue. This derestricted account of control is consistent with Howard's (1971) metagame theory and Pask's (1976, 1978) conversation theory, and is termed Ashby mapping.

Robinson illustrates his concepts with an experiment about wage negotiations between two departments of a cooperative. In Ashby's original formulation (Ashby, 1956), two players made choices in a given order of play, whereby the intersection of their choices determined the outcome. In Ashby mapping, the players select strategies rather than choosing options, while moreover the rules governing the order of play are relaxed. The nature of the original game is changed by making the outcome conditional on acceptance by the players. Thus, the situation moves from the original context of regulation and disturbance to a realistic imitation of a bargaining process. Reacting to each other's strategies, the players may now develop symmetrical metastrategies, even though their basic strategies are not symmetrical. Both strategies and metastrategies are stated by making moves that lead to conditional outcomes, and thus are public events; both the moves and the responses to these moves are known to both players. An Ashby map can thus be seen as a form of representation in which restrictions on moves are relaxed to allow strategies, and restrictions on order of play are relaxed so that outcome is conditional on symmetrical strategy or metastrategy. Using Ashby mapping, one can therefore move from an objective to a subjective control formalism; the outcome is no longer determined by the facts of the moves and the table of outcomes, but by the ability of the players to reach agreement.

Ashby mapping is thus a very useful technique for analyzing self-referentiality, both of others and of oneself, in the dynamic context of an ongoing process of negotiation where implicit goals and values continually emerge; it is not primarily a way of representing an "objective reality" but rather an interpretation of the world by those who create it.

E.   Self-Referencing and Health Care Planning

Hornung describes the construction of knowledge-based systems for the analysis of development problems in health care planning, at national and at regional and even local levels. We encounter here the same problem mentioned before: decision making and planning in health care systems take place in between the extremes of spontaneous, intuitive decisions on the one hand, and decisions based on costly, time-consuming quantitative computer-assisted studies and operations research on the other hand. Cognitive systems analysis as understood here mediates between these two extremes; it integrates general theoretical knowledge about the structure of health care systems with the available empirical knowledge of experts and decision makers about specific problems in specific countries or areas.

Health care systems are viewed as autopoietic (i.e., self-organizing and self-referential) sociotechnical systems, located at the intersection of social interaction systems, economic systems, and natural (biological) systems. The fact that they are autopoietic implies, in a planning context, the need for an active and effective participation of all members of the system for which planning is done.

Self-reference enters at several levels:

1. The level of individual learning, exemplified by the interaction of the modeler with his cognitive model.
2. The level of generating group expertise about a problem, by an interaction between the modeler, the model, and other participants in a modeling or planning group.

3. The level of self-organization in the scientific subsystem (i.e., the interaction between the modeler or modeling group and the scientific community).
4. The level of management and policy making in the health subsystem, a national system or even the international system, consisting of the interaction between modelers and decision makers at the corresponding levels.

In the context of self-reference and self-organization, computer-assisted tools of policy making and development planning obviously have to meet two basic challenges, as has already become clear from Robinson, quoted above:

They should allow for a participative planning process that takes into account the views and opinions (i.e., cognitive domains) of all the groups concerned.
They certainly should not remain the exclusive domains of technical specialists who merely present the results to the decision makers, but should rather promote, and even require, interaction and feedback among the computer, the planner, and the decision maker.

This is all the more important, as Hornung stresses, if one agrees with the thesis of Maturana and Varela (1980) that in any strict sense there is no flux of thought from one person to another, and that denotative functions of messages lie only in the cognitive domains of the observer. In this view, understanding results from cooperative behavior of two persons, and the participative interactive planning process envisaged here indeed implies such cooperation.

Hornung's qualitative systems analysis tries to utilize the advantages of both experts systems and simulation models, without the disadvantages of either. Expert systems can store a large quantity of knowledge about well-defined problems. They can provide propositions for decision making and explain how they arrive at them. The universe of possible answers is known beforehand; what is not known, however, is the answer in a particular case. Therefore, expert systems are very suitable tools for routine decision making but not for policy planning and development planning, which are concerned with nonroutine decision making.

In simulation models, only the system itself and the principles of its dynamics are known, not the universe of possible events—the entire state space of the system. This becomes gradually known only when running the model and experimenting with it. Simulation models are excellent tools for communication, since models permit information transfer by making the other person do and experience things, instead of interacting by questions and answers. However, conventional simulation models do not provide a knowledge base in the detailed way that expert systems do, while on the other hand expert systems are usually not suitable for experimentation. Within the framework of his cognitive systems analysis, Hornung developed the so-called DEDUC methodology for qualitative modeling, which distinguishes classificatory concepts (*object structures*), "if-then" statements (*implications*), and *premises*, and differentiates between an "orientor module" containing normative knowledge such as the objectives, goals, and values of the planner, and a "knowledge module" containing factual knowledge about the problem area (i.e., the internal model of the planner and, respectively, the experts).

Usually, cognitive domains imply both knowledge about reality and a normative assessment of facts. DEDUC models such cognitive systems and externalizes them in the form of computer models, such that the user is able to investigate his own externalized and objectified cognitive domain carefully and systematically. He can experiment self-referentially with a subset of his own cognitive domain turned into a computer model in order to resolve planning and policy problems. One of the advantages of Hornung's method is that models can be iteratively refined, so that construction can be started with a very simple model (rapid prototyping), which moreover can be constructed very quickly, since there is a hierarchical set of models such that the basic outline of systems models at lower hierarchical levels roughly follows from the models at the higher levels.

Contrary to classical cybernetics, which has stressed the importance of selecting the essential variables when engaging in model building, the autopoietic concept with its emphasis on dynamics insists on the importance of what Maturana and Varela have termed the essential relations.

Hornung then illustrates his modeling technique with a detailed example of the national system of Mexico and its different subsystems. Like van der Zouwen, he concludes that self-reference is at work on different levels. The science subsystem of a society brought forth cognitive systems modeling by means of which scientific knowledge is changing itself.

F. Self-Referencing and Psychological Research

Hirsig and his colleagues set off on a journey into space. They developed the hardware and software for an extremely interesting experiment to collect reliable empirical data about emotionally–motivationally determined behavior, in which subjects had to operate a spacecraft simulator. Self-reports about emotions and motives are notoriously unreliable, affected as they are by factors like social desirability and moral–ethical value judgments. Projective tests admittedly do yield empirical matter, but it is hard to code and evaluate. The reliability and validity of the data remain doubtful. Research by means of interviews, questionnaires, and so on usually taps imaginary emotional or motivational situations and gives ample opportunity for cognitive distortions. The simplest methods attempt to tap emotional states on the basis of physiological measures; but here too, interpretation of the data remains too unspecific for subtly differentiated research questions. Summarizing: the classical test–methodological conditions yield emotions only in cognitively processed form, while the direct manifestation of emotional and motivational behavior determinants presents problems in coding and evaluation.

Recent developments within the fields of interactive TV and computer games suggest a way out of this dilemma; the high degree of ego involvement observed in children and adults alike when playing these games suggests that interactive, computer-run experimental apparatus can be used in the empirical investigation of the emotional and motivational aspects of behavior.

Hirsig then set out to develop a systemic conceptual model for computer-aided, interactive experimental designs. This model contains the following elements and the interrelations between them: objective and subjectively perceived stimulus situation; the intended and actual actions of the subject and the subjectively experienced success in performing these actions; the reference values for the variables of experience and the difference with actual experience, and the possibility of modifying these reference values; and the behavioral goals and the possibility of modifying one's behavioral strategies as well as one's perceptual filters.

This model is an operationalization of the basic hypothesis, derived from stability theory, that subjects dynamically regulate their actual experience by means of their actions, in such a way that it conforms to their reference values regarding this experience. As in Robinson's Ashby mapping, a basic premise is that subjects have a sufficient amount of internal variety—in this case variety in their behavioral repertoire and behavioral strategies—to influence the stimulus situation through their actions, thus stabilizing their experiences by bringing the actual experience closer to the reference values for this experience.

The construct variable "subjectively experienced success" monitors the individual's longer-term stabilization behavior; if it remains subjectively too low, the individual has three options to still stabilize his experience at a point near his reference values:

Modification of behavioral strategies (i.e., learning)
Modification of reference values assigned to the perceived situation (i.e., adaptation of expectations)
Modification of the subject's perception (i.e., modification of the input filter in such a way that no component of the subjectively perceived situation will continue to be significant for the critical experience dimension)

In setting up their experiment, Hirsig et al. departed from the classic investigative paradigm in the field of attachment research: the opposed needs for security and exploration of small children within the context of conflict between their familiar, security-providing mothers, on the one hand, and frightening but fascinating strangers, on the other. The distances the children maintain to these two actors serve as indicators for the construct variables "security" and "arousal." For the present experiment, mother and stranger were of course substituted by more age-appropriate interaction partners. Subjects were trained to operate a spacecraft simulator and were told the experiment was intended to test its efficiency. A home base with which radio contact was maintained served as a friendly, helpful partner, while a menacing, but stationary UFO took the role of a fascinating, but dangerous object. The cockpit was realistically designed with numerous instruments and control lights and gave a view into space by real-time, computer-generated graphics.

Acoustically too, the situation was made as realistic as possible: home base became barely audible on the radio with increasing distance, while the roar of the UFO became deafening as it was approached. Warning signals from the on-board computer became louder whenever a meteorite approached the spacecraft. With meteorites, the subject could take several courses of action:

Home base offered unconditional help in any crisis situation, but in that case took
    over control of the spacecraft (supervision); with greater distance to home
    base, help took longer to arrive, but the subject's autonomy was greater.
By changing course, meteorites could be avoided.
Also, meteorites could be blasted with the cannon.

When the subject had developed his own behavioral strategy in this respect (e.g., with individually different average distances kept to home base), he was confronted with a UFO whose existence came as a surprise. And here again, individually characteristic behavior patterns developed, ranging from careful approach to outright flight. To check the core premise—that the stimulus situation, as measured by distance from home base and from unknown object, stands in a close and unambiguous relation to experienced security and experienced arousal —two physiological variables were measured during the flight: heart rate and galvanic skin response, while a hidden video camera recorded the subject's facial expressions. Individual reference values for security and arousal were indicated by the mean distance toward home base and to the unknown object. A projective test administered after the experiment tapped the subject's need for security and arousal; the results for the motivational scores on this projective test correlated highly with the results of the adventure experiment and thus indicate the high external validity of this experimental approach.

G. Self-Referencing and Economic Theory

DeVillé lands us firmly with our feet on the earth again. His contribution, entitled "Equilibrium Versus Reproduction," criticizes general equilibrium theory, considered by most economists to be an adequate theoretical description of a market-decentralized economy. Three important lessons can be learned from this critical analysis:

1. The effort to develop a theory of society that relies exclusively on methodological individualism presents unsolvable difficulties.
2. Once such methodological exclusiveness is abandoned, the sharp demarcation between economics and the other social sciences becomes untenable.

3. The construction of any adequate theory of society requires the elaboration of a dynamic theory of reproduction and transformation, combining human freedom and agency with structural constraints.

Economists often feel that neoclassical economics, since it is based on a well-developed and formalized rational choice theory, is the appropriate theoretical framework to deal with issues traditionally studied by sociologists; and some sociologists, especially those propounding rational choice theory, support this expansionist view. Reactions have come from economists and sociologists alike. Some economists, most notably the French "regulation school," question the possibility of elaborating, on the basis of the neoclassical framework, a convincing macroeconomic theory adequately representing the global functioning of a decentralized market economy. Sociologists have criticized the weaknesses of traditional economic models, where many sociological variables are either left out or kept exogenous.

DeVillé has developed, with among others Baumgartner (1986) and Burns and Baumgartner (1982), the "actor-oriented systems approach," which is based on two key ideas:

1. That individual (or collectively structured actors') behavior is fundamentally strategic, and therefore does not take its environment as given, as parametric.
2. That society can be conceived as a multilevel, hierarchically structured system. This is possible because of the existence of a complex set of rules (i.e., institutions as "rules of the games") that dominate each other according to, among other things, the power relations between social actors.

It then follows, paradoxically, that economic actors truly compete against each other precisely by trying to escape from the state of affairs defined by economists as "perfect competition." They do so also by engaging in sociopolitical competition, in ways that might even contradict the standard behavioral assumption of profit maximization. Competitive struggles are therewith structured as multilevel games. Assuming that indeed a more dynamic approach to competition requires quite different behavioral assumptions, it becomes difficult to maintain the present sharp dichotomy between economics and sociology.

The key issue in economic theory is to provide an adequate theoretical description of the global functioning of a decentralized market economy. Since Adam Smith, economic theory has tried to answer the question: Can the pursuit of self-interest by free and independent agents through voluntary and not a priori coordinated exchanges result in order rather than anarchy? Neoclassical equilibrium theory (NCGET) claims to be able to provide an affirmative answer. However, as DeVillé stresses, this claim is based on a number of unrealistic assumptions, on an equilibrium method that fails to clarify how the behavior of individuals in a nonequilibrium state of the system will spontaneously bring the system into an equilibrium state, and in a resulting ideal state that is no more than a thought experiment with a normative potential implication: if and only if the world would be like the one implied by the unrealistic assumptions made, then such a world would be characterized by "order."

NCGET started by postulating a price adjustment rule determined by the market excess demand functions: if, at a certain price level, there is an excess demand, prices will rise until an equilibrium is reached. However, since perfect competition is assumed, prices are parametric (i.e., noninfluenceable) for the agents operating in the market. To therefore answer the question of who then determines the price if no single actor can, an "auctioneer" (some centralized device) had to be postulated. This auctioneer announces prices of several commodities, calculates excess demands at these prices given the answers received, and then adjusts the prices. However, during this process, no effective trading, consumption, or production can take place.

Later theoretical developments relaxed these rather absurd and unrealistic assumptions; however, when the auctioneer and his actions are removed from the theory, no convergence from a nonequilibrium state could be proved, while even the dynamic interactions among agents were difficult to conceptualize. If one keeps the auctioneer as part of the theory, his task becomes more complicated: apart from implementing the price adjustment rule, he additionally has to decide on and enforce a rationing scheme, allocating among buyers commodities in excess demand, and among sellers commodities in excess supply. Thus, on a more general level, NCGET demonstrates the difficulties inherent in the construction of a truly dynamic theory of social systems.

In the actor-oriented systems approach, the price system is a metalevel structure of the highest possible order, acting as a constraint imposed on all individual agents and beyond their reach. The adjustment principle is the "system need," since it is the necessary structural requirement for its reproduction. In realistic systems models of dynamic social systems, one has to be careful not to attribute knowledge to agents within the model (e.g., about prices in equilibrium states) that can be acquired only by the model designer. The rationality of actors also has to be defined differently in this approach and in the NCGET models; Simon's concept of bounded rationality, based on the realization of limited availability of information and equally limited computational abilities of human agents, comes closer to the mark here.

DeVillé then sketches the outlines of an alternative research program, roughly defined as an actor-oriented evolutionary theory of a decentralized market economy. No a priori equilibrium assumptions are made here. Economic agents operate in a complex environment, characterized by "radical uncertainty," and their behavior could be described as "strategic decision making based on bounded rationality." In other words, there is no optimal strategy; "satisfactory" strategies are determined according to multilevel hierarchized criteria: for example, "at least survive, possibly expand, or even diversify." Transactions occur through the confrontation of these strategic behaviors with bargaining procedures or rules. Such again hierarchically structured rules, with varying degrees of generality (from micro to macro), can take the form of explicit rules or institutions when they are beyond the range of individual decision making.

NCGET makes a clear-cut distinction between a theory of the existence of equilibria and a theory of convergence toward those equilibria which is secondary both conceptually and in terms of the sequence of research tasks to be performed. However, there is no reason to limit oneself to the study of economic processes that converge toward NCGET equilibria. Stability of economic systems—and social systems in general—could also be conceptualized as states of the system where its core structure and processes reproduce themselves, although microunits like economic agents might find themselves in nonoptimal situations.

What is needed is an economic theory of institutions, explaining what is the minimal set of institutional mechanisms necessary for the theoretical description of the dynamic processes of a capitalist, decentralized market economy. Institutions should not be dealt with as exogenous to the system; it should be recognized that they emerge from interactive processes among agents, while at the same time posing enduring constraints on individual behaviors, and thus shaping and structuring the interactive processes between these individuals.

The neoclassical equilibrium method should be abandoned; not because it is not valid in itself, but because it imposes an untenable dichotomy between static theories and dynamic theories, between the theory of equilibrium states and the theory of processes.

Institutions can be conceived as "equilibrium solutions" of coordination problems that cannot be solved through market processes. However, in the reproduction method advanced by DeVillé, an equivalent has to be found for the equilibrium conditions in the equilibrium method. Such an equivalent might be described as follows: a system is in a process of reproduction when the institutional framework and the selection processes it entails guarantee that possibly nonoptimal but satisficing situations prevail for the "boundedly rational" individual (or collectively organized) agents—in such a way that no one will be induced to engage in strategic behavior in an attempt to change this institutional framework, but on the contrary, everyone will accept to bear the burden of its maintenance costs.

H. Self-Referencing and Economic Models

Midttun also deals with the inadequacy of much of economic theory, but with more stress on the necessity for policy makers to select sufficiently sophisticated, yet workable economic models to guide their policy decision. The problem is that economic theory has developed ideal-typical constructs with a degree of internal consistency and strong normative power, which however are bought to a large extent at the expense of realism. Often, existing economic models have a limited scope, while actor and structure assumptions make for considerable deviation from the "messy" real word. Advice sought from such idealized and limited models of the economy may be right within their limited scope, but nevertheless gives wrong guidance for the political economy as a whole.

Here, the paradox of self-referential systems, as analyzed specifically by van der Zouwen for the case of methods research, comes to the fore again: one of the reasons for the above is that models may indeed be corroborated or falsified by the very policies based on policy advice derived from them. Applying Ashby's Law of Requisite Variety, one can argue that the political governance system must have models of the political economy that are sufficiently rich to map the relevant variety found in it, if at least it is to exercise successful control.

For pragmatic purposes, economic modeling is therefore faced with a difficult tradeoff between realism and analytical simplicity. The more extensive the policy ambitions, the stronger the need for comprehensive models of the political economy to guide policy decisions in a "collectively rational" way. But the more comprehensive the models become in terms of including the multidimensional complexity of interacting political and economic processes, the less founded is the policy advice that can be derived from them. Midttun then devotes his contribution to discussing this dilemma of the tradeoff between realism and analytical simplicity in three models of political economy:

Neoclassical marginalism with its paradigm of the self-regulating market (roughly DeVillé's NCGET)
Keynesian macroeconomics, with its paradigm of the planned mixed economy
Negotiated political economy, which contains a number of post-Keynesian political science and political sociology critiques (approximately DeVillé's reproduction method)

The neoclassical paradigm of the self-regulating market is essentially a model of the parametric self-governance of the economic system, where a stable state is reached unintentionally through the interaction of economic actors within a given set of market rules. The Keynesian and later models are generally a combination of the neoclassical model and a model of economic governance through rational state intervention. The negotiated political economy perspective, finally, displays models of competitive multiple-centered governance, where economic actors engage in economic transactions but also deliberately organize to reshape market conditions and transaction rules.

These three models can be seen as successive steps in increasing systemic complexity, ranging from single-level transaction systems to multileveled and multiple-centered systems. The self-referential character of complex systems poses severe limitations on the possibility of modeling comprehensively the political economy; moving from simplistic to complex realistic modeling implies also a move from fully specified optimal solutions to conditionally specified sets of alternatives. Each of these three successive models implies a widening of systemic boundaries or the field of reference; neoclassical economics tends to restrict itself to pure market processes, Keynesianism shifted from a micro to a macro orientation and included a rational state playing an important role as an external regulator of the socioeconomic system, while the negotiated political economy perspective broadens economic analysis to encompass a number of both political and administrative elements, thus creating more fuzzy boundaries between economic and other social systems.

By making different extensions of their field of reference and varying the "tightness" of their a priori analytical assumptions, neoclassical economics, Keynesian macroeconomics, and negotiated political economy delineate different aspects of the political economy and are faced with different sets of methodological problems. Neoclassical economics is based to a large extent, for example, on assumptions of closed systems with fixed causal structures; as in much of social science, the constancy of causal relations is taken for granted, and one searches for laws of social behavior. However, as theories of the political economy become more inclusive through the widening of the systemic boundaries or the field of reference, as well as through the loosening of analytical assumptions or the inclusion of a greater degree of system multidimensionality, the analyst is increasingly faced with the complex and morphogenetic character of social systems—which precludes predictions about social processes and events in any strong sense. Keynesianism assumed a multiplier effect of the state's role in stimulating consumer demand and supplementing private investment.

This assumption was based on another implicit assumption: that the state has sufficient internal control over its own implementation process and sufficient protection against encroaching particularistic interests. The problems of economic governance in the past two decades—characterized by stagflation, stagnant economies and expectation crises—have served to underline the unrealistic nature of the above assumptions. As the public sector became large enough to influence the economy, welfare policy developed as well and turned out to be subject to particularistic claims; the close coupling of the partially contradictory goals of macroeconomic stabilization and welfare policy thus served to tie up the freedom of the state to efficiently pursue a macroeconomically motivated policy.

The negotiated political economy perspective contests the Keynesian assumption of a collectively rational state, unbound by interest conflicts within the economy in its internal decision making. In reality, such interest conflicts abound: the regulatory state apparatus is likely to act suboptimally from the viewpoint of collective rationality of society as a whole, as a result of biased political interest aggregation on the input side and implementation problems on the output side. Governance should be viewed therefore as a multiple-centered and only partially coordinated system, where the state has to govern the economy through negotiations with other interests. To become more realistic, the Keynesian model therefore has to be enlarged with a set of organizations representing market actors, as well as a negotiating arena of competing regulatory agents supplementing and/or contesting state governance.

A problem in this respect is that such a negotiated political economy tends to overallocate support to well-organized groups representing particularistic interests. The reasons should be clear:

While the interest groups have large gains and relatively small costs of mobilization, the inverse situation holds for society as a whole. Targeted public support paid out of public funds results in a considerable increase in welfare for each member of the target group at a relatively modest total cost for the system as a whole. On the other hand, to mobilize efficient support for a collectively optimal allocation of resources, if possible at all, is relatively costly. Consequently, both the distribution of payoffs and the costs of efficient mobilization favor particularistic interests.

On the implementation side, organizational inertia, the autonomy of bureaucracy, and the penetration of political interests invalidate the macroeconomic assumption of a neutral and rational state. Specialized bureaucracies and private sector representatives share common assumptions, priorities, and procedures, such that the implementation of political decisions may serve to further underline the bias toward particularism created on the political input side.

For Midttun then, self-referentiality poses limits to modeling, as also for the authors described above. In the negotiated political economy model, predictions may severely affect the very operations of the economic behavior that is being modeled. When politicoeconomic modeling becomes closely coupled to political decision making, and particularly when the policy process itself is incorporated in the model, modelers face the problem of having to make pronouncements about the actor's expected behavior despite the possibility that the actual behavior of the same actors may be heavily influenced by the cognition gained through the model and its forecasts.

This problem of self-reactivity refers to a chain of linkages between information, cognition, organization, and action. If information resulting from the forecast is fed back into the cognitive models of actors who participate in the system that is being forecasted, and if moreover those actors are organized in such a way that they can act on the basis of this information, they will then potentially be able to alter their behavior as a result of the forecast. Consequently, mapping of the system must now also include mapping of self-reactive properties—and the reactions to these reactions etc.—and all these must be handled within the model, which logically ends up in an infinite regress and necessitates an increasingly complex model that is vulnerable to validity and reliability problems.

Compared to these problems inherent in efforts to model a negotiated political economy, neoclassical economics—with its strong actor and structure assumptions and its restrictive boundary specification—certainly has the virtue of simplicity, and maintains an objective and logical basis for predictive knowledge. However, it is bought at the expense of its realism and its ability to cope with multilevel complexity. Keynesian macroeconomics was already able to deal with a richer set of properties of the real world by giving up the strong thesis of self-regulatory optimization. The negotiated political economy paradigm does not even assume rational optimization at the regulatory level, and thus makes for more realistic insight, though fewer possibilities for prediction.

While admittedly the cost of this analytical richness has been the loss of the "shortcut to predictive knowledge," the strength of the more complex models of the negotiated political economy perspective lies in their heuristic function. Outcomes may not be specified in unambiguous optimality criteria but will have the character of probabilistic, or even possibilistic or conditional statements, dependent on rationality criteria, structural assumptions, assumed goals, and values of different actor segments.

IV. EPILOGUE

In the preceding section, eight recent examples of innovative sociocybernetic research have been discussed. These examples clearly demonstrate the applicability of sociocybernetics to a wide variety of subjects within the social sciences. Moreover, they stress its specific characteristics as mentioned in Section II—characteristics that set it apart from most social science research, more often than not in a positive way. Finally, they clarify the direction in which sociocybernetics has been developing: from originally rather mechanistic, first-order cybernetics to an increasingly sophisticated second-order cybernetics, with all its implications, such as autopoiesis and self-reference, which make it eminently suitable for the subject matter of the social sciences: human individuals and groups.

Nevertheless, much remains to be desired: most research in the field is still done by cyberneticians and systems theorists rather than by social scientists, while it is generally of a theoretical nature. Consequently, the authors consider it desirable to stimulate more empirical research, especially by social scientists. Up till now, the sociocybernetic approach unfortunately has gained few adherents in the mainstream social science community, which also barely makes use of its results. Perhaps this is the case because, on the one hand, it is still relatively unknown, while on the other hand it is rarely a part of social science curricula. Another reason may be the unwarranted reproach of implicit conservatism, made by generally liberal social scientists, discussed in the beginning of Section II.

Whatever the cause, however, there is a clear task for sociocybernetics: to convince the social science community of the value of their approach.

REFERENCES

Ashby W. R. (1956). *An Introduction to Cybernetics*. London: Chapman & Hall.

Baumgartner, Thomas, and Burns, Tom R. (1982). "Wealth and Poverty Among Nations: A Social Systems Perspective on Inequality, Uneven Development and Dependency in the World Economy," in Geyer, R. F., and van der Zouwen, J. (eds.), *Dependence and Inequality: A Systems Approach to the Problems of Mexico and Other Developing Countries*. Oxford: Pergamon Press, pp. 3-22.

Baumgartner, Thomas, Burns, Tom R., de Villé, Philippe, and Gauci, Bernard (1982). "Inflation, Politics, and Social Change: Actor-Oriented Systems Analysis Applied to Explain the Roots of Inflation in Modern Society," in Geyer, R. F., and van der Zouwen, J. (eds.), *Dependence and Inequality: A Systems Approach to the Problems of Mexico and Other Developing Countries*. Oxford: Pergamon Press, pp. 59-88.

Baumgartner, Thomas (1986). "Actors, Models and Limits to Societal Self-Steering," in Geyer, F., and van der Zouwen, J. (eds.), *Sociocybernetic Paradoxes: Observation, Control and Evolution of Self-Steering Systems*. London: SAGE, pp. 9-25.

Bråten, S. (1986). "The Third Position: Beyond Artificial and Autopoietic Reduction," in Geyer, F., and van der Zouwen, J. (eds.), *Sociocybernetic Paradoxes: Observation, Control and Evolution of Self-Steering Systems*. London: SAGE, pp. 193-205.

Chomsky, N., and Miller, G. (1963). "Introduction to the Formal Analysis of Natural Languages," in Luce, R. D., Bush, R. R., and Galanter, E. (eds.), *Handbook of Mathematical Psychology*, Vol. II. New York: Wiley.

Geyer, R. F., and van der Zouwen, J. eds., (1978). *Sociocybernetics: An Actor-Oriented Systems Approach*, 2 vols. Leiden: Nijhoff.

Geyer, R. F., and van der Zouwen, J., eds., (1982). *Dependence and Inequality: A Systems Approach to the Problems of Mexico and Other Developing Countries*. Oxford: Pergamon Press.

Geyer, F., and van der Zouwen, J., eds. (1986). *Sociocybernetic Paradoxes: Observation, Control and Evolution of Self-Steering Systems*. London: SAGE.

Geyer, F., and van der Zouwen, J., eds. (1986). *Self-Referencing in Social Systems*. Salinas, CA: Intersystems.

Geyer, F., and van der Zouwen, J. (1990b). "Self-Referencing in Social systems," in Geyer, F., and van der Zouwen, J. (eds.), *Self-Referencing in Social systems*. Salinas, CA: Intersystems, pp. 1-29.

Geyer, F., ed. (1991). *The Cybernetics of Complex Systems*. Salinas, CA: Intersystems Publications.

Gierer, A. (1982). "Systems Aspects of Socioeconomic Inequalities in Social systems," in Geyer, R. F., and van der Zouwen, J. (eds.), *Dependence and Inequality: A Systems Approach to the Problems of Mexico and Other Developing Countries*. Oxford: Pergamon Press, pp. 23-34.

Howard, N. (1971). *Paradoxes of Rationality: Theory of Metagames and Political Behavior*. Cambridge, MA: MIT Press.

Lilienfeld, R. (1978). *The Rise of Systems Theory: An Ideological Analysis*. New York: Wiley.

Luhmann, N. "The Autopoiesis of Social Systems," in Geyer, F., and van der Zouwen, J.

(eds.), *Sociocybernetic Paradoxes: Observation, Control and Evolution of Self-Steering Systems.* London: SAGE, pp. 172-192.

Maturana, H. R., and Varela, F. J. (1980). *Autopoiesis and Cognition: The Realization of the Living.* Dordrecht: Reidel.

Merton, R. K. (1948). "The Self-Fulfilling Prophecy," *Antioch Rev., 8:* 193-210.

Pask, G. (1976). *Conversation Theory.* Amsterdam: Elsevier.

Pask, G. (1978). "A Conversation Theoretic Approach to Social Systems," in Geyer, R. F., and van der Zouwen, J. (eds.), *Sociocybernetics: An Actor-Oriented Systems Approach,* Vol. 1. Leiden: Nijhoff, pp. 15-26.

Prigogine, I., and Stengers, I. (1984). *Order Out of Chaos.* New York: Bantam.

Zeeuw, Gerard de (1986). "Social Change and the Design of Enquiry," in Geyer, F., and van der Zouwen, J. (eds.), *Sociocybernetic Paradoxes: Observation, Control and Evolution of Self-Steering Systems.* London: SAGE, pp. 131-144.

6

Order, Evolution, and Natural Law: Fundamental Relations in Complex System Theory

Rod Swenson   University of Connecticut, Storrs, Connecticut

I. BACKGROUND AND PREVIEW

A. Reductive Materialism and the Roots of the Modern Scientific World View

Following the virulent attacks on Aristotelian causality by Bacon and Descartes, the stunning success of Newtonian mechanics paved the way for the construction of a modern scientific enterprise, built (as Bacon claimed it should be [1]) almost entirely on efficient cause—on summativity, reversibility, and determinism.[1] The reductive materialism of this "purposeless-particle" world view effectively eliminated all goals, purposes, intentions, or other end-directed behavior from the physical world [3,4], thus radically defining the ontological foundation and epistemological thrust of modern thinking. In contrast, the physics of Aristotle, the study of the "nature" of things which dominated scientific thinking for nearly two millennia before the mechanical world view took hold, was precisely the study of ends.[2] Efficient causes, along with formal (the geometry, shape, or form of a thing or process) and material causes (the substrate from which a thing or process arises), were taken to be governed by the ends they served, or final cause. It was precisely the relation between these different kinds of cause and their interaction with respect to final cause that was understood as the subject of inquiry. Aristotelian physics was a physics of teleology, the study of nature as end-directed, and

125

thus Aristotle argued that "one only knows a thing when one knows why it is, its reason" [5].

The Aristotelian view of an active, end-directed physics sought to explicate the more general view of the Greeks that the order of the natural world emerged from chaos [6] in a process of perpetual transformation and flux, and this is precisely what was explicitly expurgated from the "dead" or static perspective of the mechanical view, which began its ascendancy in the seventeenth century. "Inquiry into final causes," said Bacon, "is sterile, and, like a virgin consecrated to God, produces nothing" (*"Nam causarum finalium inquisitio sterilis est, et, tanquam virgo Deo consecrata, nihil parit"* [6].) [7]. Boyle [8] exemplified the modern mechanical view when he compared the universe to the "ingenious clock of Strasburg-Cathedral," a comparison supported by his younger contemporary Newton. In contrast to the Greek view of flux and change, it was the immutability of nature that characterized the rise of the mechanical view: the stars, the sun, the earth, and life upon it with the exception of those portions cultivated by man (sic) were thought to be eternal [6]. The anthropocentricity of this privileged human position, which shows how deeply the pillars of the modern scientific edifice were set in a theological foundation, is obvious.

B. Self-Organization, Purposiveness, and Extraphysical Causes

It was no accident that the *why* of Aristotelian physics was reduced to the merely descriptive *how* of modern physics [4,9]—that purposiveness, or other end-directed behavior was surgically removed from the discourse of physics: it kept the watchmaker, or master designer, intact *outside* the Newtonian machine. Humans were thus dualistically situated with mind somehow outside nature and body within, manipulating the clock toward divine ends [10]. Boyle's remark that it was precisely because the universe was like the clock of Strasburg-Cathedral that it must necessarily have an intelligent creator [8] make explicit the unique marriage of materialism and theology that characterized the rise of the mechanical world view.[3] Although by conforming to the emotional requirements of the religious social ordering of the time (including the religious consciences of those doing the physics), this construction permitted stunning advances in physics, the price tag on the impoverished causal framework that this flawed materialism carried with it was an ontological dualism that has plagued future generations.[4]

By the middle of the nineteenth century the empirical facts were already more than sufficient to deny the view of an immutable nature. Kant's attack on the eternity of the solar system, made nearly a century before, was now widely accepted (although not the details of his theory). The solar system was now seen as something that had *come into being* [6] from within the context of the larger universe.

This made the idea of a single-creation event no longer tenable and showed an end-directed style of change much more closely aligned with the intuitions of Aristotelian physics than with the purposeless, reversible mechanical model. The emergence of the solar system from a previously incoherent cosmic gas necessarily meant that Earth and the order on it were not immutable either. Discoveries in the geological record confirmed that not only Earth, but the order on it (from its simplest beginnings to modern cultural systems with their human and artifactual productions) emerged progressively out of the matter and energy that had comprised this same gas. Not only was the world characterized by historical process, but this historical process was directed toward increasingly more highly ordered states. Yet given the failure of physics to causally account for this self-organizing behavior and the immediate benefits to the production and maintenance of social order derived from the promotion of anthropocentric ideologies,[5] dualism continued to thrive, in both old and new packages.

Russell [1, p. 602] has characterized Darwin as an unoriginal thinker who happened to be at the right place at the right time.[6] Darwin's theory of natural selection acting on competitive Malthusian populations in the "struggle for life" had the necessary components demanded by the social ordering of the time. It generalized Hobbes's law of *"bellum omnium contra omnes"* and Malthus's theory of population—in essence the bourgeois economy theory of competition—from human social systems to the evolution of life as a whole.[7] The attractiveness of Darwinism was that it elevated the favored ideology of the status of natural order. Its main failure, in addition to its ideological bias, was that it assumed almost all it should have otherwise explained outside its theory. This is still true today. That is, putting aside the question of sufficiency regarding a model reduced to individual competition between selfish replicating or reproducing individuals, Darwinism in both its original and modern forms assumes the "struggle for life" to begin with. The central problem that any true historical materialism or evolutionary theory must address is where, out of a "dead," purposeless world of physics, such an ordering process can come from. This unavoidably puts the fundamental question of Aristotelian final cause back on the table [15].

C. Nonequilibrium Thermodynamics: The Production of Ends Without Makers

In addition to the work of Darwin, Marx and Engels, Spencer, and many others working on theories of change, the middle of the nineteenth century saw the formulation of what Eddington [16, p. 74] has called the "supreme" law of nature, the second law of thermodynamics. The first law, which followed from the work of Meyer, Joule, Helmholtz, and others, demonstrated empirically for the first time the interrelation and unity of all dynamical processes: (1) all are embodiments of

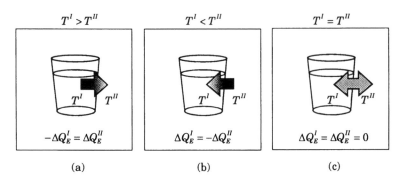

Figure 1 A glass of liquid at temperature T^I is placed in a room at a different temperature T^{II}. The disequilibrium between them (the temperature difference) defines a field potential that, in accordance with the second law of thermodynamics, produces a flow of energy as heat ΔQ_E that acts as a drain to minimize the potential—to maximize the entropy. If T^I exceeds T^{II} as in (a), the flow is from the glass to the room $-\Delta Q_E^I = \Delta Q_E^{II}$, and if T^I is less than T^{II} as in (b), the flow is from the room to the glass $\Delta Q_E^I = -\Delta Q_E^{II}$. In both cases the flow continues until $T^I = T^{II}$ and the potential is minimized (the entropy maximized) as in (c), at which time all flows stop, $\Delta Q_E^I = \Delta Q_E^{II} = 0$.

energy flows or transformations; (2) all forms of energy (e.g., mechanical, chemical, and heat) are interconvertible; and (3) the total amount of energy is conserved (remains the same). The second law, following on the work of Carnot and formulated by Thomson and Clausius, showed that all dynamical processes proceed so as to maximize the entropy, a measure of the unavailability of a system's energy to do "work" (to produce macroscopic change). Contrary to the classical mechanical model, nature was thus shown to be *irreversible*—to have a direction. The direction specified by the second law, the spreading out or dissipation of field potentials (nonequilibrium distributions of energy or "availability"[8]), is easily seen by considering a glass of liquid (tea, water, or whatever) placed in a room that is at a different temperature (see Fig. 1). If the liquid is warmer than the room, a flow of energy is produced from the glass to the room until the two are equilibrated; if the room is warmer than the liquid, a flow is produced in the other direction. The flows are the means the room–liquid system uses to maximize its entropy or equivalently to minimize its field potential, which is accomplished when the temperatures of the fluid and room are equilibrated (equal), at which time all flows (macroscopic behavior) stop.

In fact, entropy maximization is precisely a statement of final cause in the Aristotelian sense.[9] "The entropy of the world," said Clausius [20], "strives to a maximum." "Nature prefers certain states," said Planck [21], "and the measure of the preference is Clausius' entropy." The full impact of this explicit recognition of an end-directed nature was deflected by the hegemony of the mechanical view perpetuated by the interpretation of the second law due to Boltzmann [22]. Following the work of Maxwell, who had modeled gas molecules as billiard balls, and in an effort to salvage the mechanical world view, Boltzmann reduced the second law to a stochastic collision function (to purposeless mechanical collisions or efficient cause). Since when a monatomic gas is confined to a box every collision will produce a change in the velocity and direction of each molecule, all nonequilibrium energy distributions or coherent velocity distributions—molecules moving at the same speed or in the same direction—will become increasingly dispersed and irregular, leading to a final state of maximum disorder. Boltzmann recognized this state as the state of maximum entropy, and thus claimed entropy maximization, hence the second law, was simply a law of probability, the statistical result of the random collisions of elementary particles. For this reason, a collection of molecules or "bodies" "moving at the same speed and in the same direction" said Boltzmann, "is the most infinitely improbable configuration of energy conceivable" [23]—and the second law became a law of disorder.

The belief that from the standpoint of physics the production of order was "infinitely improbable" turned what Eddington [16] has called the most important scientific discovery of the nineteenth century (the second law) into the most serious roadblock yet to a nondualistic view of nature or comprehensive evolutionary theory. Physics, on this view, was not just passively disposed toward order as with the "dead" physics of the classical mechanical model, but now worked relentlessly against it. This not only reinforced the apparent justification for invoking extraphysical causes, but led theorists to speak about the various extraphysically endowed states (e.g., living systems) as "struggling against" or "paying a price" or "debt" to the laws of physics in order to "do business." Of course the problem of explaining the origin and operation of such extraphysical, purposive "debt-payers," or exactly what business they might be in (particularly in the odd sense of somehow having their existence now tied to a fight against the universal laws of nature) simply backs the theorist further into the dualistic corner [12].

Recent advances in the theory of nonequilibrium thermodynamics (the "second thermodynamics") have turned the Boltzmann conception precisely on its head, providing the basis for obliterating the untenable dualistic ontology that has hung like a great weight around the neck of the modern scientific enterprise from its beginning. The world is not reducible to the purposeless collisions of elementary particles—to a stochastic collision function or any other kind of linear, summative, aimless behavior—and this can be shown by simple and easily understood physical facts. In particular, order is no longer seen as infinitely improbable but inexorable under universal law; the world is now understood to be in the *order production business*, and it is the laws of physics that make it so. The rest of this tutorial sets forth the fundamental principles.

II. NATURAL SYMMETRY AND THE LAWS OF EVOLUTION

A. Evolution in Physics, Biology, and Culture

When we speak of evolution, or a theory of evolution, it is almost always taken to be Darwinism that we are talking about. But this fact is the result of decades of social construction. In truth Darwin never even used the word "evolution" in the first five editions of *The Origin* at all.[10] This is not because the term "evolution" was not in use. It was widely popularized in the early and mid-1850s by Spencer, who defined it as the lawful and progressive production of order from disorder, which he said held uniformly from the physical (nonliving) to the living and the cultural (human social)[11] [11,12,15,24]. The fact of the matter is that Darwin did not use the word "evolution" for the reason that he never intended to address the general problem of evolution at all: his intention was simply to show that "species" were transformed over time as the result of natural selection (a particular facet of evolution).

When the *term* evolution was historically expropriated by the proponents of Darwinism, the *idea* of evolution became effectively reduced from a spontaneous process of universal ordering to the result of natural selection acting on a population of differentially replicating or reproducing entities competing for fixed resources. The consequences of this reduction, the decoupling of the living from the physical world, are why the notion that Darwinism "owns" evolution (cf. ref. 25) must be thoroughly rejected. In assuming the "struggle for life" to begin with and avoiding the directed and global nature of terrestrial evolution as a whole, Darwinism explicitly avoids addressing the material or physical origins of such goal- or end-directed behavior and simply dualistically smuggles it into a mechanical world of physics ad hoc from outside its theory (cf. Elliot [26]). Darwinism cannot, therefore, be expected to answer the deeper questions of evolution.

The same kind of smuggling occurs with respect to cultural ordering, where the problem of order production is avoided by the assumption that culture is simply the rational creation and production of (and for the good of) man (sic). Yet this dualist deduction, which is no more than a modern construction of the same old incongruent blend of materialism and miracles discussed above, absurdly assumes that humans preceded culture—that they evolved (or miraculously appeared full-blown) and then rationally invented it! Obvious logical impossibilities aside, this view is unequivocally denied by the evolutionary facts. Members of the genus *Australopithicus* with chimpanzee-sized brains used tools for more than 2 million years before the genus *Homo* even emerged. Thus cultural evolution began long before there were any humans at all: humans, including their intentional dynamics, were a production of it [10].

B. A Selection Principle Grounded in Physical Law

Because the "mechanics" of Darwinism are carefully defined in such a way so as to avoid addressing these fundamental problems of evolution, Darwinism excludes itself a priori from any possibility of ever solving them. Because on the Darwinian view, evolution is operationally reduced to the result of "natural selection" working on a population of replicating or reproducing entities showing heritable variation and competing for the same resource (a Malthusian population), Darwinism cannot address either the evolutionary origin of the replicating ordering it assumes or the directed nature of evolution as a whole [22]. That is, while the evolutionary record shows terrestrial evolution as a progressive global phenomenon (that the Earth system at its highest level has evolved, functions, and is evolving as a single global entity characterized by increasingly more highly ordered states), Darwinism cannot address or even recognize this global evolution (in fact denies it [27]) because there is no population of competing Earth systems on which natural selection can act: the global Earth system is a *population of one.*

The "problem of the population of one," the problem of how order is selected from disorder, requires an evolutionary theory that accounts for the phenomenon of spontaneous order production, and this puts the question of purposive or end-directed physics directly back on the table [15]. In particular, it asks that what was dualistically removed from the physical world by the theological beliefs of the seventeenth century be returned to its rightful place [12]. The principle of parsimony suggests that if a world of purposeless mechanical particles (the Newtonian–Boltzmann narrative) needs miraculous makers to order it, then the physical world cannot be reducible to purposeless mechanical particles. That is, it suggests that such a description of the physical world is incomplete. More specifically, the spontaneous evolutionary ordering of the natural world suggests the operation of a *physical selection principle* (since if it does not require a population of replicating entities to act, the principle cannot be biological) that accounts for the production of ordered from disordered states. Competition[12] in this case would thus be between ordered (or macro) and disordered (or micro) modes, and such a law would turn the Boltzmann conception precisely on its head. This is indeed the case and it will be shown below.

C. Unifying the Dynamics of the Material World: Energy Is Not a Measure of the Ability of a System to Do Work

The understanding of evolution or directed change requires a clear understanding of the first and second laws of thermodynamics and their particular relation to each other. Perhaps because it is counterintuitive to describe the dissipation of a system's potential for change by the increase of a quantity, or else because end states are not as inductively obvious causes as simple cause–effect relations (efficient causes), many who take energy for granted have believed entropy to be difficult to understand. Since understanding either energy or entropy requires the understanding of both, such a belief simply indicates a misunderstanding of energy. In fact energy was not defined or understood historically until "entropy" (a word coined by Clausius [20] to sound like "energy" in order to stress the relation between the two) was also defined. It was the contribution of Clausius and Thomson to recognize that two quantities were operable in all real-world processes: one that was conserved (energy) and one that was not (entropy), and neither was intelligible without the other.

This misunderstanding is so deep that while energy is a common word even in everyday vocabulary, entropy is hardly known. Entropy is avoided altogether by ascribing all the properties of both entropy and energy to energy, although this is precisely the impossibility that lead to Clausius' and Thomson's important formulation of the two quantities to begin with. In particular (1) colloquialisms such as "consuming" or "producing" energy, (2) causal statements describing processes as being "driven by energy," (3) apparently technical definitions of energy as "a measure of the ability of a system to do work," or (4) popular admonitions about "trying to conserve energy" are either impossible or false; the first law of thermodynamics (the conservation law) says that energy is always conserved—it can never be destroyed (consumed) or created (produced)[13]; the quantity of the energy in any dynamical process is simply transformed from one configuration or form to another. For example, when fuel is used to run a car, the energy is not consumed but only transformed into other forms (e.g., heat in the air from gasoline in a tank). The same is seen with the liquid in the glass shown in Figure 1. If we build a box to enclose the glass and a portion of the air in the room so that no matter and energy can flow through the box's walls, and if the temperature of the liquid is, say, warmer than that of the rest of the air in the box, a flow of heat will be produced from the glass to the air, but the total amount of energy in the box will remain unchanged.

What changes in both cases is not the quantity of energy, which is conserved, but its quality, which is not, and it is the entropy that is a measure of the quality of the energy and motivates the change. Thus it is legitimate in both cases to talk about the dissipation, consumption, or destruction of field potentials (or "availability")—*the production of entropy*—but not about the consumption or destruction of energy. It is thus clearly seen from the case in Figure 1 that it is not the energy in the box that drives the process or provides a measure of the ability of the system to do work (produce a process): after the system has come to equilibrium and the process stops, the quantity of energy is precisely the same as it was when the liquid was warmer than the air and the process started. It is the extent to which the entropy is maximized relative to the equilibrium state, its distance from equilibrium, that determines the magnitude of the motive force or field potential. The further the system from equilibrium, the greater the force. At equilibrium there are no field potentials, and there are no flows. This is precisely the meaning of Planck's preference (see above). The conservation and interconvertibility of all forms of energy (the first law) shows the underlying unity of all natural processes (dynamics): *entropy maximization (the second law) provides their motivation* [3].

D. The First and Second Laws: Symmetry of the Laws of Physics Themselves

The preceding discussion set us up to make a fundamental point more explicit: the first and second laws of thermodynamics are not ordinary laws of physics; they sit above the ordinary laws as laws about laws expressing the dynamical symmetry of the laws of physics themselves [3,28]. The conservation principle described by the first law expresses the time-translation symmetry of the laws of physics, and the second law likewise expresses a symmetry that governs all other physical laws, but in a completely unique and powerful way. Whereas the first law is a law of equivalence, the symmetry expressed by the second law where nonequilibrium distributions of energy occur is a symmetry unfulfilled, and it is precisely this unfulfilled symmetry that underlies the preference of Planck as well as the striving of Clausius, and motivates and directs the dynamics or action of the natural world [3]. Evolution can now be understood and defined in a deeper way as *symmetry on the way to making*. The relation between the unfulfilled symmetry of the second law, of the motivation and production of self-organizing states—progressively higher order symmetries on the way to making—and the physical law that governs selection from micro to macro mode is the subject of the next section.

III. MAXIMUM ENTROPY PRODUCTION AND THE PHYSICS OF ORDER

A. Thermodynamic Systems Produce Dynamics That Reduce Their Field Potentials at the Fastest Possible Rate Given the Constraints

Because classical thermodynamics was developed in the middle of the nineteenth century as a direct result of the effort to understand and improve the efficiency of the steam engine (see, e.g., ref. 8), the production of entropy was simply taken as a nuisance to contend with. Explicating self-organization or the production of order was not part of the agenda of the early thermodynamicists; they were dealing with machines already designed and constructed according to the plans of external creators (human engineers). Understanding, however, that the symmetry described by the second law is a symmetry that in its breaking provides the origin, and in its making the end of macroscopic change, is to see the cosmic origins of evolution itself: the fundamental breaking of symmetry (that which rendered the symmetry

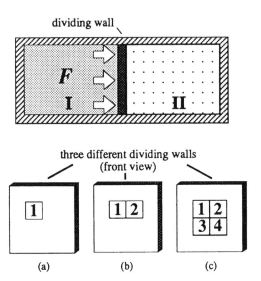

Figure 2 An adiabatically sealed chamber (one closed to the flow of energy) is divided by an adiabatic wall into two equal compartments, holding equal quantities of a monatomic gas such that the temperature in I is greater than the temperature in II, $T^I > T^{II}$. See text for discussion of (a)–(c) which show front views of the dividing wall after portions of the adiabatic seal have been stripped off.

unfulfilled) is the expansion of the universe and the disequilibrium it generates by its expansion. Herein lies the source of universal ordering.

While classical thermodynamics tells us that entropy is maximized at thermodynamic equilibrium, it tells us nothing about which path of action is selected out of those that are otherwise available to get there. Although the answer to this question is easy to demonstrate, its consequences are profound: it reveals a physical world that is not only end-directed but inherently opportunistic in obtaining its ends [3,12,15]. This flies in the face of the antiteleological or purposeless view of the physical world passed down from the dualistic foundations of seventeenth-century science. Figure 2 shows an adiabatically sealed chamber (closed to the flow of energy) divided by an adiabatic wall into two equal compartments, each holding equal quantities of a monatomic gas such that the temperature of the first chamber is greater than the temperature of the second, $T^I > T^{II}$, producing a field potential with force F. Although I and II are out of equilibrium with each other, if the constraints are left intact the system will remain the way it is and the entropy is maximized given the constraints. If, however, a section of the adiabatic seal is stripped off the dividing wall (Fig. 2a), a flow of energy in the form of heat (a drain or pathway) is immediately produced from I to II until the potential is minimized (the entropy is maximized), given the new constraints. The rate of entropy production, which can be taken as a measure of Planck's preference, is given by

$$\frac{dS}{dt} = \frac{dQ^I}{dt} \left(\frac{1}{T^I} - \frac{1}{T^{II}} \right) \qquad (1)$$

where dQ^I/dt and $(1/T^I - 1/T^{II})$ are the flow and fore, respectively.

Equation (1) shows immediately, *ceteris paribus*, that the rate of the entropy production is determined by the coefficient of conductivity of the wall. In Figure 2b a second portion of the adiabatic seal is stripped off, but the wall underneath is composed of a different material with a different coefficient of conductivity. It is easy to see that if the rate of 2 relative to the rate of 1 is sufficient to drain some quantity of the potential before 1 drains it all, then that quantity is automatically assigned to 2. If with different relative coefficients 2 can drain all the potential before 1 can drain any, the entire quantity is assigned to 2 and 1 gets none. If more drains are added (Fig. 2c), the behavior is precisely the same: regardless of the particulars of the system, not only will it produce the appropriate dynamics to minimize the potential, it will select the assembly of pathways or drains among those that are available (it will allocate its resources) to minimize the potential (maximize the entropy) at the *fastest possible rate given the constraints* [3,12,15].

B. Order Produces Entropy Faster than Disorder

This universal selection principle, the *law of maximum entropy production* [3,10,12,15,22,29,30], shows precisely why the world is in the order-production business—why order is spontaneously selected from disorder according to physical law (the selection principle sought in Section II.B): *order produces entropy faster than disorder*. Order is not improbable as Boltzmann alleged, but the inexorable product of natural law. With this single fact the dualistic edifice, built as it has been on a purposeless physical world, crumbles at its foundations. The physical world is not only end-directed but opportunistic in its end-directed behavior. The spontaneous production of order entails the transformation of field potential into the continuously coordinated or collective nonlinear ("circular") behavior of the previously disordered components, permitting the field to access a new dimension of dissipative space.

Whereas it has been understood for some time that such processes *could* occur as long as they produced enough entropy to compensate for their internal entropy reduction (see, e.g., refs. 31, 32), given Boltzmann's claim concerning the "infinite improbability" of coordinated, ordered behavior, there was no causal account of *why* such discontinuous entropy reductions ("populations of one" in the language of Section II.B) should ubiquitously and progressively occur. The law of maximum entropy production at once makes this remarkably easy to understand. Local entropy reduction (order production) occurs precisely *because* it increases the rate of entropy production of the field from which it emerges. As a result of the circular relations that define them (where effects become causes) self-organizing systems in their entification bring a new causal agency into the world—a new formal cause in Aristotle's terms. Such self-organizing systems are inherently self-amplifying sinks or drains for field potentials: the kinetic and potential energy carried in the circularity of their component relations gives them an internal (or "on-board"[14]) potential with its own internal force that acts as an internal amplifier (see refs. 12, 15, and 22 for further discussion).[15]

C. Studying the Generics in a "Simple" Physical System

Since the law of maximum entropy production is a level-independent law (invariant under transformations of scale) that acts on level-dependent substrates (material causes in Aristotle's terms), the reductionist claim that dynamics can be reduced to the laws and particles at some elementary level is rejected. The order that emerges at each level is dependent on the components and their accessible lawful relations particular to that level, and these themselves are emergent. This shows why not only ecosystems and civilizations, for example, but global evolution as a whole must proceed in levels or stages—why the components of the cosmic cloud from which the solar system emerged had to have already come from the interior of a star to produce the substrate necessary for the emergence of replicative order (life) on Earth, why you had to have prokaryotes before you could have eukaryotes, agriculture before states, quantum mechanics before an electronic media or computer revolution. Because of its invariant level-independent nature, the generic aspects of this behavior can be studied with simple physical systems under laboratory conditions. One of the best is an experiment first devised by Henri Bénard [34,35] at the beginning of this century (although he did not know the remarkable scale invariance of the results at the time).

In the Bénard experiment (Fig. 3) a viscous fluid is held in a circular container between a hot source (it is heated evenly from below) and a cold sink (it is exposed to the colder air above).[16] As long as the disequilibrium (field potential) is maintained, the system works to drain it—produces entropy—by transferring heat from source to sink. In Figure 3a heat is transferred by the incoherent, uncorrelated collisions of the molecules (conduction). The smooth and uniform macroscopic symmetry of the fluid is maintained by the microscopic disorder of the component relations: each molecule undergoes billions of collisions per second, nonaverage fluctuations are immediately damped or "sinked out," and the entire fluid and its intrinsic spacetime dimensions are describable by mean free path distances and relaxation times.[17] When the temperature of the source (hence the field force) is increased beyond a critical threshold, spontaneous order breaks the symmetry of the disordered regime as hundreds of millions of molecules exhibiting

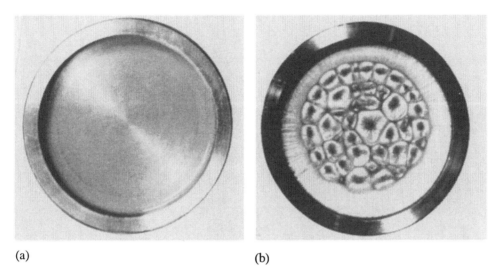

(a)   (b)

Figure 3 (a) At t_1 heat is transferred from source to sink through the disordered, uncorrelated collisions of the molecules in a viscous fluid. (b) At t_2 when the field potential is increased above a critical minimum, spontaneous order emerges as hundreds of millions of molecules start moving coherently together, producing macroscopic dynamics with an intrinsic spacetime orders of magnitude greater than in the disordered regime (see text) (From Ref. 22).

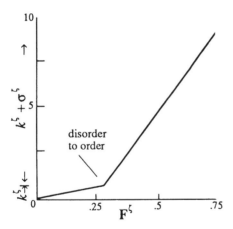

Figure 4 The discontinuous increase in the efficiency of heat transport (rate of field potential minimization) that occurs in an experiment similar to that shown in Figure 3 as a result of the transition from disorder to order: k^ξ is heat transport in the disordered regime (similar to Fig. 3a), and $k^\xi + \sigma^\xi$ is heat transport in the ordered regime (3.1×10^{-4} H (cal/cm²/s¹) plotted against field force F^ξ [36]. (From "Engineering Initial Conditions in a Self-Producing Environment" by R. Swenson, in M. Rogers and N. Warren (eds.), *A Delicate Balance: Techniques, Culture and Consequences,* Institute of Electrical and Electronic Engineers, Los Angeles, 1990, P. 70. © 1989 IEEE. Reprinted by permission.)

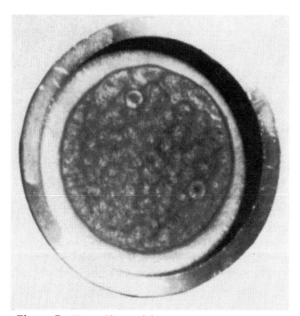

Figure 5 Two self-organizing states are seen to emerge as populations of one right after the critical threshold has been reached (prior to Fig. 3b). Other things being equal, their existence is dependent only on the fact that the macro (ordered) mode drains the field potential (pulls resources into its own coherent dynamic) faster than the micro (disordered) mode from which it emerges. There is no interaction between the two self-organizing states at this stage (From Ref. 22).

highly coordinated behavior start moving collectively together. Figure 4 shows the discontinuous increase in the rate of heat transport that results from the disorder-to-order transformation. The dissipation of field potentials (entropy production) is a function of a field's dissipative surfaces, which are dependent on its spacetime extension; order-from-disorder transformations increase these dimensions by orders of magnitude.[18]

Figure 5 shows a photograph of time slice in the Bénard experiment right after the critical threshold has been crossed[19]: two self-organizing states ("cells") are seen to have already come into being as populations of one—initially each is an individual case of micro-to-macro selection[20] with no interaction going on between them. Moments later the entire fluid is inhabited with a full population of self-organizing states (Fig. 3b). Each as a self-amplifying sink pulls resources into its production (the spacetime extension of its dissipative surfaces) at the fastest possible rate given the constraints, but now the constraints include those imposed by competition with other individuals for the same resource; the action space of these originally uncorrelated cells becomes progressively deformed (constrained) as the entire volume of fluid within the contained acts selectively as a higher level entity to maximize the spacetime extension for the fluid as a whole, given the constraints. The attractor or time-independent state in this case—the symmetry that for the time-dependent behavior was on the way to making—is a highly regular and uniform array of hexagonal cells.[21] There is not the space here to show additional photos of the remarkable evolutionary behavior that occurs in this simple fluid as it progresses toward this symmetry state (converges on its attractor), but I have published these elsewhere (see, e.g., refs. 12, 22, 30).

Two general kinds of selection may be distinguished in these evolutionary dynamics: *external selection*, which acts in the spontaneous production of order (the emergence and maintenance of a population of one) selecting macro (order) from micro (disorder); and *internal selection*, which chooses between the accessible microstates of the components and their possible relations from the population of many within that comprises the the population of one (self-organizing system). Darwinian selection is a special case of internal selection that occurs when the particular components are replicative components (when the self-organizing system is characterized by replicative ordering, e.g., the global Earth system as a whole[22]).

Another important property of the generic behavior that falls out of the physics of self-organization or spontaneous ordering is *spontaneous fission*. Because the entropy production of any growing entity depends on the extension of its dissipative surfaces, and because surface increases as the square of the linear dimensions and volume increases as the cube, as an entity isometrically increases in size, the *specific* entropy production (entropy production per unit weight) progressively goes down although the *total* entropy production increases [10,12,27,30]—that is, the internal amplifier becomes progressively less efficient. Beyond a critical size, the system becomes unstable to spontaneous fission, by which the field further elaborates its surfaces and increases its transformation of resources or field potential. This behavior too is readily observed in the evolutionary dynamics of the Bénard fluid (for photos and further discussion see refs. 10, 22, 30, and for discussion with regard to bacterial cells and global evolution as a whole see refs. 29, 30).

The evolutionary dynamics of the estimated 200-fold increase in the hominid population during the Paleolithic era is another example of the same process. The increase occurred not through a corresponding increase in the size of these ancestral villages or settlements, but through the proliferation by fissioning of their number—from something like 1500 at the beginning of the Paleolithic to some 75,000 or so at the end [37]. They grew to a certain size and divided. The work of Carneiro [37,38], demonstrating the universality (law-governed nature) of this evolutionary behavior in his study of the fissioning of autonomous villages, illustrates well the idea of level-independent laws acting on level-dependent substrates. In the Bénard example, local fluctuations (inhomogeneities) resulting from molecular collisions are damped when the field conditions are below the critical threshold, and the same is the case in the fissioning of autonomous villages: when a village is below a critical size, social interactions that can be thought of as fluctuations or deviations from the mean (e.g., adultery, theft, disharmonious acts of witchcraft) are damped. Conversely, when the village exceeds a critical size,[23] these same fluctuations are amplified to macroscopic proportions and fissioning occurs.[24]

IV. BIOLOGY AND CULTURE: HOOKING DISSIPATIVE DYNAMICS ONTO KINEMATIC FIELDS

A. Captives of Local Gradients

The emergence of replicative ordering on Earth occurred extremely rapidly in geological time after the planet had cooled sufficiently to permit it. Given the mechanism it supplied for accessing otherwise inaccessible dimensions of dissipative space—new drains or sinks for the solar potential—this is no wonder. Discussions of entropy production maximization and evolution on Earth as a global system are provided elsewhere [10,12,29,30]. In this extremely brief section the intention is to introduce the functional and generalized mechanical properties that emerged with the living from the nonliving and the cultural from the noncultural, the emergent substrates on which the level-independent evolutionary laws of physics have progressively proceeded to act.

Despite the remarkable level-independent behavior we have already discussed, if the self-organizing living are compared to the self-organizing nonliving, a striking difference is immediately apparent: the nonliving are *captives of their local gradients*, while the living are not. That is, in the case of systems like tornadoes, dust devils, and the Bénard cells we have looked at above, if we remove the local field potential (e.g., turn off the heat in the Bénard experiment), the systems "die." This is not the case with even the simplest living systems such as bacteria. When their local potentials are removed or dissipated (when they run out of food), their activity often increases [12,40].

B. Replicative Ordering: Accessing Higher Order Dissipative Space with Perception and Action

The dynamics of the living systems are coordinated with respect to information specified by kinematic fields [41,42] that permits them to "skate across" local gradients and access higher dimensions of dissipative space through the production of higher order dissipative dynamics [3,12,40]. That is, whereas in nonliving systems the dynamics are governed by local field potentials (with dimensions of mass, length, and time, viz., "mass-based" fields), the dynamics of the living are governed by nonlocal potentials linked together through observables with dimensions of length and time (kinematic or information fields). Self-organizing systems carry internal potentials ("on-board" potentials) in the kinetic and potential energy embodied in their constitutive relations, and the living hook this potential onto kinematic invariants to search out discontinuously situated potentials (resources). Bacteria, for example, are able to move away from harmful substances and find desirable resources, not only by perceiving the molecules they directly consume, but by perceiving and acting with respect to molecular gradients that allow them to discover the molecules they do consume (potentials they dissipate) and avoid those that are harmful—that provide them *information about* higher order field potentials.

This ability to act independently with respect to local potentials, and thus the facility to access higher order dissipative space, is the hallmark of the replicative order that characterizes the living. Replicative ordering requires a particular set of internal nonholonomic[25] or rate-independent constraints as part of its constitutive relations [43]; they are discrete, linear, and rate-independent relative to rest of the cell dynamics, and their constitutive relations meet a minimal condition of "semantic closure" with the rate-dependent dynamics [44] that permits their "reading" and "writing." Examples include gene sequences (harnessed by cell dynamics) and the words on this page (harnessed by cultural dynamics). Their capacity for meaning is derived from the relative thermodynamic arbitrariness of the sequences; for example, the order of the letters in the words on this page can be changed without thermodynamical consequences relative to the rate at which the words are written and read.[26] It is precisely as a result of this arbitrariness that replicative ordering is able to produce perceiving–acting systems that in their ability to behave arbitrarily with respect to local potentials are able to coordinate their dynamics with respect to higher order observables that specify higher order dimensions of dissipative space [3,12,40].

C. Second-Order Kinematics and the Rise of Culture

Learning is induced by problems, and from the physical point of view the global problem is the disequilibrium at the geo-cosmic interface [30]. Evolution on Earth can be seen as an epistemic process by which the global system as a whole learns to extend its dissipative surfaces so as to reduce the geo-cosmic potential at the fastest possible rate, given the constraints [29,30]. The ascendancy of replicative order is thus seen to be coextensive with the progressive emergence of perceiving–acting cycles, able to access higher order dissipative space by hooking new levels of dissipative dynamics to new observables. With the production of language in the emergence of culture came a qualitatively new form of replicative order that can be called "second-order kinematics" [12] or *flows about flows* (where slow flow, e.g., as in the words on this page, can be treated as no flow, or pure nonholonomic geometry). Second-order kinematics provided a new creative substrate which, as the emergence of life had done before, opened the door to the accelerated expansion of otherwise inaccessible dimensions of dissipative space. The explosion in mass communication and globalization going on at present is a new phase of matter that is precisely the latest (hypertrophied) version of this same evolutionary order-building behavior that started in terms of terrestrial evolution some 4 billion years ago on the Archean Earth.

V. CONCLUSION

While a fuller exposition is not possible here, it is hoped that the reader has been able to grasp the profound shift in the underlying assumptions regarding the nature of evolutionary ordering that has resulted from a new understanding of some deceivingly simple physical facts. Rather than being static or purposeless, the evolutionary dynamics of the natural world are now seen to be creative and purposive; the world is in the order-production business, and this can now be understood as a spontaneous search for symmetry in terms of natural law. Clearly this has profound epistemological and ontological consequences—consequences for understanding the nature of our own nondualistic being in an evolutionary (global order-producing) becoming (see refs. 10, 45 for further discussion). It is most important to emphasize the rejection of reductionism and micromechanistic determinism that the new and expanded physics provides; physics is no longer construed as being reducible to a single level of "elementary" particles. Instead, level-independent law acts on level-dependent substrates, which are themselves emergent; level-dependent behavior is coordinated and defined by the ecological dynamics particular to a given level and not reducible to any other. Creative behavior comes into the world at the discontinuities where new levels of order arise; it is here that the critical region of our evolutionary praxis resides.

ACKNOWLEDGMENTS

The author gratefully acknowledges the support of the Center for the Ecological Study of Perception and Action (CESPA) during the time this chapter was completed, and valuable interactions with Claudia Carello, R. Carneiro, Gail R. Fleischaker, H. H. Pattee, R. E. Shaw, and M. T. Turvey.

FOOTNOTES

1. "Efficient causes" are taken to be the local or proximate cause of change or mechanical agency, as in the "impressed forces" of Newton [2]. "Summativity" means that the su-

perposition principle, as it is known in physics, holds, namely that the combined effect of a number of mechanical causes acting on a population of bodies or particles equals the sum of their effects acting independently from one an other; "determinism" means that if the positions and velocities of all the bodies or particles in a system are known for any one time, all future and past states can be derived; and "reversibility" means there is no preferred direction of change, that nothing forbids reversing the signs of the equations of motion.

2. To the Greeks, physics ("phusis" or "physis") meant "nature," where the nature of a thing or process in the Aristotelian sense is the end it serves or for which it exists [1, p. 214].

3. That the physical description of the world provided by Newtonian mechanics was radically incomplete would not have been denied by Newton. Does not the world "being properly ordered," asked Newton, show the existence of an "intelligent . . . incorporeal Being?" [11] (see also refs. 12, 13).

4. Descartes, the sine qua non of dualistic philosophers, said the world was divided into the physical world or "extension" and the nonphysical world, which was "thought" or "soul," the thinking "I." While the physical world on this view was subject to deterministic mechanical laws, the nonphysical world was not. Creativity, intentionality, purposiveness, and choice were all brought into the mechanical world from the outside through the thinking "I" and its immortal connection to God.

5. Invoking extraphysical causes to explicate the natural world, as the dualist does, has played a fundamental role in the construction of world views necessary for the production of social order. Galileo's assistant (a monk) in Brecht's *Galileo* understands this well: he tries to get Galileo to suppress his work confirming the Copernican heliocentric view of the universe, pointing to the effect it would have on the peasantry who draw their strength for their "miserable lives," he says, "from the Bible texts they hear on Sunday. They have been told that God relies upon them and that the pageant of the world has been written around them" [14].

6. Engels [6, p. 155] in similar fashion characterized Newton as a "an inductive ass" and as a "plagiarizer and corrupter." Russell [1, p. 602] further generalizes his remarks about Darwin when he says that "most men who have won fame for their ideas" are not original thinkers: "As a rule, the man who first thinks of a new idea is so much ahead of his time everyone thinks he is silly, so that he remains obscure and soon forgotten. Then, gradually, the world becomes ready for the idea, and the man who proclaims it at the fortunate moment gets all the credit."

7. In fact Malthus had already claimed that the "struggle for existence" (his term) was a general property of the "animal and vegetable kingdoms" when he applied it to human social systems. Malthus's "struggle for life" appears in the full title of Darwin's *Origin* as the "struggle for life." Darwin got from Spencer the term "survival of the fittest," which he said was better than his own term "natural selection" (see refs. 12, 15).

8. Since entropy is a measure of a system's energy unavailable for producing macroscopic processes ("work"), the opposite (variously called "negentropy" [17], of "free energy") can also be called the "availability," a term introduced by Carnot [18]. Entropy maximization is thus equivalent to availability minimization or the minimization of field potentials, or to put it another way, all natural processes proceed so as to extremize avail-

ability degradation or dissipation (cf. Gaggioli and Scholten [19]) or extremize field potential minimization [12,15].

9. The "end to which everything strives and which everything serves" [2], or in Aristotle's own words, "the end of every motive or generative process" [2].

10. Nor is the word is not found in any of the 21 chapters of *The Descent of Man* [11,24] (see refs. 12, 15 for further discussion).

11. The term was originally used by Swiss performationist Bonnet, who used it to mean the "unfolding of an embryo" [24], but it was Spencer who reintroduced the term, redefined it, and first put forth a comprehensive *theory* of evolution.

12. Simply the determination of what will exist between more than one possible mode or pattern of behavior that could otherwise drain the same potential with no "end-in-view" or "end-in-mind" implied.

13. Both Matter and energy can be taken to be conserved (cannot be created or destroyed) on Earth. In stars, however, which are maintained by nuclear reactions in which matter and energy are interconverted according to Einstein's $E = mc^2$, then it is matter-energy that is conserved.

14. This excellent term used by Kugler and Turvey [31] for living systems is applicable to all self-organizing systems (see also my more extended discussion of "internal force" and "internal amplifier" with figures [12,15,22]).

15. At the risk of sponsoring unnecessary confusion for those who have not heard of Prigogine's theorem of *minimum* entropy production, which was erroneously thought to apply to order-producing systems, but to dispel confusion for those who have, a brief comment is in order (for more detail see ref. 22). The less technical reader is well-advised to simply ignore the theorem, since it makes no contribution whatsoever to the question of spontaneous ordering. It states that for a system extremely close to equilibrium with more than one force (potential) driving flows (and thus producing entropy), if one force is maintained constant but the others are allowed to dissipate, the entropy production will decrease until it reaches a minimum (relative to its earlier states) in the steady state. This statement is completely unsurprising. Since close to equilibrium the flows are a linear function of the forces, the flows will necessarily decrease as the forces dissipate until only the one force held constant remains. This tells us only that the flows are linearly dependent on the forces in the near-equilibrium regime (a fact well known since Onsager) and that potentials are spontaneously minimized—the second law. It does not tell us which flows or paths to equilibrium are selected, given these facts. The answer to that question (the one addressed in this text) is: the pathways or flows, given the constraints, that get it to equilibrium or minimize the potentials the fastest. This is the principle that accounts for ordering.

16. Following Bénard, Lord Rayleigh conducted convective experiments in containers in which the upper surface was sealed. Sometimes these two are conflated in the literature (the latter being called a Bénard convection or sometimes a Bénard–Rayleigh convection). The reader is referred to my earlier work [22] where both are illustrated and discussed in more detail than is possible here.

17. The mean free path is the average distance and the mean relaxation time the average time elapsed between interactions or collisions.

18. In the case of the Bénard experiment from of the order of 10^{-8} cm and 10^{-15} second to centimeters and seconds. The colossal magnitude of this new dynamical scale for a molecule in the fluid is equivalent to distances many times greater than the circumference of Earth and time scales greater than 4.6 billion years (the age of Earth) to humans.

19. The lawful nature of order production is seen clearly by the fact that every time the critical threshold is crossed, order inexorably emerges. The critical threshold is precisely the minimum field potential that can support the higher dissipation rate of the ordered state. This same opportunism, from the rise of replicative order and the rise of civilizations to the acceleration of global ordering today, is seen clearly in the evolutionary record as a whole (see refs. 10, 29, 30).

20. In this case competition is between conduction (disorder or micro) versus convection (ordered or macro).

21. Given the limits of space, I have chosen not to show this final state, which is quite well known and easily available. Usually it is *only* the final state that is shown, thus missing the whole directed time-dependent behavior, which is the behavior of interest with respect to evolutionary ordering.

22. The production of replicative order is order production that entails component production by replication (the system may or may not replicate or reproduce itself); for example, a cell illustrates replicative order that is also replicated, while the Earth system as a whole exhibits replicative ordering but is not itself replicated (at least not yet).

23. Villages have some minimum population at which they are viable (e.g., for the Yanomamö this is about 40–50). The critical threshold for fissioning is then necessarily 80+ [37]. I have discussed this issue of "minimal cell size" with regard to bacterial fission elsewhere [30].

24. Not only in the instance of fissioning, but with regard to the evolutionary dynamics of spontaneous order production in general, Carneiro's [38,39] elegant circumscription theory for the origin and rise of the state, which tracks the lawful relations (the universality) observed in the individual and separate instances of the emergence of civilization (order) from previously autonomous (disordered or uncorrelated relative to each other) villages, reveals the operation of the same level-independent laws [12,22,30]. Circumscription, just as in the container holding the liquid in the Bénard case, limits the rate of horizontal dissipation, so the field elaborates vertically through order production. The operation of external and internal selection is vividly played out in Carneiro's work and is seen to be one of the most characteristic level-independent dynamic invariants of global evolution as a whole.

25. Holonomic constraints are constraints that remove degrees of freedom in velocity and configuration space that do not require material instantiation (e.g., laws), and nonholonomic constraints are constraints that remove degrees of freedom in velocity space but must be materially instantiated to do so.

26. For example, the difference in the amount of entropy produced in writing or printing two alternate phrases (even if they have completely contradictory meanings) is inconsequential with regard to which one gets written, and the amount of ATP required to replicate DNA is the same regardless of the particular sequence.

REFERENCES

1. B. Russell, *History of Western Philosophy*, Allen & Unwin, London, p. 528, 1961.
2. M. Bunge, *Causality and Modern Science*, Dover, New York, 1979.
3. R. Swenson, "Gauss-in-a-Box: Nailing Down the First Principles of Action," *PAW Rev., 4*(2): 60-63 (1989).
4. R. Swenson, "Evolutionary Systems and Society," *World Futures, 30*: 11-16 (1990).
5. Aristotle, "Two Concepts: Cause and Chance." Reprinted from "*The Physics*," in *Readings in Philosophy* (J. H. Randall, Jr., J. Buchler, and E. U. Shirk, eds.), Barnes & Noble, New York, p, 70, 1967.
6. F. Engels, *Dialectics of Nature*, International Publishers, New York, p. 7, 1940.
7. F. Bacon, *De Augmentis Scientiarum*, Book II, ch. 5, 1623, in A. Woodfield, *Teleology*, Cambridge University Press, London, 1976.
8. F. A. Lange, *The History of Materialism*, Humanities Press, New York, p. 3, 1950 (translation of second edition originally published in 1877).
9. R. Rosen, "On the Scope of Syntactics in Mathematics and Science," in *Real Brains: Artificial Minds* (J. L. Casti and A. Karlquvist, eds.), North-Holland, New York, 1987.
10. R. Swenson, "Engineering Initial Conditions in a Self-Producing Environment," *Proceedings of the IEEE and SSIT Conference "A Delicate Balance: Technics, Culture, and Consequences,"* Oct. 20-21, 1989.
11. E. Gilson, *From Aristotle to Darwin and Back Again*, J. Lyon (trans.), University of Notre Dame Press, Notre Dame, IN, 1984.
12. R. Swenson, "Autocatakinetics, Yes—Autopoiesis, No: Steps Toward a Unified Theory of Evolutionary Ordering," *Int. J. General Syst.* (in press).
13. B. Weber, "Implications of the Application of Complex Systems Theory to Ecosystem," in *Proceedings of the Eighth International Congress of Cybernetics and Systems*, June 11-15, 1990, New York (F. Geyer, ed.), Intersystems, Salinas, CA, 1991.
14. B. Brecht, *Galileo*, Grove Press, New York, 1966.
15. R. Swenson, "End-Directed Physics and Evolutionary Ordering: Obviating the Problem of Populations of One," in *Proceedings of the Eighth International Congress of Cybernetics and Systems*, June 11-15, 1990, New York (F. Geyer, ed.), Intersystems, Salinas, CA, 1991.
16. A. Eddington, *The Nature of the Physical World*, Macmillan, New York, p. 74, 1929.
17. E. Schrödinger, *What Is Life?* Cambridge University Press, Cambridge, 1945.
18. S. Carnot, "Reflections on the Motive Power of Fire, and on Machines Fitted to Develop that Power." Originally published in 1824, reprinted in *Reflections on the Motive Power of Fire and Other Papers* (E. Mendoza, ed.), Dover, New York, 1960.
19. R. Gaggioli and W. Scholten, "A Thermodynamic Theory of Nonequilibrium Processes," in *Thermodynamics: Second Law Analysis* (R. A. Gaggioli, ed.), ACS Symposium Series 1222, American Chemical Society, Washington, DC, 1980.
20. R. Clausius, "Über Verschiedene für die Anwendung bequeme formen der Hauptgleichungen der mechanischen Warmetheorie," *Ann. Phy. Chem., 7*: 389-400 (1865).
21. M. Planck, *Scientific Autobiography and Other Papers*, Philosophical Library, New York, 1949.
22. R. Swenson, "Emergent Attractors and the Law of Maximum Entropy Production: Foundations to a Theory of General Evolution," *Sys. Res., 6*: 187-197 (1989).

23. L. Boltzmann, "The Second Law of Thermodynamics," *Pop. Schriften*, Essay 3, address to a formal meeting of the Imperial Academy of Science, May 29, 1886. Reprinted in *Ludwig Boltzmann, Theoretical Physics and Philosophical Problems* (S. G. Brush, trans.), Reidel, Boston, 1974.
24. R. Carneiro, "The Devolution of Evolution," *Social Biol., 19*: 248–258 (1972).
25. R. Carneiro, "The Role of Natural Selection in the Evolution of Culture" (in press).
26. H. Elliot, "Materialism," in *Readings in Philosophy* (J. H. Randall, Jr., J. Buchler, and E. U. Shirk, eds.), Barnes & Noble, New York, p. 316, 1967.
27. R. Dawkins, *The Extended Phenotype*, Freeman, San Francisco, 1982.
28. H. Callen, *Thermodynamics and an Introduction to Thermostatistics*, Wiley, New York, 1981.
29. R. Swenson, "The Earth as an Incommensurate Field at the Geo-Cosmic Interface: Fundamentals to a Theory of General Evolution," in *Geo–Cosmic Relations: The Earth and its Macroenvironment* (G. J. M. Tomassen, W. de Graff, A. A. Knoop, and R. Hengeveld, eds.), PUDOC Science Publishers, Wageningen, the Netherlands, pp. 299–306, 1989.
30. R. Swenson, "Emergent Evolution and the Global Attractor: The Evolutionary Epistemology of Entropy Production Maximization," *Proc. 33rd Annu. Meet. ISSS*, July 2–7, Edinburgh, Scotland, *3*: 46–53 (1989).
31. L. von Bertalanffy, *General System Theory*, Braziller, New York, 1968.
32. I. Prigogine,, *Introduction to Thermodynamics of Irreversible Processes*, 3rd ed., Wiley-Interscience, New York, 1961.
33. P. Kugler and M. Turvey, *Information, Natural Law, and the Self-Assembly of Rhythmic Movement*, Erlbaum, Hillsdale, NJ, 1987.
34. H. Bénard, "Les tourbillons cellulaires dans une nappe liquide," *Rev. Géneral Sci. Pur Appl., 11*: 1261–1271 (1900).
35. H. Bénard, "Les tourbillons cellulaires dans une nappe liquide transportant de la chaleur en régime permanent," *Ann. Chim. Phys. (7th ser.), 23*: 62–144 (1901).
36. W. Malkus, "Discrete Transitions in Turbulent Convection," *Proc. R. Soc. London, 225*: 185–195 (1954).
37. R. Carneiro, "Village Splitting as a Function of Population Size," in *Themes in Ethnology and Culture History, Essays in Honor of David F. Aberle* (L. Donald, ed.), Archana Publications, Meerut, India, pp. 94–124, 1987.
38. R. Carneiro, "The Chiefdom: Precursor of the State," in *The Transition to Statehood in the New World* (G. Jones and R. Kautz, eds.), Cambridge University Press, Cambridge, pp. 37–79, 1981.
39. R. Carneiro, "A Theory of the Origin of the State," *Science, 169*: 733–738 (1970).
40. R. Swenson, "A Robust Ecological Physics Needs an Ongoing Crackdown on Makers Conjured out of Thin Air," *PAW Rev., 5*(2): 110–115 (1990).
41. J. J. Gibson, *The Ecologial Approach to Visual Perception*, Houghton Mifflin, Boston, 1979.
42. P. Kugler, M. T. Turvey, C. Carello, and R. E. Shaw, "The Physics of Controlled Collisions: A Reverie About Locomotion," in *Persistence and Change* (W. Warren, Jr. and R. E. Shaw, eds.), Erlbaum, Hillsdale, NJ, pp. 195–229, 1985.
43. H. Pattee, "Dynamic and Linguistic Models of Complex Systems," *Int. J. General Syst., 3*: 259–266 (1977).

44. H. Pattee, "Cell Psychology: An Evolutionary Approach to the Symbol–Matter Problem," *Cognition Brain Theory,* 5(4): 325–341 (1983).
45. B. Weber, "Ethical Implications of the Interface of Natural and Artificial Systems," *Proceedings of the IEEE and SSIT Conference "A Delicate Balance: Technics, Culture, and Consequences,"* Oct. 20-21, 1989.

7

Are Institutions Entities of a Natural Kind? A Consideration of the Outlook for Mankind

Fenton F. Robb   The University of Edinburgh, Edinburgh, Scotland

I. INTRODUCTION

In this chapter the attempt is made to ground a theory of the emergence of social institutions from human conversational interactions in a theory of the entification and evolution of order in physical sciences. Were such an enterprise to be successful, there would seem to be at last a rational way of lowering the traditional barrier between "natural" and "moral" philosophy, that is, in modern terms, between the physical and the social sciences. Indeed such a success might also serve to endorse, if not validate, the strategic aims and endeavor of cybernetics and general systems thinking–the unification of human inquiry and the melding of knowledge from disparate disciplines–and it might serve also to question those who see regularities in history, such as those who perceive in postmodernity "a reversal of earlier tendencies to increasing differentiation" [1].

II. THE NEED FOR THEORIES OF ORGANIZATION

There are methodologies galore, and some heuristics, to discover, make, and deal with organizational problems, but few "causal explanations" of organizational behavior, grounded in nature, to which to refer when dealing with organizational problems. We need to know the limiting conditions in which our theories may work and, perhaps even more importantly, those conditions in which no theories at all can work. We need, too, some suggestions about how we may regard assertions such as that about "reversal of tendencies" above [1].

A. The Value of Theories and Laws

Generalizations, theories, laws, and explanations allow us to stop thinking about underlying causes and to get on with the job, in the belief that what we are doing can be seen as rational and justifiable, even though we may have grave doubts as to whether the theories are "true" in any absolute sense. Indeed, in the final analysis, as they say, we have to accept with Hume that there are no categorical truths to be had and that "causal explanations" are just "habits of thought" [2], "sanctified" by the institutions in society [3] and more or less "correct" [4] but useful only for the time being—until we find better explanations.

B. The Credibility of Explanations

Causal explanations are generally credible if they are founded on and consistent with what we appreciate to be the case in the natural world [3], if they are comprehensive [5], and if they are useful to ourselves [6]. Thus how we see ourselves in relation to the world about us determines what we count as a "good" theory or a "reasonable" causal explanation.

Some have seen Man as being, first, at the center of a universe created for him alone, later, as the sole embodiment of Will, and more recently as a being at the apex of historical evolution. Such anthropocentrism may be at the root of some of our problems of understanding the world around us, but, it will be argued later, it also glosses over what may be a much more important point: that there are some viewpoints from which some things can never be seen by men.

From the anthropocentric viewpoint, there is hierarchy in nature, reflecting an evolutionary chain from subatomic phenomena, through atoms, molecules, organisms, and so on, culminating in Man and, arguably, in Society and its (more worthy!) institutions.

C. Living Systems Seen as Special Cases

The inanimate world is said to be governed by the "laws" of physics and chemistry discoverable by the hard sciences. Overarching those laws is the second law of thermodynamics—roughly that things tend to run down, that every inanimate system tends toward a uniform distribution of energy, that entropy always increases.

But living systems have usually had a special position. Life processes were thought to be "different in kind" from the rest of nature. Living systems (and societies) have been seen as negentropic, running against the "arrow of time," creating order from disorder and conserving free energy [7,8].

This notion, doubtless founded in some deep primeval fear of the possible inconsequentiality of life, has justified treating living systems, organisms, as "special" cases. Living systems seem to be synthesizing the base materials of nature into sentient beings, ultimately into men. Men, in turn, create societies in order to control the natural world and bring themselves health and happiness.

D. Man Seen as Even More Special

Men are not only living organisms but, because the behavior of men is so complex and unpredictable because of "free will," men and society, it has been thought, cannot be studied in terms of natural laws. Man was a special object in the Creation, and an embodiment of the Divine Spirit. In the course of time, all will be revealed. From the vantage point at the apex of Creation, man will be lord of all he surveys. Such were the optimistic promises of the sciences and of many religions, until quite recently.

The changes in the physical sciences now open the possibility that new metaphors, perhaps more powerfully explanatory, may become available, but at the same time, there seems to come a denial of access to some important features of our world.

III. A NEW VIEW OF ENTROPY

Theory now suggests that far from being negentropic, living things, including man and society, are actually accelerators of entropy production and of the dissipation of free energy [9].

A. Living and Social Systems Are Entropy Producers

The emergences of life in its various forms and of social organization are not accidents, nor need they specifically be the manifestation of design by Divine Providence. Rather, they are among the preferred routes to maximizing entropy production selected by the characteristics of the space-time field and the energy forms available in the world here and now.

Making this move allows us to offer an alternative and much more coherent argument: there are overarching laws that govern all natural processes—man and society are objects or processes in Nature and not exceptions—man and society are governed by the same overarching laws that govern all other natural processes.

Though the social sciences do provide us with instances and insights, by distancing man and society from nature they have difficulty in generating credible laws with useful predictive value. By moving away from an anthropocentric position and by placing man in and not beyond nature, we may be able to bridge the distinction between the animate and inanimate and to discover how the natural laws may affect man in society.

B. The Law of Maximum Entropy Production

A very brief summary of the law of maximum entropy production and of the general theory of evolution being developed by Swenson [10–12] follows.

1. Incoherent Fields

All processes in the universe dissipate free energy and maximize entropy production. Such are the properties of spacetime that processes that accelerate this dissipation are preferentially selected. In any homogeneous "incoherent" field in spacetime, entropy is produced and free energy is dissipated by the microscopic interactions of the elements present.

2. The Emergence of Coherent Fields

If there is sufficient free energy available and the properties of the field allow, new entities, "attractors," [11] arise suddenly from apparently homogeneous fields. These entities that emerge are defined by the circular relations between their components. This circularity defines the coherence of the entities. Such entities are irreducible and *primitive* of their kind and are different from the processes in incoherent fields.

3. The Emergence of Irreversible Constraints

The emergence of an attractor constrains the degrees of freedom of the microscopic interactions entrained by it, and in doing this it increases by many orders of magnitude the production of entropy (and the dissipation of free energy) over that previously dissipated by the microscopic interactions between the elements. This "entification" [11] of a new attractor is an irreversible process, and it provides the preferred route to maximizing entropy production when conditions allow.

4. The Growth and Evolution of Attractors

As the circular processes of its self-production enable the attractor to entrain and constrain the microscopic interactions in its vicinity, its volume grows and its dissipative surface extends, thus increasing its rate of entropy production. However the volume grows faster than the surface and so its relative efficiency at energy dissipation declines over time. Far from equilibrium its behavior is increasingly affected by its prior states and by many small coherences in the adjacent field. Its behavior becomes unpredictable, "chaotic." Its efficiency at entropy production may eventually dwindle to a level at which, if there is still free energy available and the field allows, the emergence of another attractor is enabled. However if free energy is still available and there are not strong coherences nearby, it may remain in a state of stable chaos. If it is very far from equilibrium and if there is no further free energy available, it disintegrates. Where two or more attractors occupy the same field, that which dissipates free energy the quickest and the most efficiently will be preferentially selected. This, it is postulated, is the driving force of evolution in the natural world.

5.   The Recursive Self-Definition of Attractors

The emergent properties of an attractor are different in kind from the field from which it emerges. An attractor defines itself as an entity by the microscopic interactions it entails and constrains. But from the viewpoint of those microscopic interactions of the field from which it emerged, its entification cannot be observed. From there, all that can be observed are the new constraints imposed by it on the microscopic interactions as they are entrained by it.

It has to be said that this is a very rough and ready description of a complex cosmological theory and does little justice to its elegance and comprehensiveness.

IV.   THE EMERGENCE OF INSTITUTIONS

A.   Consiliences of Inductions

There are marked similarities between this theory about the physical world, conversion theory, and the emergence of potentially conscious systems [13], autopoiesis, the organizational closure of self-producing systems [14], the recursive loops of the viable systems model [15], the mutually amplifying processes of the second cybernetics [16], and several other models of organization offered by systems theorists. This consilience of inductions [17] has been noted elsewhere [18,19].

B.   "Institution" as a Thought Object

To anticipate difficulties arising from the common use of language, here "institution" is used in its broadest sense to embrace systems of thought, language, and conceptual structures as well as "organizations," which is here used in the narrow sense of systems of power, obligation, consensus, and consent.

1.   Conversations Make Institutions

Conversations between humans make classifications, definitions, and distinctions—they create realities and values. Institutions emerge from (microscopic) mutually amplifying conversations, agreements about realities. Emergent institutions entrain further conversations and generate communications, instructions, and fiats, and they engender and endorse actions founded on concepts formed by conversations [3,13,20].

2.   Institutions Dissipate Lifetime

Conversations dissipate the energy of human lifetime. But emergent institutions are greatly more dissipative of lifetime than the conversations that initially constituted them.

Not only is energy required to sustain conversations at the micro level, it is also required to sustain the self-productive (autopoietic) processes of the institution itself. These are the recursive loops that attenuate the noise from beyond the institution, amplify the variety of communications produced by it [15], and entrain and constrain human interactions within and beyond it, providing it with further sources of energy.

3. Feedback Generates More Distinctions

The mismatch of the outcomes of actions with the predictions implied by the institution's concepts feeds back the need for more conversations, for the promulgation of further classifications, distinctions, and values, and for more recursive loops and greater institutional complexity [9,18]. Institutionalized "truths" enacted outside an institution effectively extend its boundaries and increase its volume and surface. All these processes are dissipating human lifetime.

4. Institutions Maximize Entropy Production

Because, the theory suggests, these complex self-productive processes of institutions are vastly more dissipative of energy than the relatively simple conversations that gave rise to the institution, they are the means of maximizing entropy production.

Thus people's conversations and actions make institutions and institutions make people (i.e., categorize them) and sacrilize their actions [3]. Institutions grow by providing explanations of their universe of interest and by controlling it. As they grow, this universe of interest expands, until, maybe, the phenomena to be explained and controlled exceed the capabilities of the institution's models to deal with them.

5. Institutions Have Many Possible Futures

As an institution's ability to dissipate lifetime declines relatively, it may lose sources of lifetime, and dissipative conversations about rival models may then cause new institutions to emerge, provided there is lifetime available to support them and the as-yet-unexplained features of the field allow.

All institutional change dissipates lifetime, but if conditions in the field allow and there is free lifetime available, the emergence of new institutions is theorized to be the preferred route toward maximizing entropy production. The apparently exponential growth of institutionalized categories and classifications that pervade modern life seems to endorse this.

6. Constraining Thoughts, Conversations, and Actions

From the viewpoint of conversations, the emergence of a new institution is perceived as a new set of constraints on thoughts, conversations, and actions. Every new emergent category prescribes and proscribes what may or may not be conceivable and what actions are and are not sanctioned by institutionalized concepts.

7. The Emergence of Superordinate Institutions

At a higher level, our theory suggests, institutions interact with each other, and in their field these interactions can give rise to further institutions with different properties. These in turn entrain and constrain the institutions below them, and may further constrain the conversations between people. Among the available institutions, those that dissipate lifetime most quickly and efficiently are preferred in nature.

Hence, at the level of human interactions, there is a progressive increase in the constraints on individual thoughts and actions imposed by the emergence of institutions of which people are only dimly aware. These institutions have been called "suprahuman autopoietic" systems [19].

C. The "Invisible Hand": Of Nature, Not of Man

Hume [2] and others of the Edinburgh Enlightenment have pointed out that although institutions arise from human interactions, they do not necessarily arise from human design. Though the workings of an "invisible hand" were, in Hume's time, attributed to divine intervention or, as Hume would have it, a "propensity of human nature," we can now see them as a manifestation of the working out of a natural law, as the outcome of a propensity of nature herself, as it were.

All that we, from the microcosm of our conversations, can infer about the behavior of institutions comes from observation of the changes in the constraints and affordances imposed on us by them. We cannot properly see the world from the viewpoint of emergent institutions because our conversations are conducted at a lower logical level.

However, although we are thus prohibited from observing suprahuman systems directly, we can, with this theory and Occam's razor to hand, infer that they are governed by the same laws of entropy maximization, energy dissipation, evolution, and natural selection that affect all nature.

V. APPLICATION TO FORMAL ORGANIZATIONS

Some institutions take the form of "organizations" formed by conversations and communications that define roles and role sets [23], corporate purposes, divisions of specialisms and effort, the allocation of power, the engagement of contracts, and so on. This is consistent with our theory that organizations grow, change, and enter states of crisis. There is some evidence that this does happen [21,24,25,26]. We remark in passing that similar processes take place in systems of thought as in the sciences [27,28].

A. Two Kinds of Change in Organizations

After K. K. Smith [29], even from our microscopic viewpoint, we can be aware of two kinds of change in organizations: "morphostatic" and "morphogenetic." These are changes distinguished by their relationship with the dominant model held in view by the organization. The dominant model is that which is the most coherent and encompassing explanation believed to be true by most of those involved in and with the organization–that which is seen as the source and justification of the customs and habits that constrain and afford the interactions of the individuals within and around it.

1. Morphostatic Change

Morphostatic changes are those that take place without affecting the dominant model [5] of the organization. They involve the relatively small adjustments needed to maintain the organization in dynamic equilibrium. Within an organization, these adjustments are effected by local conversations that define and redefine roles and procedures and recognize as valid precedents established by individual conversations in response to situations not envisaged by rules and procedures.

Within an organization, such changes as these are conducted at the micro level in the organization-analogously to Kuhn's "normal" science [27]. If intervention is required, it is to try to increase understanding of the complexities of procedures, rules, and precedents and to make these more manageable by analysis and reduction. Intervention is reversible.

Mistakes can be eradicated by rewriting history and by inventing new instances and precedents. However over time the aggregation of rules and precedents increasingly complicates the dominant model and attenuates its coherence.

2. Morphogenetic Change

Morphogenetic change is of a different order. There is no slow dawning of a realization that the model held in view is inadequate. Rather, the vision of its inadequacy comes suddenly, imperatively, and unavoidably.

The change involves redefining the models of reality held in view in the organization and entails radical changes to the language in use, the values adopted and the mores of the organization-as in scientific "revolutions" [27].

Morphogenetic change arises out of overcomplexity, out of crisis in "bifurcation regions" [30] where there is great instability, where control has become attenuated, and where many small influences come to have disproportionately large and unpredictable effects.

This kind of change sometimes entails the emergence of a new logical order from the disarray caused by the mismatch between events in the real world and what was previously understood of the organization.

There are many possible routes out of crisis, among which there are the following.

Disintegration: the system collapses entirely. Then conversations and communications cease to have meaning.

Stable chaos: although there is no coherent model available, heuristic (firefighting) behavior allows the system to continue to exist but without an underlying coherent model.

Absorption: the failing model is taken over or absorbed by another "more powerful" adjacent model [15].

Emergence: some new model emerges from the substrate of the old one; this is "successful" morphogenesis.

B. Uncertainty Rules: Planning Fails

The increased significance of many small influences and the availability of sufficient free lifetime will determine which route is taken. But it is not merely the presence of these, often unnoticed and unnoticeable, influences that makes the situation inscrutable to us, it is also the sequence of their influence, the exact permutation in time, the order in which they occur as efficient causes, which makes it so.

Indeed investigation itself may become an intervention, an efficient cause of some unknown effects. Here we have a situation similar to that encountered in quantum mechanics, where the very act of measurement produces an irreversible effect on what is being measured when the system is far from equilibrium.

Chance and accident thus seem to rule the situation. But this extreme instability also forbids any useful prediction of the outcomes from a crisis. Causal models and formal planning may serve to make the situation psychologically tolerable and may help to gloss with rationality particular courses of action, but, in the event, they can provide neither credible explanation nor reliable forecast when the system is in crisis.

Thus it is that situations in which morphogenetic change is taking place may well deprive man of what was thought to be his most unique ability, that of anticipating the future. Here experience counts for nothing. Hume's skepticism is vindicated.

C. Post Hoc Rationalization

This uncertainty at the time would not, of course, prohibit accounts rationalizing what happened afterward. People are unwilling to attribute to chance events that could be construed as endowing some individuals with credit or blame.

1. The Unique Nature of Morphogenetic Change

The nature of the crisis and the emergence from it are often portrayed in heroic terms, and the crisis is used as the vehicle for the purveying of theories and magic nostrums.

So such accounts are frequently used as foundations for "practical" methodologies to be offered to organizations in supposedly similar situations. But every morphogenetic change is unique, the outcome of a concatenation of chance events. The only property common to all such change is the inherent uncertainty of what is the state of affairs, what influences may be at work, and what trajectory will be followed.

2. *The Mythical Value of Practical Experience*

This surfaces the problem of using self-styled "historical evidence," case studies, legends, and hero-myths, as precedents for action in situations that really have no observable precedent and in which no explanatory theory is possible. Whereas we may excuse, if not explain, our use of induction to make generalizations and forecasts by appeals to habit or custom in situations in which there appears to be some linearity or a vestige of order, we cannot do so when there are patently no such regularities.

VI. PRACTICAL IMPLICATIONS

Nature seems to have no preferences as to the form of energy to be dissipated. Machines, programs, experience, expertise, skills, and knowledge are all embodiments of human lifetime. Although to institutions human lifetime is merely ingredient, to the individual human, it has inestimable value.

Although forms of accounting for lifetime have been suggested at least from the days of Adam Smith, it seems that in contemporary society, all accounting can deal with are market values.

A. The Unexpressed Value of Individual Lifetime

People have finite expectations of life, often sadly unrealized because of accident or illness. The value placed by people on their own lifetime varies during life and according to circumstances. Institutionalized language in the West has no vocabulary or conceptual structure within which this can be reflected. The timelessness of indolent childhood and the urgency of living as one approaches the marginal moment cannot be expressed except in poetic terms. Yet this changing appreciation of the importance of time is one thing, perhaps the only one, we humans all have in common.

B. Institutionalized Subdivision of Human Lifetime

The only institutionalized expressions of this fundamental feature of living people are those in which institutionalized activities are directed to interacting with people in specific age groups, in the institution's interest, and none express the whole period of living.

C. Institutionalized Time

Whereas our own lifetime is finite, institutions are often, in our terms, virtually immortal. To us the value of lifetime increases at least exponentially with age. To them it seems to have a constant value over time. Institutionalized time, clock time, rules almost every aspect of human life, even in the face of natural physical rhythms.

Were we to apply some kind of life-time accounting to everyday life in organizations, we would soon come to see how they dissipate the many forms of human lifetime.

VII. CONCLUSIONS

Institutions do serve us well at times, but we should question whether the unfettered growth of institutions will ultimately serve them or us the better.

What we seem to lack is any practical alternative way of cooperating without at the same time constraining ourselves by creating institutions of cooperation that may easily come to have "lives of their own" in some sense of these words.

I have tried to avoid the tricky and probably futile task of trying to define ostensively just what is meant by institution and organization. The reasons for this retinence must now be clear; some, if not all, of these things are unobservable.

Contemporary debates about risk and failure in organizations, about the effects of organizations on the environment, on health, future generations, freedom of the individual, and so on, do reflect the increasing concern and frustration of individuals about the ways in which institutions and organizations are profligate of lifetime while at the same time reinforcing their own self-production and stimulating the production of more institutions.

Often our reactions do themselves create further organizations, which, the theory suggests, will interact with existing organizations to generate further higher level institutions. Even the quest for individual freedoms has been institutionalized into quests for particular freedoms of particular categories or groups of people, and the individual is forgotten.

A. The Pessimistic Position

If, as some believe, human lifetime should be available to people, rather than just to institutions, this theory should give cause for concern. The processes of capturing human lifetime are seen here not as being directly within human control but to be rested in nature. Institutions are seen here as spontaneously emergent properties of human and intrainstitutional conversations and communications and do not necessarily take a form of organizations that may be created by human volition to serve human ends.

The limits to human control of institutions, and the subset, organizations, have yet to be explored, but there may be ways of liberating, not just groups of people, but individuals by deinstitutionalizing society. Ivan Illich [31] has already given us some suggestions.

Even if we cannot at present prevent the growth and proliferation of institutionalized thoughts and actions and their manifestation in organizations, at least the theory warns us of its apparent inevitability. This may cause us to think twice before responding to our problems with knee-jerk reactions by trying to institutionalize them and solve them through organizational changes or through setting up new organizations to deal with them. As Douglas [3] has pointed out, institutions already make all the big decisions for us, and their influence is progressively encroaching on the other areas of individual decision making.

If we come to recognize that institutions are beyond our control, at least we may be able to starve them of human resources. We might feed them embodiments of lifetime past, experience, expertise, expert systems, machines, protocols for behavior, or programs, instead of current and future lifetimes such as we offer them at present, thus partially liberating present and future generations.

Possibly we might be able to destroy redundant institutions, which serve no discernible human purposes other than absorbing otherwise useless human lifetime. We might be able to build into their constitutions some kind of self-destruct program. This might ensure that they were offered up for sacrifice at human hands after they had had a chance to serve human ends but before their self-production processes came to dominate their behavior and ensure their escape from human control. But we have to acknowledge here a possible paradox because, at present, such a policy could be executed only through the cooperative interactions of individuals, that is, through setting up new institutions. The first institution to be destroyed by an institution formed to destroy institutions might well be itself.

We might change our minds and culture and look on institutions as undesirable aliens to be rigidly confined and sterilized by the removal of the recursive loops that sustain their autopoiesis.

The most pervasive and yet constraining of our social institutions to date is, after all, language. We now see how language is becoming ever more universal and accessible. And it is only because there is such an institution that we are able to think and talk about "liberation" at all.

B. The Optimistic Position

There is however an alternative viewpoint, which could hold that, rather than being oppressive and profligate of lifetime, the emergence of self-control in organizations is really a natural manifestation of evolutionary processes and that what emerges are not only higher but "better" life forms.

Some institutions sometimes do work to someone's advantage. They can accomplish what individuals could not accomplish without them. Often they may increase human welfare even while serving their own self-production. Maybe some people are happier and better off, whatever that means, if they are sheltered by institutions from having to take big decisions in life and if they are left to make the small ones, the ones that cannot hurt (or indeed help) them much.

If we were to abandon our traditional anthropocentric positions, we could see the emergence of institutions not as the undesirable end of human individuality, but as the early stirrings of an emergent world brain, a man–machine entity embodying and connecting all human intelligence, knowledge, and wisdom and capable of conceptualizing and solving our cultural problems just as the emergence of machines themselves made so many new things possible in our physical world.

C. A Faustian Tradeoff?

It just might be worth making a Faustian tradeoff of the loss of individuality against the material benefits and intellectual comforts that might result from the emergence of superinstitutions. However, a question that remains to be answered is this: Will we still have sufficient independence to be able to make such a choice?

REFERENCES

1. S. R. Clegg, *Modern Organizations: Organizational Studies in the Postmodern World*, Sage, London and New York, p. 1, 1990.
2. D. Hume, *Enquiries: Concerning Human Understanding and Concerning the Principles of Morals (1777)*, rev. ed., Clarendon Press, Oxford, 1975.
3. M. Douglas, *How Institutions Think*, Routledge & Kegan Paul, London, 1987.
4. H. Putnam, "The Corroboration of Theories," in *The Philosophy of Karl Popper*, (P. A. Schlipp, ed.), Open Court Publishing, La Salle, IL, pp. 221-40, 1974.
5. S. S. Bråten, "The Third Position: Beyond Artificial and Autopoietic Reduction," in *Sociocybernetic Paradoxes*, (F. Geyer and J. Van der Zouwen, eds.) Sage, Beverly Hills, CA, pp. 193-205, 1986.
6. A. Rapoport, *Operational Philosophy*, International Society for General Semantics, San Francisco, 1969.
7. W. R. Ashby, *Design for a Brain*, Chapman & Hall, London, 1952.
8. L. von Bertalanffy, "General Systems Theory," *General Syst., I*: 4 (1956).
9. F. F. Robb, "Research Note: 'On the Application of the Theory of Emergence and of the Law of Maximum Entropy Production to Social Processes,'" *Syst. Pract., 3*(4): 389-399 (1990).
10. R. Swenson, "Emergent Attractors and the Law of Maximum Entropy Production: Foundations to a Theory of General Evolution," *Syst. Res., 6*(3): 187-197 (1989).
11. R. Swenson, "Comments on Robb's Research Note: 'On the Application of the Theory of Emergence and of the Law of Maximum Entropy Production,'" *Syst. Pract., 3*(4): 401-402 (1990).
12. R. Swenson, "Order, Evolution and Natural Law: Fundamental Relations in Complex

System Theory," in *Cybernetics and Applied Systems* (C. Negoita, ed.), Dekker, New York, 1992.

13. G. Pask, *Conversation Theory*, Elsevier, Amsterdam and New York, 1976.
14. H. A. Maturana and F. J. Varela, *Autopoiesis and Cognition: The Realisation of the Living*, Reidel, Dordrecht, 1980.
15. S. Beer, *The Heart of the Enterprise*, Wiley, Chichester, 1979.
16. M. Maruyama, "The Second Cybernetics: Deviation-Amplifying Mutual Causal Processes," *Sci. Am., 51*: 164–179, and 250–280 (1963).
17. W. Whewell, *The Philosophy of the Inductive Sciences (1847)*, Johnson Reprint, New York, 1954.
18. F. F. Robb, "Morphostasis and Morphogenesis: Contexts of Design Inquiry," *Syst. Res., 7*(3): 135–146 (1990).
19. F. F. Robb, "Cybernetics and Suprahuman Autopoietic Systems," *Syst. Pract., 2*(1): 47–74 (1989).
20. N. Luhman, "The Autopoiesis of Social Systems," in *Sociocybernetic Paradoxes* (F. Geyer and J. Van der Zouwen, eds.), Sage, Beverly Hills, CA pp. 172–192, 1986.
21. C. Argyris, "Organizational Learning and Management Information Systems," *Account., Org. Society, 2*(2): 113–121 (1977).
22. F. F. Robb, "Disorder: The Paradox in the Kernel of Design Inquiry," in *Design Inquiry* (B. H. Banathy, ed.), Intersystems, Seaside, CA, 1989.
23. R. K. Merton, "The Role-Set: Problems in Sociological Theory," in *Human Aspects of Man-Made Systems* (S. C. Brown and J. N. T. Martin, eds.), Open University Press, Milton Keynes, England, 1977.
24. L. E. Greiner, "Evolution and Revolution as Organizations Grow," *Harvard Bus. Rev., 50*: 37–46 (1972).
25. A. W. Smith, "A Five-Stage Model of Management Evolution," in *General Systems Yearbook*, Vol. 27, SGSR, Louisville, KY, pp. 205–212, 1982.
26. M. L. Tushman and W. L. Moore, eds., *Readings in the Management of Innovation*, Pitman, London, 1982.
27. T. S. Kuhn, *The Structure of Scientific Revolutions*, 2nd ed., University of Chicago Press, Chicago, 1970.
28. K. Popper, "The Rationality of Scientific Revolutions," in *Problems of Scientific Revolutions* (R. Harre, ed.), Oxford University Press, Oxford, pp. 72–101, 1975.
29. K. K. Smith, "Philosophical Problems," in *Change in Organizations* (P. S. Goodman and associates, eds.), Jossey-Bass, San Francisco and London, pp. 316–374, 1982.
30. I. Prigogine, *From Being to Becoming: Time and Complexity in the Physical Sciences*, Freeman, San Francisco, 1980.
31. I. Illich, *De-schooling Society*, Penguin, Harmondsworth, 1973.

8
Intelligent Models of Economic and Social Systems

Robert W. Blanning   Vanderbilt University, Nashville, Tennessee

James R. Marsden   University of Kentucky, Lexington, Kentucky

David E. Pingry   University of Arizona, Tucson, Arizona

Ann C. Seror   Laval University, Ste-Foy, Quebec, Canada

I. INTRODUCTION

Economic and social systems—such as business organizations, free-market and centralized economics, and certain social groups—consist of networks of actors who often interact in an adaptive fashion. That is, they exchange information and act on the information so that the network exhibits an intelligence not possessed by an unorganized collection of actors. This intelligence includes the ability to respond appropriately to changing conditions, to diagnose symptoms of impending problems and to take action to mitigate or eliminate them, to learn from their own experience and the experiences of others, and to plan courses of action that meet long-term goals and avoid long-term pitfalls. But many economic and social systems do not exhibit these characteristics or are flawed in the ways in which they do exhibit them. Therefore, it would be both intellectually challenging and practically useful to understand why some systems are successful in this regard while others are not.

This chapter examines what, if anything, one can learn about the intelligent behavior of economic and social systems from the growing body of research in cognitive science and artificial intelligence. We do so by examining three topics. In Section II we attempt to explain the source of human systems intelligence by invoking the physical symbol hypothesis from artificial intelligence and extending it to include a description of economic and social systems. Then in Section III we note that with organizations, as with humans, intelligence is multifaceted, and we describe three important facets. Finally, in Section IV, we view organizational intelligence in terms of both formal and commonsense reasoning, the latter taken largely from developmental psychology.

This chapter is a synthesis of a session entitled "Intelligent Models of Economic and Social Systems," presented at the Eighth International Congress of Cybernetics and Systems, held in New York, June 11–15, 1990. The session consisted of three presentations:

1. "Human Organizations as Intelligent Systems," by Professor Blanning
2. "Intelligent Information Systems and Organization Structures: An Integrated Design Approach," by Professors Marsden and Pingry
3. "Reasoning, Artificial Intelligence, and the Organizational System," by Professor Séror

Sections II, III, and IV are based on these three presentations.

II. HUMAN ORGANIZATIONS AS PHYSICAL SYMBOL STRESSES

Students of human organizations have viewed them from many perspectives: as economic systems whose equilibria are governed by constraints not found in a free market, as networks of political actors vying for influence and control, as social institutions, and so on. One recent view arises from the widespread use of computers: organizations increasingly are being thought of as information processing systems [1–3]. One component of this is the view of organizations as intelligent information processing systems, along with the suggestion that the growing body of literature on artificial intelligence may be helpful in understanding such systems [4–8]. This research is based on the assumption that organizations possess an intelligence that exceeds (or supplements, amplifies, mediates, etc.) the intelligence of their individual members. That is, organizations can contribute to their own abilities to adapt, diagnose, learn, and plan in ways that are separate from, and in many ways independent of, the intellectual abilities of their members.

There are three ways in which an organization can contribute to its own intelligence beyond that supplied by its individual members. First, an organization's structure can guide it in responding intelligently to external stimuli. Different structures—such as centralized, decentralized, and matrix structures—are adaptive under different circumstances. Second, most organizations contain a large body of codified knowledge, in the form of manuals, memos, reports, statements, and so on, which their members invoke to direct their analyses and decisions. Codified information provides a persistent corporate memory that helps new members to draw on experience when they face unfamiliar situations. Third, organizations contain implicit knowledge in the form of role models, "war stories," and other expressions of their cultures.

A useful vehicle for understanding how structure and codified and implicit knowledge can contribute to intelligent behavior is provided by the physical symbol hypothesis. The hypothesis was developed by Newell and Simon to guide researchers in computer science as they seek to understand computers as algorithmic machines that are the proper subjects of empirical research [9]. They view computers as physical symbol systems and then state that such systems can be intelligent.

They begin with the notion of a symbol and a pattern of symbols:

A physical symbol system consists of a set of entities, called symbols, which are physical patterns that can occur as components of another type of entity called an expression (or symbol structure) [9, p. 116]

They then describe the dynamic character of these systems that allow patterns to change over time:

A physical symbol system is a machine that produces through time an evolving collection of symbol structures. [9. p. 166]

Finally, they state their hypothesis:

The Physical Symbol Hypothesis: a physical symbol system has the necessary and sufficient means for intelligent action. [9, p. 116]

We now extend this hypothesis to encompass human organizations as well. We present two such hypotheses. The first is a strong hypothesis that directly relates human organizations to algorithmic machines of the type studied by Newell and Simon, and therefore relates the empirical study of human organizations to the empirical study of more formal systems.

The Strong Hypothesis: human organizations are physical symbol systems.

The strong hypothesis presents a mechanistic, hence a positivist, view of human organizations. This is not to deny the humanity of the members of organizations, but only to suggest that organizations can profitably be studied as physical symbol systems, with the resulting advantages provided by the physical symbol hypothesis.

These advantages become apparent in the second hypothesis, called the weak hypothesis; which can be inferred by applying the physical symbol hypothesis to the strong hypothesis, or it can be regarded as an independent hypothesis capable of being investigated directly without regard to its origin.

The Weak Hypothesis: human organizations have the capacity for intelligent action.

Since these are hypotheses, they cannot be proved by rigorous logical or mathematical argument, but they can be tested. At present the most promising tests are offered by a few economists, sociologists, anthropologists, and political scientists who have been describing and modeling human systems from the perspective of artificial intelligence. The economists view markets as vehicles for intelligently coordinating transactions, with a coordination mechanism derived from first-order and other logics, often implemented by means of logic programming [10–14]. The sociologists view social systems as intelligent systems [15–17] and even ask if there can be a society of intelligent machines [18]. The anthropological view is similar, but it concerns less developed social systems, such as tribes or settlements, that specialize and exchange goods and services [19,20]. Political scientists have noticed that decentralized and weakly constrained (i.e., democratic) political systems can exhibit intelligent behavior [21] and that expert systems, and especially rule-based systems, are useful in describing them [22–25].

III. VARIETIES OF INTELLIGENT ORGANIZATIONS

In the preceding section, it was assumed that the missions of organizations are known and that intelligent organizations are ones that accomplish their missions effectively. We now consider a wider variety of possible missions and , therefore, a more global spectrum of intelligent behavior. In this enlarged framework there are three types of intelligent organization: the economically intelligent organization, the technologically intelligent organization, and the process intelligent organization [26].

The economically intelligent organization is one that makes enough profit to survive. Thus, an organization whose subunits work together to ensure the economic viability of the organization is economically intelligent. In a private corporation, this would be accomplished by selling profitable products or services and by maintaining other strategic advantages–such as tax advantages, market specialization, and barriers to competitive entry. In the case of a government or other nonprofit organization, it could be accomplished by acquiring funds from legislature, administrative bureaucracies, or other funding agencies.

The technologically intelligent organization is one that makes productive use of information processing technology (i.e., the technology of computers and telecommunications). Technological intelligence is a metaobjective—that is, it is an objective only because it aids a firm in reaching basic goals such as profit maximization and survivability. The technologically intelligent organization recognizes that competitive, social, and political conditions require that the successful organization acquire, process, communicate, and make use of information to survive and prosper, and it regards the development of effective information systems as a prerequisite to survival and prosperity.

The process intelligent organization goes beyond this. It recognizes that information must not only be acquired, processed, and communicated effectively. It must also be used effectively in decision making [27]. Such organizations, which have also been called postindustrial organizations [28], adapt their structures to the problems at hand and often display a degree of flexibility not found in more traditional organizations.

As with the application of the physical symbol hypothesis in Section II, the application of these ideas transcends the structured view of organizations traditionally adopted by management researchers. A more general view of organizations, one that accommodates decentralized structures and fluid firm/market distinctions, is now being recognized by scholars of both organizations and markets [29-31]. This view recognizes the possibility of intelligent market institutions and societies as well as intelligent corporations and government agencies. Emphasis is placed on synergies likely to take place as these various intelligent entities interact.

Since economic success is necessary for survival, we now focus on the economically intelligent organization. All organizations require resources to accomplish their mission, and the acquisition and management of these resources is of major importance. So also is the need to understand more fully the nature of economic intelligence within the firm. A promising methodological approach is offered by the discipline of experimental economics. Recent experiments in intelligent behavior [32] follow the induced-value approach of Vernon Smith [33], an approach incorporating performance-based rewards for participating human subjects. As Smith argues:

> Control is the essence of experimental methodology, and in experimental exchange studies it is important that one be able to state that, as between two experiments, individual values (e.g., demand or supply) either do or do not differ in a specified way. Such control can be achieved by using a reward structure to induce prescribed monetary value on actions [34, p. 275]

Recent technological advances have made it possible to develop networked experimentation of decision making in game theoretic and strategic settings [32,35]. The flexibility of available technology greatly enlarges both the domain of intelligent behavior that can be studied and the range of environments in which such behavior can be studied [36]. This view suggests guidelines for research and practice in this area. For example, we may expect that advances in information processing technology will require that the economically intelligent organization select two types of optimal resource mix. The first is the mix of capital and labor needed for traditional production activities, and the second is the machine–manual mix for perceiving, choosing, and manipulating production and distribution processes. To survive, the economically intelligent organization must select a machine–manual mix that allows the organization to accomplish its economic mission while remaining within the organization's economic, social, and political constraints.

IV. HUMAN ORGANIZATIONS AS COMMONSENSE REASONING SYSTEMS

In Sections II and III, we have seen that frameworks for studying intelligent organizations can be found in both economics and computer science. But they can also be found in basic notions of cognition and, especially, of reasoning and development.

It is useful to partition reasoning into two general categories—formal reasoning and everyday reasoning. Problems for which formal reasoning is appropriate are self-contained and unambiguous, with explicit premises, whereas everyday problems are open-ended, containing ambiguities and implicit premises. Much of the work on organizational intelligence referred to in Section II is based on formal reasoning—that is, organizations are modeled as sets of rules or other explicit knowledge structures, and organizational processes are modeled as formal inferential processes.

A more general approach to the modeling of human organizations and other sociocultural systems must derive from a more general approach to reasoning. Three such approaches have been identified [37]. The first is a *componential approach*, in which reasoning tasks are analyzed into components by specification of basic cognitive processes used in problem solving. This largely reductionist approach is a natural way to begin to understand organizations, since component suborganizations, decision makers, communications channels, environmental influences, and so on, must be identified in any modeling process, and this approach should help to explain individual differences between organizations as well as the ability of a single organization to perform a variety of "cognitive" problem-solving tasks. However, it is based on assumptions of independence, additivity, separability, and other simplifications that are often inappropriate of the complexities of the real world.

The second approach if the *specific rules/heuristics approach*, in which reasoning is accomplished by applying context-sensitive procedures derived through induction from prior experience with relevant situations. This approach should aid in explaining content effects of organization problem-solving process—that is, why certain organizations (with certain structures and codified and implicit knowledge) adapt well in some situations and not in others.

The third approach is the *mental models/search approach*, in which symbolic structures representing subspaces of a problem space (e.g., various diagnoses, conclusions, solutions, and scenarios) are manipulated by operators that generate a path through the problem space in an attempt to solve the problem. This relatively holistic approach has the advantage and disadvantage of extreme flexibility, since the symbolic structures and the search procedures are constructed on an ad hoc basis.

All three of these approaches, but especially the latter, are useful in describing the actions of a network of separate but interdependent actors who exchange information and act concurrently in pursuit of individual and common goals. Such an approach has also been encountered in developmental psychology. For example, Piaget has described intelligence as a process that helps an organism to adapt to its environment by constructing organized patterns of thought, or schemata, that allow the organism to establish an equilibrium with the environment. This process is implemented through a network of individual and collaborative efforts:

> In the realm of knowledge, it seems obvious that individual operations of intelligence and operations making for exchanges in cognitive cooperations are one and the same thing, the general coordination of actions to which we have continually referred being an interindividual as well as an intraindividual coordination because such "actions" can be collective as well as executed by individuals. [38, p. 360]

This combination of interindividual and intraindividual coordination is found in human, machine, and organizational intelligence.

V.   CONCLUSION

Students of human and machine cognition increasingly find it possible and even necessary to understand intelligence as a synthesis of a large number of rather simple processes, where intelligence arises primarily from the mode of synthesis rather than from the processes themselves. This is forcefully brought out in the society of mind, a perspective in which intelligence emerges from an appropriately constructed system of mindless components [39], and from the study of neuromorphic systems—systems that mimic the interactions between neurons in the brain [40].

Students of organization behavior have been less aggressive in exploring this idea, in part because the elements of human organization (people, groups, clans, departments, committees, divisions, task forces, etc.) appear sufficiently complex that it is tempting to regard organizations as simple combinations of complex entities, rather than the reverse. The tradeoff between these two perspectives is difficult to establish, and it may even be appropriate to regard organizations and other sociocultural systems as moderately complex combinations of moderately complex entities. At present we cannot demonstrate, even intuitively, whether any of these views is superior to any other, and we may find that each has merit, depending on the type of behavior one is investigating. However, we do believe that concepts from human and machine cognition, with suitable modification, will be of use in investigating the behavior of human sociocultural systems.

ACKNOWLEDGMENT

Professor Blanning's contribution was supported by the Dean's Fund for Faculty Research of the Owen Graduate School of Management of Vanderbilt University.

REFERENCES

1. G. P. Huber and R. R. McDaniel, *Manage. Sci., 32*: 572 (1986).
2. T. W. Malone and S. A. Smith, *Opin. Res., 36*: 421 (1988).
3. M. L. Tushman and D. A. Nadler, *Acad. Manage. Rev., 3*: 613 (1978).
4. R. W. Blanning, "Expert systems as an Organizational Paradigm," in *Proceedings of the Eighth International Conference on Information Systems*, Pittsburgh, pp. 232–240, 1987.
5. R. W. Blanning, "An Object-Oriented Paradigm for Organizational Behavior," in *DDS-87 Transactions*, San Francisco, pp. 87–94, 1987.
6. M. D. Cohen, in *Ambiguity and Command: Organizational Perspectives on Military Decision Making* (J. G. March and R. Weissinger-Baylon, eds.), Pittman, Marshfield, MA, p. 53, 1986.
7. M. Masuch and P. LaPotin, *Admin. Sci. 34*: 38 (1989).
8. H. U. D. Parunak, J. Kindrick, and B. Irish, "Material Handling: A Conservative Domain for Neural Connectivity and Propagation," in *Proceedings of the Sixth National Conference on Artificial Intelligence*, Seattle, pp. 307–311, 1987.
9. A. Newell, and H. A. Simon, *Commun. ACM, 19*: 113 (1976).
10. E. Hoffman, V. S. Jacob, J. R. Marsden, and A. B. Whinston, in *Artificial Intelligence in Economics and Management* (L. F. Pau, ed.), North Holland, Amsterdam, p. 1, 1986.
11. R. Krishnan, D. A. Kendrick, and R. M. Lee, *Comput. Sci. Econ. Manage., 1*: 53 (1988).
12. R. M. Lee, *Decis. Support Syst., 4: 27 (1988).*
13. R. M. Lee and G. R. Widmeyer, *J. Manage. Inf. Syst., II*: 21 (1986).
14. R. M. Miller, in *Economics and Artificial Intelligence* (J.-L. Roos, ed.), Pergamon Press, Oxford, p. 161, 1987.
15. S. Banerjee, *J. Conflict Resolut., 30*: 221 (1986).
16. R. Ennals, *Artificial Intelligence: Applications to Logical Reasoning and Historical Research*, Ellis Horwood, Chichester, 1985.
17. G. N. Gilbert and C. Heath, *Social Action and Artificial Intelligence*, Gower, Aldershot, 1985.
18. S. Woolgar, in *Intelligent Systems in a Human Context* (L. A. Murray and J. T. E. Richardson, eds.), Oxford University Press, Oxford, p. 53, 1989.
19. J. Doran, in *Intelligent Systems in a Human Context* (L. A. Murray and J. T. E. Richardson, eds.), Oxford University Press, Oxford, p. 71, 1988.
20. J. Doran, in *Quantitative Research in Archaeology: Progress and Prospects* (M. S. Aldenderfer, ed.), Sage Publications, Newbury Park, CA, p. 73, 1987.
21. C. E. Lindblom, *The Intelligence of Democracy*, Free Press, New York, 1985.
22. P. A. Anderson and S. J. Thorson, *Behav. Sci., 27*: 176 (1982).

23. D. A. Sylvan, *Behav. Sci., 32*: 212 (1987).

24. D. A. Sylvan and S. Chan, eds., *Foreign Policy Decision Making: Perception, Cognition, and Artificial Intelligence*, Praeger, New York, 1984.

25. D. A. Sylvan, A. Goel, and B. Chandrasekan, *Am. J. Polit. Sci., 34*: 74 (1990).

26. J. R. Marsden and D. E. Pingry, "The Intelligent Organization: Some Observations and Alternative Views," in *Proceedings of the 21st Annual Hawaii International Conference on System Sciences*, Vol. 35, p. 19, 1988.

27. G. P. Huber and R. R. McDaniel, *Manage, Sci., 32*: 572 (1986).

28. G. P. Huber, *Manage. Sci., 30*: 928 (1984).

29. K. M. Eisenhardt, *Manage. Sci., 31*: 134 (1985).

30. W. G. Ouchi, *Admin. Sci., 25*: 129 (1980).

31. O. E. Williamson, *Markets and Hierarchies: Analysis and Antitrust Implications*, Free Press, New York, 1975.

32. J. R. Marsden, D. E. Pingry, and E. Gardner, "The Design and Use of Laboratory Experiments in DSS Evaluation and DSS Portfolio Selection: Some Initial Results," in *Proceedings of the 1990 ISDSS conference*, Austin, September 1990, 477.

33. V. L. Smith, *Am. Econ. Rev., 72*: 923 (1982).

34. V. L. Smith, *Am. Econ. Rev., 66*: 274 (1976).

35. V. Jacob and J. R. Marsden, *J. Econ. Dyn. Control, 14*: 201 (1990).

36. E. Hoffman, J. R. Marsden, and A. B. Whinston, in *Advances in Behavioral Economics*, Vol. 2 (L. Green and H. H. Kagel, eds.), p. 1, 1990.

37. K. M. Galotti, *Psychol. Bull., 105*: 331 (1989).

38. J. Piaget, *Biology and Knowledge*, University of Chicago Press, Chicago, 1971.

39. M. Minsky, *The Society of Mind*, Simon & Schuster, New York, 1986.

40. P. K. Simpson, *Artificial Neural Systems*, Pergamon Press, New York, 1990.

9

Dynamics in a Hierarchically Organized System: Coupled Individual, Population, and Ecosystem Levels

Pierre Auger   University of Bourgogne, Dijon, France

I. INTRODUCTION

Many authors have noticed the hierarchical organization of many systems in very different scopes (e.g., physics, chemistry, biology, ecology) and many models of hierarchical systems have already been proposed. We refer to several of the past two decades works [1–6]. Usually, one distinguishes the following levels: particles, atoms, molecules, macromolecules, organelles, cells, organs, organisms. In ecology, one considers grossly the individual level, the population level, and the ecosystem level.

Groups of molecules are macromolecules. Groups of cells constitute organs, groups of organs are organisms, groups of animals are populations, groups of populations are ecosystems. One sees that there is a nearly continuous imbrication: that is, that groups of units are often themselves grouped into groups of groups to give birth to a superior level, and so on. The hierarchical system is a set of many levels of structure, imbricated the ones into the others, elements, groups, groups of groups, groups of groups of groups, and so on.

To these levels of organization of the hierarchically organized system are associated levels of description, which are called "strates" by M. D. Mesarovic et al. [2]. This means that in general, people study a particular level of organization and have developed methods, models, and theories relative to this precise level of the system. Till now, scientific searchers have focused their attention on a precise level, and few studies have been done to develop multilevel models. The aim of the present work is to contribute in this field.

II. DYNAMICS IN A TWO-LEVEL SYSTEM

Let Σ be a set with a large number of elements, which can be distributed on different discrete states. Let us consider a partition of the system Σ, that is, a set of A groups of states with N^α states in the group α. Figure 1 presents a schema of a hierarchical two-level system. Let $n_i^\alpha(t)$ be the number of elements in the ith state of the αth group at time t or state variables. We use similar notations to those in our papers, [7,8]: an upper index for the group number and a lower index for the state number.

A. Global Dynamics

The fundamental differential equations of the two-level system are the next ones:

$$\dot{n}_i^\alpha = e_i^\alpha + \sum_j a_{ij}^\alpha n_j^\alpha + \sum_\beta \sum_k a_{ik}^{\alpha\beta} n_k^\beta + \sum_j \sum_k b_{ijk}^\alpha n_j^\alpha n_k^\alpha + \sum_\beta \sum_l \sum_m b_{ilm}^{\alpha\beta} n_l^\alpha n_m^\beta \tag{1}$$

where e_i^α is a rate of exchange with the outside system for elements in state i of group α, a_{ik}^α is a transition rate from state k to i in group α, b_{ijk}^α is a rate of interaction between two elements in states j and k of group α, making the number of ele-

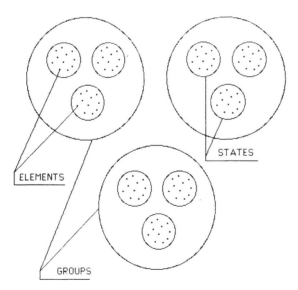

Figure 1 Hierarchically organized two-level system.

ments in state i of α vary. All the other terms are intergroup ones at rates $a_{ik}^{\alpha\beta}$ and $b_{ilm}^{\alpha\beta}$, linear and nonlinear: $a_{ik}^{\alpha\beta}$ is a transition rate from state k in group β toward state i in group α, $b_{ilm}^{\alpha\beta}$ is the rate of a reaction between elements belonging to different groups α and β $\{l(\text{in } \alpha) + m(\text{in } \beta) \rightarrow i(\text{in } \alpha) + r(\text{in } \beta)\}$. An element in the lth state of the group α reacts with an element in the mth state of another group β and it induces a transition toward states i and r. For simplicity in the notation, we forget the index r. For such a system (1), the hierarchy assumptions come next. First,

$$\text{for any } (\alpha, \beta, i, j, k, l, m), \quad |a_{ij}^{\alpha}| >> |e_i^{\alpha}|, |a_{kl}^{\alpha\beta}| \quad \text{and} \quad |b_{ijk}^{\alpha}| >> |b_{ilm}^{\alpha\beta}| \qquad (2)$$

Intragroup interactions are much more frequent than intergroup ones. Second, we assume converging intragroup motion in each isolated group. Now, let us define global variables simply as the total numbers of elements in each group α, $n^\alpha = \Sigma_k n_k^\alpha$. As a result of strong intragroup interactions with respect to intergroup ones, it can be shown that these global variables vary very slowly in time with respect to variables n_j^α (see refs. 9–11). Thus, the hierarchy in the structure of the system leads to a time hierarchy. As a consequence, we can assume that at each instant the variables n_j^α reach an intragroup equilibrium corresponding to a converging steady state point with coordinates q_i^α (stable steady state point or any rapid cyclic motion around it), which can be characterized by equilibrium frequencies or measures v_i^α:

$$v_j^\alpha = \frac{q_j^\alpha}{q^\alpha} \quad \text{with} \quad \sum_i v_i^\alpha = 1 \qquad (3)$$

In the case of a fast cyclic intragroup motion, one can consider the time-average frequencies. Then, after summation over all the states i of each group α, and substitution of $v_j^\alpha n^\alpha$ for n_j^α, one obtains group motion equations:

$$\dot{n}^\alpha = \sum_i \dot{n}_i^\alpha = e^\alpha + \sum_\beta a^{\alpha\beta} n^\beta + \sum_\beta b^{\alpha\beta} n^\alpha n^\beta \qquad (4)$$

with

$$e^\alpha = \sum_i e_i^\alpha, \quad a^{\alpha\beta} = \sum_{i\,j} a_{ij}^{\alpha\beta} v_j^\beta, \quad \text{and} \quad b^{\alpha\beta} = \sum_{i\,l\,m} b_{ilm}^{\alpha\beta} v_l^\alpha v_m^\beta$$

B. Interactions Between the Hierarchical Levels

The parameters $a^{\alpha\beta}$ and $b^{\alpha\beta}$ are frequency dependent. This means that a variation in the internal distributions of the elements inside the groups, Δv_i^α, leads to a modification of the parameters governing the collective motion. This constitutes bottom–top interactions. But, in general, the frequencies also depend on the total number of elements in each group α. A variation in the collective variables (e.g., a change in $n\alpha$ along the trajectories) modifies the internal distribution of the elements in the groups. This is the action of the superior level on the inferior level (i.e., top–bottom interactions). An interesting case appears when the functions $v_i^\alpha (n\alpha)$ are step functions. When $n\alpha$ is slowly varying, one group can jump from one local minimum to another one, leading to a sudden variation of the equilibrium frequencies v_i^α. This in turn induces a change in the collective parameters of system (4). Under these conditions, when such a "catastrophe" occurs it corresponds to a sudden change in the parameters of the collective dynamics. Intragroup frequencies work like control parameters at the global level and when they vary, a global bifurcation or even a global chaotic motion can be induced. At the collective level, it seems as if the differential systems (4) were changed suddenly. But, the changes in the global parameters are not arbitrary and are fixed by the global dynamics itself. The intragroup distributions fix the values of the global parameters. Then, the global variables change and in turn new intragroup equilibria are reached (i.e., coupled bottom–top and top–bottom interactions).

III. COUPLED INDIVIDUAL AND POPULATION KINETICS

A. Kinetics Equations

Consider a population of animals belonging to a given species and having different ages. Let α be an index for the age-classes, $\alpha \in [1,A]$, where A is the index of the last age-class. The animals can select different activities all day long, such as searching for food of different types, resting, hiding, and reproduction. We assume such well-compartmented activities. In this example, the elements of the general model are animals, the states are the activities, and the groups are the age-classes; r is the index for the activities of the animals having the age α, $r \in [1,N\alpha]$. Let $n_r^\alpha (t)$ be the number of animals having the age α and doing activity r at time t. Consider the next equations:

$$\dot{n}_r^1 = \sum_s a_{rs}^1 n_s^1 - \left(d_r^1 + N^2 b^1 \right) n_r^1 + \sum_\beta \sum_k m_k^\beta n_k^\beta, \tag{5}$$

$$\alpha \neq 1 \quad \dot{n}_r^\alpha = \sum_s a_{rs}^\alpha n_s^\alpha - \left(d_r^\alpha + N^{\alpha+1} b^\alpha \right) n_r^\alpha + \sum_k b^{\alpha-1} n_k^{\alpha-1}$$

Figure 2 represents the foregoing system of linear equations. The first equation is relative to the first age-class and the others to all age-classes different from 1. The matrices $A^\alpha = [a_{rs}^\alpha]$ describe the activity changes for animals having the age α; a_{rs}^α is the rate of transition from activity s toward activity r for animals having age α.

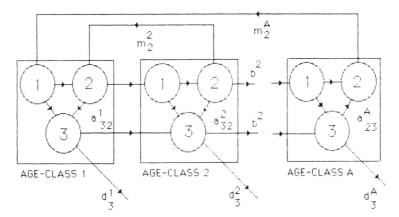

Figure 2 Coupled individual population graph.

All the other terms concern age-class changes, and d_r^α is the death rate for animals doing activity r and having age α. These rates d_r^α are activity dependent. This means that some activities can be more dangerous than others and that the death rates depend on the activities of the animals. In addition, b^α is the rate at which animals in the age-class α get older in the age-class $\alpha + 1$. As $N^{\alpha+1}$ activities can be reached in the age-class $\alpha + 1$, we multiply by the number of possible activities $N^{\alpha+1}$ in equations (5). Because m_k^β is the reproduction rate for animals having age β, it follows that activities k must correspond to reproduction. In this model, the different age-classes can contribute to reproduction.

B. Rapidly Changing Activities, Slowly Changing Age-Classes

The animals change activities several times a day, but there are relatively few changes in age-class for the 6-month and 1-year age classes. This means that there is a time hierarchy in the model:

$$\text{for any } (\alpha, \beta, r, s, k) \quad |a_{rs}^\alpha| \gg d_r^\alpha, \quad b^\alpha, \quad \text{and} \quad m_k^\alpha \tag{6}$$

The activity transition rates are very large with respect to the age-class transition rates. Under these conditions, at first order, one can neglect the age-class transitions in equations (5), giving $\dot{n}_r^\alpha \cong \Sigma_s a_{rs}^\alpha n_s^\alpha$, which are the equations describing the sequences of activities for animals aged α.

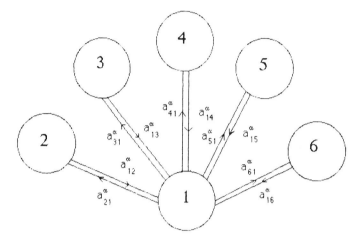

Figure 3 Individual activity graph for animals aged α.

C.   Activity Frequencies of Animals Having Age α

Let us consider the scheme of activities illustrated by Figure 3. Activity 1 is fundamental activity—for instance, hiding from predators or resting. The only possible transitions are from 1 to another activity i and then return from i to the fundamental 1. The activity sequences are described by the following equations:

$$r \neq 1, \quad \dot{n}_r^\alpha = a_{r1}^\alpha n_1^\alpha - a_{1r}^\alpha n_r^\alpha, \quad \dot{n}_1^\alpha = \sum_s a_{1s}^\alpha n_s^\alpha - \left(\sum_t a_{t1}^\alpha \right) n_1^\alpha \tag{7}$$

Activity changes are animal conservative, that is, we have $\dot{n}_1^\alpha = -\sum_r \dot{n}_r^\alpha$. A supplementary condition is required as $N\alpha$th equation, which fixes the total number of animals with the age α. Let q_r^α be the equilibrium populations corresponding to $\dot{n}_r^\alpha = 0$. Let v_r^α be the equilibrium frequency of occupation of activity r for animals having age α. This frequency is defined as the ratio of the number of animals in activity r of age-class α to the total number of animals in age-class α at equilibrium, say, q^α:

$$v_r^\alpha = \frac{q_r^\alpha}{q^\alpha} \quad \text{with } q^\alpha = \sum_r q_r^\alpha \tag{8}$$

One can calculate the frequencies v_r^α as follows (see ref. 10):

$$v_r^\alpha = \frac{a_{r1}^\alpha}{a_{1r}^\alpha + a_{1r}^\alpha \sum\limits_{s=2}^{N^\alpha} \frac{a_{s1}^\alpha}{a_{1s}^\alpha}}, \quad r \neq 1, \quad v_r^\alpha = \frac{1}{1 + \sum\limits_{s=2}^{N^\alpha} \frac{a_{s1}^\alpha}{a_{1s}^\alpha}} \tag{9}$$

Consequently, the activity frequencies are known from the assumed sequences of activity for the animals aged α.

D. Population Kinetics

Let $n^\alpha(t)$ be the whole population aged α at time t, $n^\alpha(t) = \Sigma_r n_r^\alpha(t)$. Derive them with respect to time, giving $\dot{n}^\alpha(t) = \Sigma_r \dot{n}_r^\alpha(t)$. Substitute equations (5) into them and, assuming that at each instant t, the activity distributions are the equilibrium ones defined in Section C by equations (9), substitute $v_r^\alpha n^\alpha(t)$ to $n_r^\alpha(t)$, giving the population equations:

$$\alpha = 1, \quad \dot{n}^1 = -(d^1 + B^1)n^1 + \sum_\beta m^\beta n^\beta \tag{10}$$

$$\alpha \neq 1, \quad \dot{n}^\alpha = -(d^\alpha + B^\alpha)n^\alpha + B^{\alpha-1}n^{\alpha-1}$$

The rates of death and of reproduction $d\alpha$ and $m\beta$ are given by:

$$d^\alpha = \sum_r d_r^\alpha v_r^\alpha, \quad B^\alpha = N^{\alpha+1}b^\alpha, \quad \text{and} \quad m^\beta = N^1 \sum_k m_k^\beta v_\kappa^\beta \tag{11}$$

It is interesting to see that the population parameters $d\alpha$ and $m\beta$ depend on the equilibrium activity frequencies for the animals of different ages. The preceding relations establish links between the individual and the population levels. On another hand, the system represented by equation (5) is composed of $A\,N$ equations (for A age-classes and N activities for animals in each age-class), while the system (10) is composed of only A equations. Jumping from the individual level to the population level leads to an important reduction in the number of variables and of equations. There is a reduction of the complexity of the system.

E. Coupled Individual and Population Levels

Imagine a climate variation (hard winter, hot summer). To better adapt to this new environment, the animals may change activities. Some food may become rare and another kind more readily attainable. The animals may modify their activity frequencies and as a consequence their global death rates $d\alpha$. Now, let us assume that the activity transition rates a_{i1}^α from fundamental activity 1, resting, toward all the

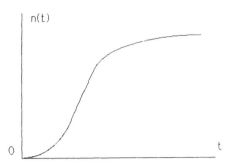

Figure 4 Qualitative aspect of the growth curve of the whole population.

other activities i are proportional to n^α. This signifies that the animals are more active when the population increases as a result of competition. We have an influence of global variable values on the intragroup equilibrium structures. It is a top-bottom coupling. In this case, one can calculate the new activity frequencies, which will be functions of the populations n^α. These new frequencies can be injected in the expressions of the global rates of death and computer simulations can be performed with several age-classes.

Without top-bottom interactions, the whole population $n(t) = \Sigma_\alpha n^\alpha(t)$ grows exponentially as a result of linear equations (10). In the top-bottom interaction case, the whole population reaches a plateau and does not explode (see Fig. 4). The originality of this model comes from the fact that usually Verlhust terms are added to the population equations in a phenomenological way.

Here, the limit in the population growth is the result of a change in the individual behavior of the animals, which modify their activity sequences with respect to the whole value of the population. Similar models can be developed to take account of the ecosystem level. In this case, one must consider the next variables $n_i^{\alpha s}(t)$, numbers of animals doing activity i, aged α, belonging to species s. A double integration leads to population or ecosystem dynamics like prey–predator models [12,13], $n_i^{\alpha s}(t) \rightarrow n^{\alpha s}(t) \rightarrow n^s(t)$.

IV. INFLUENCE OF THE ACTIVITY SEQUENCES ON COMPETITION

A. Fundamental Equations

In most models of interspecific competition, the competition between two species for the same food source leads to the extinction of one of the two competing species. These models of competition and of mutualism do not take into account the activities of the animals. Nevertheless, the animals have many different activities all day long whose sequences can also vary with seasons or else environmental changes such as pollution or climate changes. As a consequence, when one considers competition in links with activity sequences, one must consider that the animals may strongly compete for some food sources and weakly compete or even be in symbiosis for other food sources. In this section, we are going to study the influence of individual behavior on competition models. How can a change in individual behavior affect interspecific relations?

We are going to consider two interacting species 1 and 2 with activity sequences. All day long the animals can select different activities (searching for food of different types, resting, hiding, reproduction, etc.). We assume the existence of such well-compartmented activities. In this example, the elements of the general model are animals, the states are the activities, and the groups are the two species; r is the index for the activities of the animals of species 1 or 2. Let $n_r^1(t)$ and $n_r^2(t)$ be, respectively, the numbers of animals of species 1 and 2 doing activity r at time t. Consider the following dynamical differential equations:

$$\frac{dn_r^1}{dt} = \sum_s a_{rs}^1 n_s^1 + r^1 n_r^1 \left[\frac{1 - n_r^1}{K^1} + \sum_s b_{rs}^{12} n_s^2 \right] \tag{12}$$

$$\frac{dn_t^2}{dt} = \sum_s a_{ts}^2 n_s^2 + r^2 n_t^2 \left[\frac{1 - n_t^2}{K^2} + \sum_s b_{ts}^{21} n_s^1 \right]$$

Matrices $A^\alpha = [a_{rs}^\alpha]$ describe the activity changes for animals of species $\alpha = 1$ or 2; a_{rs}^α is the rate of transition from activity s toward activity r for animals of species α; r^α is the linear birthrate for animals of species α; and K^α is the carrying capacity for animals of species α. These terms are positive parameters and do not depend on the activity of the animals. In addition, $b_{rs}^{\alpha\beta}$ are competition parameters between species α doing activity r and species β doing activity s. These parameters are assumed to depend on the activity of the animals. We are going to assume that the animals are in strong competition for some couples of activities, and in weak competition for others. In the strong competition case, the parameters $b_{rs}^{\alpha\beta}$ will be more negative, and in the weak competition case, the parameters $b_{rs}^{\alpha\beta}$ will be less negative.

As before, the animals change activities several times per day, but there are relatively few changes in age-class for the 6-month and 1-year age classes with respect to the competition and mutualism terms. This means that there is a hierarchy in the order of magnitude of the parameters of the model:

$$\text{for any } (\alpha, r, s), \quad |a_{rs}^\alpha| \gg r^\alpha \tag{13}$$

The linear terms concerning the activity transitions are assumed to be very large with respect to the linear birthrates of the species. The second-order nonlinear terms are also assumed to be perturbations with respect to linear ones. As a consequence, we consider a neighborhood of the variables in which the activity terms are dominant in equations (12).

B. Strong or Weak Competition

Now, we assume constant activity frequencies v_i^α. By use of the general method recalled in Section IV.A, we get the differential equations governing the time evolution of the species populations:

$$\frac{dn^1}{dt} = r^1 n^1 \left[\frac{1 - n^1}{K^1} + b^{12} n^2 \right] \tag{14}$$

$$\frac{dn^2}{dt} = r^2 n^2 \left[\frac{1 - n^2}{K^2} + b^{21} n^1 \right]$$

In equations (14), we have replaced n_r^α by $v_r^\alpha n\alpha$ so that the global interspecific terms b^{12} or b^{21} are given by the next relations—that is, depend on the activity frequencies:

$$b^{12} = \sum_{r,s} b_{rs}^{12} v_r^1 v_s^2 \quad \text{and} \quad b^{21} = \sum_{r,s} b_{rs}^{21} v_r^2 v_s^1 \tag{15}$$

It is interesting to see that the global interspecific parameters depend on the equilibrium activity frequencies for the animals of species 1 or 2. The preceding relations establish links between the individual and the population and ecosystem levels. On another hand, the system represented by equations (12) is composed of $2N$ equations for two species and N activities for animals in each species) while the system represented by equations (14) is composed of only two equations. Jumping from the individual level to the population and ecosystem levels leads to an important reduction in the number of variables and of equations.

As noticed previously, the parameters b_{rs}^{12} and b_{tu}^{21} can be more or less negative. For some couples of activities, the animals may strongly compete, and these parameters are more negative, and for other activities the animals may weakly compete, and these parameters are less negative. As a consequence, the values of the global parameters b^{12} and b^{21} are not fixed but, rather, depend on the activity frequencies v_r^1 and v_s^2 of the animals of both species. Grossly, if the animals engage in activities with strong competition, the global parameters will be more

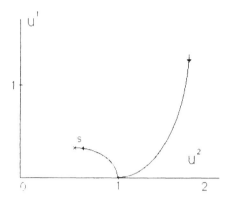

Figure 5   At first, species 1 is becoming extinct. Then, near extinction, animals of species 1 modify their individual behavior. This modifies the parameters and the trajectory, which is evolving toward a stable steady state point S.

negative. On the contrary, if the animals select activities with weak competition, the global parameters will be less negative. The characteristic of strong or weak competition is not fixed once and for all, but it will be fixed by the activity sequences of the animals. These sequences will fix the activity frequencies, which are weights in the global parameters equations. Furthermore, if the animals change their activity sequences, this will also change the global parameters of interactions between the species.

C.   Computer Simulations for Two Competing Species

In these simulations, we consider two populations that can compete either strongly or weakly. Equations (14) are nondimensionalized by considering new variables and parameters a^{12} and a^{21} linked to b^{12} and b^{21}, for further details, see Murray [13]. For this new system, there exist four steady states $(0,0)$, $(1,0)$, $(0,1)$, and (u_1^*, u_2^*). In competition models, the parameters a^{12} and a^{21} are negative. In the competition case, one can show that except when a^{12} and a^{21} exceed -1, the steady state point (u_1^*, u_2^*) is unstable, and depending on the initial conditions or on the values of the parameters, the system evolves toward either $(1,0)$ or $(0,1)$, both of which are stable. This means that only one species can survive except when a^{12} and a^{21} exceed -1, for which even in competition the two species can coexist; see Murray [13]. Figure 5 presents a computer simulation of these equations. The initial conditions are $(2,2)$. The simulation shows that the system evolves toward the steady state $(0,1)$. Species 1 is extinct and has been supplanted by species 2. Now, near extinction, suppose that the animals of species 1 modify their activity transition graph. This will modify their activity frequencies and as shown by equations (15), it will modify the parameters b_{12} and b_{21} and, as a consequence, also the parameters of the nondimensionalized equations a_{12} and a_{21}. Figure 5 shows a second trajectory drawn from the initial point (1.00124, 0.0001) near extinction of species 1, with other values of the interspecific parameters corresponding to weak competition. This trajectory shows that the two species are now going to coexist. Indeed, in this case a_{12} and a_{21} exceed –1, and the steady state point (u_1^*, u_2^*) = (0.714, 0.357) is stable.

Through this example, we would like to show that a change in the average individual behavior of the animals may strongly modify the stability and the structure of the ecosystem. By selecting new activities, a species that is becoming extinct, or some individuals of this species, can survive and find a new equilibrium. This example is a typical case of what can be called an interaction between the individual and population levels.

It seems to us that the problem of the evolution or of the stability of the ecosystem cannot be considered from a global point of view only and that the interactions between the individual, population, and ecosystem levels must be taken into account. A change in each of these levels will have an impact on the other levels. The whole evolution is governed by these coupled evolutions.

V. CONCLUSION

It is possible to realize computer simulations of global equations at the population level and to simulate top–bottom and bottom–top couplings. It is also possible to apply this general model of a hierarchically organized system to other fields than ecology. For instance, one can study hierarchically organized sets of neurons, or the coupling between biochemical and cellular kinetics. We have already developed such models in various fields [11].

The theoretical frame we have proposed here can be used to study complex systems composed of a large number of elements and presenting a hierarchical structure. These systems could not be studied very easily in another manner. Indeed, if the system contains many possible states, it corresponds to it a set of a very large number of coupled differential equations. The computer simulation of such a system would need a great deal of computer time, and the results (if obtained) would be very difficult to use because there would be too many data. On the contrary, if the hierarchical partition corresponds to few groups with many states in each of them, one obtains a set of a few differential equations and an important reduction in the number of variables. If one is able to separate the levels well, the complexity of the system is much reduced. In this way, this work is a contribution to the general complex systems theory [14,15].

REFERENCES

1. T. F. H. Alllen and T. B. Starr, *Hierarchy: Perspectives for Ecological Complexity*, University of Chicago Press, Chicago, 1982.

2. M. D. Mesarovic, M. Mako, and Y. Takahara, *Theory of Hierarchical, Multilevel Systems*, Academic Press, New York, 1970.

3. H. H. Pattee, *Hierarchy Theory: The Challenge of Complex Systems*, Braziller, New York, 1973.

4. H. A. Simon, *The Sciences of the Artificial*, MIT Press, Cambridge, MA, 1969.

5. P. Weiss, *Hierarchically Organized Systems in Theory and in Practice*, Hafner, New York, 1971.

6. L. L. Whyte, A. G. Wilson, and D. Wilson, *Hierarchical Structures*, Elsevier, New York, 1969.

7. P. Auger, *Int. J. General Sys.*, 8: 82 (1980).

8. P. Auger, *Sys. Res.*, 7(4): 221–236 (1990).

9. P. Auger, *Math Biosci.*, 65: 269 (1983).

10. P. Auger, *Syst. Res.*, 3: 41–50 (1986).

11. P. Auger, *Hierarchically Organized Systems: Dynamics and Thermodynamics: Applications in Physics, Biology, and Economics*, Pergamon Press, Oxford, 1989.

12. R. M. May, *Theoretical Ecology: Principles and Applications*, Blackwell, Oxford, 1976.

13. J. D. Murray, *Mathematical Biology*, Springer Verlag, New York, 1980.

14. G. J. Klir, *An Approach to General Systems Theory*, Van Nostrand Reinhold, New York, 1969.

15. G. J. Klir, *Architecture of Systems Problem Solving*, Plenum Press, New York, 1985.

10

Knowledge Measurement, Cognitive Complexity, and Cybernetics of Mutual Man–Machine Adaptation

Yan M. Yufik   Institute of Medical Cybernetics, Inc., Washington, D.C.

Thomas B. Sheridan   Massachusetts Institute of Technology, Cambridge, Massachusetts

Valery F. Venda   University of Manitoba, Winnipeg, Canada

I. INTRODUCTION

The subject we are going to explore has grown from predominantly practical concerns: how to improve the design of modern machines so that they complement rather than thwart cognitive skills of their operators; how to diagnose such skills and monitor their progress in the course of operator training and, last but not least, how to organize training to ensure its efficiency and acceptable cost in terms of time, resources, and sheer human aggravation.

The design of machines by one part of the humankind to confuse another part can be traced back to the Stonehenge era. Since then, machines have improved in many respects except one: their operation can be as mind-boggling as the mysteries of ancient civilizations. Ancient engineers inspired awe in their fellow tribesman by concealing the purpose of their creations. Modern designers are more sophisticated and often manage to cause sustained bewilderment in the users even after the purpose of the system is uncovered.

The first line of defense lies in the manuals: there are many ways to make them impregnable. The second line is in the training. By limiting training to standard procedures, users are left helpless to counter variations in the system conditions. Finally, the operation of the system can be made counterintuitive, so that every function is an entrapment, and users are never certain about what action causes what results. Make any operational error fatal, and you will complete the list of engineering tricks as it appears to almost any novice contemplating a power plant control room, a crew station in a modern aircraft, or even some unpretentious home device accompanied by a hundred-page manual.

On a more serious note, there is something profoundly puzzling in the fact that the engineering mind creates artifacts that consistently defy user understanding. A trivial solution to this puzzle is that of professional specialization: engineers are responsible for the functionality and physical efficiency of their systems, and almost never for their operability. Until recently, concerns about excessive cognitive complexity of system operation entered the design scene under the name of technical aesthetics, which itself connotes something superfluous and inconsequential for the system functioning. Recently, however, in Chernobyl and Three Mile Island, consequences of operator confusion were demonstrated quite dramatically.

Ruling out engineering conspiracy, the solution of the puzzle should be sought in the very nature of the cognitive processes involved in machine design and operational decision making. What are the factors that make systems and control situations complex? What cognitive mechanisms are invoked by the operators to overcome complexity? How can knowledge of these mechanisms be used to guide the training of operators and to augment their decision making? Unfortunately, these authors are not aware of any comprehensive theory addressing this problem in its entirety. However, it might be useful to review some of the recent experimental findings and theoretical developments intended to account for new data on operator performance in complex man–machine systems. This chapter attempts such a review, which is offered, of course, not as a definitive answer to the foregoing questions but rather as a catalyst for further discussion.

The chapter proceeds in the following order. We start by reviewing experimental results concerning operator training in complex interactive tasks. Next we present some general ideas of knowledge measurement, establishing a framework in which the results can be discussed. Within the knowledge measurement framework, we propose a computational model of a cognitive process manifest in the operator's behavior. Namely, we try to model the formation of chunks, that is, components of operator cognitive models that represent clusters of strongly interacting system variables and are processed as cohesive wholes when solving control tasks. We suspect that chunking is largely responsible for overcoming complexity and performance improvements in the course of operator training. The chapter concludes by briefly indicating research directions in knowledge measurement concerning cognitive skills diagnosis, operator training, and interface design.

II. THE DYNAMICS OF OPERATOR TRAINING
IN COMPLEX INTERACTIVE TASKS

Experimental data indicate several stages in acquiring expertise in controlling complex systems (Dreyfus and Dreyfus, 1980; Yufik, 1982; Yufik and Sheridan, 1985, 1986; Rasmussen, 1986; Venda, 1982).

To a novice just entering the first stage of training, a complex system appears mostly as a tangled web of control variables. Interactions among the variables are not at all clear. The immediate outcome of any action is uncertain, let alone its remote consequences. As a result, the variables appear almost random; that is, they seem to assume their values arbitrarily within some physically admissible ranges. The trainee's attention span is limited to only a few characteristics of the system status.

Under these circumstances, no planning is possible beyond, typically, a one-step response to local changes in the system conditions. Although limited in scope, such responses consume a great deal of mental energy because of vacillation among competing decision alternatives. Only rarely can the operator state prerequisites and consequences of control actions; thus the choice of actions can be attributed to conjecture rather than to any form of disciplined reasoning. With the trainee's continuing exposure to new tasks, however, the chances of making satisfactory choices rapidly improve, preparing for the transition to the next stage in the training process.

At the next stage, the preferred strategy is procedure selection; that is, the trainee learns standard control procedures, which tend to be memorized and retrieved as separate, rigid entities. This means that if any action in a procedure happens to be unavailable and possible substitutions are not specified in advance, the whole procedure becomes unimplementable and is rejected. If several procedures share the same control sequence, these commonalities can interfere with performance by diverting the flow of actions into a wrong alternative path. Substantial mental effort is still spent in recognizing procedures appropriate for the situation at hand, and in retrieving them completely and without confusing the order of actions.

The next stage, witnesses qualitative improvements in the operator's performance, caused, presumably, by a change in perception of the system. The system now appears as a dynamic whole where individual procedures have merged in a connected graph. This change from a fragmented to a holistic, coherent view of the system occurs gradually and in several ways.

First, the operator becomes capable of planning and inferring side effects of control actions. When standard procedures are unavailable, collaterals can be found on-line (i.e., without being prescribed in advance). Second, the operator can establish multiple global objectives and prioritize them according to relative impact on the overall system mission and other criteria (e.g., safety). Third, the operator becomes aware of and can articulate his or her planning strategy, indicating, for example, the list of priorities and possible courses of action. For example, the operator might choose to address the most critical objective first, or to start with the least risky action (Yufik, 1982). Awareness of alternative strategies is associated with the capability to change them deliberately, as a form of metaplanning.

Fourth, the view of the system takes advantage of commonalities across the range of procedures, in that subsets of strongly interrelated variables are grouped into cohesive units, or chunks. In the planning process such units participate as functional wholes, in that the unit's input associates directly to its output, without the necessity of tracing actions within the unit. With this, performance becomes not only more robust but more fluent and appreciably less strenuous.

At the final stage, a new form of behavior emerges to replace planning and metaplanning. The operator becomes seemingly capable of making direct associations between the overall control situations and appropriate responses. The impression is that a large dictionary of situation–response pairs has been acquired, along with the capability to recognize critical situational features directly associated with an appropriate decision (Shively and Kirlik, 1990). As described by Dreyfus and Dreyfus (1980):

> Up to this stage, the performer needed some sort of analytical principle (rule, guideline, maxim) to connect his grasp of the general (typical, whole) situation to a specific action. Now this repertoire of experienced situations is so vast that normally each specific situation immediately dictates an intuitively appropriate action.

When looked at more closely, the operator's intuitive grasp reveals important fine-grain detail; that is, it quickly converges on a small subset of variables crucial for the response formulation. The capability to grasp the overall situation and simultaneously to focus on its essential, strategic constituents, thus filtering noise and circumventing inconsequential variables, is the most important benefit of the emergent holistic perception. This capability, we believe, underlies expert performance in any complex domain.

For example, early observations of chess players revealed that "the most important psychological feature in the learning of chess (and it seems equally true of all other learning) is the progressive organization of knowledge, making possible the direction of the player's attention to the relations of larger and more complex units" (Cleveland, 1907). This observation was corroborated by many later studies of chess problem solving, and it was concluded that "a master usually examines only a handful of possible moves. The trick is that his mode of perceiving the board is like a filter: he literally does not see bad moves when he looks at a chess situation no more than chess amateurs see illegal moves when they look at the chess situation" (Hofstadter, 1979).

To the extent that attentional energy is not wasted over irrelevant detail, expert performance becomes highly efficient while demanding a relatively low effort. In our view, the prevailing cognitive mechanism underlying performance at this stage is that of gestalt-directed processing, of which chunking is a special form. Like planning, this mechanism operates on the graph. Unlike planning, it operates simultaneously on the entire graph. Instead of sequential tracing of links, the graph is partitioned into cohesive components amenable to simultaneous manipulation. Later, we will put forth several hypotheses as to how this mechanism works. Some preliminary comments are due here.

III. GESTALT-DIRECTED PROCESSING

Webster's dictionary defines gestalt as a "structure, configuration or pattern . . . so integrated as to constitute a functional unit with properties not derivable by summation of its parts." For example, chess players when presented briefly with snapshots of chess positions can recognize them as favorable for whites or blacks without being able to identify individual pieces and their respective places. Inversely, multiple arrangements of pieces can be constructed as sample instances of a position with some predefined characteristics. Apparently, gestalts of chess positions capture general regularities in the patterns of pieces allocation. In this respect, "highly revealing was the fact that masters' mistakes involved placing whole groups of pieces in the wrong place, which left the game strategically almost the same, but to a novice's eye, not at all the same" (Hofstadter, 1979).

Take now a more graphic example of gestalts depicted in Figure 1. In the center of the picture one can see two standing nuns, surrounded by other figures. Parts of the central composition can be recombined to reveal the face of Voltaire. To trigger the recombination, a hint might suffice suggesting, for example, that heads of the nuns appear as eyes. Following that, different objects simultaneously assume identities of facial features arranged in a cohesive unit, in that objects within the unit are, in a sense, attracted more strongly to each other than to the external objects in the face surrounding. With some effort, however, experienced subjectively as redirection of attention, these internal relations can be broken. They then dissolve into the background, and the original scene with two nuns is brought back to the fore. As any exhibition of modern art readily demonstrates, an arbitrary set of objects can be arranged to suggest a likeness of a human face, and vice versa, facial relations can be recombined to transfigure the image of a face into a collection of objects. The point of this example is that gestalts, once formed, become accessible for recall. Different gestalts can be called in turn to assume control, and will partition the input differently.

In other words, gestalts can be abstracted from the input and can be projected onto the input. Whether the projection is subjectively convincing depends largely

Figure 1 *The Slave Market with Disappearing Bust of Voltaire*, Salvador Dali, 1940, oil on canvas. Fragment.

on the overall context in which the projection occurs rather than on the material contained in the input. This explains why "the detailed properties and features we ordinarily see in an attended figure are, in a sense, 'optional.' They do not arise automatically just because the relevant information is available in the icon, but only because part of the input was selected for attention and certain operations then performed on it" (Neisser, 1967).

To elaborate further on the chess example, note that in chess theory individual pieces are assigned relative values (a queen carries 9 points, a pawn is valued at 1 point, etc.), although position analysis, obviously, cannot be reduced to the summation of points. Instead, such analysis involves partitioning of the positions into structural elements so that they can be arranged into a recognizable combination. The success depends largely on the partitioning strategies available to the player. As players themselves put it, "no one can say a priori whether a given position contains a combination or not. We must learn to find and create combinations that we can use . . ." (Pelts and Alburt, 1987).

Figure 2 *Study of Regular Division of the Plane with Birds*, M. C. Escher, 1938. India ink, pencil, and water-color.

The picture in Figure 2 is partitioned in two combinations of figures presenting remarkable perceptual discontinuity. The combination made of black westbound birds suppresses the combination made with white eastbound birds, or the other way around, depending on the viewer's perspective. Note that each perspective can be invoked at will, entailing different picture partitioning and, consequently, different interpretations.

Consider now examples of operator errors in controlling complex systems (Sheridan, 1980). At Three Mile Island, an unusual combination of system indications was misinterpreted to signify a properly sealed pressurizer vessel with excessive auxiliary cooling water entering the system (see below, Figure 5). In reality, the vessel was open and boiling dry. Efforts to shut off the imaginary outside water supply only precipitated the loss of water from inside the vessel, leading to the reactor failure. This and other errors cited by Sheridan (1980) occurred when "operators were performing a familiar task, which they kept doing as usual in the face of conditions that turned out to be unusual." The assumption of usual conditions determined the perspective in which the set of system variables was partitioned into subjectively meaningful groups. This partitioning was internally consistent, but misleading. It determined how the overall system status was perceived, suppressing the competing alternative perspectives.

The major conclusion from the examples above is that the capability to overcome "functional fixedness" (Dunker, 1945)—that is, to reorganize operational problems by considering different organizations of relations among the problem components—is crucial to the efficiency of operator performance. Nobody can say a priori whether the reactor control board contains a combination of instrument readings signifying an abnormal system condition. Similar to chess players, operators need the capability to find and create combinations that they can use to diagnose the system status.

Deficit in the volitional control of this capability is at the root of difficulties experiences in learning other complex skills. Studies of high school students (Landa, 1976) implicated this deficit as one of the major infirmities obstructing problem solving. For example, in geometry tests some students failed when tests required "active cognitive operations in order to isolate some element of a figure (a segment, for example) from the context in which it appears and to include it in different contexts." By contrast, good performers were not dominated by the "protrusive" features of the problems.

Experiments and observations of this type strongly suggest a basic cognitive mechanism capable of abstracting structural invariants from a family of input patterns, and, inversely, arranging new inputs to comply with these invariants. This mechanism comprises a number of strategies that gradually come under volitional control and are used to partition inputs into components, followed by arranging these components into coherent structures perceived as functional units.

Stated differently, the mechanism develops descriptions of gestalts along with some descriptions of generic components and procedures for putting them together. To maintain cognitive economy, the descriptions and procedures should be minimal. More precisely, they should contain the details necessary and sufficient to serve the purpose for which the gestalt can be called. We define the operation of this mechanism as gestalt-directed processing, and we suspect that this mechanism is responsible for expert performance, rather than a buildup of large situation–action vocabularies.

Instead of compiling such vocabularies, operators might learn several basic strategies sufficient to partition and organize input under a small number of typical constraints. In this way, a large variety of situation–action instances can be generated dynamically, with the help of a few fundamental partitioning and integration operations. In the sections that follow, we focus on a special case of these operations and make some proposals regarding their possible computational nature.

To summarize, experimental data suggest that the development of operational expertise progresses through four major stages: disjointed actions, disjointed procedures, planning and metaplanning, and gestalt-directed processing. The most significant change in operator cognitive behavior throughout these stages is gradual transition from a fragmented view of the system and sequential processing of individual variables, to a holistic situation assessment and simultaneous manipulation of cohesive groups of variables. The latter strategy appears computationally more efficient when implemented on "human hardware" (vs. computer).

IV. TRANSFORMATION THEORY OF LEARNING (TTL)

In terms of the overall dynamics of the training process, the key observation is as follows (Venda, 1986b, 1990). Within each stage, operator performance can improve until it reaches some relative efficiency peak. If the performance demands continue to increase—for example, because of growth of problem complexity or time pressure—the efficiency might decline. Ultimately, the operator becomes incapable of any further improvement unless the transition occurs to the next, more efficient performance stage, as Figure 3 illustrates.

Characteristically, at each stage there are certain short periods, called transformation points, most favorable for the change of strategy. At such points three conditions are met. First, the present strategy is sufficiently mastered to be abstracted

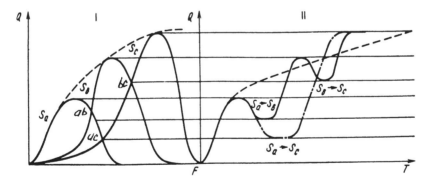

Figure 3 Transformation of cognitive strategies in the course of training: Q, performance efficiency; F, task complexity; T, time. (I) Efficiency curves for S_a, S_b, and S_c, where the transformation points are ab, bc, and ac. (II) Performance dynamics due to strategy transformations. (After Venda, 1990.)

from the training samples and applied to any new instances of the task. Second, the old strategy acquires elements that can be extended and generalized to serve as a basis for the new strategy. Third, the task demands are high enough to motivate the transition, but not so high that they become overwhelming.

According to the transformation theory of learning (TTL), the art of training requires exact diagnosis of the trainee's strategies, adjustment of the timing and training tasks to the trainee's subjective pace, and organization of feedback to establish the trainee's awareness of the strategies employed at each stage. Training technology based on these criteria yields appreciable time savings in comparison with conventional training methods, and produces robust skills withstanding the stress of external conditions (Venda and Yufik, 1990a).

Local oscillations in performance efficiency might take place also within a single stage, where the operator can choose among several decision strategies of the same general type. Here, local efficiency peaks might be also followed by partial performance degradation, until a strategy modification is accomplished that is better tuned to the task detail. Importantly, radical change of strategies and transition to the next training stage require a substantial concentration of effort. When attempting this radical change, the trainee often slides back to previously mastered strategies, until the new form of behavior stabilizes. Within a stage, performance improves gradually through less strenuous search for strategy modifications. Since temporal efficiency drops are caused by strategy transitions, learning curves become manifestly nonmonotonic when tasks acquire the level of complexity necessitating such transitions to produce acceptable performance. When demands are lowered and/or the task is simplified, perfection of a single strategy might suffice to meet the demands, and monotonic character of the learning curves is resumed.

The transformation learning theory runs against the traditional theory of Ebbinghaus suggesting smooth exponential growth of performance efficiency in the course of training. However, the transformational law has been confirmed by multiple experiments and seemingly transcends in its applicability the boundaries of any particular system behavior. Instead, we believe, this law reflects fundamental regularities in the way a complex adaptive system of any nature responds to the changing environment.

Researching the determinants of operator behavior, Venda (1990) has found that training dynamics depend on the operator's capability to group control variables into functional units. Training proceeds apparently in the same way as the development of reading skills, that is, by progressing through stages in which the student learns to recognize letters, syllables, and then words as cohesive units, and to assemble these units into meaningful sentences. Acquisition of each strategy results in some local peak in the performance efficiency. However, efficiency declines with the increase of task demands (e.g., required reading speed), as shown in Figure 4.

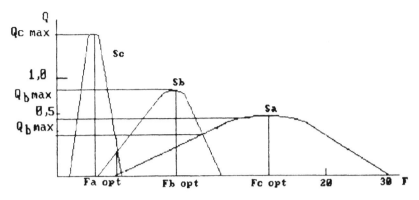

Figure 4 Relative efficiency of reading strategies: S_a, by letters; S_b, by syllables; and S_c, by words. F is the optimal number of units in the input.

One can learn to extract content from the text by glancing through groups of words and paragraphs. Further improvements of reading skills come usually at the expense of specialization. As the story goes, John F. Kennedy could comprehend a newspaper page at a glance, provided, however, that the page was dedicated to political news. Given any other subject, his performance degraded to an ordinary level. This example points at an important tradeoff: although the mechanism underlying expert performance appears to be universal, the computational detail of its operation might be domain-specific. (This would explain why governments are not run by chess grandmasters.)

In studying operator performance in complex man–machine systems, we want to determine what functional units are acquired by the operators, and what strategies are applied to manipulate these units in making control decisions. This is a tall order. In the remainder of this chapter we discuss how this problem is approached in the emerging discipline of knowledge measurement.

V. KNOWLEDGE MEASUREMENT AND GRAPH-BASED REPRESENTATION OF OPERATOR COGNITIVE MODELS

A. Graph-Based Representation of Conceptual Structures

Understanding of complex systems involves several levels of abstraction (Rasmussen, 1986). The lowest level concerns the physical details of system organization (shape, size, position of controls, etc.). The next level above represents functional components as assemblies of subcomponents and elementary parts (pumps, valves, vessels, control instruments, etc.). The next level represents generic system functions, and finally, the top level represents global criteria of system functioning (e.g., efficiency) and reflects the overall system role in some general mission during which the system might interact with other mission participants.

In our view, however, the operator decision process rarely involves this entire abstraction hierarchy. Instead, it is confined primarily to an intermediate level representing interactions among the system functional variables. The natural tendency to minimize cognitive effort favors "shallow" cognitive models, retaining mostly the detail necessary and sufficient for making control decisions.

This means that operator decisions are preoccupied with the variables that can be accessed through instruments and are amenable to active control. Our assumption is that cognitive models serve to support reasoning about available actions and their outcomes, rather than "deep" reasoning concerned, for example, with the underlying physical causes. This assumption has been justified by direct experiments (e.g., Venda, 1982) and by the experience of interface designers in complex systems, such as nuclear power plants (e.g., Nelson, 1980). Recent theories of operator cognition shift emphasis from qualitative models of physical laws (Underwood, 1982; de Kleer and Brown, 1983) to representing physical causality simply as an ordering relation. "But causality is an ordering relation in physical systems. A switch causes a pump to operate, which causes coolant to flow, which causes heat removal, which controls the reaction temperature, and so on" (Moray, 1990). Ordering relations on sets are generally expressed as directed graphs.

Figure 5 presents a diagram of a nuclear reactor core cooling system, showing the major physical components and their functional interrelations (Yufik and Sheridan, 1986). When control decisions are being made, this information needs to be translated by the operator into the order in which control devices have to be operated so that the values of system variables can be changed in the desired direction. Figure 6 illustrates possible results of such translation.

We believe that operator cognitive models integrate the results of such translations into conceptual structures organized as directed and labeled graphs similar to the one shown in Figure 6. Nodes in these graphs represent functional variables, while links represent their interactions. Decision making can be represented as various forms of graph traversal. This means that when considering a procedure in response to the system conditions, the operator mentally traces various paths in the graph, either in step-by-step fashion or by applying some form of simultaneous graph manipulation.

Imagine now that in the operator model of system interactions weights are associated with the graph links reflecting the subjective "strength" of interactions these links represent. Let this "strength" be determined by the relative frequency with which the variables co-occur across the range of admissible control procedures. This means that a close-to-zero weight will be assigned to the link in the

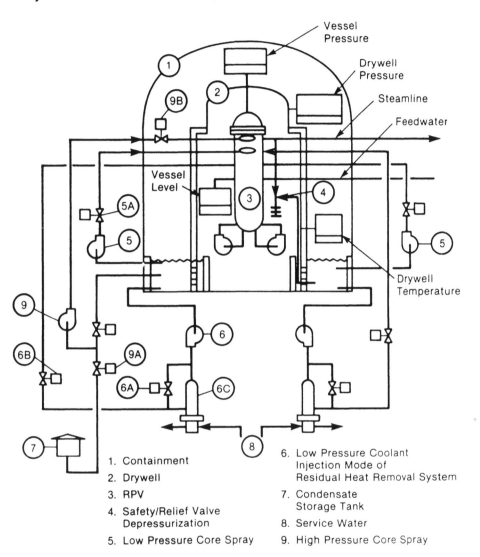

Figure 5 Reactor core cooling system.

1. Containment
2. Drywell
3. RPV
4. Safety/Relief Valve Depressurization
5. Low Pressure Core Spray

6. Low Pressure Coolant Injection Mode of Residual Heat Removal System
7. Condensate Storage Tank
8. Service Water
9. High Pressure Core Spray

200

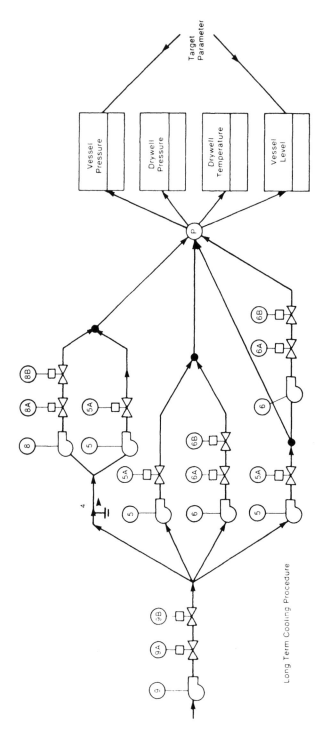

Figure 6 Reactor cooling procedures.

absence of any interaction among the variables, except on rare occasions. Assigning of the maximum weight, on the other hand, suggests that in the operator's perception, adjustment of one of the linked variables is always preceded or followed by the adjustment of another. The distribution of weights, we believe, has a strong influence on the way the graph is manipulated. Subjectively, strongly connected variables are experienced as being closely associated, in that, for example, recollection of one variable instantaneously brings to mind another one. By contrast, recollection of weak associations requires time and appreciable mental effort. The distribution of weights changes in the course of training and subsequent practice, as new interactions are recognized by the operator and as previously acknowledged interactions are reinforced or weakened. As a result, the strategy of graph manipulation also changes. We suspect these changes of being largely responsible for improvements in an operator's performance efficiency.

In the next section, we propose a computational hypothesis as to how the distribution of weights impacts operator decision making. However, before turning to specifics, we would like to generalize the foregoing discussion and formulate the overall framework of knowledge measurement. We will do this by comparing objectives and methods of knowledge measurement to those of knowledge engineering.

B. Objectives and Methods of Knowledge Measurement

Knowledge measurement (as introduced in Yufik 1989, 1990a) borrows its representation formalism mainly from the activation graph (Anderson and Bower, 1973; Norman and Rumelhart, 1975; Anderson, 1976, 1980; Yufik, 1981; Hunt and Lansman, 1986) and conceptual structure theories (Sowa, 1984). Simply speaking, knowledge measurement represents cognitive models as directed, weighted and labeled graphs (Yufik, 1990,b,c; Yufik et al., 1992). Compare this representation to the representation schemes adopted in knowledge engineering.

Knowledge engineering aims at computational simulation of expert reasoning patterns. For example, the operator reads displays, infers system status, and generates a plan of control actions. A knowledge-based model of the operator is designed, given display readings at the input, to generate at the output system diagnosis and operational plan approximately those produced by the expert. The computational mechanism responsible for the input–output mapping in the model is inference operating on rule-based or frame-based knowledge structures.

In Figure 7, frames represent control variables in a nuclear power plant. Each frame is a data structure composed of multiple data elements (slots). In each frame, slots are provided for the name of the variable, its possible states, the likelihood of state transitions, and other parameters associated with the variable. Computation is accomplished via exchange of messages in the input frames. This

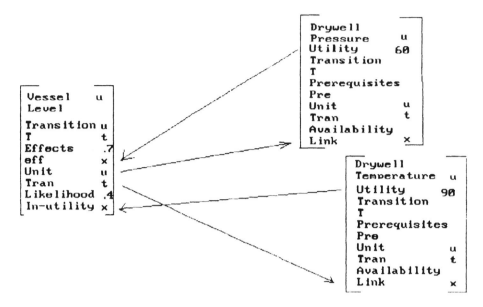

Figure 7 Frame-based representation of nuclear plant interactions. (After Yufik and Sheridan, 1986.)

means that modification of data elements in the input frames is transmitted to other frames according to the message exchange rules, resulting in the computation of output values. If these values are found in the proximity of response patterns produced by the human expert, the computation is considered to be successful. More generally, a successful knowledge engineering project results in a computational mechanism capable of generating a sufficiently wide variety of input–output associations, judged to be appropriate by a consensus of domain experts. These associations constitute the object of study in knowledge engineering.

The purpose of knowledge measurement is different. First, there is no attempt to reproduce exact reasoning patterns. Second, the object of study is the overall organization of knowledge structures, and changes of the organization in the course of operator training. The dynamics issue also concerns prediction of mental workload experienced by expert and novice operators. Summarily, knowledge measurement is interested in the topology of knowledge structures (cognitive models), their dynamics in the course of training, and the mental effort invested in the manipulation of these structures. This agenda is almost orthogonal to that of knowledge engineering. Accordingly, the representation formalism adopted in knowledge measurement is different.

Let the system of frames above be simplified in the following manner. Frames

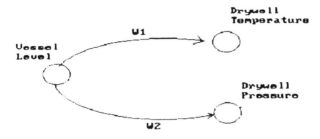

Figure 8 Collapse of frames into labeled nodes.

are collapsed and replaced by labeled nodes, as in Figure 8. Each node is associated with a system variable, and weights are assigned to the links according to the subjective strength of interactions among the variables these links represent. Individual data elements are no longer present in the structure of nodes; consequently, a detailed inference computation is no longer available. This means, for example, that relations among the states of variables cannot be inferred, and only partial ordering among the variables is represented. This representation sacrifices the detail necessary for precise inference. Instead, it allows a more global view of the organization of the knowledge structure and its dynamics. First, we can establish what fragments the knowledge structure is composed of, and how these fragments are interconnected (if at all).

> [Students'] knowledge is quite incoherent, consisting largely of various disconnected knowledge fragments (many of them incorrect). As a result, students are unable to deal with situations deviating slightly from standard situations previously encountered by them; they fail to detect inconsistencies; and they encounter paradoxes which they cannot resolve (Reif, 1987).

To account for performance deficiencies at early training stages, the knowledge fragments have to be explicitly represented.

Note that in knowledge engineering, disjointed knowledge fragments emerge only as intermediate results in the construction of the knowledge base; by themselves they are of little interest. Second, we can find out how the knowledge fragments and their interconnections change in the course of training. This deals, in part, with the clustering of nodes into cohesive, strongly connected groups based on the subjective strength of intervariable interactions. Third, we can predict the operator mental workload and its dynamics based on the gradual changes in the overall structure topology. In short, knowledge measurement provides tools for cognitive diagnosis and assessment of cognitive dynamics in the course of novice-to-expert transition, rather than for high fidelity simulation of expert reasoning.

The remainder of this chapter considers an aspect of cognitive diagnosis that is concerned with the formation of cohesive clusters of variables in the operator cognitive model of the system. As indicated earlier, we consider such clusters or "chunks" to be a special form of gestalt underlying operator decision making.

VI. DIAGNOSIS OF CHUNKS IN THE OPERATOR COGNITIVE MODELS

A. Computation of Chunks

We hypothesize two operations on graphs: partitioning of graphs into chunks to represent persistent domain interactions, and manipulation of chunks to solve domain tasks (Yufik, 1987, 1988, 1990c).

The concept of chunks is not new. However, our definition of the mechanism for chunk formation is new. Traditionally (Laird, 1983; Rosenbloom, 1983) chunks are associated with hierarchical problem-solving architectures, being used in the context of a universal sub-goal-forming process. These architectures account for the power law of practice, for example, in learning simple perceptual motor skills. It was demonstrated, however, that in learning complex procedural skills the power law does not apply (Venda, 1990). At the same time, it transpired in our studies that chunks might not be formed in the result of multilevel subgoaling. Rather, we suppose, chunks emerge as "strongly" connected clusters of variables in a simpler graph-based architecture.

Somewhat paradoxically, a simpler cognitive architecture seems to yield more complex behavior. It is encouraging that the possibility of single-level processing has been suggested earlier in the neuropsychological literature as an alternative to the hierarchical schema of cognition (e.g., Broadbent et al., 1978). At any rate, our single-level chunking hypothesis needs further theoretical development and experimental validation. The major points of this hypothesis are summarized next.

We define a "chunk" as a group of "strongly" connected links in a weighted graph. In Figure 9, weights W_i ($i = 1, 2, \ldots, 6$) are associated with the links in the chunk, while weights V_j ($j = 1, 2, \ldots, 5$) are associated with the links in the cutset (i.e., a subset of links separating the chunk from the rest of the graph). We say that a group of links constitutes a chunk if and only if

$$\sum_{i = 1, \ldots, 6} W_i > \sum_{j = 1, \ldots, 5} V_j$$

In other words, by definition a "chunk" is a subset of the graph such that the cumulative weight of links in the subset is greater than the cumulative weight of links in the corresponding cutset.

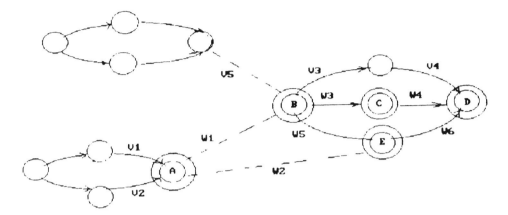

Figure 9 Integration of knowledge fragments and formation of chunks. Chunk contains nodes A, B, C, D, and E. Broken lines indicate interactions among original fragments. Weights W_1, W_2, ..., W_6 are assigned to links in the chunk; weights V_1, V_2, ..., V_5 are assigned to links in the cutset; and $\Sigma_{i=1,...,k} W_i > \Sigma_{j=1,...,q} V_j$ where k is the number of links in the chunk and q is the number of links in the cutset.

Our basic assumption is that cognitive models are formed as a result of integrating initially disjointed knowledge fragments into a connected structure, which is subsequently partitioned into a small number of cohesive chunks M (supposedly, $M \leq 7 + 2$) such that interactions within the chunks are stronger than interactions between the chunks, allowing chunks to be manipulated as wholes. Figure 9 illustrates this process.

In other words, according to the chunking hypothesis the tendency in the formation of cognitive models is to represent the system as a connected structure composed of minimally interdependent functional units. Ultimately, decisions within such units become automated, and only transitions among the units have to be decided on. This latter problem is further simplified if the units can be arranged in a linear chain. If the controlled system is amenable to this type of representation, it will lend itself easily to the operator's control. In this case, the average subjective complexity of control tasks can be expected to decline rapidly in the course of operator training. Otherwise, the system control will be perceived as counterintuitive and confusing (Yufik and Hartzell, 1989).

One can envision a number of optimization criteria for computing chunks, representing different idiosyncratic cognitive styles. Examples might be as follows.

1.   The operator might intend to obtain the most "distinct" chunks, so that each chunk is appreciably heavier then the cutset connecting it to the rest of the

graph. This criterion can be formulated as a max–min partitioning problem: partition graph G into M chunks such that the form

$$F = \{\min (W_m - V_m)\} \qquad m = 1, \ldots, M$$

is maximized. Here, W_m and V_m are cumulative weights of the mth chunk and mth cutset, correspondingly.

2.   The operator might try to minimize the overall interdependence among the chunks, which translates into minimizing the cumulative weight of all the cutsets in the graph. This criterion can be formulated as a minimization partitioning problem: partition graph G into M chunks such that the form

$$F = \left\{ \sum_{m = 1, \ldots, M} V_m \right\}$$

is minimized.

Of course, the use of optimization models does not imply that the actual decision process involves optimization calculations. The assumption is only that the overall organization of the decision process, whatever the underlying neural mechanism of this process might be, can be approximated with the help of weak optimization criteria. By the same token, English grammar approximates the overall organization of speech patterns produced by a native speaker, whatever the actual underlying mechanism of speech production might be, and regardless of the speaker's awareness of a single grammar rule.

The chunking process can be viewed as a direct result of the quintessential gestalt mechanism as described, for example, by Goldschlager (1984): a set of simultaneously active points on a local cortex forms a corporate memory, in that future activation of any subset entails set completion, which is activation of the entire set. Also, if activation occurs in a specific sequence, the same sequence will be reproduced during the set completion. Chunking as defined here represents a form of set completion in ordered sets.

B.   Computation of Chunk Manipulation Strategies

The process of chunking on graphs describes gradual changes in the organization of the operator's cognitive model. As indicated earlier, solving control tasks involves operations on the model, which can be represented as various forms of graph traversal. Simply speaking, a path in the graph defines an admissible sequence of control actions, and graph traversal implies obtaining such a path under the constraints imposed by the task at hand. Depending on the constraints, a single path or a group of paths (hyperpath) will deliver the task solution (Yufik and Sheridan, 1986; Yufik, 1987, 1988, 1990c).

The traversal operations involve manipulation of chunks and can be formulated as follows: for a graph G with M embedded chunks, find a hyperpath such that

chunks $M_i \ldots M_j$ are traversed,
chunks $M_i \ldots M_j$ are circumvented, or
chunks $M_1 \ldots M_q$ are traversed and chunks $M_q \ldots M_j$, are circumvented.

There are reasons to believe that expert performance can be accounted for in terms of chunk manipulations: first, the expert recognizes a cohesive group of variables as dominating the task, and then the solution is formed based on this dominating group (i.e., including or excluding the group, depending on the task content).

For example, in medical diagnosis the doctor learns to isolate a cohesive group of symptoms $s(A)$ as caused by the disease A. When diagnosing a new patient, the doctor will often assert A, and then proceed to interpret the remaining symptoms based on this assertion (Yufik and Zhelesnyak, 1989). In chess, the player identifies a group of pieces as dominating the position and concentrates on the moves afforded by the pieces. In system control, an experienced operator learns to recognize a combination of symptoms as indicative of a safety-related problem. When responding to a new task, operation plans are formed to include actions that in earlier cases were found to be helpful in addressing this problem. By the same token, actions that might exacerbate the problem are excluded from consideration (Yufik and Sheridan, 1986). This model of chunk manipulation seems to corroborate the recognition-primed decision model (Klein, 1988) and other current views on proficient decision making.

C. The Dynamics of Rechunking

Consider the graph in Figure 10. Earlier (Fig. 9) this graph contained an embedded chunk with nodes A, B, C, D, and E. Let the operator embark on new tasks where link BF is often exercised in conjunction with other links in the chunk. As a result of new experiences, the subjective weight of link BF has increased, which might entail the emergence of a new chunk with nodes A, B, C, D, E, and F.

According to the basic definition, the sum of weights of the internal links in the chunk exceeds the cumulative weight of links in the cutset.

$$R = \sum_{i=1,\ldots,7} W_i - \sum_{j=1,\ldots,6} V_j, \quad R > 0$$

This means, in fact, that the value of R should exceed some minimum threshold $R > R_{\min}$ before a new chunk can emerge. The same would apply to the entire graph with M embedded chunks. Note that in a fragmented structure, rechunking might occur in different fragments independently, while in a connected structure the ten-

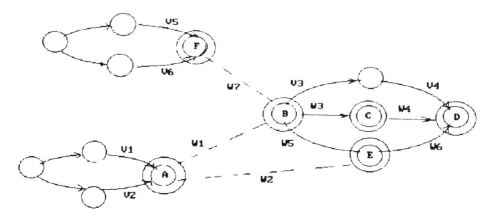

Figure 10 Rechunking as a result of new experiences.

dency will be, probably, towards simultaneous rechunking throughout the entire graph.

More precisely, until the value of R only slightly exceeds R_{min}, one can expect interference between the old and emerging chunks when neither of them is perceived consistently. This interference corresponds to the declining performance efficiency periods in the strategy transformation diagrams in Figure 3.

After the value of R has considerably exceeded the threshold, $R \gg R_{min}$ (subjective minimum threshold), new chunks will stabilize, and efficiency will start to improve, until the potential for improvement associated with the current chunking schema is exhausted, and a new cycle of rechunking takes place.

Consider now a different circumstance under which rechunking might occur. Assume that the operator is capable of changing the distribution of weights at will—for example, by assigning a greater weight to one of the links. In principle, in a well-connected structure even a single weight adjustment might entail the emergence of new chunks throughout the graph. Subjectively, this will be experienced as reinterpretation of the entire system of relationships represented by the graph. As a result of rechunking, these relationships will be perceived in a different perspective.

For example, when contemplating the scene in Figure 1, a hint about the heads of the nuns causes higher weights to be assigned to relationships that were previously ignored, thus elevating them from the background. This redistribution of weights entails rechunking and allows the image of Voltaire's face to emerge. Similarly, voluntary redistribution of weights when contemplating interactions among system variables might entail a new interpretation of the system status.

To summarize, it appears that chunking as hypothesized in knowledge measurement offers a computational account of some of the holistic phenomena that clearly manifest themselves in system control and in other domains. To validate this account, methods are needed to diagnose chunks in the cognitive models. In general, knowledge measurement involves the following forms of cognitive diagnosis:

Acquisition of underlying graphs and distributions of weights
Acquisition of changes of graph topology and modifications of weight distributions in the course of training
Analysis of graphs to determine partitioning into chunks at various training stages
Acquisition of strategies used to manipulate chunks in solving control tasks
Assessment of subjective rechunking thresholds
Determination of differences among novice and expert chunking and chunk manipulation strategies
Determination of the dynamics of cognitive complexity of control task

VIII. COGNITIVE COMPLEXITY

A. What Is Complexity?

The discussion of cognitive models was intended to provide some motivation enabling us to respond to the challenges presented at the beginning:

What are the factors that make systems and control situations complex? What cognitive mechanisms are invoked by the operators to overcome complexity? How can the knowledge of these mechanisms be used to guide the training of operators and to augment their decision making?

This time, we need to go beyond general considerations. We need not only to answer the questions above, but also to quantify the answers so that measures of complexity can be established and applied to inform operator training and interface design.

Before attempting such measures, we need to clarify the notion of complexity. Perhaps no other term in the cybernetics and psychological literature has been used as loosely as this one. Resorting again to Webster's dictionary for a definitive explanation, we find "complex" defined as "composed of two or more parts" and "hard to separate, analyze or solve." Complex is also synonymous with "intricate" and "knotty." The former suggests "such interlacing of parts as to make it nearly impossible to follow or grasp them separately," while the latter implies "complication and entanglement that make solution or understanding improbable."

Several aspects of these definitions are worthy of special note. First, complexity is viewed as a property of the object itself, dependent on the number of parts the object consists of. At the same time, complexity refers to the way the object is perceived by an outside observer, in whose eyes the "interlacing" of parts makes it difficult to separate one part from another or, more generally, to understand the object altogether. In other words, complexity seems to relate most closely to the comprehensibility of the object's overall organization, as determined, on the one hand, by the interrelations among the object's constituent parts, and, on the other hand, by the observer's cognitive capacity. This broad definition of complexity needs to be made more narrow for a measure of complexity to emerge. How can one measure the relative comprehensibility of an object's organization? How does the perception of the object change when its organization starts to "make sense"? Let us look at some anecdotal examples of insightful comprehension.

Young Karl F. Gauss (who later proved to be one of the most potent mathematical minds of all times) astounded his teachers by solving instantaneously the problem of summing up all the integers from 1 to 100. While his less perceptive fellow students were struggling laboriously through the sequence of step-by-step additions (1 + 2 = 3, 3 + 3 = 6, 4 + 6 = 10, 5 + 10 = 15, etc.), calculating intermediate sums and adding them to consecutive integers in the {1, 100} set, Gauss had noticed and made efficient use of an organizational pattern in the set. Namely, he noticed that 1 + 99 = 100, 2 + 98 = 100, . . ., 49 + 51 = 100. This observation reduced the problem of 99 summations to just three trivial operations:

$$\sum_{\{1, 100\}} I = (49 \times 100) + 50 + 100 = 5050$$

The trick that Gauss employed was partitioning the set into 49 equivalent groupings, or "parts." In the result, his representation of the set contracted to the form expressed by the summation formula above.

Note that although Gauss's partitioning is immanent to the organization of the integer set, it is by no means apparent and does not arise automatically. In this sense, the partitioning is "optional" and can be attributed to the keenness of Gauss's perception as much as to the innate properties of integers.

Obviously, the partitioning produces substantial savings in the mental effort required to solve the summation problem. Take as a reference base the effort needed to follow the least imaginative but apparent route to solution, which is consecutive summation of all the integers. Let's associate a unit of expended mental energy with a single most elementary mental step, in this case, the summation of two integers. Gauss's contracted representation of the set reduces sharply the number of such steps. Consequently, from the cognitive economy standpoint, his is a very efficient representation. As a matter of fact, the representation cannot get any more efficient, since no further contraction is possible. In other words, Gauss's partitioning accomplishes the minimal—the shortest possible representation of the set organization—necessary and sufficient to yield the solution of the problem at hand.

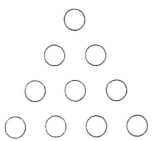

Figure 11   Ten coins forming a pyramid.

Consider another example presented in Figure 11. Ten coins are arranged in a pyramid. The problem is to turn the pyramid upside down by changing the positions of a minimal number of coins. The initial tendency is to imagine the moves of each and every coin separately from the rest of the arrangement. It does not take long to recognize the resulting "complication and entanglement that make solution or understanding improbable." However, the solution becomes obvious when a cohesive group of seven coins is perceived at the center of the pyramid. With this, the pyramid arrangement is partitioned in two parts: the central group forming a stationary "disk," and three peripheral coins that can be rolled freely along the disk's circumference. This view of the arrangement allows one to orient the pyramid in any direction, as Figure 12 demonstrates.

Note that partitioning deems the number of coins and their positions in the central disk unimportant, since no repositioning of these internal coins is required. The amount of detail necessary and sufficient to solve any reorientation problem becomes limited, in fact, to the current and desired positions of the external coins.

Again, as in the preceding example, an insight into the problem produces a more succinct, compressed representation of object's organization. This represen-

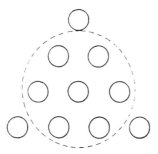

Figure 12   Partitioning of the pyramidal arrangement into central stationary "disk" and movable peripheral coins.

tation excludes unnecessary detail by making use of some cohesive groupings of the object's constituent elements. Manipulation of such groups instead of the elements serves to minimize the number of mental operations required for problem solution.

We can state now that when an object can be viewed as a set of elements, the object's complexity is bounded by two characteristics: the number of elements distinguished in the set, and the number of groups into which the set can be partitioned. The partitioning criterion is, of course, a function of the problem situation in which the object is considered. This last observation seemingly dims perspectives for a general method for computing the lower complexity bound, since such computation appears to depend on the conditions peculiar to each specific problem. However, there is an ingenuous way to deal with this difficulty and to generalize the computation of the lower complexity bound (Kolmogorov, 1987).

B. Kolmogorov's Complexity Measure, or Algorithmic Entropy

Instead of object X, one can consider its possible descriptions (representations). The shortest description sufficient to reconstruct the object is called Kolmogorov's complexity of the object $K(X)$, or its algorithmic entropy (Kolmogorov, 1987).

More generally, let the descriptions take the form of binary arrays. For example, create a checklist of possible features that can be observed in various objects. Then the description of a specific object can be obtained by checking 1 when the feature is present and 0 if otherwise.

In this way, the object becomes described as a binary string X. If one checks the presence of combinations of features, two- and multidimensional arrays will be obtained. To substantiate the concept of object reconstruction, consider a computer program (which is also a binary string) such that when executed on a general-purpose computer will cause printout of the string X. The shortest possible such program (containing the minimum number of bits) defines Kolmogorov's complexity $K(X)$ of the string X.

Assume that description X can be partitioned into a set $X = \{X_1, X_2, \ldots, X_n\}$, each part X_i having complexity $H(X_i)$. Each X_i, in its turn, comprises a certain number of some basic low level elements. To reconstruct X, descriptions of all the parts will be needed plus the description A of their interrelationships sufficient for assembling parts back into X. Then, Kolmogorov's complexity of X can be computed as follows (Chaitin, 1974):

$$K(X) = \min\left[H(A) + \sum_{i=1}^{n} H(X_i) \right]$$

where minimization is taken over all possible nonoverlapping partitions of X. Description of each part is presumed to be separate and self-contained, that is, making no reference to other descriptions.

Computed in this manner, $K(X)$ defines the shortest, most economical description of X as an organized whole composed of distinct, nonoverlapping parts. For comparison, consider an object that appears to be totally unstructured and disorganized, with no perceptible regularities in the arrangement of its elements. If no groupings of elements can be observed in X—that is, if no partitioning can be established—the description of X will have to address each individual low level element and reference its position with respect to other elements. The length of this description will determine the upper bound of the object's complexity, or $U(X)$.

To compress this description, one has to make use of the internal regularities and whole–part relationships in the object. Such regularities will be manifest in the object's description in the form of repetitive binary sequences. For example, let $X = 1011001011101010$. This sequence can be reformulated by using "hypersymbols" (Nicolis and Prigogine, 1989), such as $a = 1011$, $b = 0010$, $c = 1110$, and $d = 1010$. Then the contracted description of X reads as $X = abcd$. The $K(X)$ computation implies maximum utilization of the regularity patterns discernible in the object's organization. Thus, Kolmogorov's complexity $K(X)$ established the lower bound of object's complexity as perceived and comprehended by an ideal observer.

We maintain that cognitive models of complex systems evolve toward the lower complexity bound. This evolution is mandated by cognitive economy, as can be seen from the following elementary analysis. Let each bit in the description of X represent a state of a control variable (e.g., 1 = "normal" and 0 = "abnormal"), states of X that can be distinguished by the operator. The initial information content of X is determined by the number of variables and equals e.g., 16 bits. This means that to identify the state of the system, the state of each of the 16 variables has to be assessed, one step at a time.

In this way, potentially up to 2^{16} states can be distinguished. Assume now that variables are grouped in functional chunks and that each of the "chunks" a, b, c, and d is associated with, for example, four different states. The information content of X is reduced then to $4 \times \log 4 = 8$ bits, which potentially allows the isolation of only 2^8 system states. Finally, let the operator learn to recognize the state of X instantaneously; that is, let all the chunks lump together into a single functional unit associated with, for example, only 16 states of special significance. The information content is now reduced to $\log 16 = 4$ bits. The amount of information processing work required for state identification is in direct proportion to the information content of state description. Consequently, reduction of the information content translates into savings of mental effort. However, the savings come at the expense of specialization and dramatic narrowing of the range of possibilities "selected for attention" (Neisser, 1967).

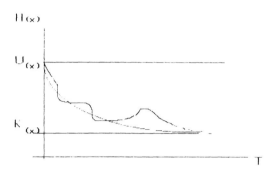

Figure 13   Dynamics of an object's complexity as perceived by the observer: $U(X)$ and $K(X)$ are upper and lower complexity bounds, T is observation time.

Figure 13 suggests an approximation for the general low of an object's comprehension. Initially, no organization is apparent, which corresponds to maximum complexity $U(X)$. Gradually, various regularity patterns are identified, causing complexity $H(X)$ to decline approaching asymptotically the level of $K(X)$. The irregular line presents a more realistic picture of the comprehension progress, and contains plateaus and temporary comprehension reversals. These correspond to a nonideal observer showing no progress or temporarily losing sight of the organizational patterns. During such periods of comprehension reversal, the observer understands the object in terms of the less significant whole–part relationships.

Nested arrangements of the type shown in Figure 14, and dubbed holons by Arthur Koestler, are the quintessential expression of the whole–part relationship. Holons exhibit "intermediary structures on a series of levels of ascending order of complexity: sub-wholes which display, according to the way you look at them, some of the characteristics commonly attributed to wholes and some of the characteristics commonly attributed to parts" (Koestler, 1967).

Kolmogorov's theory of complexity offers quantification of Koestler's general observation on the nature of whole–part relationships in nested structures. In this, a concept of complexity diameter will be useful. Let complexity diameter of a holon $Hd(X) = D$ be determined as the minimum number of bits needed to describe X as an assembly of independent parts $X_1, X_2, \ldots, X_n$, each a part of diameter $Hd(X^i) < D$. Establish an arbitrary threshold value $\bar{D}$ such that $Hd(X_i) < \bar{D}$, and consider the changes of $Hd(X)$ when d varies from 0 to $\bar{D}$. As d increases, the description of X can take advantage of internal patterns of progressively larger complexity diameter. Therefore, $Hd(X)$ will show a decline each time d increases past the diameter of every significant structural pattern in the holon. Thus, computation of $Hd(X)$ as a function of d is analogous to scanning the nested structure for the purpose of obtaining its complexity "spectrum" (Chaitin, 1978).

To conclude this subsection, two more issues should be given attention, namely, complexity of gestalts and partitioning criteria. Both issues concern the essence of whole–part relationships and lead to some concessions outside the computational formalism.

First, consider the complexity of gestalts. We have determined that the experience of an object's complexity hinges on the observer's capability of applying progressively more efficient (i.e., tending to minimize the overall description length) object partitionings producing self-contained, independent parts. As Section III suggested, gestalts contain minimal descriptions of generic components and procedures for putting components together. Accordingly, gestalts can be viewed as maximally compressed models of objects, that is, representations of minimal attainable complexity. Ultimately, well-formed gestalts resist partitioning and strive to preserve their integrity until a sufficient effort is invested in overcoming this resistance. Until gestalts break down and dissolve into the background—that is, as long as they are perceived as functional wholes—they can be assigned zero complexity.

Second, consider the issue of partitioning criteria. What criteria can govern the partitioning process, besides the formal description minimization principle? Clearly, in reality some external constraints are applied, limiting the number of possible partitionings. Takeforexamplethisstringofletters. When trying to comprehend the string, you partition it in such a way that parts form meaningful words and combine into a meaningful sentence.

Accordingly, one can expect that in any domain, the semantics will enter the partitioning process in the form of constraints limiting the space of possibilities.

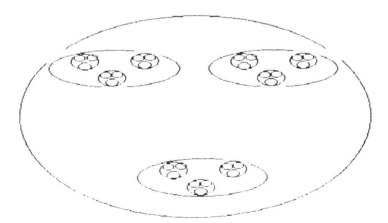

Figure 14 Nested structures, or holons according to Koestler (1967).

The chess game again provides compelling evidence of the development of such constraining mechanisms with practice:

> Master-level players have built up higher level organization in the way they see the board; consequently, to them bad moves are as unlikely to come to mind as illegal moves are, to most people. . . . The distinction can apply just as well to other intellectual activities—for instance, doing mathematics. A gifted mathematician doesn't usually think up and try out all sorts of false pathways to the desired theorem, as less gifted people might do; rather, he just "smells" the promising paths, and takes them immediately. (Hofstadter, 1979)

It appears that a general, situation-independent partitioning mechanism develops in conjunction with the capability of assessing situational constraints and applying them to limit the amount of computation and optimize the partitioning outcome.

To recapitulate, we postulated a chunking mechanism underlying the learning processes, and described this mechanism in terms of graph partitioning. More precisely, we limited our analysis to a special form of learning, that is, acquisition of cognitive skills necessary to control complex systems. The essence of the assumption is that this type of learning involves the development of "shallow" cognitive models, followed by their partitioning into cohesive components, or chunks. Stated differently, this learning relies almost exclusively on comprehension of whole–part relationships in complex nested structures. Next, we pointed to Kolmogorov's theory as a source of computational methods to assess the complexity of such structures.

The assumption here is that the dynamics of learning can be expressed in terms of Kolmogorov's complexity minimization. Ultimately, this assumption implies a general underlying mechanism driving the partitioning process toward minimizing Kolmogorov's complexity of cognitive models, under the constraints derived from the problem semantics. Next we explore the consequences of our assumption in the domain of operational control.

C. Cognitive Complexity of Operational Control

In the remaining space of this chapter, we outline the general direction of the complexity assessment proposal, leaving the mathematical detail to a more technical presentation (Yufik and Sheridan, 1991).

Let the graph of a cooling procedure in Figure 6 coincide with the operator's model of the reactor at some stage in the operator's training. This means that each time it is necessary to implement a cooling procedure, the operator mentally traces links in the graph, moving from one operation to another in a step-by-step fashion. For the sake of generality, the graph is reproduced in Figure 15.

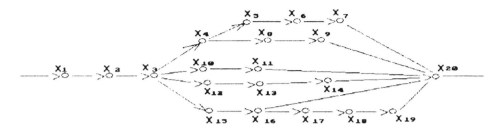

Figure 15 Graph representation of cooling procedures.

The organization of an n-node labeled graph $G = (X,L)$, where X is the set of nodes and L the set of links, can be exhaustively described by the adjacency matrix, which is an $n \times n$ matrix $A = [a_{ji}]$ with entries

$$a_{ij} = \begin{bmatrix} 1(x_i, x_j) \\ 0 \end{bmatrix} \quad \begin{array}{l} \text{if } (x_i, x_j) \ \varepsilon \ L \\ \text{if } (x_i, x_j) \ \varepsilon \ L \end{array}$$

More simply, the entry is 1 if there is a link between x_i and x_j (x_i is adjacent to x_j), and 0 if otherwise. A fragment of the adjacency matrix for graph Figure 6 is represented as follows.

	X_1	X_2	X_3	X_4	X_5	X_6	$\cdots$	X_{17}	X_{18}	X_{19}	X_{20}
X_1	0	1	0	0	0	0		0	0	0	0
X_2	0	0	1	0	0	0		0	0	0	0
X_3	0	0	0	1	0	0		0	0	0	0
X_4	0	0	0	0	1	0		0	0	0	0
.											
.											
.											
X_{16}	0	0	0	0	0	0		1	0	0	1
X_{17}	0	0	0	0	0	0		0	1	0	0
X_{18}	0	0	0	0	0	0		0	0	1	0
X_{19}	0	0	0	0	0	0		0	0	0	1
X_{20}	0	0	0	0	0	0		0	0	0	0

The length of this description can be equated simply to the size of the matrix, that is, $H(X) = n \times n$. (More precisely, Kolmogorov's complexity of a random $n \times n$ matrix computes as $K(X) = n + H(n) + 0(1)$. However, for the purposes of making a point in this discussion, a more elementary approximation will suffice.)

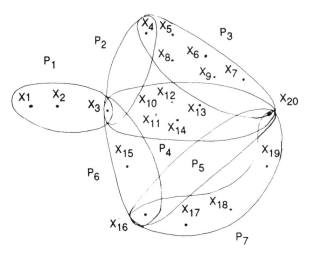

Figure 16 Hypergraph representation of overlearned cooling procedures.

Assume now that as a result of training, some of the constituent subprocedures merge into chunks; that is, they become overlearned to the extent that they no longer require step-by-step tracing for their implementation. Psychologically, this degree of cohesiveness in the representation of procedural relations is experienced as "continuous movement of imagination, in which intuition of each relation is simultaneous with transition to the next" (Descartes, 1638). Mathematically, formation of cohesive components, or chunks comprising multiple "strongly" connected links, can be represented as transformation of the ordinary graph $G = (X, L)$ into a hypergraph $F = X, P)$ where hyperlinks $P_i P$ contain subsets of X so that $P_i = X$. In Figure 16, which illustrates this transformation, the hypergraph F includes seven hyperlinks $P_1, \ldots, P_7$, each representing a cohesive chunk. The hypergraph organization is described by the matrix that follows, reflecting participation of individual nodes in the hyperlinks.

	X_1	X_2	X_3	X_4	X_5	X_6	$\cdots$	X_{17}	X_{18}	X_{19}	X_{20}
P_1	1	1	1	0	0	0		0	0	0	0
P_2	0	0	1	1	0	0		0	0	0	0
P_3	0	0	0	1	1	1		0	0	0	1
P_4	0	0	1	0	0	0		0	0	0	1
P_5	0	0	0	0	0	0		0	0	0	1
P_6	0	0	1	0	0	0		0	0	0	0
P_7	0	0	0	0	0	0		1	1	1	1

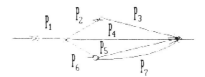

Figure 17 Nodes in hyperlinks are lumped together as a result of contraction.

The hypergraph presents, in a sense, a simplified, large-grain abstraction of the original graph topology. The simplification is achieved by combining "strongly" connected links, as well as by eliminating "weak" links with weights falling below some relative threshold values. The lower level relations among individual nodes are no longer reflected in the hyperlink organization (see Fig. 17). Therefore, formation of hyperlinks seems to be an adequate representation of the transition from sequential, step-by-step processing to simultaneous manipulation of node groups, perceived and processed as integrated, dynamic wholes.

Obviously, the hypergraph description is more economical than that of the original ordinary graph; compare the corresponding matrices. Further hypergraph contraction entails enfolding of hyperlinks, which can be represented as coalescence of their internal nodes. In essence, contraction is a form of homomorphic (many-to-one) mapping among the node sets. Such mappings underlie the formation of gestalts, since "mathematically, the gestalt mechanism is required to reduce sets of very large cardinality to output sets of cardinality one (i.e., the single name of the input) . . ." (Routh, 1985). And vice versa, each hyperlink can unfold into a subset of an ordinary graph. Such enfolding and unfolding creates nested structures of varying complexity, as measured by the size of corresponding matrices.

To summarize, the discussion above puts forth an approach to assessing the cognitive complexity of operational control. Namely, complexity of the operator's model of the controlled system is computed based on the matrix descriptions of procedural graphs with chunks embedded in the graph structure. In this, the emergence of chunks is represented as formation of hypergraphs, where hyperlinks represent chunks in the original ordinary graphs.

D. Experimental and Theoretical Evidence in Support of the Complexity Hypothesis

Here we want to state one more time the essence of the proposed cognitive mechanism and to inspect available evidence supporting its plausibility. Of course, we also want to assess the shortcomings of the proposal and to establish the limits of its applicability.

In a nutshell, the proposal advances four basic assumptions (Yufik and Sheridan, 1991).

First, we suggest that cognitive models are developed to represent significant domain relationships and are organized and processed as graphs.

Second, we hypothesize an underlying cognitive tendency toward contracted, concise representations retaining the detail necessary and sufficient for solving domain tasks with minimum expenditure of mental effort. The proposed mechanism of model contraction is chunking, which transforms ordinary graphs into hypergraphs based on the distribution of weights on the graph links. This process accounts for the transition from sequential to simultaneous model processing.

Third, we assume that the dynamics of contraction can be expressed as minimization of Kolmogorov's complexity of graphs, with chunks embedded in the structure.

Fourth, we suggest that the chunking mechanism gradually comes under the operator's volitional control, which is experienced subjectively as the capability of "selecting for attention" various groups of graph components. In terms of graph manipulation, this capability is represented as volitional redistribution of weights in the graph, causing new chunks to emerge from the background.

By way of supportive evidence, we can point to vast amounts of experimental data on operator behavior which can be consistently interpreted in terms of graph-based organization of operator cognitive models (Venda, 1982). Some of the other major results amenable to this interpretation or explicitly relying on it are referenced in Yufik and Hartzell (1989). Venda (1982) introduced 15 experimentally determined psychological factors of complexity affecting the efficiency of operator performance in solving control tasks. The list of factors includes the number of control elements in the system, the number of alternative procedural paths leading toward the task solution, and the degree of interference (i.e., relative overlapping of the alternative paths). All these factors relate to the connectivity and other topological properties of the underlying graph models.

Complexity measure derived from the Kolmogorov algorithmic theory can be viewed as an integrative characteristic of graph complexity subsuming, in fact, Venda's partial complexity factors. It also appears that some of the general principles of user-centered design (Norman and Draper, 1986) can be interpreted in terms of Kolmogorov's complexity reduction. Nonmonotonic reduction of Kolmogorov's complexity caused by rechunking roughly corresponds to the experimentally observed dynamics of learning in performing complex tasks, for example, in the simultaneous compensatory tracking of dynamic signals on several displays, as shown in Figure 18.

Similar dynamics was observed in learning to control complicated technological processes. In these experiments formation of chunks was determined with the help of eye tracking techniques. The subjects were learning to solve a variety of control problems using mnemoshemes, which are functional graphical represen-

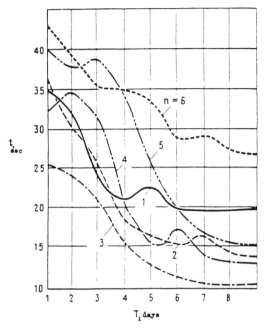

Figure 18 Experimental data for a compensatory tracking task: one to six signals were observed simultaneously. T indicates the duration of practice, and t the mean tracking time per signal. (After Venda, 1986b.)

tations of the technological processes. Three distinct solution strategies were observed at subsequent learning stages. First, subjects perceived and operated each individual control element separately. Next, they formed small functionally connected subsets of elements. Finally, the schema was partitioned into larger chunks amenable to simultaneous perception and manipulation (Venda, 1986b). Undoubtedly, these results are in general correspondence with the proposed chunking theory. However, at this moment we do not yet have sufficient data to compare in detail the observable dynamics of the chunking process with what our theory would predict based on the covariation of system variables in the control procedures.

Our proposal emphasizes the role of "shallow," horizontal cognitive models in attaining competent performance in operational control. This means that, in our view, the operator's model of the system evolves to represent system behavior primarily as admissible mappings between control actions and the system input/output characteristics. It is rare, we believe, for the operator to be compelled to infer the course of actions from general laws responsible for the system internal conditions. One reason is that such an inference might not be specific enough to dictate concrete operational responses. Another reason concerns the higher cost of such an inference in terms of the necessary investment of mental energy. The latter point is supported by the following data.

Vekker (1976) reports extensive experiments on the thermodynamics of elementary cognitive operations, primarily of the word association type. The subjects were presented with word stimuli and had to respond by forming two types of association. First, the required responses were of the horizontal type (i.e., establishing whole-part or object-property relationships). Second, the subjects responded with "vertical" associations (e.g., of the gender-species type). Responses of the second type proved to be considerably more demanding, according to the local temperature, skin galvanic resistance, and other measurements indicative of the energy expenditures required of the organism in support of the cognitive activity.

Broadbent (1966) pointed to some inherent limitations in hierarchical recall: namely, items classified in a hierarchy are accessible down only one branch. Therefore, when the cue that labels the branch is forgotten, the item cannot be recalled. By comparison, a horizontal matrix structure appears to be more robust, since items can be reached through two retrieval cues. The hierarchical and matrix retrieval organizations were compared experimentally in Broadbent et al. (1978), where words were recalled after presentation in either a hierarchical or a matrix fashion. The difference of performance became apparent in large structures containing multiple word clusters: the matrix organization demonstrated more uniform and, on the average, more reliable performance.

Perhaps the most decisive study of matrix memory organization as being responsible for superior performance in recall and input categorization was undertaken by Shabelnikov (1982). Young children were trained to categorize matrix arrangements based on a combination of features, as Figure 19 explains. Children were presented with various matrix arrangements, to be assigned to one of five categories (hammer, envelope, star, etc.) based on the combination of features (presence or absence of shading) in positions 1, 2, and 3. Initially, children proceeded in the categorization tasks by considering features separately, from left to right. That is, following the categorization tree, they identified categories allowed by the first feature, then proceeded to name the categories allowed by the second feature, and finally identified the category associated with the given combination of all three features. Training involved several phases, characterized by the degree of process internalization. The children learned first to suppress verbalization, and then to suppress the tendency to point to the pictures in the course of matrix analysis. Finally, they were able to categorize arrangements almost instantly, responding simultaneously to the entire feature arrangement.

Figure 20 shows the dynamics of learning. The experiments demonstrated that simultaneous categorization required memory organization where decision alter-

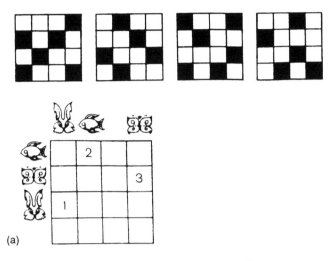

(a)

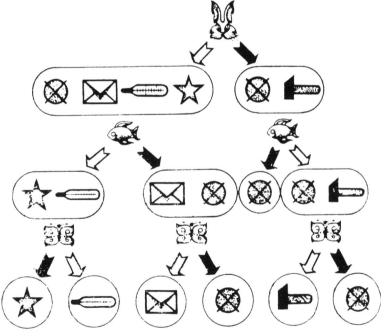

(b)

Figure 19   Categorization of matrix arrangements by young children. (a) Stimulus and identification of stimulus features. (b) Categorization rules based on combinations of significant features (positions 1, 2, and 3).

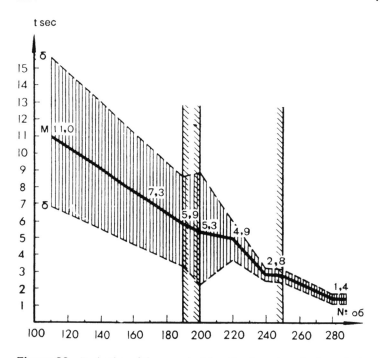

Figure 20 Reduction of time required for stimulus categorization: t is the categorization time, N the number of stimulus presentations. The phases were as follows: I, suppression of verbalization phase; II, suppression of pointing phase; and III, simultaneous processing phase.

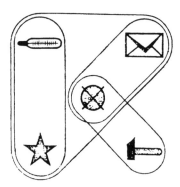

Figure 21 Folding of categorization rules into a compact nested structure. (After Shabelnikov, 1982.)

natives folded into integrated structures of the type shown in Figure 21, which is a hypergraph presenting a succinct "horizontal" description of the overall organization of the features set.

E.   "Shallow" Cognitive Models of System Operation

Let us pause here to look more closely at the concept of "shallow" cognitive models. In line with the tradition in cybernetics that can be traced back to Ashby (1956), cognitive models are viewed as mental structures isomorphic (having one-to-one correspondence) or homomorphic (having one-to-many correspondence) to the objects they represent. A model might be isomorphic to the system organization at the level of minute physical detail. However,

> for many purposes mental models will be homomorphs, not isomorphs of the physical systems. The higher the level of the abstraction hierarchy at which a person thinks about the system, the fewer the elements there are to think about.
>
> A "cooling system" may contain several "pumps." A "pump" may contain several "glands." A "gland" may contain several "seals." Thus it is advantageous for an operator to think about a system as high up in the hierarchy as possible to reduce his mental workload and the amount of data he must carry in his working memory. The higher levels of the abstraction hierarchy are formed from the lower levels by many-to-one mappings that develop during formal training or informal experience with the plant. That is, higher levels of abstraction are homomorphs of lower levels. They preserve the causal relations between the subsystems but with the loss of detail. (Moray, 1990)

This description captures the essence of "shallow" modeling. Imagine projecting (mapping) representation structures at several abstraction levels onto a single plane. Clearly, the projection will form a nested arrangement—for example, of a holon type—since homomorphs as defined in the description reflect nothing other than part–whole relationships, indicating, for example, that "pump" is one of several distinct parts contained in the "cooling system." This relationship is concrete, in that any ambiguity can be resolved simply by pointing at components and their parts.

For comparison, consider a multilevel representation of species–gender relationships, such as "'pumps' are 'hydraulic devices.'" Now, there is no straightforward way to superimpose representation levels. Potentially, an infinite variety of devices might be classified as "hydraulic." Since neither commonalities nor distinctions among these varieties are specified, there are no rules to distinguish pumps from other gadgets, which makes device identification less than 100% certain. More generally, both terms in the relationship refer to abstract classes rather than to concrete objects. To appreciate the resulting difficulty in mapping one rep-

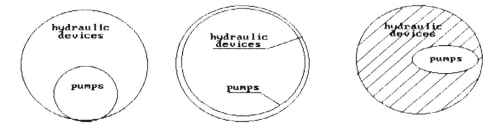

Figure 22 Diagrams representing the relationship "pumps belong to the class of hydraulic devices."

resentation level onto another, consider the following readings of the "*a* belongs to the class *b*" relationship:

All pumps are hydraulic devices.
Only pumps are hydraulic devices.
Most of the hydraulic devices are not pumps, etc.

The diagrams in Figure 22 represent these interpretations. To eliminate ambiguity, a complete list of all possible classes of hydraulic devices is needed, along with exhaustive descriptions of device features (class attributes), allowing both definite attribution of any device to one of the classes and maximal separation (clear distinction) between the classes. Otherwise, some residual ambiguity will always remain, entailing uncertainty in the mapping decisions.

The foregoing analysis of cognitive models assumes that for the sake of comprehensibility, models of complex systems reduce relationships among abstract classes to "shallow" relationships of the whole–part type among concrete and fully specified objects. Ultimately, such "shallow" relationships become represented as nested structures with distinctly separable components. Comprehensibility of such structures was demonstrated by Shapiro (1983), who studied computer induction of decision rules, using chess endgames as an experimental test-branch. A special emphasis was placed on the human understandability of the induced rules, beside their correctness and efficiency. Two modes of rule induction were compared for the King vs. Pawn and King (KPK) endgame: unstructured and structured induction.

In the first mode, rules were generated from an unstructured file of endgame examples. In the second mode, an expert player was first asked to partition the file in a number of classes or subproblems with a KPK ending (e.g., pawn-can-run, rookpawn, etc.), providing an exhaustive list of attributes uniquely specifying each class, as Figure 23 shows.

The partitioning process is schematically shown in Figure 24. First, the expert

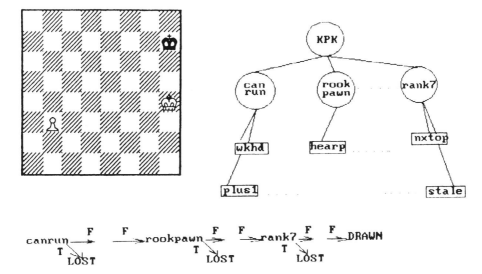

Figure 23 Expert partitioning of the KPK endgame into simpler subgames. Subgames are circled: canrun, pawn can run game; rookpawn, rook game; and rank7, pawn on the 7th rank game. Primitive attributes are boxed: wkahd, the White king is ahead of the pawn; plus1, the distance of the pawn to the queening square is greater than the Black king's affective distance plus 1; nearp, the Black king is nearer the pawn than the White king; stale, initial stalemate condition; nxtop, the White king can force its way next to the pawn. (After Shapiro, 1983.)

establishes a set of attributes and splits the problem "P" by attributes a_1, a_2, a_3. Then the subproblems are further split using the lower level attributes. Finally, an ordered structure is formed by grouping significant attributes and omitting the insignificant ones. Then the structured file is submitted for rule induction.

In the case of unstructured induction, a set of rules is generated that is "complete, correct, and efficient—but a failure as an expert system. To the expert such a ramifying and formless decision-structure is opaque, unmemorisable and not mentally checkable." However, "structured induction prepartitions the domain in a procedural hierarchy of subdomains, for each of which a relatively small and linear (and hence transparent) decision tree can be induced" (Michie, 1985). The organization of the resulting rule set proved to be fully comprehensible to other experts and ordinary players. That is, they could memorize the rules and apply them to generate and "check mentally" sequences of moves.

Note that expert partitioning of the examples file produced an ordered set of distinctly separable subproblems, each associated with a finite list of attributes and a linear checklist exhaustively specifying each subproblem. In this way a class

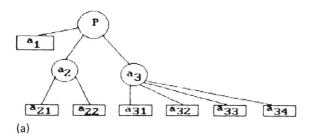

(a)

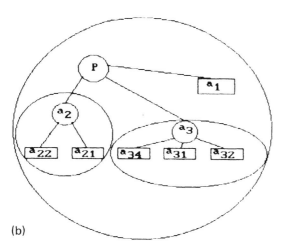

(b)

Figure 24 Decomposition diagram for hypothetical program P. (a) Decomposition by attributes only. (b) Grouping and ordering of subproblems. (After Shapiro, 1983.)

of endgames is represented, in a sense, as a whole–part schema for an assembly of completely defined procedural components. Apparently, such schemes underlie superior performance in chess. According to recent studies by (Koedinger and Anderson, 1990) they play a significant role in general problem solving, e.g. in finding geometry proofs.

Expert behavior in chess problem solving and other domains demonstrates, in our view, the cognitive system's propensity to organize models as "shallow" nested structures. As Vekker's data (Vekker, 1976) indicate, the underlying cognitive motivation is parsimonious: operations on the descriptions of whole–part relationships in such structures are less demanding than operations on the descriptions of generic classes.

By contrast with "shallow" models, abstraction hierarchies that cannot be unequivocally "compressed" into a single-level arrangement can be called "deep" models. The difference between the models is rooted in two alternative ways of constructing a set: one way is to provide a complete list of all the set elements, while another is to give a generic rule by which an arbitrary object can be judged as a member or nonmember of the set (Cantor, 1885). The latter mechanism appears to be cognitively more taxing. The difficulties are exacerbated when rules allow for graded set membership (rather than full-or-none) (Negoita and Ralescu, 1975).

"Shallow" models employ the former mechanism of set construction and support associative, combinatorial reasoning about concrete concepts referencing finite sets with completely defined organization. It is this form of reasoning, we believe, that is exploited most heavily in system control. Mathematically, associative structures can be expressed as lattices (Moray, 1990). More generally, they are expressed as weighted and labeled graphs.

In summary, it appears that cognitive mechanisms invoked to overcome complexity are capable of abstracting patterns of regularity in the objects or procedures and then representing the organization of patterns in the form of compact nested structures amenable to simultaneous processing. The tendency is to obtain structures with minimally overlapping components, which causes a gradual reduction of the representation complexity and, accordingly, improved processing efficiency. Objects and procedures that can be represented in this fashion appear comprehensible. This conclusion, in fact, parallels Webster's definition of complexity cited at the beginning Section VII. However, our research goal was to substantiate this definition by proposing psychological mechanisms and measures of complexity.

There are reasons to believe that cognitive apparatus can indeed assess the level of input complexity on some subjective scale and adjust to this level automatically. For example,

> experimental data indicates that [the] visual system is capable of adjusting to the perceptual and semantic complexity of the informational field. This adjustment is somewhat similar to the system fine tuning to accommodate light signals of various intensity. Adjustment to the light intensity changes the dilation of the pupil, while adjustment to the field complexity causes changes in the duration of eye fixations which carry from fragments of seconds in elementary visual tasks to several seconds in more complex situations. (Gordon and Zinchenko, 1974)

One of the objectives of knowledge measurement is to establish the level of complexity a given task will present to an average operator, and then to predict performance and the dynamics of complexity reduction experienced in the result of training.

A recent examination of the computational complexity of visual tasks (Tsotsos, 1989) revealed a fundamental role of complexity satisfaction as one of the reasons the vision architecture evolved into its current form. The study also argued for the importance of attentional mechanisms as the basic means of making visual search computationally tractable. In this regard, the results of the study are resonant with the ideas in this chapter. However, they also point to the limitations of our proposal: namely, our proposed complexity assessment approach, and knowledge measurement in general, are concerned with the organization and processing of conceptual models, representing interrelationships among logical, rather than physical domain entities. Although it is difficult to separate conceptual and perceptual cognitive mechanisms [e.g., Tsotsos (1989) bounds the feasibility of visual search on the abstraction of prototypical visual knowledge and exploitation of the semantic content], still an operator can develop a model of interactions among the control variables (e.g., in a power plant) without visualizing the plant itself.

Such a model might suffice for operation planning. However, exercising of these plans requires participation of visual and motor–kinesthetic cognitive levels. Interaction among these levels is studied in a unified theory of cognitive processes (Vekker, 1976), postulating distinct "languages" for each cognitive level and determining comprehension as resulting from successful interlevel translation. Our approach does not account for the additional complexity, arising at the visual and motor–kinesthetic levels and in the course of interlevel translation.

The diagnosis of cognitive complexity is addressed by, for example, Yufik and Hartzell (1989). The computational details of diagnostic techniques will be published elsewhere (Yufik et al, 1992). In the remaining space of this chapter we indicate our overall diagnostic setting and some possible applications of the results.

VIII. COGNITIVE DIAGNOSIS AND MUTUAL MAN–MACHINE ADAPTATION

We view cognitive diagnosis as a subset of knowledge measurement, concerned with the cognitive complexity and, in a sense, cognitive deficiencies, responsible for excessive errors, delayed responses, and the like. Knowledge measurement establishes the organization of cognitive models and strategies employed in their manipulation.

The diagnostic process consists of analyzing operator responses to a series of control tasks and questions aimed at explicating latent psychological factors responsible for the performance efficiency. The diagnostic setting includes computer-administered adaptive questionnaires and mimic displays presenting a simplified diagram of the controlled system organization, as shown, for example, in Figure 5. When solving control tasks, the operator is requested to indicate the following:

1. What instruments are relevant to the task.
2. What actions and in what order have to be taken to solve the task.
3. Alternative task solutions.
4. Immediate prerequisites and consequences of each individual action.
5. Second-order prerequisites and consequences of each action.
6. Critical, or mandatory actions.
7. Noncritical auxiliary actions, etc.

Task solutions are indicated as sequences of instrument manipulations and display readings. To record inputs, including the time of each entry, touch screens or light pens can be used. From these inputs, the operator's model of interactions among the system variables is reconstructed.

To assess the subjective "strength" of interactions, the techniques of concept sorting and proximity rating are employed. The operator is presented with an electronic archive (see, e.g., Gaines and Sharp, 1987) of notecards, each depicting an individual instrument. The cards must be sorted by the operator into groups according to the participation of the corresponding control variables in the tasks. Then a target variable (e.g., notecard depicting the corresponding instrument) is presented, and the subject is requested to rate other variables with respect to the target one, giving a value between 0 (no interaction) and 10 (strong interaction). The proximity measures contribute in the computation of chunks and rechunking thresholds.

When obtained from a sufficient variety of sample control tasks, the results of computation reveal operator strategies and their transformations. Consequently, the results can be used to inform training and facilitate operator adaptation to the system.

Let us consider briefly the application of knowledge measurement in training. The purpose of training is twofold: to accelerate the trainees' progress toward the acquisition of expert decision strategies applied in the handling of standard situations, and to enhance the trainees' capability to depart from fixed strategies in nonstandard (e.g., emergency) situations.

The first objective is served by diagnosing the strategy currently being exercised by a trainee and by establishing conditions favorable for orderly strategy transformations. This includes identification of transformation points (see Fig. 3) and adjustment of the succession of training tasks according to the trainee's advances in reaching these points.

The second objective implies enhancement of the trainee's ability to redirect attention to significant features of the emergency situation related to the crucial aspects of the overall system status, such as system safety. Experiments with power plant operators have demonstrated (Frolov et al., 1989) the tendency to overreact to emergency conditions by diffusing attention among multiple, often insignificant plant parameters, at the same time concentrating on local remedial actions limited to compensating for the deviations of some local conditions of secondary importance. Increasing operator's awareness of the regular and emergency strategies, and training in voluntary switching from one to another, proved to result in appreciable performance improvements. In this way, knowledge measurement contributes in the adaptation of the operator to the variety of conditions peculiar to the controlled system.

At the same time, the results of knowledge measurement can help in adapting the system to the operator by modifying the interface according to the operator's model of system interactions, as depicted in Figure 25.

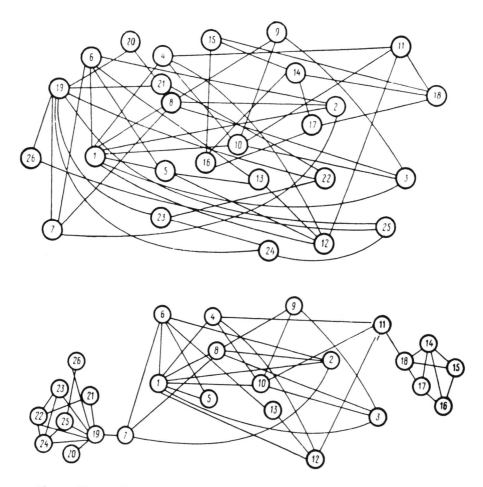

Figure 25 Modification of display layout according to operator perception of system interactions.

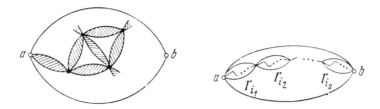

Figure 26 Hypergraph organization of display layout. Groups of variables are lumped into hyperlinks.

One of the objectives of knowledge measurement in the layout design is to prevent conflicts between the organization of the operator's cognitive model of the system (as determined by the covariation of system variables and complexity reduction tendency), on the one hand, and the organization of displays (as determined by other factors influencing the design, e.g., available space), on the other. This objective is accomplished by determining the decomposition of cognitive models into minimally overlapping, strongly connected chunks, and mapping this decomposition onto the display layout. Figure 25 depicts the resulting display simplification and disentanglement of intervariable relationships. More generally, such mapping produces hypergraph structures, of the type shown in Figure 26. This design approach is now being considered for the development of multifunction displays (Yufik and Sheridan, 1991), based on the premise that in cognitive models, patterns of screen sequences become represented as simultaneous hypergraph structures of the type above, which makes the overall organization of patterns amenable to expedient recall and mental navigation.

To summarize, knowledge measurement appears to promise a host of methods and computational tools for the development of symbiotic man–machine systems. However, much work remains to be done for this promise to be realized in concrete methods for operator training and interface design.

IX. CONCLUSION

We conclude this chapter by setting our sights beyond the limits suggested by the referenced data and mathematical considerations. As indicated earlier, we have reasons to believe that our major theoretical premise summarized as the transformational theory of learning and the horizontal chunking concept transcend the boundaries of man–machine systems and capture some basic regularities underlying the adaptive behavior of complex systems of any nature, including biological, physical, and social systems. Without further details, we would like to offer a hypothetical formulation of two fundamental laws: the law of mutual adaptation and the law of transformations (Venda and Yufik, 1990a,b).

The law of mutual adaptation suggests that the existence and development of any system is a process of mutual adjustment between the system as a whole and its environment. In other words, for a system to survive, not only does the system need to adapt to the environment, but the environment should also be capable of adapting to the system. As a result, they establish a form of balanced reciprocal relationship, entailing efficient and reliable system functioning. If the environment does not change to accommodate the system, the system's adaptation resources might be overstretched, causing malfunction or total breakdown. For example, a machine adapts to the operator through the interface and decision aids. A corporation adapts to the capabilities of individual business units, while requiring a certain degree of compliance between the unit's strategy and the corporate objectives. An inflexible policy placing the entire adaptation burden on a single party has a small chance to succeed.

The law of transformation indicates that first, adaptation of any system to the environment requires mutual adjustment of internal components within the system. Second, the cumulative effect of continuous local adjustments throughout the system amounts to discrete periodic transformations of the overall system organization. Third, only co-occurrence of certain internal developments and external conditions makes such transformations possible.

Understanding the adaptation laws and their quantification through knowledge measurement opens, we believe, a new way to design and manage man–machine–environment systems, capable of survival and efficient functioning under a broad variety of conditions.

ACKNOWLEDGMENTS

This work has been supported in part by contract NAS2-13823 from NASA Ames Research Center to the Institute of Medical Cybernetics, Inc. Our sincere thanks are due to Jim Hartzell, Carolyn Banda, Barry Smith, Kevin Corker, and Betsy Constantine of NASA Ames for their continuing interest. The first author is indebted to Don Norman of the University of California, San Diego, for extending his kind help and encouragement when they are needed most.

REFERENCES

Ashby, W. R. (1956). *Introduction to Cybernetics*. London: Chapman & Hall.

Anderson, J. R. (1976). *Language, Memory, and Thought*. Hillsdale, NJ: Erlbaum.

Anderson, J. R., and Bower, G. H. (1973). *Human Associative Memory*. Washington, DC: Winston.

Anderson, J. R. (1980). "Cognitive Psychology and Its Implications." San Francisco, CA: W. H. Freeman and Company.

Broadbent, D. E. (1966). "The Well-Ordered Mind, *American Educational Research Journal*, Vol. 3, 281-295.

Broadbent, D. E., Cooper, P. J., and Broadbent, M. H. P. (1978). "A Comparison of Hierarchical and Matrix Retrieval Schemes in Recall," *J. Exp. Psychol. Hum. Percept. Performance, 4*: 486–497.

Cantor, G. (1885). "Set Theory," in *Collection of Works by G. Cantor* (in Russian). Moscow: Nauka (1985).

Chaitin, G. J. (1974). "Information-Theoretic Computational Complexity," *IEEE Trans. Inf. Theory, IT-20*: 10–15.

Chaitin, G. J. (1978). "Toward a Mathematical Definition of *Life*." In Levine, D. and Tribus, M. (eds.) "The Maximum Entropy Formalism." Cambridge, MA: MIT Press.

Cleveland, A. A. (1907). "The Psychology of Chess and of Learning to Play It," *Am. J. Psychol.*, pp. 269–308.

de Kleer, J., and Brown, J. S. (1983). The origin, form and logic of qualitative physical laws. Xerox PARC, Cognitive and Instructional Sciences.

Descartes, R. (1638). "Rules for the Direction of the Mind." In: Descartes, R. 1954. *Philosophical Writings*. Nelson and Louis, Ltd., New York.

Dreyfus, S. E., and Dreyfus, L. H. (1980). "A Five-Stage Model of the Mental Activities in Direct Skill Acquisition," University of California, Berkeley, Operations Research Center.

Duncker, K. (1945). "On Problem-Solving," *Psychol. Monog., 58*: 270.

Frolov, K. V., Diakov, A. F., and Venda, V. F. (1989). "Ergonomic and Psychological Factors of Safety and Efficiency of Power Plants," *Electrichestvo, 2*: 1–7 (in Russian).

Gaines, B. R., and Sharp, M. (1987). "A Knowledge Acquisition Extension to Notecards," in *Proceedings of the First European Workshop on Knowledge Acquisition for Knowledge-Based Systems*, Reading University.

Goldschlager, L. M. (1984). "A Computational Theory of Higher Brain Function," STAN-CS-84-1004, Stanford University, Stanford, CA.

Gordon, V. M., and Zinchenko, V. P. (1974). "Systemic-Structural Analysis of Cognitive Processes," *Ergonomics, 8.*

Hofstadter, D. (1980). *Godel, Escher, Bach: An Eternal Golden Braid.* New York: Vintage Books.

Hunt, E., and Lansman, M. (1986). "Unified Model of Attention and Problem Solving," *Psychol. Rev., 93*(4): 446–461.

Klein, G. A., Calderwood, R., and Clinton-Cirocco, A. (1986). "Rapid Decision Making on the Fire Ground," in *Proceedings of the 30th Annual Meeting of the Human Factors Society*, pp. 576–580.

Klein, (1988). "Recognition-primed decisions." (Manuscript).

Koedinger, K. R., and Anderson, J. R. (1990). "Abstract Planning and Perceptual Chunks: Elements of Expertise in Geometry," *Cognitive Sci., 14*: 511–550.

Koestler, A. (1967). *The Ghost in the Machine.* London: Hutchinson.

Kolmogorov, A. N. (1987). *Theory of Information and Theory of Algorithms.* Moscow: Nauka (in Russian).

Laird, J. E. (1983). *Universal Subgoaling*, Ph.D. thesis, Carnegie-Mellon University, Pittsburgh.

Landa, L. N. (1976). *Instructional Regulation and Control. Cybernetics, Algorithmization and Heuristics in Education.* Englewood Cliffs, NJ: Educational Technology Publications.

Michie, D. (1984). *The Fifth Generation.* Paris: CGS Institute.

Moray, N. (1990). "A Lattice Theory Approach to the Structure of Mental Models," *Phil. Trans. R. Soc. London B, 327:* 577–583.

Negoita, C. V., and Ralescu, D. A. (1975). *Applications of Fuzzy Sets to Systems Analysis.* Basel: Birkhäuser.

Neisser, U. (1967). *Cognitive Psychology.* New York: Appleton-Century-Crofts.

Nelson, W. R. (1980). "Response Trees for Emergency Operator Action at the LOFT Facility," presented at ANS/ENS Topical Meeting on Thermal Reactor Safety, Knoxville, TN.

Nicolis, G., and Prigogine, I. (1989). *Exploring Complexity.* New York: Freeman.

Norman, D. A., and Draper, S. W., eds. (1986). *User-Centered System Design: New Perspectives on Human–Computer Interaction.* Hillsdale, NJ: Erlbaum.

Norman, D. A., Rumelhart, D. E., and the LNR Research Group (1975). *Explorations in Cognition.* San Francisco: Freeman.

Pelts, R., and Alburt, L. (1987). *Comprehensive Chess Course.* New York: Chess Information and Research Center, N.Y.

Rasmussen, J. (1986). *Information Processing and Human–Machine Interaction.* Amsterdam: North Holland.

Reif, F. (1987). "Cognitive Principles for Instructional Design," Final Report on ONR contract N00014-83-K-0598, University of California, Berkeley.

Rosenbloom, P. S. (1983). *The Chunking of Goal Hierarchies: A Model of Practice in Stimulus–Response Compatibility.* Ph.D. thesis, Carnegie-Mellon University, Pittsburgh.

Routh, R. L. (1985). *Cortical Thought Theory: A Working Model of the Human Gestalt Mechanism.* Dissertation, Air Force Institute of Technology, Wright–Patterson Air Force Base, Ohio.

Shabelnikov, V. K. (1982). *Formation of Quick Thought. Psychological Mechanisms of "Direct" Object Comprehension.* Alwa Ata, Mektey (in Russian).

Shapiro, A. D. (1983). *The Role of Structured Induction in Expert Systems.* Dissertation, Edinburgh University, UK.

Sheridan, T. B. (1980). "Human Error in Power Plants," *Technol. Rev.* 822–33.

Shirley, R. J., and Kirlik, A. (1990). "Transition of Knowledge Representation in Decision Makers: From Novice to Expert. *Proc. 8th International Congress of Cybernetics and Systems,* Hunter College, N.Y., p. 152.

Sowa, W. F. (1984). "Conceptual Structures." "Information Processing in Mind and Machine." Addison-Wesley Publishing Company, Inc.

Tsotsos, J. K. (1989). *Analyzing Vision at the Complexity Level.* University of Toronto, Canada(Manuscript).

Underwood, W. E. (1982). "A CSA Model-Based Nuclear Power Plant Consultant," in *Proceedings of the National Conference on Artificial Intelligence,* pp. 302–305.

Vekker, L. M. (1976). *Psychological Processes,* Vol. 2. Leningrad: Leningrad University Press (in Russian).

Venda, V. F. (1982). *Engineering Psychology and Synthesis of Information Representation systems*. Moscow: Machiuostroeuie (in Russian).

Venda, V. F. (1986a). "On the Laws of Mutual Adaptation in Man-Machine and Other Systems," in Karwowski, W. (ed.), *Trends in Ergonomics*. Amsterdam: Elsevier, North Holland.

Venda, V. F. (1986b). "On Transformation Learning Theory," Behav. Sci., 31(*1*): *1–11*.

Venda, V. F. (1990). *Systems of Hybrid Intelligence*. Moscow: Machiuostroeuie (in Russian).

Venda, V. F., and Yufik, Y. M. (1990a). "Functional and Psychological Complexity of Mental Activities," in *Proceedings of the 8th International Congress on Systems and Cybernetics*, Hunter College, New York.

Venda, V. F., and Yufik, Y. M. (1990b). "Man-Machine Mutual Multilevel Adaptation in Organizational Design and Management, in *Proceedings of the Third International Symposium on Human Factors in Organizational Design and Management*, Kyoto, Japan, pp. 337-341.

Yufik, Y. M. (1981). "Simulation of Cognitive Strategies and systems with Virtual Structure," Technical Report, Cognitive Science Institute, University of California, San Diego.

Yufik, Y. M. (1982). "Cognitive Models of Supervisory Control," Technical Report, General Atomic, San Diego, CA.

Yufik, Y. M. (1987). "Graph-Theoretic Approach to Heuristic Configuration Design," Technical Report, FMC Artificial Intelligence Center, Santa Clara, CA.

Yufik, Y. M. (1988). "Graph-theoretic models of cognitive dynamics." Institute of Medical Cybernetics, Inc.: Philadelphia, PA.

Yufik, Y. M. (1989). "Emerging Technology of Knowledge Measurement," presented at the 1989 National Conference on Cybernetics, Newport Beach, VA.

Yufik, Y. M. (1990a). "Application of Cognitive Modeling and Knowledge Measurement in Diagnosis and Training of Complex Skills," in *Proceedings of INTERACT 90, UK*, pp. 887-892.

Yufik, Y. M. (1990b). "Computational and Cognitive Models of Configurative Synthesis," in *Proceedings of the IEEE International Symposium on Intelligent Control*, Philadelphia.

Yufik, Y. M. (1990c). "Knowledge Measurement," presented at the Gordon Research Conference on Communication and Control in Complex Systems, Tilton, MA.

Yufik, Y. M., and Hartzell, E. J. (1989). "Design for Trainability: Assessment of Cognitive Complexity in Man-Machine Systems," in Salvendy, G., and Smith J. (eds.), *Designing and Using Human–Computer Interfaces and Knowledge-Based Systems*. New York: Elsevier, pp. 160-167.

Yufik, Y. M., and Sheridan, T. B. (1983). "A Framework for the Design of Operator Planning/Decision Aids," *Trans. Am. Nuclear Soc.*, 45: 360-362.

Yufik, Y. M., and Sheridan, T. B. (1985). "Intelligent Decision and Training Aid with Optimization Based Inference Engine," in *Proceedings on Aerospace Applications of Artificial Intelligence*, pp. 277-286.

Yufik, Y. M., and Sheridan, T. B. (1986). "Hybrid Knowledge-Based Decision Aid for Operators of Large-Scale Systems, in *Large-Scale Systems*, Vol. 10. Amsterdam: North Holland, pp. 133–146.

Yufik, Y. M., and Zhelesnyak, J. (1989). "Knowledge and Information: Knowledge Acquisition and Manipulation in Knowledge Processing Systems for Oncological Decision Making," in *Proceedings of the Twelfth International Congress on Cybernetics*, Belgium.

Yufik, Y. M., and Sheridan, T. B. (1991). "A Technique to Assess the Cognitive Complexity of Man-Machine Interface." Institute of Medical Cybernetics, Inc. Report to U.S. Army and NASA Ames Research Center.

Yufik, Y. M., Sheridan, T. B., and A3I Design Team (1992). "Knowledge Measurement and Complexity of Interactive Tasks," *Int. J. Human-Computer Interaction* (in press).

11
Pullback Versus Feedback

Constantin Virgil Negoita   Hunter College,
City University of New York, New York, New York

I. INTRODUCTION

This chapter considers an evaluation to be an axiological option, a mental construction, an arrangement, a form. Roughly speaking, an evaluation and the set of all evaluations have the same structure, that is, constants and operations (such as the greatest lower bound, less-than-or-equal), subject to some laws, commutative or associative. Any collection of evaluations is closed under such a set of transformations; that is, each evaluation can be obtained from other evaluations of the same collection using an operation. It is the aim of this chapter to exploit such a structure.

Human systems also can be understood by looking at evaluation processes. We speak about processes to emphasize that a sequence of states or a dynamic system is involved. We shall also show that evaluations by synthesis can be described by a suitable structure, looking carefully at the operation of regression toward a constant.

Multiple evaluations are associated with undecidability generated by conflict, not governed by the principle of the excluded middle.

II. PURPOSE AND DIALECTICAL LOGIC

Human systems have fascinated philosophers for centuries. We must say at the outset that the concept of purpose is very meaningful and satisfactory for a modern theory of human systems management.

It is well known [1] that there is a distinction between the functional analysis of an entity and a behavioral approach. In the former the main goal is understanding of the intrinsic organization of the entity studied, that is, its structure. The behavioral approach consists of the examination of the output of the object and of the relation of this output to its input. The behavioristic method of inquiry omits the specific structure. Purposeful behavior is directed toward a final condition in which the behaving entity reaches a predetermined correlation with respect to another entity. All purposeful behavior has been considered to require feedback; that is, the behavior of an entity is said to be controlled by the margin of error at which the entity stands with reference to a relatively specific goal at a given time. Consequently, teleology often has been defined as "purpose controlled by feedback."

In this model the knotty problem of consciousness, which is so relevant to human behavior, was bypassed. In this chapter the definition is enlarged by adding "purpose controlled by pullback," in trying to cope with this knotty problem.

In purposive action theories, individual actors are said to control certain events. In theories involving systems, by contrast, causal relations are described as being autonomous. Neither the autonomous nor the action approach affords a wholly adequate frame-work for the explanation of human systems management. This chapter introduces a new theoretical framework based on a new concept of control. Central to this framework is a dialectical logic.

Aristotelian logic is based on the law of the excluded middle (X cannot be A and non-A at the same time). In opposition to this is what one might call dialectical logic, assuming that A and non-A do not exclude each other as the predicates of X. The axiom of the dialectical logic is felt to be "natural." To make the axiom more understandable, I shall mention a nice story of several men who were asked to describe an elephant in the dark. One, touching the legs, described the animal as a pillar. Another, touching an ear, described a fan. A third, touching the trunk, described the animal as a water pipe. In the search for unity behind the diversity, conflicting evaluations reflect the nature not of things but of the perceiving mind. Conflict is a category of man's mind, not in itself an element of reality. Dialectical logic is concerned with the relationship between the diversity of a phenomenon and its unity. In short, dialectical thought leads to a synthesis.

The element formed and the process of its formation called synthesis are inseparable, meaning that the dialectical logic expresses a philosophy of phenomenology.

Identity is not something given or defined. It is something that has to be continually achieved.

Thus the essence of dialectical analysis lies in the fact that it forces reformulations and transformations of the presently accepted and artificially fixed images. The important aspect of system analysis is the development of a unique description. Our inability to make precise descriptions forces us to deal with partial descriptions. If we explore the mode of cognition as a procedure of describing complex systems, and how natural language is involved in this process, we can see that humans cope with complexity by synthesizing partial representations and that learning implies conceptualization, which is concerned with getting a feel for the whole. Each word of natural language is inherently vague. It is an essential characteristic of a vague concept that the boundaries of the domain of its applicability are not fixed. Inexact concepts are associated with undecidability generated by conflict.

The existence of a conflict at one level generates a synthesis at the higher level. This movement from one level to another can be described as the dynamics of a system. As a result of such movement, a compact representation is achieved. Conceptualization is thus viewed as a dialectical process.

Dialectical processes are present in many problems in management sciences. Planning is a notorious example. In a multicriterion optimization problem there is no distinction between the means and the ends; we speak about their confluence. To solve multicriterion decision-making problem means to move the decision to a higher level (i.e., across and between the means and ends). The reason for aggregating imprecise evaluations is to achieve robustness, to cope with situations that cannot be foreseen in detail.

III. SYNTHESIS BY PULLBACK

The formalization of dialectical logic rests on the contention that our intuitively generated systems can be represented as structures. This analysis leads to a pyramid of relations that contract the set of evaluations into an abstract unity. The formal structure evolved, representing the levels of interrelation brought into awareness through synthesis, can take the form of a lattice: a set with any two elements having a least upper bound and a greatest lower bound.

Any evaluation is concerned with a collection X of objects and their ordering. The order is usually derived from another collection, which has already been ordered. Evaluation means order transfer, a kind of reasoning by analogy. An evaluation induced by the lattice L with structure S can be viewed as a function $X \to L$. The set $F(X)$ of all evaluations defined on the same collection X also has structure S with all constants and operations defined pointwise. For example, since L has a least element, $F(X)$ also has a least element.

In $F(X)$ three fundamental notions that define a dynamic process can be identified: state, stage, and transition. Our lattice $F(X)$ describes a change viewed as a sequence of states. The states are evaluations, dynamics is conflict resolution (incorporation of alternate evaluations into a new one), and stage indicates the level of synthesis.

We shall use these ideas to motivate the following construction. The order relation in the lattice will be designated by an arrow. By convention, if an evaluation f_1 is transformed into the evaluation g, we write $f_1 \rightarrow g$. For every two arrows $f_1 \rightarrow g$, $f_2 \rightarrow g$ there are two arrows $p \rightarrow f_1$, $p \rightarrow f_2$ indicating the pullback of f_1 and f_2 over g. If we put all this information together we get a quadrangle: two paths from p to g are in evidence. From point p one can reach g by following either path f_1 or path f_2. Many elements of the lattice satisfy this condition, but we shall be looking for the one having the property of being *as close as possible* to both f_1 and f_2. An aggregate evaluation of the collection X is achieved by assembling all partial evaluations. Initial evaluations $f_1: X \rightarrow L$ and $f_2: X \rightarrow L$ are consequently reconciled in a higher synthesis $p: X \rightarrow L$, X being described by its characteristic function g.

To illustrate, we shall give an example of fuzzy programming [2]. Let us consider two evaluations, a constraint $f_1: R \rightarrow L$ and an objective function $f_2: R \rightarrow L$, where R is the real line. Since these two evaluations operate to achieve their own independent ordering, conflict might develop between them. The absence of conflict would imply that a change in each of the initial evaluations would cause an identical change in an overall evaluation p obtained by a composition law given by the operator "minimum: (i.e. $p(x) = f_1(x) * f_2(x)$, where * stands for "minimum"). We speak of confluence because this operator preserves monotonicity; that is, a decrease in each of the initial evaluations would not cause a corresponding increase in the overall evaluation.

The principle of pullback acts as a recursive formula producing a sequence of terms. The sequence begins with two singular evaluations f_1 and f_2. The process of synthesis is an operation transforming f_1 and f_2 into p_1. Repeating this operation on p_1 (i.e., p_1, p_2) will give p_3, and so on. In the limit, the synthesis process produces a sequence of terms representing a continual expansion of perspective moving from level to level and taking on the values of the positive integers varying from zero to infinity ($F(X)$ is an infinite set).

We have tried to give an account of the process of synthesis. The principle of pullback serves to set up the condition for the transcendence of the conflicting evaluations. The initial step is the assertion of f_1 and f_2, which are subjective axiological options. Thus we have one reality X, two forms, and their pullback. The pullback couples an evaluation f_1 and evaluation f_2 together in such a way that it is not possible for a completely determined system to appear, that is, a system in which reference to either evaluation f_1 or f_2 but not both can be made. Ambiguity must be present because no final distinction into separable evaluations such as f_1 and f_2 can be achieved. The notion of blurring [3] is relevant to our model. A coarsely sampled and quantitized portrait could be recognized more easily if viewed at a distance. This has been practiced by painters for a long time. They "pull back" to understand the whole.

It is obvious that a continued synthesis will generate a hierarchy of vague concepts. Everything partial such as f_1 and f_2 is unstable. Only through a process of continual synthesis are all conflicts canceled. Synthesis as a cancellation retains only the previous state as a perspective of orientation. Unity is therefore a transcendence of what is unified. Synthesis takes an immediately given evaluation f_1 and places this evaluation in context with f_2 such that the result is neither f_1 nor f_2 as such but the transcending and unifying relation p. The movement of synthesis is therefore a continual movement of canceling conflicts.

IV. STRUCTURAL STABILITY AS A PURPOSE

Pullback was presented as an act that covers both the process and its attainment. It is an attribute of a process that it has a duration. An attainment can only be dated. In this framework the process of synthesis could be characterized as a struggle for conflict resolution between multiple evaluations. The distinction between campaigning and winning could, for example, be signified by the terms "process" and "attainment."

If the set of evaluations is evolving, we should be able to formalize the fact that partial synthesizing follows a directional adjustment, moving the synthesis toward the initial element of the lattice. The new evaluations are melted away to preserve a unique view toward a unique reality. The aim of pullback is to bring the new evaluations into intelligible relations with the old ones. This is hermeneutics, a philosophy of understanding. Unfolding of evaluation implies contraction, etymologically pulling-back. Back, because the movement in the lattice is toward the initial element.

First, there is the sense of conflict. Zeleny calls it the motivating tension, the dissatisfaction with the status quo of the current multiplicity [4]. We think that the underlying source of the presynthesis conflict is the structural instability. Because of the conflict experienced among different evaluations, one starts searching for a new evaluation that is structurally stable (i.e., unique and covering a large family of particular evaluations).

Every evaluation is a model, in the broad sense of the word, a conceptual image intended to capture certain aspects of reality. What the evaluator is looking for is a unique and all-embracing evaluation. Repeated disequilibria result in a continuous process of modification of a global image. Dynamic pullback strives for the maintenance of structural stability by establishing the equilibrium.

We obtain a natural notion of dynamics in this setting. Our approach contrasts with the usual approach, the behavioristic one, to the study of purpose. Precisely, the problem is the following: one is given an evaluation $e: X \rightarrow L$, inducing an order on X. We say that $x \leq y$ if $e(x) \leq e(y)$ in L. We say that the map $m: R \rightarrow X$ is an admissible path for e if for every $t_1, t_2 \in R$ $t_1 \leq t_2$ implies $m(t_1) \leq m(t_2)$, that is, $e(m(t_1) \leq e(m(t_2))$. Suppose z is a maximal element in X according to the order introduced by L. Therefore if $e(z) \leq e(x)$, then $z = x$ and we say that m ends.

The equilibrium is defined as the element $x \in X$ for which there is no such m. A movement along an admissible path is implicit in any evaluation.

Now, consider the set of all evaluations $F(X)$. We have seen that this set is also a lattice. On $F(X)$ we have a binary operation $* : (f_1, f_2) \rightarrow f_1 * f_2$, associative and communicative defining an aggregation. A potential function $F(X) \rightarrow L$ was put in evidence.

If we explicitly define a potential function, $E : F(X) \rightarrow [0,1]$ (viewed, for instance, as an entropy), then if $e \in F(X)$ is an evaluation, $E(e)$ is a measure of that evaluation.

A cognition process is a system under a potential, that is, an admissible path. It is assumed that a state of knowledge is a point in $F(X)$, that is, an image or an evaluation of the reality X. One considers changes in $F(X)$ that will increase the horizon of each point or decrease E on $F(X)$.. A state $e \in F(X)$ is called structurally stable or in equilibrium if it has the property that there is no $e' \in F(X)$ with $E(e') \geq E(e)$. The idea is that if e is not stable, some synthesis will take place and tend to make it stable [5].

In this example a collection of partial evaluations is given, and, according to simple interaction rules between them, a new evaluation can emerge spontaneously. In fact, the structure explains the purposeful system controlled by the differences between the actual state and the constant of the structure, the ideal state. Purposefulness implies the will to eliminate the ambiguity introduced by partial evaluations. The process aims at a conflict resolution and is evolving in a hierarchy of evaluations. Caught in ambiguity, there is a possibility to resolve it, moving in the hierarchy [6].

V. MANAGEMENT OF HUMAN SYSTEMS

It is proposed that the principle of pullback can be generalized in the field of management sciences. In fact, to manage, to exercise control, to influence humans, means to determine images (mechanical systems have controllers that determine positions). Imaginative contrivances distinguish human action from mechanical behavior. Models are proper to a conscious praxis of human beings. Humans erect the model in their imagination before they construct it in reality. But image construction is a process; that is, it involves states, stages, and transitions. We can now consider the sequence of such states. The sequence implies that the system is heading somewhere and that we can explain how the system gets from its present state to wherever it is going [7].

All human systems operate and exist in a fluctuating environment. They cope with the fluctuations through a process of learning. In other words, they are open systems. To reduce the influence of fluctuations, the evaluator searches for structurally stable evaluations or images, trying to stay out of trouble. The learning process is necessary for humans to remain stable under unusual or even new conditions. The emergence of stable patterns of evaluation, of stable images, of stable horizons, can be viewed as a process of conflict resolution by synthesis. It is the supreme tendency of humans to remove conflicts and come to a temporary rest at a state of equilibrium. Hence, it appears that the unfolding of an image amounts to attempting or seeking this point of equilibrium [8].

So far we have considered the human system generating its own evaluations. In fact, an evaluation, an image, can be suggested or communicated from without. A human being cannot separate himself from his culture, no matter how hard he might try. He cannot be exempt from an intellectual influence. He is, consciously or unconsciously, captive of his own created paradigms. The external system can bring forward, cause to appear, create, or give rise to an image in the managed system either by deliberately supplying its own partial images (in given sequences), by freezing the system into fixed images, or by imposing standardized evaluations.

We now turn to the concept of feedback. According to the feedback control law, the external system would make the managed system less sensitive to the uncontrolled images through making use of the most up-to-date information about its current state. If a disturbance occurs, the error is processed and a correction implied to the input of the managed system so that the actual state is kept near the desired state. This procedure is not adequate for describing human system management. Each human being is an irreversible product of his particular history. Anything done to a person cannot be entirely undone (a machine can be cleared and reset) [9].

"Image" describes that tacit perimeter of a viewpoint. The event of understanding an instruction is one in which a person opens himself up to new perimeters and thereby extends or broadens his image to include the new one. Image is the range of vision that includes everything that can be seen from a particular point or level. This is the reason we speak of possible expansion of image, of the opening of a new horizon, of narrowness of mind. As stated before, a hermeneutical problem, an interpretation problem, arises when one becomes aware of an incongruency between two images, as occurs when hearing a new instruction. Interpretation is the process through which we seek to resolve this incongruency. The two images—the one of the external system and the one of the managed system—merge in the event of understanding. In the initial stage of a managerial event, the two horizons, the two images, are recognized in their distance from each other. Because one's own image is not closed or fixed but capable of movement and expansion, understanding the new image, the external image is possible. One cannot simply leave behind his own horizon of meaning, his library of images, to enter totally into the context within which the instruction stands; rather his own image must be broadened so that it eventually fuses with that of the external system. Through the interpreter's encounter with the external image, a new and more comprehensive image is formed. To place oneself in the external situation that is to be understood results ultimately in the attainment of a higher synthesis that overcomes not only one's own particularity but also that of the others.

The structure of human systems, being that which guarantees the unity of evaluation in the bond of synthesis, requires the manager of a human system to take it into account. Every effective manager thus creates a body unified by a common creed, a body of actors, or doers, who perform in a play.

The concept of pullback suggests an understanding of the process of management as a cultivation of an open system according to its natural structure. Therefore, culture—that is, the way in which constituent evaluations are joined together at a given time and place—could be formalized if the natural structure were detected. *Getting things done through people seems to be an adequate definition of human systems management.* Getting things done with people is the mechanistic vision. Perhaps the reader of these lines will be sufficiently intrigued to sally forth and tackle these vexing problems for himself.

VI. CONCLUSIONS

A structural approach seems to be suitable for understanding management processes of human systems. The structuralistic method leads to formalization not by avoiding intuition, but by following and enhancing it. It is our opinion that the structuralistics approach and the preceding ideas are forerunners of a general trend in the foundations of cybernetics, which will necessarily be forced to take much greater technical cognizance of conflict resolution and structural transformations.

REFERENCES

1. C. V. Negoita, ed., *Proceedings of the Eighth International Congress of Cybernetics and Systems,* Hunter College, New York, June 11–15, 1990.
2. C. V. Negoita, *Management Applications of System Theory*, Birkhäuser Verlag, Basel, 1979.
3. C. V. Negoita, and D. A. Ralescu, *Applications of Fuzzy Sets to System Analysis*, Birkhäuser Verlag, Basel, 1975.
4. C. V. Negoita, *Fuzzy Systems*, Abacus Press, London, 1981.
5. C. V. Negoita, *Expert Systems and Fuzzy Systems*, Benjamin/Cummings, Menlo Park, CA, 1985.
6. C. V. Negoita, and D. A. Ralescu, *Simulation, Knowledge-Based Computing, and Fuzzy Statistics*, Van Nostrand, New York, 1987.

7. C. V. Negoita, *Pullback*, Vantage Press, New York, 1986.
8. C. V. Negoita, *Cybernetic Conspiracy: Mind Over Matter*, Falcon Press, Phoenix, AZ, 1988.
9. C. V. Negoita, *Connections*, Carlton Press, New York, 1990.

12
Parallel Distributed Processing

Alex M. Andrew   Viable Systems, Devon, United Kingdom

I. RATIONALE AND MOTIVATION

The past decade has seen a strong revival of interest in *neural computing*. The idea that certain computing tasks are best performed by brainlike artifacts was popular in the early days of cybernetics, particularly the early 1950s, but it fell into disfavor. The tasks considered were mainly in the general area understood by *artificial intelligence* (AI), and in the late part of that decade it was found to be more profitable to concentrate on what has been termed the *heuristic programming* approach. The parting of the ways is acknowledged, for example, in the introduction to the famous collection edited by Feigenbaum and Feldman [1].

The new approach is compatible with existing computer technology of the kind conveniently referred to as embodying "von Neumann" architecture. (In fact, as emphasized by Roska [2], it is rather unfair to von Neumann that his name has come to be the customary way of referring to this restricted view of computing. He presented an admirably clear description of it, but was fully aware of its restrictions.)

Within the so-called von Neumann framework, the needs of AI have stimulated much valuable work aimed at overcoming the limitations. This has been acknowledged in a jocular but apposite reference [3] to AI as the "department of clever tricks" of computer science; many techniques that were originally explored in an AI context are now standard features of software practice.

Even so, it has become apparent that there are strong reasons for exploring possibilities outside the "von Neumann" framework, and a notable development was that of the *connection machine* [4]. Parallel operation has also found its way into standard computing technology, under such headings as *digital array processor, pipeline machine, data-driven architecture*, and *concurrent* versions of Prolog, Pascal, etc. The Japanese "Fifth-Generation Project" [5] has embodied, from the start, the assumption that parallel operation would be exploited.

Since the brain operates in a highly parallel fashion, discussions of parallel operation invariably evoke comparison with the nervous system, regardless of whether the artificial realization has the form of a neural net. It has also been realized that the real brain embodies even more "clever tricks" than are known to workers in mainstream AI, so there is much interest in *parallel distributed processing* (PDP), with the explicit intention of investigating and modeling nervous system operation.

The term has been used to denote a particular group of researchers and as the title of a collection of their papers [6]. Other important recent collections and monographs in the subject area may be mentioned [7–11]; the list is certainly not exhaustive.

Apart from the insight they may give into neurophysiological mechanisms as such, the potential advantages of the PDP approach can be discussed under two headings, namely the enhancement of computing power and imitation of the "clever tricks" of the brain that still put it well ahead of mainstream work in AI. These can be placed under the general heading of *flexibility*.

A. Computing Power

It is generally recognized that the impressive computing power of the brain is due to its powerful implementation of parallel distributed processing. The advent of robotics has highlighted the computational complexity of many everyday tasks. It is, for example, difficult to build an automatic table-tennis player, even using the latest computer technology. The brain, however, is able to achieve the result on the basis of computing elements that are at least a thousand times slower in their individual responses than are the elements of artificial systems.

The remarkably high response speed of neural processors has been noted by Marr [12], Sejnowski (see ref. 6), and others [13]. It has implications for the kinds of coding that can be hypothesized in nervous pathways and for other aspects of neural processing.

As Hillis [4] has pointed out, most of modern computing technology is clearly inefficient, since storage depends on silicon devices that are similar to those that perform the computing function. For want of suitable ways of organizing parallel operation to be effective, most computers operate in the inefficient "von Neumann" serial fashion. This means that most of the silicon is idle most of the time.

B. Flexibility

However, the advantages of parallel processing are not only those attributable to better utilization of the computing elements. For many tasks, a form of representation other than the linear one of "von Neumann" machines is obviously preferable. A two-dimensional (or higher) array of numbers *can* be stored perfectly well in linear storage, but it is obvious that many operations depending on "neighborhood relationships" become extremely tedious.

In conventional computing technology the situation is improved, as far as two-dimensional arrays are concerned, by the use of a digital array processor. Processing of visual images, and other sensory data mapped on a surface, is also much more "natural" when the data are represented in two dimensions and processed in parallel over the entire area. Not only is the processing much faster, it is also more robust and potentially adaptive (flexible) because of the way the hardware matches the problem. The matter of adaptation will be discussed again in Section III.B.

II. THE CURRENT POSITION

The revival of interest in neural computing can be attributed to three things, as follows (1) powerful computers are now available, and simulation studies that would have been unthinkable a few decades ago can now be carried out fairly readily; (2) there have been certain new theoretical developments — one that is widely held to constitute a breakthrough is by Hopfield [14]; and (3) certain limitations of the "mainstream" approach have become apparent.

A.   AI Stagnation

Of the three reasons for renewed interest, my own somewhat skeptical view is that the most significant is (3). The relative stagnation of mainstream AI (despite a lot of talk that would suggest otherwise!) has recently been acknowledged by Boden [15].

B. Evolution

Since the brain has "clever tricks" that are still mysterious to us, an obvious way to try to make progress is to consider the conditions under which biological intelligence may have evolved. The response time constraint [13] is clearly important here, since operation must have been compatible with it at all stages of evolutionary development. Evolutionary considerations have been stressed in earlier discussions [16–18], and more recently by Lenat [19], though mainly with reference to a relatively late stage of evolution.

C. Nervous System

Attention to biological systems has mainly been with reference to the brain, hence the nervous system. The origins of the "clever tricks" are presumably to be found in stages of development that are prior to the emergence of spoken language. It is for this reason that Kilmer et al. [20] focused attention on the *reticular formation* of the brain stem, a phylogenetically ancient neural structure.

A slightly worrying observation is that remarkably complex behavior is shown by unicellular organisms [21], suggesting that the origins of the special features of biological processing may even be preneural. This aspect is discussed in a little publicized letter from von Neumann to Norbert Wiener, quoted in the recent biography by Masani [22]. Von Neumann suggests the study of viruses as a better starting point than neural nets. However, the idea that intelligence is likely to be understood through an appreciation of evolutionary mechanisms remains unchallenged.

III. CONTINUITY

A great deal of confusion can be attributed to a curious reluctance to recognize the importance of *continuity* in intelligence [23-27]. The kind of continuity that is important is not that of the differential calculus, but rather continuity "in the large," as implicit in extrapolation, interpolation, and ranking of values. As Lenat [19] points out, evolution depends on such continuity, and this indicates its strong relevance to the present discussion. The topic has also been discussed by MacKay [28] and as *heuristic connection* by Minsky (see ref. 1).

A. Obvious Continuity

Continuity enters in simple way into motor control and various regulatory functions. These are not usually considered to be manifestations of intelligence, even though the human capacity for acquiring manual skill by practice has not been imitated in artifacts. Continuity also enters in a fairly obvious way into any form of pattern classification, since there has to be some criterion of similarity according to which any pair of patterns belonging to the same class scores more highly than does a pair from distinct classes.

It is easy to feel that the current successes of neural computing techniques, in practice, stem from their exploitation of rather obvious continuous criteria. A deeper understanding of intelligent processes requires examination of the evolutionary transition from obvious continuity to more subtle forms.

B. Hidden Continuity

There is a widespread assumption that thinking is essentially "logical," in the sense that it manipulates discrete concepts without regard to the continuous aspects that allow interpolation, extrapolation, and ranking. The evolutionary view suggests that, on the contrary, "intelligence" has evolved as an extension of these continuous regulatory processes, and continuity still plays an essential part in it.

The importance of continuity is indirectly acknowledged in recent discussions of *fuzzy sets and systems* [29,30], where reference is made to *linguistic variables*. It has also been argued [31,32] that the formulation of the argument in these discussions is misleading from the evolutionary point of view. The usual approach is to introduce the idea of a *fuzzy set* as fundamental, and to relate this later to the idea of a *linguistic variable*. This is because the emphasis tends to be on *uncertainty* rather than *continuity* as such, and because the thinking is influenced by the persistent prejudice that intelligence must be based on "logic" as commonly understood.

From the evolutionary viewpoint, it would seem to be more useful to regard the *linguistic variables* as fundamental. In fact, the appreciation of new continuous variables to be evaluated probably should be seen as a form of concept formation at least as important as that of discrete yes/no concepts. Since it is useful to apply these ideas to prelinguistic evolutionary development, the choice of term is rather unfortunate; a better defining adjective might have been chosen from *relevant, significant, heuristic, interesting,* or *worthy*.

Once a new variable has been accepted as *relevant*, one or more fuzzy concepts are immediately suggested by application of the heuristic rule stressed by Lenat [19]:

Examine extreme cases.

For most practical purposes, the implications of the evolutionary viewpoint are not greatly different from those of standard *fuzzy* theory. However, the evolutionary argument differs in acknowledging the value of *relevant* (or *linguistic*, except that they can arise prelinguistically) *variables* even where these do not correspond to important *fuzzy concepts* in the accepted sense.

The distinction is important in considering the evolution of the important manifestations of *hidden continuity* effective in analogical reasoning [27,28]. According to the evolutionary argument, inferences based purely on "logic," as implemented in *expert systems*, must fail to exploit certain of the brain's "clever tricks" and the failure cannot be remedied by "fuzzification" alone.

IV. SUCCINCTNESS

There is no doubt that discrete yes/no concepts are important — the argument is that regulatory activity, concerned largely with continuous variables, is more primitive. It is important to consider the steps by which largely conceptual processing evolved from the more primitive kind. The continuous aspects of conceptual thinking can then be seen as a genetic legacy.

The development can be seen as part of a general tendency to find *succinct* representations [17]. The term *succinct* was first used in the AI context by Banerji [33] and has been employed in a specific context by Rothenberg [34]. A great deal of relevant discussion appears in the early work of Gordon Pask [35].

A. Concept of a Concept

The evolution of conceptual thinking from essentially regulative processing can be epitomized as evolution of the *concept of a concept* [18]. The tendency to operate in terms of concepts is a general principle which, once evolved, is retained only if it proves useful. All concepts are subjected to a similar survival criterion.

B. Wandering Correlators

Most theories about self-organization in neural nets specify conditions under which the strength or *weight* of connections should be modified, and these are readily extended to give conditions for the establishment of new connections where none had existed. Usually the condition can be expressed as a level of correlation between activity on the two sides of the actual or proposed connection.

Since the number of potential connections is enormous, it is unlikely to be feasible to compute all potentially relevant correlation levels all the time. Instead, there can be some kind of *wandering correlator* [26], sampling pairs of signal points either at random or under the guidance of heuristics yet to be discovered.

Mobile elements of this sort are a feature of many proposals for self-organizing networks, including that of Buller [36].

The operation of *wandering correlators* could result in improved *succinctness*. In an extreme case, a section of net might come to compute a function that is redundant because it corresponds exactly to one already available at another point in the net. It is not difficult to visualize pruning mechanisms that would simplify the net once the correspondence had been detected by a *wandering correlator*. Principles determining pruning of networks and other adaptive changes in connectivity are best described under the heading of *significance feedback*.

V. SIGNIFICANCE FEEDBACK

Self-organization in networks requires a mechanism to preserve pathways and computing elements whose outputs are, in some sense, useful to an overall goal. Operation of the mechanism requires appropriate feedback, and the term *significance feedback* was coined by Andrew [37,38]. In a simple form such feedback is implicit in the computation of *worth* in a *pandemonium* [39]. In recent years the idea has reemerged under the name of *back-propagation*, or *error propagation*, as discussed by Rumelhart, Hinton, and Williams in reference 6.

Marvin Minsky's discussion of the *credit assignment problem* in reference 1 clearly shows the need for some sort of *significance feedback* throughout a net, so the important question is not whether such feedback is operative, but what form it takes. The idea behind the discussions of *significance feedback* is that networks might incorporate identifiable pathways mediating this function. There has been little attempt to identify such pathways in living systems, but speculation is encouraged by the fact that mammalian nerves contain numerous fine fibers to which no other function has been ascribed. Experimental findings by Professor Pat Wall and his group [40] show that these fibers play *some* important role in neural organization.

In its simple ("scalar") form, *significance feedback* provides an indication of the *worth* of the information conveyed in an associated forward-going path. In its "vector" form it provides an indication of how the signal might have differed so as to have greater worth.

The general idea is capable of considerable elaboration. The worth of a forward-going signal is increased if it is accompanied by some means of assessing its reliability or importance. The importance of such "feedforward of significance" can be illustrated by McCulloch's analogy of a group of men hunting a bear. He uses this in introducing his principle of "redundancy of potential command" [41].

When one of a group of hunters actually sees the bear, he is likely to shout to the others in a tone of voice that indicates his confidence. He becomes, temporarily, the effective leader of the group. At least, he does if the others take him seriously — his feedforward of significance has probably been assessed by his fellows (as in the cautionary tale of the boy who cried "wolf") and given a low rating if he is overimaginative. The feedforward (tone of voice) indication is meant to facilitate the assessment of significance of the message conveyed in the shout. However, the feedforward indication is itself assessed by a nested *significance feedback* mechanism.

Such recursive operation of significance-indicating subnetworks appears to be a usual feature of biological adaptation. It is illustrated, though with reference to only a small depth of nesting, by the various discussions referred to here.

VI. CONCLUSION

This "tutorial" has indicated many more open problems than solutions, but in a tutorial survey that is probably no bad thing. I hope the point of view I have outlined is appropriate and conducive to further progress.

Time alone will tell whether the current revival of interest in neural computing stems from fresh insights, or whether the techniques will in due course be found to be of limited value, as was the case with the *perceptron* idea [42,43]. (The reference is meant to be the *simple perceptron* as treated by Minsky and Papert, and to which the famous training algorithm, with its associated convergence theorem, strictly applies. Without this restriction the term does not have a precise interpretation. Later developments of the principle are reviewed in the following two chapters, respectively by Roman Swiniarski and Constantine Manikopoulos.)

Whatever the outcome in the short term, longer term implications should not be forgotten (a comment that applies to the *perceptron* principle, also). The long-term significance has been indicated in Section II. Since the brain still has "clever tricks" to be discovered, there is a strong case for considering the evolution and nature of biological information processing, both in the context of neural nets and more widely.

This is not to deny the immediate practical value of neural computing, as emphasized, for example, by Aleksander [44,45] and by Kohonen [46]. Attention to continuous variates, as discussed in Section III, provides a way of integrating the different approaches. The current applications of neural computing tend to utilize the forms of continuity referred to as *obvious continuity*, manifested in pattern classification and regulatory tasks. To gain insight into the special capabilities of the brain, it is necessary to ask how the exploitation of obvious continuity has facilitated the evolution of systems exploiting the hidden kind.

REFERENCES

1. E. A. Feigenbaum and J. Feldman, eds., *Computers and Thought*, McGraw-Hill, New York, 1963.
2. R. Roska, in *Discrete Event Systems: Models and Applications* (P. Varaiya and A. B. Kurzhanski, eds.), Springer Verlag, Berlin, p. 225, 1988.
3. R. Forsyth and C. Naylor, *The Hitch-Hiker's Guide to Artificial Intelligence*, Chapman & Hall, London, 1985.
4. W. D. Hillis, *The Connection Machine*, MIT Press, Cambridge, MA, 1985.
5. *Proceedings of International Conference on Fifth-Generation Computer Systems 1988*, edited by ICOT, Ohmsha, Tokyo/Springer Verlag, Berlin, 1988.
6. D. E. Rumelhart, J. L. McClelland, and the PDP Research Group, *Parallel Distributed Processing*, MIT Press, Cambridge, MA, 1986.
7. G. E. Hinton and J. A. Anderson, eds., *Parallel Models of Associative Memory*, Erlbaum, Hillsdale, NJ, 1981.
8. G. Palm and A. Aerten, eds., *Brain Theory*, Springer Verlag, Berlin, 1986.
9. R. M. J. Cotterill, ed., *Computer Simulation in Brain Science*, University Press, Cambridge, 1988.
10. M. A. Arbib, *The Metaphorical Brain Vol. II, Neural Networks and Beyond*, Wiley, New York, 1989.
11. R. Pfeifer, Z. Schreter, F. Fogelman-Soulié, and L. Steels, eds., *Connectionism in Perspective*, North Holland, Amsterdam, 1989.
12. D. Marr, *Vision*, Freeman, San Francisco, 1982.
13. A. M. Andrew, in *Parallel Problem Solving from Nature*, (H.-P. Schwefel and R. Männer, eds.), Springer Verlag, Berlin, p. 254, 1991.
14. J. J. Hopfield, *Proc. Natl. Acad. Sci. USA*, 79: 2554 (1982).

15. M. Boden, in *Artificial Intelligence and Applied Cybernetics* (M. Ghosal, ed.), South Asian Publishers, New Delhi, p. 1, 1989.

16. A. M. Andrew, in *Improving the Human Condition — Quality and Stability in Social Systems* (R. F. Ericson, ed.), SGSR, Liouville/Springer Verlag, Berlin, p. 444, 1979.

17. A. M. Andrew, in *Applied General Systems Research* (G. J. Klir, ed.), Plenum Press, New York, p. 553, 1978.

18. A. M. Andrew, in *Applied Systems and Cybernetics* (G. E. Lasker, ed.), Pergamon Press, New York, p. 607, 1981.

19. D. B. Lenat, in *Machine Learning* (R. S. Michalski, J. G. Carbonell, and T. M. Mitchell, eds.), Springer Verlag, Berlin, p. 343, 1984.

20. W. L. Kilmer, W. S. McCulloch, and J. Blum, *Int. J. Man–Machine Stud.* *1*:279 (1969).

21. K. L. Bellman and L. J. Goldberg, *Am. J. Physiol.,* *246*:R915 (1984).

22. P. R. Masani, *Norbert Wiener 1894–1964*, Birkhäuser Verlag, Basel, 1990.

23. P. S. Churchland, *Neurophilosophy — Toward a Unified Science of the Mind/Brain*, MIT Press, Cambridge, MA, 1986.

24. A. M. Andrew, in *Cybernetics and Systems Research* (R. Trappl, ed.), North Holland, Amsterdam, p. 19, 1982.

25. A. M. Andrew, *Int. J. Syst. Res. Inf. Sci.* *2*:143 (1987).

26. A. M. Andrew, *Self-Organizing Systems*, Gordon & Breach, London, 1989.

27. A. M. Andrew, *Continuous Heuristics — The Prelinguistic Basis of Intelligence*, Ellis Horwood, Chichester, 1990.

28. D. M. MacKay, in *Mechanisation of Thought Processes*, Her Majesty's Stationery Office, London, p. 55, 1959.

29. L. A. Zadeh, *Int. J. General Syst.,* *17*:129 (1990).

30. W. Pedrycz, *Fuzzy Control and Fuzzy Systems*, Research Studies, Taunton, MA/ Wiley, New York, 1989.

31. A. M. Andrew, *Kybernetes,* *19*(4):65 (1990).

32. A. M. Andrew, *Int. J. General Syst.,* *18*(2):175 (1990).

33. R. B. Banerji, *Theory of Problem Solving*, Elsevier, New York, 1969.

34. D. Rothenberg, in *Formal Aspects of Cognitive Processes* (T. Storer and D. Winter, eds.), Springer Verlag, Berlin, p. 72, 1975.

35. G. Pask, *Information Processing 1962* (IFIP Proceedings), North Holland, Amsterdam, p. 482, 1962.

36. A. Buller, "*A Subneural Network for Highly Distributed Processing*," submitted (Technical University of Gdansk) for Congress.

37. A. M. Andrew, "Significance Feedback in Neural Nets," Report of Biological Computer Laboratory, University of Illinois, 1965.

38. A. M. Andrew, in *Advances in Cybernetics and Systems Research, Vol. 1* (F. Pichler and R. Trappl, eds.), Hemisphere, London, p. 244, 1973.

39. O. G. Selfridge, in *Mechanisation of Thought Processes*, Her Majesty's Stationery Office, London, p. 511, 1959.

40. P. D. Wall, M. Fitzgerald, and C. J. Woolf, *Exp. Neurol.* *78*:425 (1982).

41. W. S. McCulloch, in *Self-Organizing Systems* (M. C. Yovits and S. Cameron, eds.), Pergamon Press, New York, p. 262, 1960.

42. F. Rosenblatt, *Principles of Neurodynamics*, Spartan Books, New York, 1961.
43. M. Minsky and S. Papert, *Perceptrons*, MIT Press, Cambridge, MA, 1969.
44. I. Aleksander and P. Burnett, *Reinventing Man*, Kogan Page, London, 1983.
45. I. Aleksander and H. Morton, *An Introduction to Neural Computing*, Chapman & Hall, London, 1990.
46. T. Kohonen, *Associative Memory*, Springer Verlag, Berlin, 1977.

13
Introduction to Neural Networks

Roman Swiniarski   San Diego State University, San Diego, California

I. ARTIFICIAL NEURAL NETWORKS: INTRODUCTION

Advances in the technology of very large scale integrated (VLSI) systems have led to greatly revitalized interest in artificial neural networks. The computational capabilities of neural networks, as asynchronous, massively parallel distributed processing systems, have been a great inspiration in designing novel artificial neural networks, which have been applied successfully in pattern recognition, classification, signal processing, adaptive control, robotics, vision, and so on.

By analogy to the human brain, an artificial neural network (hereafter called "neural network") is considered to be a system of many highly interconnected, simple "neuronlike" adaptive elements that interact using weighted connections. Each element (neuron) output (for some dynamic neuron just internal state) has a certain activity level that is the function of inputs received from the other units and the strength of the connection of the neuron with the given input (represented by the connection weight). For dynamic neurons, the output is a function of the input and the internal state (which stores the history of previous activity). The many different models of neural networks depend on the model of a simple neuron and the mechanisms of processing (e.g., synchronous or asynchronous). Some of models (Rumelhart and McClelland, 1986; Widrow and Winter, 1988) assume a perceptron or adaline-like type of static, memoryless model of neurons. Others, for example, Hopfield–Grossberg dynamic models (Hopfield, 1982, 1984; Cohen and Grossberg, 1983), assume that the simple neuron can be represented by a simple dynamic element (with internal memory and of course internal state) described by a simple, first-order nonlinear differential equation. The primary output of the neuron (by analogy to the activation rate of the neuron) is passed by the "squashing" nonlinear function (output limiter), which produces the final output of the neuron. This output (logically single) can be then duplicated and can be connected to the input of the another neurons.

Two major groups of neural networks are frequently considered. First, the static, feedforward neural networks with static, memoryless neurons, have found great and promising applications, particularly in pattern recognition and signal processing (Rumelhart and McClelland, 1986; Lipmann, 1987). The second type of dynamic neural network (Hopfield, 1982, 1984), with dynamic neurons, has been applied as a new massively parallel technique of solving hard, NP-complete combinatorial optimization problems (e.g., the traveling salesman problem). These two types of popular neural networks are discussed in Sections II and III.

II. STATIC, FEEDFORWARD NEURAL NETWORKS

To date the static, multilayered, feedforward back-propagation neural networks have evoked great interest mainly in classification and other patternlike recognition processes (Werbos, 1974; Rumelhart and McClelland, 1986; Lipmann, 1987). We will discuss the most frequently used back-propagation learning rule of neural networks (Werbos, 1974; Rumelhart and McClelland, 1986).

A. Neural Network Architecture

The static (memoryless), feedforward back-propagation neural network (Fig. 1) is considered to be a multilayered system of interconnected simple perceptron-or adaline-type, neuronlike processing elements, with weighted interconnections. This network has an input layer (on the bottom), where the input vector is presented to the network. Then the next intermediate layers follow, ending with the top output layer producing the output of the neural network. Connections within a layer or from higher to lower layers are forbidden (i.e., there is no feedback present in this network); however, connections can skip some intermediate layers. The input and the all intermediate layers, except the output layers, are called "hidden layers," since unlike the output layers, their outputs are not directly "observable," and in the training session direct knowledge about their desired output is not given explicitly. The processing of information by static, feedforward back-propagation neural networks is generally defined as fully concurrent and asynchronous. However, for some simulation purposes it is assumed that neural networks process information sequentially, layerwise, from the bottom (input) layer to the output layer. In this processing scheme it is assumed that all elements within a given layer process input signals and produce output in parallel

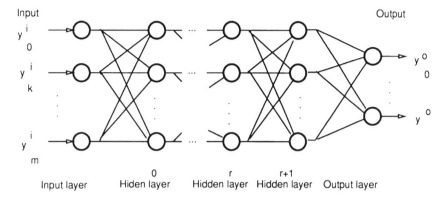

Figure 1   Feedforward neural network

(asynchronously). In some models the input layer is considered simply to receive the input vector (linear unit), but generally we can assume that this layer also performs processing.

In some applications (pattern recognition) the inputs to the neural networks are assumed to be binary, while other application (signal processing) assume analog inputs. The intermediate output of the jth neuronlike adaptive element (Fig. 2) is described by the following linear function (weighted sum of inputs):

$$x_j = \sum_{i=1}^{l} w_{ji} y_i \ + \ w_{j0} y_{j0} \tag{1}$$

where w_{ji} ($i = 1, \dots, l$) are the weights associated with the inputs y_i ($i - 1, \dots, l$) to the jth neurons (outputs of the previous layer neurons), and the term $w_{j0} y_{j0}$ (here we will assume that $x_{j0} = 1$) play the role of threshold (Widrow and Winter, 1988).

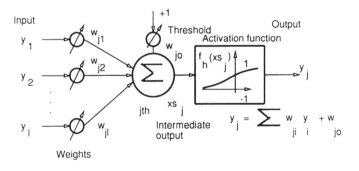

Figure 2   A neuronlike element.

Here "bias" (or threshold) is defined in the same way as a regular neuron's input. This provides a flexible way to teach thresholding elements, also. The total output y_i of the neuron considered is obtained by passing the intermediate output x_j by some "squashing" nonlinear element, implementing some saturation nonlinear function $f_h(x_j)$ (by analogy to the neuron activation rate). The two types of nonlinear saturation function $f_h(x_j)$ are mostly considered in neural network architectures. For some classification processing purposes, the saturation function is considered to be a hard limiter, defined in the following way:

$$y_j = f_h\left(\sum_{i=1}^{l} w_{ji}y_i + w_{j0}y_{j0}\right) \tag{2}$$

$$y_j = \begin{cases} +1 & \text{class 1} \ (when \ \sum_{i=1}^{l} w_{ji}y_i + w_{j0}y_{j0} > 0) \\ -1 & \text{class 2} \ (otherwise) \end{cases} \tag{3}$$

Frequently the saturation function $f_h(x_j)$ is considered to be a differentiable sigmoid-type function (smoothed version of step function), for example, a logistic function (Fig. 2)

$$y_j = f_h(x_j) = \frac{1}{1 + e^{-x_j}} = \frac{1}{1 + \exp\left(-\sum_{i=1}^{l} w_{ji}y_i + w_{j0}y_{j0}\right)} \tag{4}$$

or a hyperbolic tangent function. We can easily find that a simple neuronlike element with hard limiter can perform linear classification processing. The input vector (input pattern) can be classified into two distinct classes: class 1 ($y_j = -1$) and class 2 ($y_j = 1$). The classifying hyperplane (which classifies analog or binary input vector into classes 1 and 2), corresponding to the critical threshold condition (when the analog intermediate output of neuron is zero), can be easily found as $\sum_{i=1}^{l} w_{ji}y_i + w_{j0}y_{j0} = 0$. The more complicated nonlinear classification can be obtained by multiple-neuron, multiple-layered networks (Widrow and Winter, 1988; Lipmann, 1987). The neuronlike elements with smooth sigmoid-type saturation element function can be used more flexibly for classification as well as for nonlinear mapping with the analog outputs, which is important in such applications as adaptive control or signal processing (Rumelhart and McClelland, 1986). In the foregoing description of neuronlike elements, we used the term "adaptive neuronlike elements." The term "adaptive" reflects the possibility of tuning (adapting) the neuron weights, during the learning session, to properly perform the desired processing of input signals (e.g., classification of input patterns).

B. Learning Techniques for Neural Networks

The neural network, as a system of highly interconnected adaptive neuronlike elements, can be trained to accomplish the particular processing of input signals (e.g., for input pattern recognition). The architecture of the network (i.e., structure of layers; neuron type, connections, and strength) determines the network processing capabilities. For the network topological structure that has been determined, the training can provide a way of adapting the interconnection strengths to perform the required task better. The interconnection weights represent some kind of "memory" (even though the static feedforward network is a memoryless system). The network can be trained to accomplish a given input signal processing task. The learning procedures for neural networks fall into two broad major categories: supervised (Rumelhart and McClelland, 1986) and unsupervised (Widrow et al., 1973) learning. The most popular and very natural technique, called supervised learning, is based on the existence of a teacher, which specifies the desired output for the given individual input to the network (input pattern). the training case c is defined as the input–desired output pair:

$$C_c = \{y_{i,c}^I, d_{j,c}\} \quad (i = 1, 2, \ldots, m; \quad j = 1, 2, \ldots, n, \quad c = 1, 2, \ldots, s) \tag{5}$$

where $y^I \in R^m$ denotes the network's input vector [with the elements $y_{i,c}^I$ and $d_{j,c}$ ($j = 1, 2, \ldots, m$)] the network's desired (ideal) output for the given input from the training case C_c. The output of the network is described by vector $y_c^o \in R^n$ with elements $y_{j,c}^o$ ($j = 1, 2, \ldots, n$). The training set

$$TR = \{(y_{1,i,c}^I, d_{j,c}); (i = 1, 2, \ldots, m; \quad j = 1, 2, \ldots, n, \quad c = 1, 2, \ldots, s\} \tag{6}$$

contains the s training cases C_c.

The teacher, which can be considered to be a nonlinear mathematical formula, control law, or human expert decision, determines the desired output for a given input. The major advantage of neural networks consists of their generalization properties. The generalization, potentially, may guarantee the correct action of networks even for input patterns for which no training has occurred. Of course the quality of the training technique and the training set is crucial in achieving the high generalization feature of trained networks. Training constructs the specific interconnection strengths (weights) that capture regularity in the input signals.

The other important stream of learning algorithms (Widrow et al., 1973) assumes no ideal teacher for each training case. This, biologically very natural, unsupervised learning deals with situations in which the desired output is not known a priori, or the desired output is known after a series of inputs. This difficult learning technique is under intensive research and can create a surprisingly strong methodology for the training of neural networks to act in unknown or variable environments, without the precise goal and structure of control algorithms (Widrow et al., 1973).

1. Error Back-Propagation Learning

In a form of supervised learning that has gained great popularity recently, the case input is provided to the network input, and the real network output is computed and compared with the desired output known from the training case. The error then can be back-propagated from the last output layer of neurons to the neurons in the intermediate hidden layer. This technique is based on the known gradient descent based LMS (least mean square of errors) error minimalization procedure (Werbos, 1983; Rumelhart and McClelland, 1986; Widrow and Winter, 1988). The main difficulty arising in the application of the LMS technique to neural networks lies in the fact that only output layer neuron errors are given explicitly, as these neurons are fully observable, and desired output is predefined by the teacher in the training case C_c. In this technique the output layer neurons are back-propagated sequentially to the previous layer neurons, until the input layer neurons are reached. The error terms, obtained this way for each neuron, then are used to adopt the weights of the connections associated with the technique called "back-propagation error" learning (Rumelhart and McClelland, 1986), which can be described briefly as follows. The goal of training is to find the set of weights that ensure that for each input the network output will be the same or sufficiently close to the desired ideal output. A measure that describes the imperfection of networks with a given set of weights for all s training cases in the given training set is given by the following error performance criterion:

$$E = \frac{1}{2} \sum_{c=1}^{c=s} \sum_{j=1}^{n} (d_{j,c} - y_{j,c}^o)^2 \qquad (7)$$

where $y_{j,c}^o$ is actual network's output for the input from case C_c, and $d_{j,c}$ is the desired output for this case.

Our goal of finding the set of weights guaranteeing minimization of output errors is the classical static minimization problem with the criterion of total network error E. To minimize the criterion E, the gradient descent method can be adopted. To apply this method, we have to find the partial derivative of E with respect to each weight in the network (i.e., the contribution of each weight to the total error) $\partial E / \partial w_{ji}$ and find the adjustment of weights as a function of this term, for example, $\Delta w_{ji} = -\eta \partial E / \partial w_{ji}$. For all training sets this is simply the sum of the partial derivatives for each case (for a batch learning technique). However, in some implementations of the error back-propagation learning method, the partial derivatives $\partial E / \partial w_{ji}$ are computed sequentially for each training case C_c, and weights are then adjusted by a slight amount related to the error condition of the case.

Network error can be minimized by proper training sessions. Each session starts from arbitrary initial values of the weights (set randomly). Then these values are systematically changed—for example, after each training case—according to the weight adaptation rule. Computation of partial derivatives $\partial E^c / \partial w_{ji}$ requires evaluation of $\partial E^c / \partial y_j$, which creates some difficulties for neurons in the hidden layers (for which the desired outputs are not given explicitly in the training case). Using the chain rule of partial derivatives, we can easily find for the output layer neurons:

$$\frac{\partial E^c}{\partial w_{ji}} = \frac{\partial E^c}{\partial x_j} \frac{\partial x_j}{\partial w_{ji}} \tag{8}$$

where the jth output layer neuron error term is defined as follows:

$$\delta_o^j = -\frac{\partial E^c}{\partial x_j} = (d_j - y_j^o) y_j^o (1 - y_j^o); \quad \frac{\partial x_j}{\partial E^c / \partial w_{ji}} = y_i \tag{9}$$

where y_i is the input to the jth output neuron from the previous ith hidden layer neuron, amplified by weights w_{ji}.

The error term for the jth neuron in the jth layer is thus given by

$$\delta_r^j = -\frac{\partial E^c}{\partial x_j} = -\frac{\partial E^c}{\partial y_j} \frac{\partial y_j}{\partial x_j} = \left[\sum_{k=1}^{Nr} \delta_k^{r+1} w_{kj} \right] y_j (1 - y_j) \tag{10}$$

where index k denotes all N_{r+1} neurons of higher layer $r + 1$ connected to the jth neurons of layer r, which are under considerations.

Having error terms for given training case computed for the all neurons in the network, and the real outputs of neurons, the adaptation of weights associated with each neuron can be realized. One of the most frequently used weight adaptation technique relies on the following formula:

$$w_{ji}(t + 1) = w_{ji}(t) + \eta \delta_j y_j + \beta (w_{ji}(t) - w_{ji}(t - 1)) \tag{11}$$

where the term η is the learning procedure tuning parameter, and β (momentum term) is the exponential decay tuning factor from the range [0, 1]. The size of training set, the tuning parameters η and β, as well as the initial estimate of weights, are selected experimentally. No formal proof of error back-propagation convergence exists. The achievement of local minima is possible. Current research on feedforward neural networks focuses on the problem of optimal network architectures, fast and efficient (escaping from local minima) training techniques, and generalization.

III. HOPFIELD DYNAMIC NEURAL NETWORK

A. Introduction

The Hopfield-type dynamic neural networks have a long history as analog computers constituted as electrical networks consisting of interconnected amplifiers. The massively parallel, asynchronous analog form of processing has been recently revitalized with the hope of practical VLSI implementation as universal electronic chips. As analog computers have been widely used to model dynamic systems, the Hopfield neural networks have emphasized their ability to solve hard optimization problems. The Hopfield dynamic neural networks (Hopfield, 1982, 1985) are based on the paradigm of the natural tendency of evolving dynamic systems toward the internal states associated with the minimal energy defined in the system. Computations by dynamic network, being in fact an analog electrical circuit, are carried on truly concurrently and asynchronously.

1. Architecture and Dynamics

The simple neuronlike element in dynamic neural networks represents from the functional point of view a simple first-order continuous time dynamic system with an internal feedback and one internal state $x_i(t)$. The neuron output is defined by the continuous nonlinear activation function of its internal state $y_i(t) = f_h(x_i(t))$.

In Hopfield neural networks the simple neuron is implemented by electronic amplifier, with additional circuitry providing integration of input currents. The output of amplifier $y_i(t)$ is saturated, and it is defined rather in the category of static input–output relations of amplifier characteristics, mainly as a function $y_i(t) = f_h(x_i(t))$, where $x_i(t)$, denotes the amplifier input voltage (internal state of neuron) and y_i denotes the amplifier output voltage.

The N neurons constituting a network (Fig. 3) are interconnected (generally fully) via the weights (modeling a synaptic connection). The output of the neurons is fed back to their inputs and to the inputs of the other neurons. The environment influences the networks by special control input signals I_i. It is also assumed that there is a way to set the initial internal states of all neurons (initial state of the neural network).

The following model (Fig. 3) describes the neuron's motion in the time domain

$$C_i \frac{dx_i(t)}{dt} = -\frac{1}{R_i} x_i(t) + \sum_{j=1}^{N} w_{ij} y_j(t) + I_i \qquad (12)$$

with output signal defined as $y_i(t) = f_h(x_i(t))$. In equation (12), R_i is a parallel combination of neuron resistance ρ_i and is entirely connected to the neuron resistors R_{ij} ($j = 1, 2, \ldots, N$) (modeling the synaptic strength)

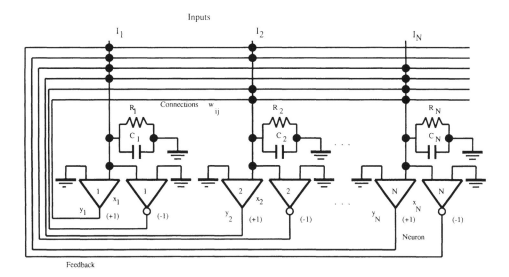

Figure 3 A dynamic Hopfield neural network.

$$\frac{1}{R_1} = \frac{1}{\varrho_i} + \sum_{j=1}^{N} \frac{1}{R_{ij}} \qquad (13)$$

For simplicity we will assume that the activation output functions f_h are the same for all neurons, that the basic electrical circuitry for the neurons is the same (i.e., $R_i = R$ and $C_i = C$), and that the neurons are current independent. Dividing the foregoing model of neurons by C and redefining the notations $w_{ij}y_i = w_{ij}/C$, $I_i = I_i/C$, we can obtain the following model of neuron motion:

$$\frac{dx_i(t)}{dt} = -\frac{1}{\tau}x(t) + \sum_{j=1}^{N} w_{ij}y_i(t) + I_i; \quad x_i(t_0) = \xi_i \qquad (14)$$

with a time constant of neuron $\tau = RC$ and output function $y_i(t) = f_h(x_i(t))$. The output activation function is usually considered to be a sigmoid "smooth" function (Fig. 4), for example, or an offset hyperbolic tangent with a "temperature" factor modeling the steepness of characteristic

$$y_i(t) = f_h(x_i(t)) = \frac{1}{2}\left[1 + \tan h\left(\frac{x_i(t)}{T}\right)\right] \qquad (15)$$

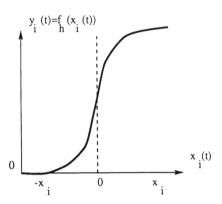

Figure 4 Output activation function.

In many applications it is assumed that the connection matrix w_{ij} $(i, j = 1, 2, \ldots, N)$ is symmetric $(w_{ij} = w_{ji})$ and that it has on a main diagonal zeros $(w_{ii} = 0)$ that describe the situation when there is no feedback from the neuron output y_i to its input.

Strength of connection (a synapse) is implemented by a conductance w_{ij} which connects one of the two jth neurons' output y_i to the input of the ith neuron (feedback). This connection is made with resistor $R_{ij} = 1/w_{ij}$. If the synapse is excitatory $(w_{ij} > 0)$, this resistor is connected to the normal output (+1) of the jth neuron. For the inhibitory connection (inhibitory synapse $w_{ij} < 0$), the connection is made to the inverted output of the jth neuron. The weight matrix w_{ij} $(i, j = 1, 2, \ldots, N)$ defines connectivity among the neurons of the networks. Some synaptic connections may be set to zero, to model lack of influence from the output of a given jth neuron to the activity of the ith neuron ("no feedback connection"). The total (net) input current to any ith neuron (and thus input voltage) is the sum of currents flowing through the set of resistors connecting its input to the outputs of the other neurons.

For the "high gain" limit of output function, the neural network will go to the stable states x^s (and thus outputs y^s) corresponding to the energy minima. These stable states will occur only for the network states that produce output signals at the 2^N "corners" of the space $[y_{i,min}, y_{i.max}]$, $(i = 1, 2, \ldots, N)$.

2. Analog Computation by Dynamic Neural Network

The dynamic neural network may be used to compute the solution of a specific temporal pattern processing or "hard" optimization problem by:

1. Choosing connectivity matrix w_{ij} $(i = 1, 2, \ldots, N)$ and input bias currents I_i $(i = 1, 2, \ldots, N)$, specific for the computational problem and designed through ana-

lyzing the energy function corresponding to the problem and resulting stable states, providing a local minima of the energy function.
2. Implementing the network with designed connectivity weights and the input bias current (in VLSI circuits, analog machine, or digital computer simulation program).
3. Running the network starting from an initial internal state.

The properly designed network will evolve (autonomously) from the initial states $x(t_o)$ or corresponding $y(t_o)$ to the final stable states x^s (observed as the saturated outputs y^s in the corner of 2^N hypercube). These stable states y^s are considered to be the solution of the problem. Normally, these states are selected using the binary code of the final result.

3. Energy of the Dynamic Neural Network

Recall again the model of neuron dynamics (constituted with the amplifier). A Liapunov function for the neural network may be defined as a scalar energy function of the neural network. For amplifiers with a continuous sigmoid activation function we can write the following Liapunov function:

$$E = -\frac{1}{2} \sum_{i=1}^{N} \sum_{j=1}^{N} w_{ij} y_i(t) y_i(t) + \sum_{i=1}^{N} \left(\frac{1}{R_i} \right) \int_0^{y_i(t)} f_h^{-1}(y)dy - \sum_{i=1}^{N} y_i I_i \quad (16)$$

The second term in this energy equation represents an energy associated with the internal amplifier activity with amplifier resistance R_i. This term may be neglected for the hard limiter at the output or for the "high gain operation region" of the amplifier.

4. Evolution of the Network Toward the Stable State Corresponding to Minimum Energy in the System

The neural network will evolve toward the states guaranteeing the minimum energy (possible local) of the system. The time derivative of the network's Liapunov function for the symmetric synaptic connectivity ($w_{ij} = w_{ji}, i = 1, 2, \ldots, N$) leads us to the conclusion, fundamental for the dynamic neural network, that $dE/dt \leq 0$; $dE/dt = 0 \rightarrow dy_i(t)/dt = 0$ for all i. It means that the time evolution of the network is a motion in the state space (trajectory) that seeks out minima in the energy function E and comes to a stop at such states (stable state, no movement of state $[dy_i(t)]/dt = 0$). This is a fundamental conclusion for the dynamic neural network. The network will evolve to the stable states located in the corners of an N-hypercube limited by the asymptotes of neuron activation functions, and these states give the minimum energy in the network.

We see that stable states located in the corners of an N-hypercube will require, instead, "binary" coding of the computational "input data" and the analog computation "results." We can model the desired stable network states, providing the appropriate values for the connection weights. These values may be derived by analyzing the performance criteria of a computational problem and comparing these values to the values in the standard network energy function. This is a paradigm of analog computation.

B. Application of Hopfield Dynamic Neural Network in Combinatorial Optimization

Dynamic neural networks tend to the "binary" stable states that which correspond to the network energy function minima, and this is the basis analog computation. The stable states (results) may be "programmed" by selecting the weight values, depending on the computational problem. A dynamic neural network with specially selected connection matrix w_{ij} and input bias current I_i ($i, j = 1, 2, \ldots, N$) can be used to compute solutions to specific optimization of mapping problems.

1. The "Programming" of the Dynamic Neural Network

Let us assume that the optimization computational problem is precisely defined. The optimization computational problem first must be coded in a form suitable for neural network processing. This frequently requires finding the binary code for the input data and the result.

Together with the coding phase, the formulation of the example optimization performance criteria must be carried on. This phase requires formulating the optimization performance index with respect to the selected technique of "binary" coding of the computational result. Comparison of this performance criterion with the standard energy function in the network allows us to define the specific weight values, which guarantees the convergence of the network to the stable states corresponding to the optimal solution.

2. The Traveling Salesman Problem

The traveling salesman problem belongs to the class of "hard" combinatorial optimization problems. From the point of view of computational complexity, it is NP-complete computational. Computational complexity depends exponentially on the size of the problem (number of cities). The traveling salesman optimization problem may be mathematically formulated as follows. We are given a finite set of n cities (denoted later by X and Y) $CI = \{A, B, C, \ldots\}$ and the set of pairwise distances between cities $DI = \{d_{AB}, d_{AC}, \ldots, d_{BC}, d_{BD}, \ldots\}$. The distances between the cities also may be represented by an $n \times n$ square matrix, rows and columns representing the cities, and the elements being the distances. The cities and the distances between them form the optimization system and the parameters.

The goal of optimization is to find a closed tour that starts from one city, visits each city once, returns to the starting city, and has the shortest total path length possible among all the paths that might have been chosen. The optimization performance criterion (scalar value) is the length of tour path consisting some sequence in which the cities are visited. The solution of the traveling salesman problem is the ordered list (sequence) of the cities visited in the tour that provides shortest of all tour paths.

Binary coding of the solution relevant for neural processing. The solution of the traveling salesman problem, an ordered list of cities visited in sequence, must be "binary coded" into stable states of the neural network. Hopfield and Tank (1985) have proposed a two-dimensional scheme (square matrix) for the binary coding of a solution in which a row represents one city and a column (position) represents the position of this city in the optimal tour sequence. The neural network will consist of $n \times n$ neurons. Physically our network will consist of course one layer, but logically it will be considered to be a square matrix $y_{x,i}$, $X \in \{A, B, C, \ldots\}$; $i = 1, 2, \ldots, n$. Each city will be represented by n network neurons (one row of the matrix) $y_x = (y_{x,1}, y_{x,2}, \ldots, y_{x,n})$. The final location (in the optimal sequence) of any individual city is specified by the output states of a set of n neurons in the corresponding row. The coding scheme for the traveling salesman problem is quite natural, since any individual city can be in any one of the n possible positions in the tour list (sequence).

For the legible tour we should have one 1 in each row and only one 1 in each column, since only one city may be placed in the sequence position represented by column. Of course the legible tour should have n 1's in the neuron matrix.

A legible tour may be presented as the following neuron state array (e.g., for a 5-city problem)

	1	2	3	4	5
A	0	1	0	0	0
B	0	0	0	1	0
C	1	0	0	0	0
D	0	0	0	0	1
E	0	0	1	0	0

The array above says that the tour starts from the city C, since the row representing this city has 1 on the first position. Then the tour goes from C to city A, since row A has 1 on the second position, from A to E, from E to B, and from B to D. The last part of tour is from the city D to C (starting city). From the legible tours, we should find that having shortest path length.

The design of the energy function. We must find the energy function (and thus the necessary weights) of the network in which the lowest energy-stable state corresponds to the shortest path. Comparing this energy function with the standard energy functions of n^2 neuron neural networks, we can find the required values of the weights. The energy function design procedure may be divided logically into two phases. In this first phase, we should provide an energy function term guaranteeing that stable states corresponding to the legible tours will be obtained. In the second phase, we must include a term guaranteeing that from the legible stable states those providing the shortest path will provide the minimum value of energy in the network (our solution).

To elicit the stable, legible states and the states among the $n!$ legible states that will have shortest path, thus providing a minima for this term, the following energy function is considered:

$$E^{TSP} = E_{123} + E_4 = \frac{\alpha}{2} \sum_{X=X_i}^{X_n} \sum_{i=1}^{n} \sum_{j+1, i! = j}^{n} y_{X_i} y_{X_j}$$

$$+ \frac{\beta}{2} \sum_{i=1}^{n} \sum_{X=X_i}^{X_n} \sum_{Y=Y_i, Y \neq X}^{Y_n} y_{X_i} y_{Y_j} \tag{17}$$

$$+ \frac{\gamma}{2} \left(\sum_{X=X_i}^{X_n} \sum_{i=1}^{n} y_{X_i} - n \right)^2 + \frac{\zeta}{2} \sum_{X=X_i}^{X_n} \sum_{Y=Y_i, Y \neq X}^{Y_n} \sum_{i=1}^{n} d_{XY} y_{X_i} (y_{Y_{i+1}} + y_{Y_{i-1}}) \tag{18}$$

The first three terms in the energy equation favor the legible states and last term the shortest path.

For the sufficiently large α, β, γ, all low energy states of the networks described by the energy function above will belong to the legible states of a valid tour. The total energy of that state will be the length of the tour (since first three terms will be 0 for the legible stable states) and the states with the shortest path will be the lowest energy states.

Design of the connection weights. Having a final energy function E^{TSP} for the traveling salesman neural network, we can now find the corresponding connection matrix (values of the connection weights) equalizing this energy equation with the standard equation

$$E = -\frac{1}{2} \sum_{i=1}^{N} \sum_{j=1}^{N} w_{ij} y_i(t) y_j(t) - \sum_{i=1}^{N} y_i I_i \tag{19}$$

for the energy in the $N = n \times n$ neuron neural network. Using a "city row"–"position column" matrix coding technique for the traveling salesman neural network architecture, we can find the following connection weights:

$$w_{Xi, Yj} = -\alpha \delta_{XY} (1 - \delta_{ij}) - \beta \delta_{ij} (1 - \delta_{XY}) - \gamma - \zeta d_{XY} (\delta_{j,i+1} + \delta_{j,i-1}) \tag{20}$$

where the Kronecker delta is defined as follows

$$\delta_{ij} = \begin{cases} 1 & \text{if} \quad i = j \\ 0 & \text{otherwise} \end{cases} \qquad \delta_{XY} = \begin{cases} 1 & \text{if} \quad X = Y \\ 0 & \text{otherwise} \end{cases} \qquad (21)$$

We can see that each required connection from the output of some neuron to the input of another neuron contributes to the total value of the input, with amounts proportional to the values of $\alpha, \beta, \gamma,$ or ζ and neuron output. These amounts constitute the final connection weights. Neural network design thus is ready to solve the traveling salesman problem for given "input data" embedded in the weight values. The network will start with some initial internal state and will evolve (autonomously) toward the stable state in the corners of $n \times n$ hypercube. This stable state is our solution—it represents the binary-coded tour (sequence of visited cities) with the shortest path.

To solve the problem for a different set of cities and a different distance matrix, we would simply expand the network and modify the weights.

REFERENCES

Anderson, J. A., and Rosenfeld, E. eds. *Neurocomputing: Foundation of Research.* Cambridge, MA: MIT Press.

Cohen, M. A., and Grossberg, S. (1983). "Absolute Stability of Global Pattern Formation and Parallel Memory Storage by Competitive Neural Networks," *IEEE Trans. Syst. Man. Cybern., SMC-3*: 815–826.

Grossberg, S. (ed.), *Neural Network and Natural Intelligence.* Cambridge, MA: Bradford Books, MIT Press.

Hopfield, J. J., (1982). "Neural Networks and Physical Systems with Emergent Collective Computational Abilities,"*Proc. Natl. Acad. Sci. USA, 79:* 2554–2558.

Hopfield, J. J., (1984). "Neurons with Grade Response Have Collective Computational Properties Like Those of Two-State Neurons," *Proc. Natl. Acad. Sci. USA, 81:* 3088–3092.

Hopfield, J. J., and Tank, D. W. (1985). "Neural Computation of Decisions in Optimization Problems," *Biol. Cybern., 52:* 141–152.

Hopfield, J. J., and Tank, D. W., (1986). "Computing with Neural Circuits: A Model," *Science, 233:* 625–633.

Lippmann, R. P., (1987). "An Introduction to Computing with Neural Nets," *IEEE ASSP Mag.,* April, pp. 4–22.

McCulloch, W. S., and Pitts, W. (1943). "A Logical Calculus of the Ideas Imminent in Nervous Activity," *Bull. Math. Biophy., 5:* 115–133.

Minsky, M., and Papert, S. (1969). *Perceptrons: An Introduction to Computational Geometry.* Cambridge, MA: MIT Press.

Rosenblatt, R., (1959). *Principles of Neurodynamics.* New York: Spartan Books.

Rumelhart, D. E., and McClelland, J. L. (1986). *Parallel Distributed Processing: Explorations in Microstructure of Cognition,* Vol. 1: *Foundations,* Vol. 2: *Psychological and Biological Models,* Cambridge, MA: MIT Press.

Rumelhart, D. E., Hinton, G. E., and Williams, R. J., (1986). Learning Representation by Back-Propagation Errors," *Nature, 323*(9): 533–536.

Swiniarki, R. (1991). "Adaptive Neuromorphic Self-Tuning PID Controller Uses Pattern Recognition Approach," *Adv. Modeling Simulation, 23*(4): 47–64.

Tank, D. W., and Hopfield, J. J. (1986). "Simple 'Neural' Optimization Networks: An A/D Converter, Signal Decision Circuits, and Linear Programming Circuits," *IEEE Trans. Circuits Syst. CAS-33*: 533–241.

Werbos, P. (1974). *Beyond Regression: New Tools for Prediction and Analysis in the Behavioral Sciences,* Ph. D. thesis, Harvard University, Cambridge, MA.

Widrow, B., (1987). "The Original Adaptive Broom Balancer," presented at the IEEE Conference on Circuits and Systems, Philadelphia.

Widrow, B., and Winter, R., (1988). "Neural nets for Adaptive Filtering and Adaptive Pattern Recognition," *IEEE Comput.,* March, pp. 25–39.

Widrow, B., Gupta, N.K., and Muitra, S. (1973). "Punish/Reward: Learning with Critic in Adaptive Threshold Systems," *IEEE Transaction Syst. Man. Cybern., SMC-3*: 455–465.

14

Neural Network Vector Quantization in Image Coding

Constantine N. Manikopoulos New Jersey Institute of Technology, Newark, New Jersey

I. INTRODUCTION

Over the past two decades, all around the world, there has been a constantly escalating demand for high quality visual information. The delivery of such communication services has been made technologically feasible by the growing availability of optical fiber links and the rapid development of sophisticated very large scale integrated (VLSI) devices. As quality video services become more desirable, concern for transmission efficiency has heightened. This is because images require large bandwidths for transmission. Despite the large bandwidth of modern communication links (i.e., optical fibers), the demand for enhanced video services continues to outstrip channel capacities. This makes efficient image compression a necessity. Thus, recently, much work has been devoted to the development of image coding techniques that accomplish large compression on image data with good pictorial quality. Similar demands for compression exist in maintaining large databases of images, a task that also finds many commercial applications. Compression, when applied to images, is usually known as *image coding*.

II. VECTOR QUANTIZATION

Digital transmission of images is expected to provide flexibility, reliability, and cost effectiveness, with the added potential for communication privacy and security through encryption. The conversion of an analog signal into a digital one consists of two parts: *sampling* and *quantization*. Sampling converts a continuous time signal into a discrete time signal by measuring the signal value at regular intervals of time. Quantization converts a continuous amplitude signal into one of a set of discrete amplitudes, thus resulting in a discrete amplitude signal that is different from the continuous amplitude signal by the quantization error or noise.

When each of a set parameters is quantized separately, the process is known as *scalar quantization*. When the set of parameters is quantized jointly, as a single vector, the process is known as *vector quantization* (VQ).

The research in VQ-based techniques has a long history. In 1965 Forgy [1] developed a clustering algorithm that is known in the pattern recognition literature as the *K*-means algorithm. In an unpublished paper in 1957, Lloyd had independently developed the same algorithm but for the scalar quantization problem and a known distribution (Lloyd's paper has recently been published [2]). The application of this algorithm to a training sequence along with VQ has been termed, the generalized Lloyd algorithm in much of the information theory literature. In 1980, Linde, Buzo, and Gray, in a widely read paper [3], showed that the algorithm works with a large class of distortion measures, including measures that are not metric, so the algorithm is currently called the *LBG* algorithm. Since then, VQ has received much attention resulting in numerous coding methods.

A.   Image Coding with Vector Quantization

Image data compression methods can be classified in two basically different categories. In the first category are methods that directly exploit redundancy in the data. They operate in the spatial domain. In the second category, compression is achieved by an energy-preserving transformation of the given image into another array such that maximum information is packed into a minimum number of samples. Such techniques are called transform coding. Other image data compression algorithms exist, as well, which use a combination of these two methods. VQ belongs in the first category.

VQ is one of the most efficient coding techniques, especially at high compression ratios, because it permits a large number of image pixels to be encoded at once. Many methods have been proposed, such as mean/shape VQ [4], classified VQ [5], interframe VQ [6,7], predictive VQ [8], transform VQ, and subband VQ [9]. Generally, these techniques can achieve a good image quality at a bit rate between 0.25 and 1 bit/pixel.

III.   A NEURAL NETWORK APPROACH TO VECTOR QUANTIZATION

A.   Introduction to Neural Networks

There are several descriptions or definitions of a neural network. Kohonen [10] wrote, "The artificial neural networks are massively parallel interconnected networks of simple (usually adaptive) elements and their hierarchical organizations which are intended to interact with the objects of the real world in the same way as the biological nervous systems do." Neural network taxonomies may be devised on the basis of a number of descriptors (topology or architecture, type of inputs handled, learning algorithms, tasks performed, etc.). For example, six important neural net structures have been described by Lippman [11] that can be used for pattern classification. These networks are highly parallel building blocks that illustrate neural net components and design principles and can be used to construct more complex systems.

Among these six models, the Hopfield, Hamming, and Carpenter–Grossberg networks use binary inputs, while single-layer and multilayered perceptron networks and the self-organizing feature map (SOFM) network admit continuous inputs. From another point of view, the networks can be divided into two groups according to training mode, namely those trained with and without supervision. Networks trained with supervision, such as the Hopfield network and perceptrons, may be used as associative memories or as classifiers. These networks are provided with side information or labels that specify the correct class for new input patterns during training. Most traditional statistical classifiers, such as the Gaussian classifier, are trained with supervision using labeled training data. On the other hand, however, some networks, such as Kohonen's SOFMs. are trained without supervision. No information concerning the correct class is provided to these networks during training.

The SOFM may be used as a vector quantizer or cluster generator in pattern recognition tasks. The first report of successfully using the SOFM algorithm for image coding appeared in the *Proceedings* of SPIE'88. N. M. Nasrabadi and Y. Feng [12] reported that good performance can be obtained with SOFM-based vector quantization for still images. Then Manikopoulos and Li [13] proposed a scheme for adaptive image sequence coding with the neural network VQ (NNVQ). Subsequently, Li and Manikopoulos [14] utilized neural net based nonlinear prediction to enhance the effectiveness of DPCM coding of images.

Vector quantization can be regarded as a process of pattern classifying and matching. This pattern matching task, in some applications, does not require very high precision. Neural networks, consisting of analog computational elements, can accomplish basic matching and classification of patterns. This represents an alternative to traditional VQ, which may be implemented with high speed but lower resolution analog neural circuits.

B. Vector Quantization with Self-Organized Feature Maps

The SOFM is an unsupervised neural net based clustering algorithm that can be used to design a VQ. It differs from the LBG algorithm in that the former forms a codebook continuously, while the latter does it iteratively, in "batch" mode; this has important theoretical and practical consequences. In applying the SOFM, for every input vector, the weight between each input node and the corresponding selected output node is updated by encouraging a shift toward the input vector. Given a training sequence with a stationary probability density function $p(x)$, the algorithm can form an ordered "image" of $p(x)$ onto the weights of the networks, something like the set of the codevectors in the LBG algorithm.

The strength of the connection between each input node i and output node j is represented by a weight w_{ij}. These weights represent the degree of influence exerted from input to output. Let us consider codebook generation with NNVQs based on the use of the SOFM. As mentioned, the SOFM is a self-learning, clustering algorithm, which changes the values of the weights, during training, in a manner that can be specified by the following system equation:

$$w_{ij}(t + 1) = w_{ij}(t) + \alpha(t)\,(x_i - w_{ij}(t)) \qquad j \in N_c \tag{1}$$

Where $\alpha(t)$ is an adaptation function (usually it is a monotonically decreasing function), $w_{ij}(t)$ is the weight between input node i and output node j at training epoch t, and N_c is the topological neighborhood around the best representation weight vector. For vector quantization, the system equation (1) is modified as follows:

$$\mathbf{w}_j(t + 1) = \mathbf{w}_j(t) + \alpha(t)\,[\mathbf{x} - \mathbf{w}_j(t)] \tag{2}$$

$$\mathbf{w}_i(t + 1) = \mathbf{w}_i(t), \qquad \text{for all } i \neq j$$

That is, only the nearest representation weight is updated each time.

By borrowing from the vector quantization terminology, we may call the set of the weights $\mathbf{w} = [\mathbf{w}_j, j = 1, 2 \ldots, N]$ the codebook, where $\mathbf{w}_j = [w_{1j}, w_{2j}, \ldots, w_{Kj}]$ is the jth representation vector, called codevector.

A simple architecture of NNVQ (Fig. 1) consists of an input layer of a small number of nodes K and an output layer of a large number of nodes N. The K input nodes receive the K components of the input vectors. The N output nodes represent each of the N codevectors of the resulting codebook. Although very similar to the standard SOFM, it differs from it in that adaptation is taking place. Each input node is connected to every output node by a connection of adjustable strength. It is the values of the connection strengths, or weights, w_{ij}, which adaptively self-organize to reflect the best representations of the input vector patterns. The starting values of these weights, w_{ij}, can be random small quantities.

The NNVQ design procedure, based on a training sequence, is described as follows:

0. Initialization: given a training sequence, vector size K, and codebook size N; initialize the weights with random values.

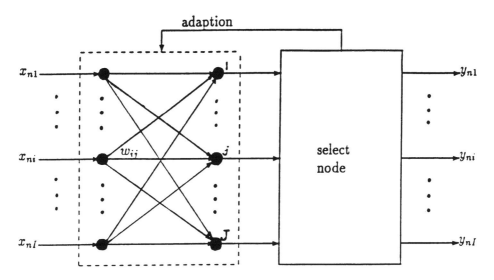

Figure 1 The generic architecture of an NNVQ. It consists of a single layer of fully connected processing neurons, as shown. Each output node corresponds to a distinct representation vector.

1. Introduce the component values of a new vector u_t to the input nodes, where $t = 1, 2, \ldots, Q$ designates a member of the training set.

2. Calculate the distances d_{tj} between the input vector and every output vector node, where $j = 1, 2, \ldots, N$ denotes the output node, or equivalently, the resulting representation vectors.

We may write:

$$d_{tj} = \sum_{i=1}^{K} (u_{ti} - w_{ij})^2 \qquad (3)$$

Identify the output node, j_{min}, which gives the lowest distance value.

3. Adjust the weights of node j_{min} by encouraging a shift toward the input vector u_t. This modification may extend, as well, to the group of nodes comprising a small neighborhood E, around j_{min}. We may explicitly describe the adjustment operation by:

$$w_{ij}(t + 1) = w_{ij}(t) + \alpha_h(t) (u_{ti} - w_{ij}(t)) \qquad (4)$$

for $j = j_{min}$, and for all $j \in E$. The modification factor $\alpha_h(t)$ for a node $j_h \in E$, is given by $\alpha_h(t) = \alpha(t)/h$, for $h = 1, 2, \ldots, H$ (ordered by ascending distance from

j_{min}), where H is the total number of nodes comprising the neighborhood E. Here, both the size of the neighborhood E and the adjustment factors α_h decrease slowly with time. Explicit expressions for them, as used in our simulation, are given below.

4.   Return to 1 until the training set is exhausted.

IV.   PERFORMANCE OF THE NNVQ

A.   Distortion Measures Used with NNVQs

The NNVQ can work in the same way as an ordinary vector quantizer. Given an input vector, the best reproduction vector can be found by using the nearest neighbor rule, that is,

$$Q(\mathbf{x}) = \mathbf{w}_j \qquad \text{if } d(\mathbf{x}, \mathbf{w}_j) \le d(\mathbf{x}, \mathbf{w}_i) \qquad \text{for all } i \ne j \qquad (5)$$

Here, $Q(x)$ represents the transformation that vector quantizes its argument (i.e., it assigns a representation vector to its argument), and $d(x,y)$ represents the value of the metric operating on its two vector arguments—the distortion measure.

Two distortion measures have been used in the simulation experiments. They are as follows:

Absolute distance measure (ADM)
Definition $d_a(\mathbf{x}, \mathbf{w}) = |\mathbf{x} - \mathbf{w}|$
With the ADM, the peak-to-peak signal/noise ratio (SNR) is defined as follows:

$$PSNR_a = 20 \log_{10}\left(\frac{255^2}{E[d_a(\mathbf{x}, \mathbf{w})]} \right) \qquad (6)$$

With ADM, very robust performance has been achieved with a high *SNR*.

Mean Square Error (MSE) measure.
Definition: $d_m(\mathbf{x}, \mathbf{w}) = (\mathbf{x} - \mathbf{w})^2$
The corresponding peak SNR is defined as follows:

$$PSNR_m = 10 \log_{10}\left(\frac{255^2}{E[d_m(\mathbf{x}, \mathbf{w})]} \right) \qquad (7)$$

The MSE has found the widest application of all measures, to date.

B. Convergence of the NNVQ

Associated with each weight $\mathbf{w}_j$, there is a Voronoi region S_j defined as follows:

$$\mathbf{x} \in S_j \qquad \text{if f} \quad d(\mathbf{x}, \mathbf{w}_j) \leq d(\mathbf{x}, \mathbf{w}_i), \text{ for all } j \neq i \qquad (8)$$

Vector $\mathbf{w}_j$ is a variable during the training phase; its asymptotic value can be found by the conditional expectation of equations (2).

$$E[\mathbf{w}_j(t + 1)|\mathbf{x} \in S_j] = E[\mathbf{w}_j(t)|\mathbf{x} \in S_j] + \alpha(t)E[\mathbf{x} - \mathbf{w}_j(t)] \qquad (9)$$

When $\mathbf{w}_j$ reaches its equilibrium value,

$$E[\mathbf{w}_j(t + 1)|\mathbf{x} \in S_j\} = E[\mathbf{w}_j(t)|\mathbf{x} \in S_j] \qquad (10)$$

It follows that

$$\mathbf{w}_j = E(\mathbf{x}|\mathbf{x} \in S_j), \qquad \text{as } t \to \infty \qquad (11)$$

This means that the equilibrium value of $\mathbf{w}_j$ coincides with the centroid of the subset S_j.

Because the weight is updated with every input vector, the NNVQ converges to the asymptotic value much faster than the iterative LBG algorithm. Figure 2 illustrates the convergence phase of the two algorithms, both starting with the same initial codebook. It is clear that when convergence (i.e., the "knee" of the training curve,) has been reached, the NNVQ gets there about five times faster. This ratio of convergence speeds becomes higher as the size of the vectors increases. Eventually, the times needed for convergence by the LBG algorithm become untenable, in practice.

C. Optimality of the NNVQ

A vector quantizer is said to be an optimal quantizer if the overall average distortion is minimized over all N-level quantizers. There are two necessary conditions for optimality:

1. The quantizer is realized by using a minimum distortion or nearest neighbor selection rule

$$Q(\mathbf{x}) = y_j, \qquad \text{if } d(\mathbf{x}, y_j) \leq d(\mathbf{x}, y_i), \qquad \text{for all } j \neq i \qquad (12)$$

2. Vector y_j should be chosen in such a way that

$$E[d(\mathbf{x}, y_j)|\mathbf{x} \in S_j] = \min E[d(\mathbf{x}, \mathbf{u})|\mathbf{x} \in S_j] \qquad (13)$$

From equations (5) and (11), we can see that the NNVQ, based on the SOFM algorithm, also satisfies these two necessary conditions for optimality.

For a Gaussian memoryless source, Table 1 gives some simulation results for both algorithms. The results indicate that the NNVQ and the LBGVQ are essen-

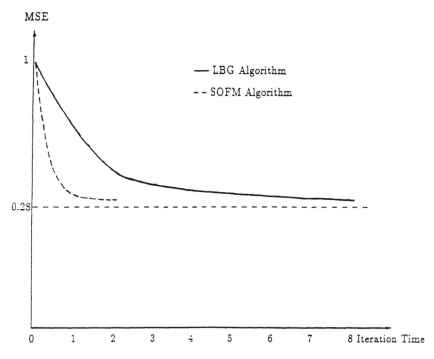

Figure 2   The convergence phase of the two algorithms, the LBG and the SOFM. Both algorithms start with the same initial codebook. The SOFM, which is based on a neural net, converges much faster.

Table 1   Comparison of LBG and SOFM for a Gaussian Memoryless Source.[a]

K	N	LBG (mse)	SOFM (mse)
2	4	0.350	0.351
2	8	0.192	0.191
4	16	0.320	0.310

[a]The length of the test sequence is 9600 vectors, all outside the training set.

tially equivalent in performance, as far as the mean square error is concerned. Of course, the NNVQ provides a number of other advantages over LBGVQ: speed of convergence, ease of adaptivity, and the capability to train large vectors without combinatorial explosion.

V. IMPLEMENTATION OF NNVQ

Obviously, an NNVQ can be implemented in the same way as an LBG VQ. That is, given an input vector, find the nearest weight vector in series, and then code the index of the nearest weight vector. The computational cost will also remain the same.

However, vector quantization can be regarded as a pattern classifying and matching process. And this pattern matching task, in some applications, does not require very high precision. Neural networks, consisting of analog computational elements, can accomplish basic pattern matching and classifying tasks. Thus, alternatively, a VQ may be implemented with high speed but lower resolution analog neural circuits.

Two methods have been studied for the implementation of NNVQ which can accomplish the vector quantization process with very high speed suboptimal performance.

A. Cascade Method

The cascade network method implements a VQ in two parts. The first part calculates the value of every output node in parallel. This is shown in Figure 3. Let input x represent voltage, and the weight w_{ij} represent the conductance between input node i and output node j. Each output

$$Y_j = \sum_{i=1}^{K} X_i w_{ij} \quad j = 1, 2, \ldots, N$$

represents the projection of the input vector X onto the codevector w_{ij}, which is actually a kind of distortion measure between the input vector and each codevector. Obviously, the node with largest output value may be regarded to be the optimal output node whose corresponding weight vector matches the input vector best. The corresponding node label is selected and coded by a channel codeword in the second part of the NNVQ.

At the decoder, the input vector can be reconstructed by a table lookup procedure.

B. Direct Mapping Method

Basically, an encoding process with vector quantization can be divided into three steps: (1) convert the analog signal to digital data, (2) find the nearest codevector

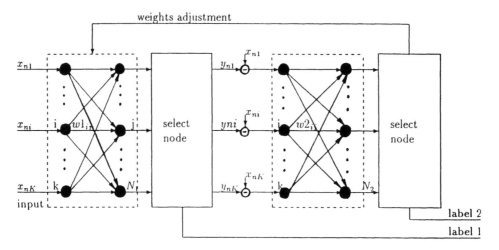

Figure 3   The architecture of a two-stage neural network cascade VQ.

to the input vector by searching the whole codebook, and (3) code the nearest codevector by the corresponding codeword. The encoder can be represented by a black box with analog signal as the input and a binary index codeword as the output. An important research goal is to implement the black box with a multilayered neural network.

According to our computer simulation results to date, after proper training, the neural network can correctly find 79% of the nearest codevectors. The total performance is about 0.85–1.5 dB less than that of full search VQ. This performance is comparable to that of a number of suboptimal search algorithms. But it can accomplish the VQ process without delay, except for a negligible propagation time.

VI.   ADAPTIVE IMAGE CODING WITH NNVQ

By their very nature, image sequences involve continuous change. This may be a change of scenery as new objects or actors enter the picture, or it may be due to motion of the entities in the image. Regardless of the cause, the originally devised codebook may be, and indeed often is, soon rendered ineffective. A number of frames later, the distortion in the picture rises and the pictorial quality of the image deteriorates. Thus, it is important to provide a means of updating the codebook to keep up with the changes in the image. Up to now, this has been accomplished by a number of adaptive algorithms, mentioned previously. An example is the class of algorithms known as motion compensation. The disadvantage of these algorithms is that it is difficult to design them to be fully adaptive in the sense of effectively

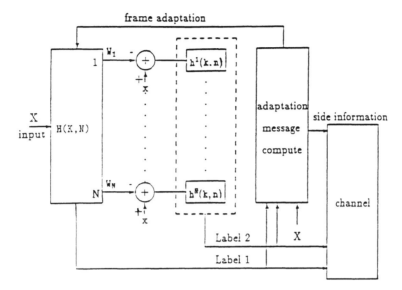

Figure 4   The architecture of an ANNVQ.

compensating for all types and rates of motion. If the attempt is made, the bit rate for transmission rises to excessively high levels.

In response to these adaptation requirements, a new method for encoding an image sequence, termed adaptive neural net vector quantization (ANNVQ), has been devised. Its architecture is shown in Figure 4. It is designed for use in encoding image sequences. This, also, is based on Kohonen's SOFM but differs from it in that after training the initial codebook a modified form of adaptation resumes, to allow responses to scene changes and motion. This neural net algorithm has the potential to circumvent motion problems. This is because the neural net does not need to respond to change according to one or more particular formulas, but rather according to very general prescriptions, where the magnitude of the response is determined by the recent encoding history. The main advantages are high image quality with modest bit rate and effective adaptation to motion and/or scene changes, with the capability to keep the image quality constant by quick adjustments of the instantaneous bit rate. This is a good match to packet-switched networks, where variable bit rate and uniform image quality are highly desirable.

A.   ANNVQ Codebook Design and Adaptation

In Kohonen's SOFMs, the adaptation of the codebook terminates after the training set has been processed. In contrast, the present algorithm, ANNVQ, resumes a modified version of codevector adaptation to respond to scene changes and motion. In designing the algorithm, which adapts to changes in image sequences, it is important to keep the bit rate constant. Thus, the codebook should not be updated by the introduction of new codevectors. Rather, updating should be accomplished by modifying the codevectors that are no longer effective in their encoding task toward new codevector values better suited to encoding the new image frames. The measurement of encoding effectiveness can be achieved by keeping track of the distortion resulting whenever one of the codevectors is actually employed for encoding an incoming source vector. Thus, we may define arrays, $D(j)$, $R(i,j)$, and $F(j)$. The first one, $D(j)$, stores the accumulated distortion due to the use of representation vector j, as each source vector, v_j, comes through. Array $R(i,j)$ accumulates the totals of the components i of vectors v_j. The last one, $F(j)$, counts the total number of times representation vector j has been utilized. At some point, codebook regeneration (i.e., updating of the codebook) takes place. The trigger point of regeneration is determined, either a priori, by the number of source vectors processed, or adaptively, when the level of total distortion D_{total} or peak distortion D_{peak} accumulated in the encoding process reaches a threshold value. In our work, the distortion is quantified in terms of the Euclidean distance between the elements involved. Thus, the distortion contribution, d_{lj}, of the jth codeword in the codebook is given by:

$$d_{lj} = \sum_{i=1}^{k} (u_{li} - w_{ij})^2$$

We may write $D(j) = \sum_{l=1}^{L} d_{lj}$, where L is the total number of vectors encoded by the codevector j. In other words, $L = F(j)$. It is these L vectors that are contributing to the distortion accumulating at node j. Now, it is evident that

$$D_{\text{total}} = \sum_{j=1}^{N} D(j) \qquad D_{\text{peak}} = \max \{D(j)\}$$

In the present work, the regeneration process is triggered when the total distortion D_{total} rises above a preset threshold D_{th}. Essentially, D_{th} sets the desired upper limit in distortion for the coding process. Whenever the codebook regeneration process is triggered, the algorithm that effects this proceeds as follows:

1.   Compute the effective distortion generation rate g_j for every node. This is provided by $g_j = D(j)/F(j)$.

2.   Sort out the nodes with distortion above a preset threshold level d_{th}. These comprise the ordered set of nodes of increasing distortion designated by j_m, for $m = 1,2, \ldots, M$ such that $g_{jm} > d_{th}$. Here, $J_M = j_{max}$, where g_{jmax} is the maximum of the whole list. The magnitude of the threshold d_{th} is predetermined by a compromise between the desired pictorial quality and bit rate.

3. Compute the centroid, $c_{i,jm}$, of the source vectors processed by node j_m. This is given by

$$c_{i,jm} = R(i, j_m)/F(j_m), \qquad m = 1, 2, \ldots, M$$

4. Modify the ineffective codevectors. To accomplish this, adjust the weights of node j_m by encouraging a shift toward the centroid, $c_{i,jm}$. We may explicitly describe the adjustment operation by:

$$w_{ij}(n + 1) = w_{ij}(n) + \beta(c_{i, j} - w_{ij}(n))$$

for $j = j_m$. Here, the adjustment factor β is a constant and n signifies a source vector outside the training set.

5. Transmit to the decoder the indices of the nodes j_m under modification, and the magnitude of the coefficients of the corresponding centroids $c_{i,j}$. The decoder is initially endowed with the modification rule, so it can duplicate the adjustment process in the encoder precisely.

6. Reinitialize $D(j)$, $R(i, j)$, and $F(j)$, and return to the encoding process.

B. Results of Simulations Carried Out with the ANNVQ

The codebook size employed was 256, suited to practical implementations. The specific values of the adjustment factors $\alpha(k)$ and β used in the simulation were $\alpha(k) = 0.1e^{-k/1000}$ and $\beta = 0.5$. The size of the neighborhood E was determined by $H(k) = 2 + 50e^{-k100}$. When adapting the codebook vectors, only two bits per component were transmitted to the decoder, for a total 32 bits for each centroid value.

Both numerical and pictorial results have been obtained. The bit rate R is made up of two parts: $R = R_1 + R_2$, where $R_1 = (log_2 256)/16 = 0.5$ *bit/pixel*, and $R_2 =$ adaptation overhead rate. The latter cannot be computed explicitly, since it is image dependent. It rises in high detail or rapid motion regions of the images, while it may fall to zero whenever there is low detail and little motion occurs. However, the average value of R_2, according to our simulation experiments, is 0.026 bit/pixel.

Figure 5 depicts the value obtained of $PSNR_m$ for ANNVQ, in a simulation experiment. It is found to be about 31.5 dB with adaptation and 30.5 dB without adaptation, outside the training set. Frames 1–10 have been used to provide the training set. The dashed line marks the separation of the training set from the test set.

The ANNVQ can devise a successful codebook of representation vectors. The value of $PSNR_m$ obtained, which is about 30.5 dB outside the training set, is more than adequate for a number of image transmission tasks. Importantly, it stays at that level during frames 11–20, which are outside the training set and during which adaptation occurs. Without adaptation, the $PSNR_m$ starts to decline.

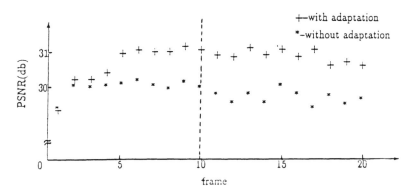

Figure 5   The value obtained of PSNR$_m$ for an ANNVQ, over 20 frames of a sequence. The dashed line separates the training set from the test set.

VII.   IMAGE CODING WITH CASCADE NNVQ

Cascade VQ, or multistage VQ, is a kind of suboptimal technique intended to reduce the storage as well as computational cost in image transmission. As the name implies, cascade VQ consists of a sequence of VQ stages, each operating on the residual of the preceding stage. However, cascade VQ working in this way will result in a large degradation in performance. This is because after each stage, the residuals are pooled together to form the input to the next stage. In general, the probability density functions (pdf) of the residuals from different clusters of the preceding stage will be different, and pooling them together will result in a single pdf that will lose many of the dependencies that existed in the initial clusters.

Here, we present a two-stage cascade NNVQ.

Although vector quantization has been applied to difference signals in a number of ways, the cascade NNVQ, which also operates on the residuals of the previous stage, is different in several aspects, as described below:

1.   The cascade NNVQ is designed with the SOFM algorithm.

2.   Associated with each output node, an independent subnetwork has been developed that operates only on the residual from that cluster. Therefore, the dependencies that existed in the initial cluster will never be lost.

3.   The absolute distance distortion measure is used, which has been found to be a better distortion measure in this task.

4.   An efficient method of adaptation has been developed.

A.   Structure of the Cascade NNVQ

Let the first-stage network network be $H(K,N)$. Let **W** denote the set of the weights, $\mathbf{W} = [\mathbf{W}_1, \mathbf{W}_2, \ldots, \mathbf{W}_N]$. Associated with jth output node of the first stage, there is a subnetwork, denoted as $h^j(K,n)$, where the set of the weights of $h^j(K,n)$ is denoted as $\mathbf{w}^j = [\mathbf{w}^j_1, \mathbf{w}^j_2, \ldots, \mathbf{w}^j_n], j = 1,2, \ldots, N$.

For the first stage,

$$Q(\mathbf{x}) = \mathbf{W}_j, \qquad \text{if } \mathbf{x} \in S_j, \qquad j = 1, \ldots, N$$

Where S_j is the Voronoi region of $\mathbf{w}_j$.

Then, the difference between $\mathbf{x}$ and $\mathbf{W}_j$ is taken as the input to the corresponding subnetwork.

$$q(\mathbf{x} - \mathbf{w}_j) = \mathbf{w}^j_l, \qquad \text{if } \mathbf{x} \in S_j \quad \text{and} \quad (\mathbf{x} - \mathbf{W}_j) \in s_l \qquad (14)$$

The reconstruction vector of $\mathbf{x}$, therefore, is

$$\mathbf{x}_c = \mathbf{w}^j_l + \mathbf{W}_j \qquad (15)$$

Recall that to adapt the weight $\mathbf{W}_j$, we need to find the deviation $\mathbf{x} - \mathbf{W}_j$. From equation (6), we have

$$\mathbf{x} - \mathbf{W}_j = \mathbf{w}^j_l + \mathbf{e}_j \qquad (16)$$

where $\mathbf{e}_j$ is the quantization error.

To adapt $H(K,N)$ frame by frame, we should find the average deviation of $\mathbf{x}$ and $\mathbf{W}_j$. According to equation (7), we have

$$E[\mathbf{x} - \mathbf{W}_j | \mathbf{x} \in S_j(F)] = E[\mathbf{w}^j_l | l \in V_j(F)] + E[\mathbf{e}_j | \mathbf{x} \in S_j(F)] \qquad (17)$$

where $S_j(F)$ is the subset of S_j at the Fth frame and $V_j(F)$ is the set of all l's.

According to the large number theory, $\mathbf{e}_j$ must be a Gaussian random variable with zero mean. But in a small frame, $E[\mathbf{e}_j]$ may not be negligible. Thus, it may be transmitted to the decoder once per frame as side information.

The first-stage network is adapted once per frame by

$$\mathbf{W}_j(F + 1) = \mathbf{W}_j(F) + \beta\{E[\mathbf{w}^j_l | l \in V_j(F)] + E[\mathbf{e}_j | \mathbf{x} \in S_j(F)]\} \qquad (18)$$

where β is an adaptation constant.

The total bit rate is

$$R = R_1 + R_2 + R_f \text{ bits/sample} \qquad (19)$$

where $R_1 = (log_2N)/K$, $R_2 = (log_2n)/K$, $R_f = (N \cdot B)/N_F$, B is the number of bits needed for the transmission of $\mathbf{e}_j$, and $N_F = NP$ is the number of pixels in one frame.

B. Simulations Performed with the Cascade NNVQ

Simulations have been carried out with a network made up from a first-stage denoted by $H(16,32)$, and a second stage consisting of 32 subnetworks described as $h^j(16,j)$ for $j = 1, \ldots, 32$. Thus, there is a distinct subnetwork for each output node of the first stage. The architecture of the two-stage cascade neural net utilized here was depicted in Figure 3.

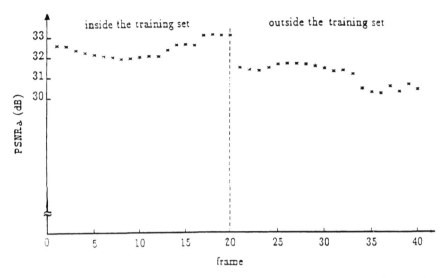

Figure 6   The value obtained of PSNR$_a$ for a two-stage ANNVQ, over 40 frames of a sequence.

The neural network is initialized by randomly choosing 32 vectors from the first 20 frames. Then, the weights are updated based on the image data of the first 20 frames. The adaptation function is chosen as a monotonically decreasing function

$$\alpha(t) = 0.1 \times 1.15^{-t}$$

Each subnetwork is trained in the same way.

The error $E[e_j]$ is transmitted to the decoder with $B = 16$ bits/vector. So the total bit rate is

$$R = 0.3125 + 0.3125 + 0.0476 = 0.673 \text{ bit/sample}$$

β was chosen to be 0.1.

Figure 6 illustrates the performance of a two-stage cascade NNVQ, in terms of the PSNRα, over the 40 frames of the sequence. The absolute distance measure has been employed. The first 20 frames of the sequence have been utilized as the training set. The dashed line marks the separation of the training set from the test set.

The compression values achieved with this sequence (i.e., about 15), resulting at a compressed transmission rate of about 160 kbit/s, with a PSNRα of about 31–32 dB, are quite significant, if we judge them by keeping in mind the low redundancy initially present in the image sequence. Individual frames of the sequence, original and reconstructed, have been compared, as well as the whole sequence depicted in real time. The pictorial quality of the sequence is quite good for a videoconference session.

SUMMARY

The NNVQ is a new vector quantizer quite useful in encoding still pictures as well as image sequences, based on neural networks. It is a class of quantizers similar in philosophy to the LBG algorithm, but of considerably less computational burden for large vectors, if implemented with neural networks, as well as offering faster convergence. The NNVQ can be applied to data compression of a large variety of sources, (still pictures, image sequences, speech data, quantized radar signal signatures, etc.). ANNVQ is an adaptive extension of NNVQ. The learning algorithm utilized in the ANNVQ, in this work, is based on the self-organizing feature maps (SOFM), a neural network type of clustering algorithm developed by Kohonen. There is considerable conceptual correspondence to the LBG VQ clustering algorithm, as well as important differences. They are similar, functionally, in that they both map input image blocks into best representation vectors, thus achieving compression. As far as performance is concerned, the compression levels accomplished to date are quite comparable.

In applying the ANNVQ, in contrast to the SOFM, adaptation of the codebook does not cease after training; rather, it resumes, to respond to local detail, scene changes, or motion. The onset of adaptation may be triggered on the basis of either the accumulated distortion during the encoding process or a given number of image data processed (i.e., a frame of a sequence). The adaptation of the codebook is fairly straightforward to incorporate in the ANNVQ scheme, in a rather natural and smooth manner. Although the formulation of similar adaptation can possibly be devised for the LBG VQ algorithms, it would be more ad hoc and abrupt.

The ANNVQ also differs from the LBG algorithm in that the former forms a codebook continuously, while the latter does it iteratively, in "batch" mode. This is important, because it makes possible the generation of codebooks with large condevectors, (i.e., of dimensionality > 25) in practically available times. This task has proven, heretofore, very difficult to accomplish with the LBG algorithm. Yet it is at the heart of obtaining higher encoding efficiencies. Also, in applying the SOFM, during training, adjustment proceeds over a neighborhood around the best representation vector, the size of which shrinks slowly to zero as a function of training epochs. This constitutes another significant distinction between the LBG and SOFM algorithms, which renders them, in principle, very different. In some of the earlier approaches to neural network vector quantization, the initial size of the neighborhood was very small, which rendered the two approaches (neural net and LBG) indistinguishable, for all practical purposes. In this work, the initial size (i.e., 50) is large enough for the two algorithms to operate in distinctly different manners. Simulation experiments, which have been carried out for a Gaussian memoryless source, have shown that the SOFM NNVQ works as well as the LBG VQ, as far as the resulting distortion is concerned. It performs considerably better with respect to convergence time required in compiling an acceptable codebook. This disparity grows further as the dimensionality of the input vectors increases.

Simulation experiments have been performed with ANNVQ as well as cascade NNVQ in coding a videoconference sequence. The results, numerical and pictorial, have been found to be quite good. The image sequence consists of 40 frames each of size 112×96 pixels. It was segmented into 4×4 contiguous blocks of pixels. The uncompressed transmission rate of the sequence utilized (i.e., 112×96 at 30 frames/s or, equivalently, 322 kpixel/s) is very low, as appropriate to a videoconference sequence. Thus, the initial redundancy and pixel correlation here is small compared to other sequences, which utilize a much larger number of pixels per frame. Also, this sequence is characterized by considerable amount of motion. Therefore, the overall compression values achieved with it, about 15, resulting at at compressed transmission rate of about 160 kbits/s, with a peak signal-to-noise ratio of 31–32 dB, are quite significant, if we judge them by keeping in mind its uncompressed transmission rate level. The pictorial quality of the sequence has also been judged to be quite good for a videoconference session.

REFERENCES

1. E. W. Forgy, *Biometrics, 21*: 768 (1965).
2. S. P. Lloyd, *IEEE Trans. Inf. Theory, IT-28*: 129 (1982).
3. Y. Linde, A. Buzo, and R. M. Gray, *IEEE Trans. Commun., COM-28*: 84 (1980).
4. R. L. Baker and R. M. Gray, "Image Compression using Non Adaptive Spatial Vector Quantization," in *Proceedings of the Sixteenth Conference on Circuits, Systems, and Computers*, pp. 55–61, 1982.
5. B. Ramamurthi and A. Gersho, *IEEE Trans. Commun., COM-34*: 1105 (1986).
6. M. Goldberg and H. F. Sun, *IEEE Trans. Commun., COM-34*: 703 (1986).
7. C. Manikopoulos, J. Li, and G. Antoniou, "Neural Net Adaptive Encoding of Image Sequence Data," *J. New Generation Comput. Syst.*, 4:99 (1991).
8. H. M. Hang and J. W. Woods, *IEEE Trans. Commun., COM-33*: 1208 (1985).
9. J. W. Woods and S. D. O'Neil, *IEEE Trans. ASSP, 34*: 1278 (1986).
10. T. Kohonen, *Self-Organization and Associative Memory*, Berlin: Springer-Verlag, 1984.
11. R. P. Lippmann, *IEEE ASSP Mag.*, April 1987, p. 4.
12. N. M. Nasrabadi and Y. Feng, "Vector Quantization of Images Based Upon a Neural Network Clustering Algorithm," in *Proceedings of Visual Communications and Image Processing*, Boston, pp. 207–213, 1988.
13. C. N. Manikopoulos and J. Li, "Adaptive Image Sequence Coding with Neural Network Vector Quantization," *Proceedings of the International Joint Conference on Neural Networks*, Washington DC, pp. II-573, 1989.
14. J. Li and C. Manikopoulos, "Nonlinear Prediction in Image Coding with DPCM," *IEE Electron. Lett.*, 26:1357 (1990).

15
Theory of the Fuzzy Controller: A Brief Survey

James J. Buckley University of Alabama at Birmingham, Birmingham, Alabama

I. INTRODUCTION

This chapter is a tutorial on the modern fuzzy controller. To start with, we should understand how a basic fuzzy controller operates. By a basic fuzzy controller we mean an elementary fuzzy controller with no "extras." An "extra" is something that has been added to the basic fuzzy controller to enhance its operation. The internal workings of a basic fuzzy controller are discussed in detail in Section II; we deal with Sugeno's fuzzy controller separately from the other elementary fuzzy controllers. In Section IV we survey the "extras," which include self-organizing, adaptive, predictive, self-regulating, fuzzy model based, and neural fuzzy controllers.

The applications of the fuzzy controller have far outstripped its theory. In Section III we survey the known theoretical results on the fuzzy controller. These include (1) the functional relationship between the defuzzified output and all the inputs to the fuzzy controller, (2) limit theorems, and (3) stability. An important aspect of this survey is to be able to point out areas needing future study. Suggestions for future research are also contained in Section III. Section V contains a brief summary and our conclusions. One conclusion is that for the fuzzy controller to truly generalize control theory, it must process fuzzy data for control of man-machine systems.

II. HOW IT WORKS

In this section we discuss the internal workings of a basic fuzzy controller. We divide the discussion into two parts: first the usual fuzzy controller, and second, Sugeno's fuzzy controller [1-3].

A. Basic Fuzzy Controller

An elementary fuzzy controller is comprised of (1) input, (2) fuzzy numbers, (3) output, (4) rules, (5) evaluation, and (6) defuzzification.

1. Input

Let us assume that the process has only one state variable. If $y(t)$ is the process output at time t, let sp be the set point, or target value for $y(t)$, and let Δ be the sampling period for the process. At times $t = \Delta, 2\Delta, \ldots$, an input translator computes numbers r_i, $1 \le i \le n$, from $y(t)$, all scaled to be in some interval, for input to the fuzzy controller.

It is common to first compute $y_i(t) = (i-1)$th derivative of error $= y(t) - sp$, $1 \le i \le n$, where the 0th derivative of error is just error, at $t = \Delta, 2\Delta, \ldots$. Of course, the input translator can only approximate $y_2(t), y_3(t), \ldots$ at discrete times $t = \Delta, 2\Delta, \ldots$. We call $y_2(t)$ "rate" and $y_3(t)$ "rate of change of rate," at $t = \Delta, 2\Delta, \ldots$. There are scaling constants c_i, $1 \le i \le n$, so that $r_i = c_i y_i(t) \in [-1, 1]$, $1 \le i \le n$, at $t = \Delta, 2\Delta, \ldots$. In this section we assume that r_1 = scaled error and r_2 = scaled rate are the only inputs to the fuzzy controller both in $[-1, 1]$.

2. Fuzzy Numbers

There are N fuzzy numbers $\overline{R}(j)$, $1 \le j \le N$, with membership functions $y = \mu(x|\overline{R}(j))$, equally spaced in $[-1, 1]$. It is assumed that they cover the interval so that given an x in $[-1, 1]$, there is at least one j so that $\mu(x|\overline{R}(j)) > 0$. These fuzzy numbers will define the linguistic variables used in the antecedents of the fuzzy control rules. In this section, for simplicity, we assume that $N = 3$ so we may interpret these fuzzy numbers as $\overline{R}(1)$ = "negative," $\overline{R}(2)$ = "zero," and $\overline{R}(3)$ = "positive." $\overline{R}(1)$ will be centered at $x = -1$, so we can use only the right half of $\overline{R}(1)$; $\overline{R}(2)$ is centered at zero; and $\overline{R}(3)$ is centered at $x = 1$, with only its left half used.

All our fuzzy numbers will be continuous and normalized. In computer applications usually discrete approximations are employed, but in this chapter we always use continuous fuzzy numbers.

3. Output

Let us assume that the fuzzy controller has only one output to be inputted to the process. The primary output from the fuzzy controller is a fuzzy set $\overline{O}$, called the Output fuzzy set, whose elements are fuzzy numbers $\overline{O}(l)$, $1 \le l \le L$. So the Output fuzzy set may be written as

$$\overline{O} = \left\{ \frac{\Delta(1)}{\overline{O}(1)}, \ldots, \frac{\Delta(L)}{\overline{O}(L)} \right\} \tag{1}$$

where $\Delta(l)$ is the membership value of $\overline{O}(l)$ in $\overline{O}$. The fuzzy numbers $\overline{O}(l)$ define the linguistic variables used in the consequence of a fuzzy control rule.

4. Rules

The cells in the fuzzy controller table are described by vectors $w = (x_1, x_2)$ with $x_i \in \{1, 2, 3\}$. Let W denote all such vectors. W is a listing of all the cells in the fuzzy controller table.

Example 1. If $w = (1,3)$, then the antecedent of this fuzzy control rule is

$$\text{if} \qquad [r_1 = \overline{R}(1)] \qquad \text{and} \qquad [r_2 = \overline{R}(3)], \quad \text{then}, \ldots \tag{2}$$

We may translate equation (2) to be

$$\text{if} \qquad [r_1 = \text{negative}] \qquad \text{and} \qquad [r_2 = \text{positive}], \quad \text{then}, \ldots, \tag{3}$$

where $r_1(r_2)$ is scaled error (rate).

The fuzzy controller table has a conclusion function $\Psi : W \rightarrow \{ \overline{O}(l) | 1 \leq l \leq L \}$.

Example 2. Continuing Example 1, suppose $L = 5$ and $\Psi(1,3) = \overline{O}(4)$. If we interpret the fuzzy numbers $\overline{O}(l)$ as $\overline{O}(1) =$ "negative large," $\overline{O}(2) =$ "negative small," $\overline{O}(3) =$ "zero," $\overline{O}(4) =$ "positive small," and $\overline{O}(5) =$ "positive large," then this fuzzy control rule is

$$\text{if} \qquad [r_1 = \text{negative}] \qquad \text{and} \qquad [r_2 = \text{positive}], \quad \text{then}$$
$$\text{Output = positive small} \tag{4}$$

So, the fuzzy control rules are completely specified by Ψ. Special fuzzy controller rules are determined by special functions Ψ, which could be linear, quadratic, etc. Ψ is linear if $\Psi(w) = a_1 x_1 + a_2 x_2 + c$ where the a_i and c are integers not all zero. By $\Psi(w) = \alpha$ we mean $\Psi(w) = \overline{O}(\alpha)$ with $\alpha \in \{1, 2, \ldots, L\}$. A commonly used linear Ψ is $\Psi(w) = 2N - (x_1 + x_2) + 1$. If Ψ is linear, we write $\Psi =$ "linear," and if Ψ is the special linear conclusion function $2N - (x_1 + x_2) + 1$ we write $\Psi =$ "linear*."

Example 3. If $N = 3$ and $\Psi =$ linear*, then $\Psi(1,1) = 7 - 2 = 5$, $\Psi(1,2) = \Psi(2,1) = 4, \ldots, \Psi(3,3) = 1$. The translation for $w = (3,2)$ is

$$\text{if} \qquad [r_1 = \text{positive}] \qquad \text{and} \qquad [r_2 = \text{zero}], \quad \text{then}$$
$$\text{Output = negative small} \tag{5}$$

since $\overline{O}(2) =$ "negative small."

5. Evaluation

There are two basic methods of evaluating the fuzzy control rules: expert system procedures and approximate reasoning/fuzzy logic procedures.

Expert systems. Given r_1 and r_2, the fuzzy control rules are evaluated producing the membership values $\Delta(l)$ of the fuzzy numbers $\overline{O}(l)$ in $\overline{O}$. This method has been employed in the fuzzy controllers discussed in references 4–15. Let T be some t-norm, and C a co-t-norm, extended by associativity, if necessary, to be functions of three or more arguments.

For a fuzzy control rule $\Psi(x_1,x_2) = \alpha$ we first evaluate the antecedent as $\gamma(x_1 x_2)$ $= T(\mu(r_1|\overline{R}(x_1)),\mu(r_2|\overline{R}(x_2)))$. For example, if $w = (3,2)$, then $\gamma(3,2) = T(\mu(r_1|\overline{R}(3)),\mu(r_2|\overline{R}(2)))$. t-Norms are generally used to evaluate statements connected by "and." Next, we find all antecedents with the same conclusion by computing $\Gamma(\alpha) = \{w|\Psi(w) = \alpha\}$, for α in $\{1, 2, 3, \ldots, L\}$. Then $\Delta(l) = C\{\gamma(w)|w \in \Gamma(\alpha)\}$. We set $\Delta(l)$ to be zero when $\Gamma(\alpha)$ is empty.

Example 4. This continues Examples 1 through 3. We have $L = 5$ and $\Psi =$ linear*. So $\Gamma(1) = \{(3,3)\}$, $\Gamma(2) = \{(3,2), (2,3)\}$, $\Gamma(3) = \{(3,1), (2,2), (1,3)\}$, $\Gamma(4) = \{(1,2), (2,1)\}$, and $\Gamma(5) = \{(1,1)\}$. It follows that $\Delta(3) = C(\gamma(3,1), \gamma(2,2), \gamma(1,3))$.

In this way, given the input r_1 and r_2, the fuzzy controller constructs the Output fuzzy set $\overline{O}$.

Approximate reasoning. Most elementary fuzzy controllers use this procedure for evaluating the rules to produce an Output fuzzy set. The idea is to interpret a fuzzy control rule as an implication in approximate reasoning and to use Zadeh's compositional rule of inference [16–18] to evaluate the inference given the inputs r_1 and r_2. Consider the rule

$$\text{if } [r_1 = \overline{R}(1)] \quad \text{and} \quad [r_2 = \overline{R}(3)], \text{ then Output} = \overline{O}(4) \tag{6}$$

We first combine the fuzzy numbers $\overline{R}(1)$, $\overline{R}(3)$, and $\overline{O}(4)$ to obtain a fuzzy relation $\overline{R}_{13}$ on R^3. If $\mu(y_1, y_2, y_3|\overline{R}_{13})$ is the membership function for $\overline{R}_{13}$, then $\mu(y_1, y_2, y_3|\overline{R}_{13})$ is in $[0, 1]$ for real numbers y_1, y_2, y_3. There are many methods for computing $\overline{R}_{13}$ (see ref. 19 for a survey), and the initial method in reference 20 was

$$\mu(y_1,y_2,y_3|\overline{R}_{13}) = \min(\mu(y_1|\overline{R}(1)), \mu(y_2|\overline{R}(3)), \mu(y_3|\overline{O}(4))) \tag{7}$$

This is done for all rules producing fuzzy relations $\overline{R}_{11}, \overline{R}_{12}, \ldots, \overline{R}_{33}$ on R^3 (recall that we are assuming that $N = 3$). We may next combine all these relations into one relation $\overline{R}$ on R^3. One possible procedure for obtaining $\overline{R}$ is

$$\mu(y_1,y_2,y_3|\overline{R}) = \max_{i,j}(\mu(y_1,y_2,y_3|\overline{R}_{ij}) \tag{8}$$

Given r_1 and r_2, then the Output fuzzy set $\overline{O}^*$, different from $\overline{O}$ in the "Expert Systems" section above, is

$$\mu(y_3|\overline{O}^*) = \mu(r_1,r_2,y_3|\overline{R}) \tag{9}$$

Another method of calculating $\overline{O}^*$ is [21,22] to use the numbers $\gamma(x_1,x_2)$ computed in the "Expert Systems" section above to weight the fuzzy numbers $\overline{O}(l)$ in the consequence of a rule and the $\overline{O}^*$ is the union of the weighted fuzzy numbers. For the rule in equation (6) we would first calculate $\overline{O}^*(4) = \gamma(1,3)\overline{O}(4)$ and then

$$\mu(y|\overline{O}^*) = \max_l(\mu(y|\overline{O}^*(l))) \tag{10}$$

We have presented only two of the numerous methods investigated for calculating an Output fuzzy set $\overline{O}^*$ using the approximate reasoning interpretation of the fuzzy control rules.

6. Defuzzification

Defuzzification is simply a mapping of $\overline{O}$, or $\overline{O}^*$, into the interval $[-1, 1]$. Let δ be the value of this mapping. If $u(t)$ is the input to the process at time t, then $u(t) = u(t - \Delta) + K\delta$ at $t = \Delta, 2\Delta, \ldots$, where K is another scaling constant. The defuzzification will depend on the Output fuzzy set, or on the evaluation procedure.

Expert system. We will define only two of the commonly used defuzzifiers. Let $cv(l)$ be a central value of $\overline{O}(l)$, $1 \le l \le L$. A central value of $\overline{O}(l)$ is a point (may be unique) where the membership function for $\overline{O}(l)$ is one. Then a linear defuzzifier for $\overline{O}, \delta = $ linear, equals $cv(1)\Delta(1) + \cdots + cv(L)\Delta(L)$. If sum (Δ) is the sum of the $\Delta(l)$, then a nonlinear defuzzifier for $\overline{O}$ is $\delta = \delta_2^* = $ (linear) / sum (Δ), also called a center of gravity defuzzifier.

Approximate reasoning. Two typical defuzzifiers for $\overline{O}^*$ are (see ref. 23 for a survey of other defuzzifiers) the average of maxima and the center of gravity. The average of maxima procedure sets δ equal to the average of all the values, where the membership function for $\overline{O}^*$ takes on its maximum value. The center of gravity method has δ equal to the center of gravity of the fuzzy set $\overline{O}^*$.

B. Sugeno's Controller

The discussion above explains how almost all elementary fuzzy controllers operate except, most notably, Sugeno's controller. In Sugeno's controller a fuzzy control rule becomes a fuzzy process law like

$$L_3: \text{if } [r_1 = \text{negative}] \quad \text{and} \quad [r_2 = \text{positive}], \text{then} \\ y_3 = c_{03} + c_{13}r_1 + c_{23}r_2 \tag{11}$$

That is, the consequence becomes a function of the inputs. The process laws are numbered $L_1, L_2, \ldots$, and L_3 in equation (11) would be a typical process law. The constants c_{ij} may be determined from knowledge of the process, trial input-output data, etc. In fact, in one study [1] the parameters c_{ij} are computed using trial input-output data, to minimize output error. Other functions of the inputs r_i can be used for y_i [3].

We evaluate the antecedent in each fuzzy process law as in the "Expert System" subsection of Section II.A.5, obtaining the $\gamma(x_1, x_2)$ numbers. Also, the y_i

values are obtained, given r_1 and r_2, for each process law. Then a defuzzified value δ may be computed as follows:

$$\delta = \frac{\Sigma\gamma(x_1, x_2)y_i}{\Sigma\gamma(x_1, x_2)} \tag{12}$$

In equation (12) the sums are over all process laws and the contribution $\gamma(x_1,x_2)y_i$ in the numerator has both $\gamma(x_1,x_2)$ and y_i coming from the same process law. For example, from process law L_3 in equation (11) we would have $\gamma(x_1,x_2)y_i = \gamma(1,3)y_3$.

C. Extensions

The basic fuzzy controllers described above may be extended in various directions and still be considered to be elementary fuzzy controllers. The process can have multiple outputs and inputs. The process may have two or more state variables, and we could compute scaled error, scaled rate, etc. for each process output for input to the fuzzy controller. Also, there would be an Output fuzzy set $\overline{O}_k$, or $\overline{O}_k^*$, corresponding to each process input that would need to be defuzzified. We could employ any number N of fuzzy numbers for each controller input, and the scaled intervals for the variables and fuzzy numbers can be $[-M, M]$ for any $M > 0$. In the expert system evaluation of the fuzzy control rules, we may use different t-norms for different rules (mixed fuzzy logic). All these variations still produce an elementary fuzzy controller.

III. RESEARCH RESULTS

We will classify the research results on the theory of the fuzzy controller into three categories: functional relationship, limit theorems, and stability.

A. Functional Relationship

Suppose the fuzzy controller has one Output fuzzy set, which is defuzzified to a value δ in $[-1, 1]$. If the inputs to the fuzzy controller are $r_1, r_2, \ldots,$ then this research area is concerned with finding the structure of a function F where $\delta = F(r_1, r_2, \ldots)$. That is, find the functional relationship between the defuzzified output and all the inputs. Finding the functional relationship between δ and the inputs is what has been called [24] the algebraic model of the fuzzy controller.

All the results discussed below relate to an elementary fuzzy controller, which employs the expert system method of evaluating the rules. In the initial research in the functional relationship area of the fuzzy controller [15], the authors wanted to find evaluation methods (t-norms and co-t-norms) that produce a linear controller. We say the fuzzy controller is a linear controller if

$$\delta = \Sigma \tau_i r_i \tag{13}$$

where the sum is over all inputs and the τ_i are constants. Otherwise, we would say that the fuzzy controller is a nonlinear controller. In the research of Siler and Ying there were two inputs, three triangular fuzzy numbers ($N = 3$) for each input, $\Psi = linear^*$, $\delta = $ linear, and the Output fuzzy set had five triangular fuzzy numbers. They found that mixed fuzzy logic (using a different t-norm for different fuzzy control rules) did produce a linear controller but, more importantly, one obtains a linear controller when $T = PAND$ and $C = LOR$. This last result was generalized [11,4] to processes with multiple state variables, controllers with two or more Output fuzzy sets, any number of triangular fuzzy numbers for each input, $\Psi = $ linear, and $\delta = \delta_2^*$. It is interesting to note that the mixed fuzzy logic result does not generalize and appears to be a singular result for the particular fuzzy controller considered in this research.

The next set of results for the two-input case were for the smallest fuzzy controllers, which has only two fuzzy numbers ("negative" and "positive") for each input. All fuzzy numbers are triangular. If $\Psi = linear^*$, $T = $ min, and $C = $ max, then we obtained a linear controller for $\delta = $ linear [12] but a nonlinear controller when $\delta = \delta_2^*$ [6]. Zadeh logic ($T = $ min, $C = $ max) is very important, since it has been used extensively in applications. Therefore, the results above ($\delta = \delta_2^*$) have been extended [6] to larger fuzzy controllers having any number of triangular fuzzy numbers for each input, and we found a closed-form expression for F in $\delta = F(r_1, r_2)$, compared it to the PI controller, and analyzed its nonlinearities.

In the two input case, if $\delta = F(r_1, r_2) = \beta_1 r_1 + \beta_2 r_2$, where the β_i are functions of r_1 and r_2, we call the fuzzy controller a nonlinear PI controller. We have showed [12] that the smallest fuzzy controller, triangular fuzzy numbers, $\Psi = linear^*$, $\delta = \delta_2^*$, but $T = $ min and $C = LOR$, is a nonlinear PI controller.

Now let us turn to the three-input case but only one state variable and only one Output fuzzy set. Almost nothing has been published on the three input case. A summary of some isolated results and some conjectures is presented in reference 15.

B. Limit Theorems

A few researchers have noticed that if they increased the number of fuzzy numbers used for each input, hence increased the number of fuzzy control rules, there was little or no change in control of the process. This led us to the following "central limit" type results for the fuzzy controller. These results hold for the expert system method of evaluating the fuzzy control rules, any number of inputs, any type of fuzzy number, $\Psi = linear^*$, any t-norm, any co-t-norm, and any defuzzifier. As before, N denotes the number of fuzzy numbers used for each input. For one state variable and one Output fuzzy set, we showed [9] that as $N \to +\infty$, δ becomes a linear function of all inputs. This result was later generalized [5] to multiple state variables, Ψ = linear and multiple Output fuzzy sets. These theorems show that fuzzy controllers with linear conclusion functions become linear controllers as the number of fuzzy control rules grow.

C. Stability

Stability of the fuzzy controller still remains a major unsolved problem. If $e(t)$ is error = $y(t)$ - (set point) at $t = \Delta, 2\Delta, \ldots$, then one definition of stability would be to say that the fuzzy controller is stable if $e(n\Delta) \to 0$ as $n \to +\infty$. However, without a specific process (model), or even a fuzzy model of the process, to work with, it seems impossible, in general, to show $e(n\Delta) \to 0$ as $n \to +\infty$ [26]. We suggested [10] a fuzzy goal for stability in that the membership value for this fuzzy goal is near one (zero) when "setting-in time" is short (long).

A number of other authors have considered the stability problem for the fuzzy controller. Modeling simple fuzzy controllers as multilevel relay controllers was done [27] to investigate the stability of the controller. Other authors [28] extended this work to further study the stability of the fuzzy controller. Daley and Gill [29] state that they employed Liapunov's second method to identify a stable choice of scaling factors. A more theoretical study of stability in fuzzy systems [30] has received further analysis [31]. Also, definitions for stability for the fuzzy controller have been introduced [32,33]. A new approach [34] entails looking at the stability of a two-input fuzzy controller, which employs the approximate reasoning method of evaluating the rules, using bifurcation theory, but the process is assumed to be governed by a given differential equation.

However, in the final analysis discussion of stability of the fuzzy controller may be irrelevant [26], since stability analysis relies on the availability of a mathematical model of the process and fuzzy controllers have achieved their success most notably in the absence of such a model.

D. Other Research

There has been limited research on the first two research areas discussed above. A thorough study on how an elementary fuzzy controller performs under various methods of evaluating the rules (approximate reasoning method), different defuzzifiers, and various types of fuzzy numbers has been reported [19,23,35,36]. In another pair of studies [37,38], the authors first consider how the compositional rule of inference and the defuzzifier effect control and second investigate how the scaling constants and the fuzzy control rules will effect the defuzzified output. Manipulating the scaling constants and the defuzzifier to improve performance has also been discussed [10,39].

There are a couple of papers [40-42] with results similar to those mentioned above about the functional relationship between δ and the inputs. In these reports the authors do analyze the difference between the defuzzified output δ and the P,

PI, and PID controllers for one, two, and three inputs, respectively. They believe their results will help in studying the stability of these fuzzy controllers.

In the initial paper on taking the limit of a fuzzy controller, as the rules grow without bound [43], the author showed that in the limit, as the quantization levels of the input and output variables become infinitely fine, the fuzzy controller approaches the PI controller.

Overall, the research results on the theory of the fuzzy controller are scarce compared to the numerous applications papers.

E. Future Research

First we must continue to extend the results summarized above on the fuzzy controller that uses the expert system method of evaluating the rules. The two-input case can be further studied using different types of fuzzy numbers (besides just triangular), other types of defuzzifier, other fuzzy logics for evaluating the rules, and more fuzzy numbers per input. Considerable effort needs to be put on the three-input case to see what, if any, results for the two-input case generalize to three inputs. For three inputs we want to know:

1. When is it a linear controller? And if it is nonlinear, compare it to the PID controller.
2. When is it a nonlinear PID controller?

In the area of limit theorems, we would like to find necessary and sufficient conditions on a fuzzy controller so that it approaches a linear controller as the rules grow without bound. It would be nice to know something about the rate of convergence for the limit theorems discussed above. Finally, do we obtain a limiting result that depends only on the structure of the conclusion function? That is, if the conclusion function is quadratic, will the defuzzified value approach a quadratic function of the inputs as the number of rules grows without bound?

Next we turn to the basic fuzzy controller whose rules are evaluated using the approximate reasoning procedure. Almost nothing is known about functional relationship and limits for this fuzzy controller. Therefore, a top priority is to derive these results, for two and three inputs, for this type of fuzzy controller.

The problem of stability of the fuzzy controller also has top priority. Almost any new results in this area are welcome.

All the foregoing research projects would start assuming one state variable (one process output) and one Output fuzzy set (one process input) and then generalize to multiple outputs and inputs where possible.

IV. EXTRAS

By an "extra" we mean something that has been added to the basic fuzzy controller described above to enhance its performance. There are a number of items one must choose to set up a basic fuzzy controller. We called these items "variables." Fuzzy controller variables include (1) the number of inputs (error, rate, . . .) to compute per process state variable, the input scaling constants and the corresponding scaled interval(s), and the sampling interval; (2) the number and type of fuzzy numbers to use for each input; (3) the number and type of fuzzy numbers to use for each Output fuzzy set; (4) the fuzzy control rules (both the cells in the fuzzy control table and the conclusion function(s)); (5) the method of evaluating the fuzzy control rules given the inputs; (6) the defuzzifiers; and (7) the output scaling constant(s). When something is added to the basic fuzzy controller to adjust, or change, some of these variables in order to alter the control of the process, we call the "something" added an "extra." In computer applications we have the added variable of how to discretize the continuous fuzzy numbers.

In the first paper with an "extra" [44], the authors describe a self-organizing fuzzy controller (SOC); see also reference 45. Construction of the set of fuzzy control rules is obviously a crucial aspect of fuzzy controller design. An SOC attempts to automate the task of constructing the rule base by using a higher level set of rules, which can modify existing rules or create new rules. The metarules (higher level rules) are based on acceptable process response, which requires at least a crude model of the process. After this publication, the literature on automatically changing some of the variables mentioned above to achieve better control has grown quite large. In this section we can only briefly survey some of the results in this area.

Perhaps a good place to start is to determine how to change the scaling constants to obtain better performance. In reference 10 the authors discuss varying the output scaling constant and the defuzzifier to meet certain fuzzy goals. The fuzzy goals include "fast" rise time and "small" overshoot. Other authors [46] describe a self-regulating fuzzy controller (SRC) that can vary all the scaling constants (see also ref. 47). Also, in both references 46 and 47, the authors consider changing the consequence of a fuzzy control rule (the conclusion function discussed above) to improve control.

Another variable to consider is the shape of the fuzzy numbers used for the inputs and used in the Output fuzzy set. An adaptive fuzzy controller (AFC) modifies the values of some of its variables to automatically adjust to changing process conditions (different set point). Bartolini et al. [48] explain how to change the shape of the fuzzy sets based on the current performance of the fuzzy controller. They call their system a performance AFC (PAFC). See also reference 49.

An AFC may vary any variables to adapt to changing conditions. In the 1980s a controller was proposed [50,51] that selects the best control action (process input) based on a fuzzy model of the process and a performance measure. No fuzzy control rules are needed. At each control instant the controller surveys all possible control actions, uses the fuzzy process model to predict their effect at the next sampling time, and chooses the action that produces the best result with respect to the performance measure. These authors might call their method a fuzzy model based controller (FMC). Besides having the adaptive feature, this procedure may be used for self-tuning to a particular process.

Another title given to a fuzzy controller, which is to change the values of some of its variables, is predictive fuzzy controller (PFC). Yasunobu et al. [52,53] have discussed a PFC in which the system first predicts (through simulation) the result of each fuzzy control rule, then evaluates a performance index corresponding to each control result, and then chooses the rule to execute that has the best comprehensive evaluation. This controller is similar to the AFC described above. The simulation may be done employing test data gained from experienced operators.

Many other procedures are possible for determining how to vary the variables, and in one mixture of fuzzy control and nonfuzzy control [54], the nonfuzzy controller switches control between three separate fuzzy controllers. A new idea is to combine neural networks with a fuzzy controller where the neural net may be used for computation and learning. Some authors [55–57] consider embedding a neural network in the fuzzy controller to enhance control of a process. In particular, two papers [56,57] propose a neural network for using trial data to design the shapes of the fuzzy numbers and the conclusions of the fuzzy control rules (Sugeno-type controller). We will call this controller a neural fuzzy controller (NFC).

All the foregoing descriptions of additions to the fuzzy controller have a similar theme: vary some of the variables (discussed above) to achieve a "better" controller, where a "better" controller is measured with respect to some (fuzzy or nonfuzzy) criteria. However, they all process real numbers. That is, the input to the fuzzy controller and its defuzzified output is always real numbers. We have argued [7] that for the fuzzy controller to generalize control theory, it should be able to process fuzzy sets. This means that the input to the fuzzy controller may be a fuzzy set (representing a linguistic variable) and the output of the fuzzy controller for input to the process can also be a fuzzy set in the form of a linguistic variable. This idea has recently been developed [8] for control of man–machine systems.

V. SUMMARY AND CONCLUSIONS

We started this brief tutorial on the fuzzy controller with a detailed description on how an elementary fuzzy controller operates. Basic fuzzy controllers may be divided into two groups depending on how the fuzzy control rules are evaluated: (1) as production rules in an expert system or (2) as implications in approximate reasoning. We discussed Sugeno's fuzzy controller separately, because its structure does not fit into the general description of basic fuzzy controllers.

We next surveyed the known results on the theory of the fuzzy controller. The first topic was determining the form of F, where F is the functional relationship between the defuzzified output and all the inputs to the fuzzy controller. The results here were only for the expert system method of evaluating the rules and were mostly concerned with determining, for small (two inputs and a few fuzzy numbers for each input) fuzzy controllers, when the fuzzy controller is a linear controller (F is linear). More general results were found for the limit theorems. It has been shown, for the expert system method of rule evaluation, and a linear fuzzy control rule table, that as the number of rules grows without bound, F becomes linear. The last research area discussed was that of stability. Except for a few isolated results, a general theory of stability for the fuzzy controller is unsolved. After looking over the known research results on the theory of the fuzzy controller, it becomes clear what areas are of immediate concern for future study. Suggestions for future research were summarized at the end of Section III.

The discussion up to this point has been about a basic fuzzy controller with no "extras." An "extra" has been defined as anything added to the basic fuzzy controller that modifies some of its variables to achieve "better" control. The variables in an elementary fuzzy controller include the scaling constants, the number and type of fuzzy numbers used to define the linguistic variables, the fuzzy control rules, the method of evaluation, and the defuzzifiers. A "better" controller is determined with respect to some criteria such as performance indices. This is the major area of current research on the application of the fuzzy controller and is growing rapidly. A brief survey of some of these "extras" was presented in Section IV.

However, all these fuzzy controllers, with or without additions, process only real numbers. It seems that a *fuzzy* controller should also be able to process fuzzy information. To the author, who suggests [8] a generalization of the traditional fuzzy controller to a fuzzy input/output controller that will process linguistic variables for the control of man-machine systems, it seems that the fuzzy controller will achieve its true power only when it is allowed to also process fuzzy data.

REFERENCES

1. M. Sugeno and M. Nishida, "Fuzzy Control of Model Car," *Fuzzy Sets Syst., 16*: 103–113 (1985).
2. M. Sugeno and G. T. Kang, "Fuzzy Modeling and Control of Multilayer Incinerator," *Fuzzy Sets Syst., 18*: 329–346 (1986).
3. M. Maeda and S. Mrakami, "A Design for a Fuzzy Logic Controller," *Inf. Sci., 45*: 315–330 (1988).
4. J. J. Buckley, "Further Results for the Linear Fuzzy Controller," *Kybernetes, 18*: 48–55 (1989).
5. J. J. Buckley, "Fuzzy Controller: Further Limit Theorems for Linear Control Rules," *Fuzzy Sets Syst., 36*: 225–233 (1990).
6. J. J. Buckley, "Nonlinear Fuzzy Controller," *Inf. Sci.,* Vol. 60, no. 3, December 1991. To appear.
7. J. J. Buckley, "Fuzzy vs. Non-Fuzzy Controllers," *Control and Cybern., 18*:127–130 (1989).

8. J. J. Buckley, "Fuzzy I/O Controller," *Fuzzy Sets Syst.*, *43*:127-137 (1991).

9. J. J. Buckley and H. Ying, "Fuzzy Controller Theory: Limit Theorems for Linear Fuzzy Control Rules," *Automatica, 25*: 469-472 (1989).

10. J. J. Buckley and H. Ying, "Expert Fuzzy Controller," *Fuzzy Sets Syst.*, *44*:373-390 (1991).

11. J. J. Buckley and H. Ying, "Linear Fuzzy Controller: It Is a Linear Non-Fuzzy Controller," *Inf. Sci., 51*: 183-192 (1990).

12. J. J. Buckley, W. Siler, and H. Ying, "Fuzzy Control Theory: A Nonlinear Case," *Automatica, 26*: 513-520 (1990).

13. H. Ying, W. Siler, and D. Tucker, "A New Type of Fuzzy Controller Based Upon a Fuzzy Expert System Shell FLOPS," in *Proceedings of the International Workshop on Artificial Intelligence for Industrial Applications*, IEEE, pp. 382-386, 1988.

14. H. Ying, L. Sheppard, and D. Tucker, "Expert-System-Based Fuzzy Control of Arterial Pressure by Drug Infusion," *Med. Prog. Technol., 13*: 203-215 (1988).

15. W. Siler and H. Ying, "Fuzzy Control Theory: The Linear Case," *Fuzzy Sets Syst., 33*: 275-290 (1989).

16. L. A. Zadeh, "Outline of New Approach to the Analysis of Complex Systems and Decision Processes," *IEEE Trans. Syst. Man. Cybern., SMC-3*: 28-44 (1973).

17. L. A. Zadeh, "The Concept of a Linguistic Variable and its Application to Approximate Reasoning," Parts I-III, *Inf. Sci., 8*: 199-249, 301-357 (1975), *9*: 43-80 (1975).

18. L. A. Zadeh, "A Theory of Approximate Reasoning," in *Machine Intelligence* (J. Hayes, D. Michie, and L. I. Mikulich, eds.), Vol. 9, Halstead Press, New York, pp. 149-194, 1979.

19. M. Mizumoto, "Fuzzy Controls Under Various Fuzzy Reasoning Methods," *Inf. Sci., 45*: 129-151 (1988).

20. S. Assilian and E. Mamdani, "An Experiment in Linguistic Synthesis with a Fuzzy Logic Controller," *Int. J. Man-Machine Stud., 7*: 1-13 (1974).

21. E. H. Mamdani, J. J. Ostergaard, and E. Lembessis, "Use of Fuzzy Logic for Implementing Rule-Based Controllers for Industrial Processes," in *Fuzzy Sets and Decision Analysis* (H. J. Zimmermann, L. A. Zadeh, and B. R. Gaines, eds.), North Holland, Amsterdam, pp. 307-323, 1984.

22. M. Sugeno, "An Introductory Survey of Fuzzy Control," *Inf. Sci., 36*: 59-83 (1985).

23. M. Mizumoto, "Fuzzy Controls Under Various Defuzzifier Methods," in "Proceedings of the International Workshop on Fuzzy System Applications," Iizuka, Japan, August 20-24, 1988.

24. M. Braae and D. A. Rutherford, "Theoretical and Linguistic Aspects of the Fuzzy Logic Controller," *Automatica, 15*: 553-577 (1979).

25. J. J. Buckley, "Theory of the Fuzzy Controller: An Introduction," in *Proceedings of the Eighth International Congress on Cybernetics and Systems*, Hunter College, New York, June 11-15, 1990.

26. E. H. Mamdami, "Advances in the Linguistic Synthesis of Fuzzy Controllers," *Int. J. Man-Machine Stud., 8*: 669-678 (1976).

27. W. J. M. Kickkert and E. H. Mamdani, "Analysis of a Fuzzy Logic Controller," *Fuzzy Sets Syst., 1*: 29-44 (1978).

28. K. S. Ray and D. Dutta Majumder, "Application of Circle Criteria for Stability Analy-

sis of Linear SISO and MIMO Systems Associated with Fuzzy Logic Controller," *IEEE Trans. Syst. Man. Cybern., SMC-14*: 345–349 (1984).

29. S. Daley and K. F. Gill, "The Fuzzy Logic Controller: An Alternate Design Scheme?" *Comput. Ind., 6*: 3–14 (1985).

30. R. M. Tong, "Some Properties of Fuzzy Feedback Systems," *IEEE Trans. Syst. Man. Cybern., SMC-10*: 327–330 (1980).

31. A. Cumani, "On a Possibilistic Approach to the Analysis of Fuzzy Feedback Systems," *IEEE Trans. Syst. Man. Cybern., SMC-12*: 417–422 (1982).

32. J. B. Kiszka, M. M. Gupta, and P. N. Nikiforuk, "Some Properties of Expert Control Systems," in *Approximate Reasoning in Expert Systems* (M. M. Gupta, A. Kandel, W. Bandler, and J. B. Kiszka, eds.), North Holland, Amsterdam, pp. 235 ff, 1985.

33. M. M. Gupta, G. M. Trojan, and J. B. Kiszka, "Controllability of Fuzzy Control Systems," *IEEE Trans. Syst. Man. Cybern., SMC-16*: 576 (1986).

34. S. Kawase and N. Yanagihara, "On the Stability of Fuzzy Control Systems," in *Proceedings of the Third IFSA Congress*, Seattle, WA, Aug. 6–11, 1989, pp. 67–70.

35. M. Mizumoto, "Fuzzy Controls Under Various Approximate Reasoning Methods," in *Proceedings of the Second IFSA Congress*, Tokyo, July 20–25, 1987, pp. 143–146.

36. M. Mizumoto, " Improvement Methods of Fuzzy Controls," in *Proceedings of the Third IFSA Congress*, Seattle, WA, Aug. 6–11, 1989, pp. 60–62.

37. M. Braae and D. A. Rutherford, "Fuzzy Relations in a Control Setting," *Kybernetes, 7*: 185–188 (1978).

38. M. Braae and D. A. Rutherford, "Selection of Parameters for a Fuzzy Logic Controller," *Fuzzy Sets Syst., 2*: 185–199 (1979).

39. J. B. Kiszka, M. E. Kochanska, and D. S. Sliwinska, "The Influence of Some Parameters on the Accuracy of a Fuzzy Model," in *Industrial Applications of Fuzzy Control* (M. Sugeno, ed.), North Holland, Amsterdam, pp. 187–230, 1985.

40. P. Z. Wang, H. M. Zhang, and W. Xu, "Pad-Analysis of Fuzzy Controllers' Stability," unpublished manuscript.

41. P. Z. Wang, H. M. Zhang, and W. Xu, "Analysis of a New Fuzzy Controller: FOCS2000," in *Proceedings of the Third IFSA Congress*, Seattle, WA, Aug. 6–11, 1989, pp. 208–211.

42. P. Z. Wang, H. M. Zhang, Z. G. Wu, and W. Xu, "PAD-Analysis of Stability of Fuzzy Control Systems," in *Proceedings of NAFIPS '90*, Toronto, Canada, June 6–8, 1990, pp. 354–357.

43. P. J. MacVicar-Whelan, "Fuzzy Sets for Man–Machine Interaction," *Int. J. Man–Machine Stud., 8*: 687–697 (1976).

44. T. J. Procyk and E. H. Mamdani, "A Linguistic Self-Organizing Process Controller," *Automatica, 15*: 15–30 (1979).

45. K. Sugiyama, "Rule-Based Self-Organizing Controller," in *Fuzzy Computing* (M. M. Gupta and T. Yamakawa, eds.), North Holland, Amsterdam, pp. 341–353, 1988.

46. X. T. Peng, S. M. Liu, T. Yamakawa, P. Wang, and X. Liu, "Self-Regulating PID Controllers and Their Application to a Temperature Controlling Process," in *Fuzzy Computing—Theory, Hardware, and Applications* (M. M. Gupta and T. Yamakawa, eds.), North Holland, Amsterdam, pp. 355–364, 1988.

47. X. T. Peng, "Generating Rules for Fuzzy Logic Controllers by Functions," *Fuzzy Sets Syst., 36*: 83-89 (1990).

48. G. Bartolini, G. Casalino, F. Davoli, M. Mastretta, R. Minciardi, and E. Morten, "Development of Performance Adaptive Fuzzy Controllers with Application to Continuous Casting Plants," in *Cybernetics and Systems Research* (R. Trappl, ed.), North Holland, Amsterdam, pp. 721-728, 1982.

49. K. S. Ray and D. D. Majumder, "Structure of an Intelligent Fuzzy Logic Controller and Its Behavior," in *Approximate Reasoning in Expert systems* (M. M. Gupta, A. Kandel, W. Bandler, and J. B. Kiszka, eds.), North Holland, Amsterdam, pp. 593-619, 1985.

50. B. P. Graham and R. B. Newell, "Fuzzy Identification and Control of a Liquid Level Rig," *Fuzzy Sets Syst., 26*: 255-273 (1988).

51. B. P. Graham and R. B. Newell, "Fuzzy Adaptive Control of a First-Order Process," *Fuzzy Sets Syst., 31*: 47-65 (1989).

52. S. Yasunobu and T. Hasegawa, "Predictive Fuzzy Control and Application for Automatic Container Crane Operation systems," in *Proceedings of the Second IFSA Congress*, Tokyo, July 20-25, 1987, pp. 349-352.

53. H. Oshima, S. Yasunobu, and S. Sekino, "Automatic Train Operation system Based on Predictive Fuzzy Control," in *Proceedings of the International Workshop on Artificial Intelligence for Industrial Applications*, IEEE, pp. 485-489, 1988.

54. T. Terano and S. Masui, "Manual Control of an Intrinsically Unstable System and Its Modeling by Fuzzy Logic," *Inf. Sci., 45*: 249-273 (1988).

55. M. M. Gupta, W. Pedrycz, and J. B. Kiszka, "Fuzzy Control: From Fuzzy Controllers to Cognitive Controllers," in *Proceedings of the Third IFSA Congress*, Seattle, WA, Aug. 6-11, 1989, pp. 258-261.

56. I. Hayashi, H. Nomura, and N. Wakami, "Artificial Neural Network Driven Fuzzy Control and Its Application to the Learning of Inverted Pendulum System," in *Proceedings of the Third IFSA Congress*, Seattle, WA, Aug. 6-11, 1989, pp. 610-613.

57. H. Takagi and I. Hayashi, "NN-Driven Fuzzy Reasoning," *J. Approximate Reasoning*, 5:191-212 (1991).

16

From Symbol Manipulation to Understanding Cognition: A Critical Introduction to Cognitive Science from a Computational Neuroepistemology Perspective

Markus F. Peschl University of Vienna, Vienna, Austria

I. INTRODUCTORY REMARKS

This chapter presents an introduction to *cognitive science* (and cognitive modeling); I shall *not* however, follow the traditional approach of this discipline, because this seems to be very problematic for several reasons, as discussed in the course of this chapter. Generally speaking, we understand cognitive science as the *continuation of traditional epistemology* in the context of modern *(natural) scientific knowledge* (especially of neuroscience, computer science, and cybernetics). In contrast to this approach, traditional cognitive science is dominated in most cases by the methods and concepts of computer science; epistemological or philosophical questions are only of second-order interest if they are interesting at all. This seems to be quite unjustified, because the questions cognitive science is concerned with are very old and have a rich tradition in philosophy and epistemology.

To make clear the implicit assumptions and basic problems of cognitive science, the traditional approach to this discipline is discussed in the first part of this chapter. The most important points of criticism are the unjustified *dominance* of computer science (and its implications), the lack of interdisciplinary cooperation, and the reduction to *symbol manipulation*. The assumptions and methods, which in most cases are applied *implicitly* and *without reflection* are critically reviewed from an *interdisciplinary* perspective. Arguments from computer science, philosophy, epistemology, and the philosophy of science, as well as from semiotics, will be used to make explicit the inadequacy, insufficiencies, and problems of the traditional approach to cognitive science.

As an implication of this criticism an *alternative* concept is sketched (see Section IV): this approach is called *computational neuroepistemology (CNE)*, and it represents an answer, an alternative, and possibly a solution to the problems and to the inadequacy of traditional cognitive science as discussed earlier in the chapter. CNE investigates the very *basic* problem of *knowledge, knowledge representation, language, communication,* etc.; knowledge is not reduced to symbolic or natural language knowledge (as is done in AI and traditional cognitive science); we rather try to find a bridge spanning the gap between very primitive forms of knowledge (simple behavior), over linguistic structures to scientific knowledge.

Computational neuroepistemology is based on epistemological, computer science as well as on neuroscience issues and considerations. It understands itself as an alternative concept of the traditional cognitive science approaches, which apply the paradigm of symbolic representation. It is an alternative to the "orthodox" symbol manipulation processes dominating almost all computational models of cognition. The number of participating disciplines is reduced to three (neuroscience, epistemology, and computer science). Each of these disciplines plays a characteristic role in the interdisciplinary discourse of the CNE approach. It enables a more adequate investigation, description, explanation, model, etc. of cognitive phenomena, because each of these disciplines has the same weight in the discussion—a sophisticated system of self-organization of the three disciplines guarantees a well-balanced interdisciplinary discourse. The most important points and implications of this approach can be summarized as follows:

Computer science represents a quite young paradigm, which plays a central role in the CNE approach: it provides *parallel distributed processing (connectionism, PDP).* Its combination with neuroscience offers very interesting possibilities in the investigation of the relation between neural and "mental" processes (*"mind and body"*).

A *constructivist* view is assumed: epistemology offers very interesting concepts combining natural scientific knowledge (e.g., neuroscience, second-order cybernetics) with epistemological ideas of constructivism (Maturana, 1970, 1983; von Foerster, 1973, 1984; Maturana and Varela, 1975, 1980; von Glasenfeld, 1976, 1981, etc.).

The interaction of these three approaches and disciplines (connectionism, neuroscience, and constructivism) has very interesting implications for the central question of *knowledge representation* in cognitive science, neuroscience as well as in artificial intelligence.

Computational neuroepistemology represents a *bottom-up* approach: the aim is to understand the *basic* processes of language, knowledge, communication, and so on; that is, we are not interested in complex problem-solving or chess-playing strategies, etc. (as AI is), but rather in the (basic *neural*) processes responsible for these abilities. As shown in Sections IV and V, the computational neuroepistemology approach tries to model cognition on the more basic level of neural activities from the bottom up (not on a symbolic level in the top-down manner).

II. FIELDS IN TRADITIONAL COGNITIVE SCIENCE

Before discussing the methods and (implicit) assumptions of traditional cognitive science in detail, we are going to have a look at the most important fields of research in this discipline, to get an overview of the scope and interests. We will see that a wide spectrum of phenomena, disciplines, and methods is involved in the investigation of cognitive processes; their *complexity and diversity* makes cognitive science such a fascinating field of research. Traditional cognitive science can be divided into the following areas (this enumeration covers the most important fields of current research): perception and vision; problem solving, thinking, and reasoning; motor control; language; and learning.

A.   Perception and Vision

One part of cognitive science investigates and simulates the *peripheral perception system*. Our knowledge is determined by the structure of our nervous system and by the experiences—the system of perception, thus, plays a key role as it determines how we are perceiving our environment. This fact is in most cases underestimated and ignored. The sensory system, however, enables to recognize an object *by integrating different modalities* (shape, color, touch, motion, etc.). One of the most important sensors represents the *visual system*—it dominates (along with the acoustic system) our perception of the world. It is investigated quite well by neuroscience, and we do know a lot of visual processing in the brain (see, Hubel and Wiesel, 1962, 1965, 1968).

The *visual system* is also the most popular field of interest in cognitive science. In the beginning the idea of pattern recognition was in the fore–generally speaking, the problem is to discern a structure from an array of intensities. This problem has been solved by mathematical and statistical methods; close relations to neuroscientific issues can be found. D. Marr is one of the most important exponents in this field (Marr, 1982). In the course of development, the question of *understanding* pictures became increasingly interesting. This implies that these primary pattern recognition systems had to be connected to knowledge-based and knowledge-processing machines. There are many applications in this field, such as in medicine (medical information processing, automatic recognition of waveforms in EEGs and ECGs, etc.), in the earth and space sciences (classification of pictures), in radar and sonar, and in promoting a better understanding of the visual system by simulating simple artificial visual systems.

B. Problem Solving, Thinking and Reasoning

Problem solving is one of the most fascinating areas being investigated by cognitive science. A given problem has to be solved by finding or constructing a solution; this process has to be done automatically by making use of different reasoning techniques. These techniques depend on the kind of knowledge representation used for representing the problem, the phenomena, or the domain. AI has demonstrated that problems can be solved by *searching* in a big searching space (this strategy is applied in most computer games, such as chess). The problem is to draw conclusions from given facts. From a principal point of view, the different forms of reasoning, problem solving, etc. are strongly related because-if we are assuming a symbolic knowledge representation-they always represent a sort of *classification* of given facts.

Other problem-solving techniques have also been developed, such as applying rules (e.g., in expert systems) or inferring in a semantic network. The models of the connectionist approach represent a very promising alternative, because they make use of an alternative kind of knowledge representation. We have to differentiate, however, between different forms of PDP networks being applied to problem-solving tasks.

C. Motor Control

The field of motor control investigates all the output (i.e., motor) functions in natural and artificial systems to communicate the cognitions being processed inside the organism/machine to its environment. Motor systems have different tasks to fulfill:

On the one hand, they have to enable the organism or machine to move around in his or her or its environment.

On the other hand, the motor system has to move the sensory organs to acquire information *actively* from the environment.

It has to be seen that there is a close relation between the input and output side of the organism/machine, which are connected with respect to two factors:

The mechanism responsible for reasoning, planning etc.
The environment in which the organism/machine is acting (Fig. 1)

In many cases and models this closed feedback loop is not taken into consideration. As will be discussed in Section IV, this causes many problems in attempting to adequately simulate, understand, and explain basic problems of cognitive processes.

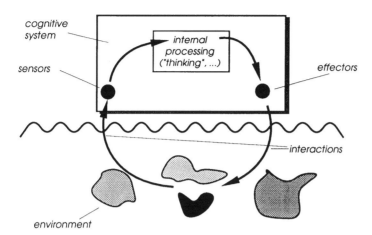

Figure 1   The closed feedback loop: sensory–reasoning mechanism–motor output–environment–sensory– . . . of an organism/machine acting in an environment.

Robotics can be seen as a part of this research area—the interesting point is, as on the input side, the combination of motor systems with knowledge-based systems. *Autonomous vehicles* are one result of this combination: they are capable of traveling from one specified location to another without external assistance.

D.   Language

Language and verbal communication are among the most important and characteristic abilities of the human species. Linguistics and cognitive psychology have a long tradition in investigating this phenomenon. Natural language processing (NLP) is the formulation and investigation of computationally effective mechanisms for communication through natural language. Three disciplines are involved in the investigation of the phenomenon of language in cognitive science. We will see in Section III that these three disciplines also contribute to traditional cognitive science.

The development of computer systems for understanding natural language has become one of the central topics of research in artificial intelligence as well as in cognitive science, because it has very interesting applications in the field of computer science, especially in human–computer interface research; natural language interfaces facilitate interaction with the computer, because the user does not have to learn complicated commands and parameters, but communicates by making use of his or her natural language. This implies the need for a very complex theory explaining the phenomenon of language and how it can be understood and processed by computers. Traditional cognitive science tries to model these phenomena by making use of grammatical theories that easily can be implemented in computers. Noam Chomsky and his generative grammars offer one of the most important foundations in this field of research (see Chomsky, 1980). If we want to understand this phenomenon, it is not enough to involve only computer scientists and linguists; there is a need of interdisciplinary cooperation. As discussed in Section V, we have to involve philosophers and researchers from *semiotics* and neuroscience. Models have been developed (with more or less success) for understanding language, for *analyzing* syntax and semantics, and even for artificially *generating* text. Machine translation represents another field of interest, which is related to natural language understanding.

E. Learning

Learning has been investigated by psychology for a long time, and it has turned out to be one of the most difficult issues in cognitive science (as well as in AI). *Machine learning* tries to automatically acquire knowledge by making use of computational methods. There exist different techniques and principles such as learning from examples, learning by doing, learning by analogy, learning by discovery, and learning in problem solving. Many attempts have been made in the field of *machine learning*; the results are quite poor, however.

Again the *connectionist* approach has brought about very interesting results, such as learning from examples and generalizing (e.g., the NETtalk of Sejnowski and Rosenberg, 1986, 1987; the past tense model of Rumelhart and McClelland, 1986). The PDP approach provides very powerful learning rules allowing the system to adapt to its environment. From a neuroscience point of view, we have to look very critically at these models, because they represent only very abstract simulations of natural neurons and learning processes. We take this problem into consideration in our computational neuroepistemology approach by involving neuroscientists in the interdisciplinary discourse (see Section V).

III. TRADITIONAL COGNITIVE SCIENCE:
A "PSEUDOINTERDISCIPLINARY" DISCOURSE?

After having viewed the most important domains of research in traditional cognitive science, I want to present and discuss the methodology and organization of this discipline. As shown in Section II, a multitude of disciplines is involved in the process of research in cognitive science. Normally the following disciplines are assumed to contribute (and receive) their knowledge to (from) cognitive science: *(cognitive) psychology, computer science (AI), linguistics, philosophy and neuroscience* (Winograd and Flores, 1986; Stillings et al., 1987; Posner, 1989; Simon and Kaplan, 1989; Osherson, 1990; Varela, 1990). To widen the spectrum, one might also include the (theory of the) arts, (second-order) cybernetics, anthropology or economics.

The five disciplines mentioned above represent the principal contributors to cognitive science; their interactions constitute the fuzzy concept for the—so called—interdisciplinary enterprise cognitive science (Fig. 2). Having a closer look at the reality of cognitive science's *interdisciplinarity* (for instance, by examining its models, publications, presentations, etc.), one can see, however, that the word "interdisciplinarity" often is abused as an "advertisement" for the title of a project, or a book. What is called "interdisciplinary" in many cases represents nothing but a short reference to a result, method, or experiment from another discipline that is distantly related to the topic of the paper, project, book, etc. It turns out that two kinds of scientific cooperation are mixed up under the name of "interdisciplinarity."

Multidisciplinarity   This kind of cooperation between different disciplines is "practiced" in most cases. It reduces "interdisciplinarity" to the indiscriminate quoting of results from other disciplines to justify one's own experiments, etc. It could be compared to observing another discipline from a safe distance to see whether one's own results are of any relevance; one does not dare to risk a closer interaction, because one fears that one's own results could be wrong or of less relevance. In many cases the observer does not even understand the paradigm (*and* its *problems*) the other scientist is working in; the observer indiscriminately makes use of (abuses) results that fit into his or her own research.

Evidence for the dominance of this form of cooperation also can be observed in many publications giving an introduction to cognitive science: there is always one editor and a number of contributors, each of whom describes the contribution to cognitive science from the perspective of *his or her* discipline. In only a few

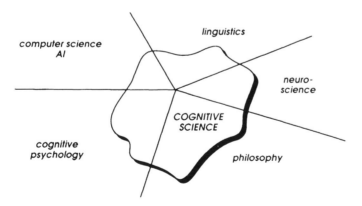

Figure 2   The "interdisciplinary" interaction of different disciplines participating in the discourse of cognitive science.

cases—describing the interaction of these disciplines—can "real" interdisciplinarity be found.

Interdisciplinarity   This case of scientific cooperation claims a *consequent integration and reflection* of methods, results, etc.; it assumes that all disciplines participating in the interdisciplinary discourse are willing to get involved in a *critical* discussion with the other disciplines. This calls for well-balanced relations between the participating disciplines and a common level of discussion (Section V). Such cooperation may even go so far that one discipline has to give up its current research paradigm if the arguments of the other disciplines are found to be conclusive. As we will see in Section V, the concept of an alternative approach to cognitive science (i.e., computational neuroepistemology) provides a mechanism (i.e., self-organization) that may force the participating disciplines to change their paradigm (or to leave the interdisciplinary discourse) if their results are not compatible with those of the other disciplines.

Traditional approaches to cognitive science do not provide such mechanisms, because there has not really been an intensive and explicit discussion about the methods and the cooperation between the disciplines. Interdisciplinarity, as suggested in the CNE approach, may avoid "dead ends" such as the research paradigm of orthodox AI because of a consequent discourse; that is, the results of interdisciplinary discussions are *consequently integrated* in the research being done by one's own discipline. Only if these two criteria (*consequent integration and reflection on the paradigm, methods, etc.*) are fulfilled, success in interdisciplinary cooperation seems to be possible—otherwise we fall back to a multidisciplinary enterprise, as described above.

A.   The Contribution of the Disciplines Involved in Traditional Cognitive Science

Interdisciplinarity (multidisciplinarity) is characteristic of cognitive science. That is why we now discuss briefly the contributions and interactions of the most important disciplines involved in the discourse of traditional cognitive science.

1.   Computer Science and Artificial Intelligence

I have already mentioned the *unjustified dominance* of computer science, its concepts and methods. As shown in Section V, aspects of neuroscience as well as of epistemology will become (are) at least as important as the computational issues in our alternative concept of computational neuroepistemology. Nevertheless, close relations between AI (which has been so called since about 1956) and cognitive science can be found.

Computer science has a very strong influence on the conceptions of the models being simulated in cognitive science, because the *information processing* metaphor is the (implicit) foundation of this approach to understanding and simulating cognitive processes. In the traditional understanding, however, the concept of information processing is reduced to manipulating meaningless symbols on a syntactic level. The traditional von Neumann architecture largely determines —because of its generality and plasticity—the kind of processing. As we will see in Section IV, the symbolic paradigm (physical symbol systems hypothesis) is the result of this influence; it is very problematic, however, to reduce cognitive processes to such a paradigm. That is why, in the computational neuroepistemology approach we are following another path, which is inspired by neuroscience and epistemology rather than by the concepts, ideas, architectures, etc. of traditional computer science (Section V).

2. (Cognitive) Psychology

Psychology is far from being a unified discipline. There is a multitude of fields, specializations, and approaches. Psychology's aim is, in short, to formulate theories about the (human) mind and behavior in order to predict, verify, cure, and so on.

The so-called *information processing* revolution of the 1950s and 1960s brought about a (paradigmatic) *shift* in the goals, research methods, and experiments (Simon and Kaplan, 1989). Before this time the dominance of behaviorism prevented most researchers from investigating the processes inside the brain and from thinking about internal representations. After this revolution, however, cognitive processes were understood as *information processes* operating on internal representations—they could be simulated on a computer. During this time the physical symbol systems hypothesis (Newell and Simon, 1976; Newell, 1980) was vaguely formulated for the first time—it was based on the assumption of viewing thinking as a process of manipulating symbols.

Many (cognitive) models and concepts have been developed since this time (see, e.g., Anderson, 1988; Mandl and Spada, 1988). In most cases the models are based on the assumptions mentioned above (von Neumann computer architecture). Insofar as cognitive psychology represents the precursor of cognitive science, it is very closely related to it, and many similarities can be found in the methods, assumptions, results, and models of these disciplines.

3. Philosophy

Philosophy plays a central role in cognitive science, although its interesting contributions have been suppressed by computer science issues.[1] Nevertheless philosophy was one of the first disciplines to recognize and discuss the problem of cognition, mind and body, etc.—the philosophers (e.g., Descartes, Kant, Leibnitz, Bacon, Hume) soon found out that the problem of *(knowledge) representation*

---

[1] F. Varela (1990) often points out the central role of the (European) *tradition* being provided by philosophy.

seems to be central. Especially *epistemology*, investigating the structure and development of *knowledge*, can contribute to increasing what we learn about and from cognitive science: "The advent of machine intelligence forced radical reconsideration of the mind–body problem [, of the concepts of language and knowledge as well as of cognition][2] . . . " *Simon* and *Kaplan*, 1989, p. 6).

Another contribution coming originally from philosophy is the field of *logic*. It has developed into a mathematical discipline and represents the basis for all kinds of "intelligent" systems making use of production rules and the symbol-manipulating approach. The *philosophy of science* plays an important role in organizing, controlling, regulating, etc. the process of discourse in the interdisciplinary discussion. It is also very interesting with respect to its theories concerning the development of science and knowledge.

4. Neuroscience

In traditional cognitive science, neuroscience plays only a second-order role, because the gap between the very basic neural (and "unintelligent") processes of cognition were of no interest (or at least of low priority) to AI people and to cognitive scientists, who are interested in more spectacular results of abstract problem solving or medical diagnoses. The knowledge provided by neuroscience is far from describing or explaining "higher" cognitive phenomena—it is capable of investigating only relatively small networks of neurons that represent and are responsible for simple forms of behavior, perception, knowledge, etc.

Developments in the past few years, however, have brought about an interesting turn: the connectionist (or PDP) approach offers very interesting results for neuroscientists as well as for cognitive science. We will take this into account when developing an alternative approach to cognitive science (Section V). Neuroscience is interested in the information processes in (natural) neural networks and their realization in the neural "wet ware." Unlike most approaches in traditional cognitive science and orthodox AI, however, they do not assume that cognitive processes can be reduced to symbol manipulation. They are rather in search for the (biological) *substratum* of cognitive processes; their aim is to explain how neural information processes represent, process, and otherwise deal with knowledge (*Sejnowski* et al., 1990).

5. Linguistics

Cognitive science is interested in linguistics because its domain of research is *language*, which seems to be the most important (and efficient) medium for transferring information and knowledge between (human) organisms. That is why cognitive science tries to understand how linguistic knowledge is represented in the mind. Linguistics is closely linked to AI because the two disciplines act on the

---

[2]Bracketed note by the author.

same level of abstraction (i.e., logic and symbols). *Chomsky* (1980) represents one of the most famous exponents in this discipline. Computational linguistics and psycholinguistics have developed specialized fields linked to cognitive science—both are interesting for cognitive science because of their results concerning linguistic behavior.

In this context one has to see the important and interesting contributions coming from *semiotics*, which originally emerged from linguistics. Semiotics understands language, communication, and each kind of interactive behavior, pattern, etc. as a process of *using symbols*; symbols are, of course, not reduced to linguistic symbols, but rather represent a very general and wide spectrum of behavioral activities (visual, olfactory, acoustic, etc. patterns) *based on a code* and on a system of *references*. Its knowledge represents one basis for our investigations concerning communication, language, etc., and the cognitive activities associated with these phenomena. Semiotics can help us to better understand the problems of traditional cognitive science (and AI), which is based on symbolic knowledge representation (Section IV.A). To avoid these problems, it seems to be very interesting to integrate semiotic concepts in the development of our alternative approach to cognitive science (CNE).

As has been shown in this section, interdisciplinary discourse is often very difficult. The main reason for the problems seems to lie in the different levels of discussion: that is, neuroscientific investigations deal with a domain or level of argumentation completely different from, for instance, orthodox AI. A real interdisciplinary discussion can take place only if everybody participating in the discourse is capable of contributing and "receiving" knowledge on the same level, that is, only if the knowledge provided by the different disciplines is useful for the others. The paradigm of symbol manipulation, for instance, will never be compatible with results from neuroscience. In Section IV I am going to discuss the assumptions made by traditional cognitive science as a means of making clear why this conception of cognitive science seems not to be adequate for the investigation of *basic* questions of what is knowledge, cognition, language, etc.

IV. TRADITIONAL ASSUMPTIONS AND THE SYMBOLIC PARADIGM: RESULTS OF A NAIVE UNDERSTANDING OF COGNITION

Having a closer look at the models of cognition provided by cognitive science (e.g., *Stillings et al.*, 1987; *Anderson*, 1988; *Mandl* and *Spada*, 1988; *Posner*, 1989), one can see that they are, in many cases, based on implicit assumptions that seem to be questionable: the representation of knowledge is reduced to the *symbolic* paradigm. That is why I am going to examine this processing paradigm provided by computer science from an interdisciplinary point of view, to reveal the problems and the *inadequacy* of this approach to understanding, describing, and simulating cognitive processes.

A.   Some Semiotic Considerations on Symbols

Before looking at the paradigm, we have to discuss some basic questions concerning the concept of a *symbol*, of *language*, and of *knowledge*. *Symbols* play a central role in traditional cognitive science because they are used as basic representational structures in most models provided by the traditional approach; the concept of a symbol, however, is in most cases applied *without reflection* and *naively*. That is why we are going to discuss this central form of *symbolic* representation from a *semiotic* perspective, which can help us to better understand the problems and the (wrong) assumptions associated with this approach.

Generally speaking, we are talking of a *symbol s* whenever a certain pattern *s* stands for something else. This pattern is chosen (or evolved) in most cases *arbitrarily* and refers to an object (in the environment) *o*, to another symbol, etc. This does not mean, however, that we can equate the objects *o* with the symbols *s* (and vice versa); we rather have to see that the problem is more sophisticated than we had assumed at first glance. There is *no direct relation* between the object *o* and the symbol *s*. We can find a third instance in between; it is called the *meaning m*, or the "sense," the "concept," the "mental image," etc. Hence, the object *o*, the meaning *m*, and symbol *s* are involved in the process of *designation* (i.e., the process of understanding the meaning of a symbol). As can be seen in Figure 3, these three components can be arranged in a triangle, which is called the *semiotic triangle*, after *Richards* (*Eco*, 1972, 1973). These three components can be differenti-

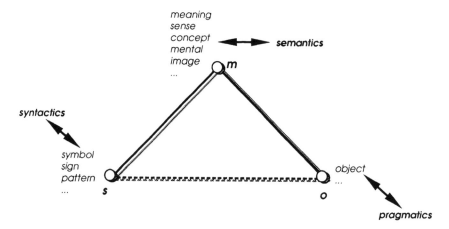

Figure 3   The semiotic triangle.

ated in the light of the traditional differentiation of semantics, syntactics, and pragmatics.

What are the implications of this differentiation for our considerations concerning the traditional cognitive science approach? It becomes clear that a symbol does not directly refer to an object. As Figure 3 indicates, there is the instance of "meaning" *m* between *o* and *s*. The point *we* (i.e., users of computational neuroepistemology) are interested in is this third element of *meaning*, which seems to play a central role in the question of what *knowledge* is, because it represents the "*connection*" between *s* and *o*. This connection is not "*given*," but rather the result of a process of *active construction* (in our brains), adaptation, learning, etc.; it depends individually on the experiences and on the phylogenetic structures of the organism. This implies that we can no longer talk of a language or of a symbol system consisting of symbols that have a "fixed" or standardized meaning. The meaning *always* depends on the *individual* as well as on the *consensual use* of the symbols. That is why we must, rather, investigate the process of how, for instance, a symbol gets its meaning or how the relation between the use of a symbol, the object, and the meaning is established, etc. (computational neuroepistemology). This implies that we need to focus on the domain of *pragmatics* and *semantics* instead of the investigation of syntactical structures, as traditional cognitive science does. The pragamatical aspects as well as the problem of meaning can be integrated and modeled in the approach of *computational neuroepistemology* (*CNE*) by making use of the methods of parallel distributed processing (connectionism), combined with constructivist concepts of epistemology and neuroscience (*Peschl*, 1990a–c).

Traditional cognitive science, however, is not really interested in or does not even realize these problems, because its methods reduce these questions to *symbol manipulation*; that is, it operates exclusively in the symbolic domain (*s*, left corner of the semiotic triangle). If these practitioners reduce cognitive processes to symbol manipulation, they do not see that they are assuming, if they go on thinking consequently, that, for instance, the computer symbol "**apple**" has its meaning in *se*; that is, they are making the error equating the symbol with the meaning and the object (Section IV.B). Of course, traditional cognitive science and AI have recognized the problem of *semantics*—however, the solution is based again on *syntactic* structures and methods of manipulating symbols; that is, semantic information has been added by establishing new *symbolic* relations, descriptions, predicates, etc. (e.g., in semantic networks, frames, scripts, etc.), implying that this problem has not been solved in any way. Rather, it has been hushed up and covered by adding complex syntactic structures pretending to be semantic knowledge. The problem of processing knowledge in traditional cognitive science is shown below in Figure 4, where we can see that the semantic and pragmatic aspect is completely omitted from the process of manipulating syntactic knowledge.

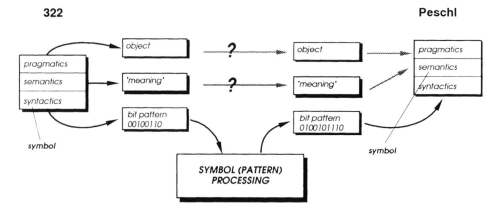

Figure 4 Symbolic knowledge processing and knowledge representation in traditional cognitive science.

B. Symbolic Knowledge Representation: The Paradigm of "Explicitness" and Linguistic Transparency

What are the implications for cognitive science from our considerations in the preceding section? As we have seen, cognitive science is dominated by the concepts and ideas of computer science; the *von Neumann* architecture (based on *Alan Turing's* ideas) has a strong *influence* on the way traditional cognitive science solves the problem of *knowledge representation* (Fig. 4).

1. The Problem: Restriction to Explicit (Linguistic) Knowledge

Programming conventional computers is inspired by the following idea: if a problem can be formulated in an *explicit* manner, it can be mapped to and processed by a computer program; we call this the concept of "*explicitness*" or, as Clark describes it, *linguistic transparency* (Clark, 1989). "*Explicit*" means that the phenomenon, problem, process, etc. can be described in the domain of natural language and, thus, represents the foundation for being transformed and mapped to the domain of formal computer languages. The *von Neumann* architecture supports this idea of explicitness because it is based on the assumption that everything that can be formalized is capable of being computed by this universal (processing) mechanism. This implies that the problem x has to be given at least in a natural language description. This represents the *minimal* requirement for being processed (or solved) by a conventional computer program (written in C, Pascal, LISP, Prolog, etc.), which is based on explicit data structures and processes.

Think, for instance, of the development of a program p_x for solving, processing, etc. a problem or phenomenon x. We can observe the following steps

One of the first steps is to clarify the problem; this means that one tries to formulate the "idea" or "feeling" of the x in natural language. The result is a description d_x in natural language.

The next step is to *refine* this description by splitting the problem x into smaller pieces x_i. The result of this process is the description of a process scheme $\{d_{x_1}, d_{x_2}, \ldots, d_{x_n}\}$.

After the problem x has been broken into small pieces, the pieces have to be refined to minimal process structures that can be mapped to a formal (programming) language; this requires a differentiation in the *process structure* and the (more static) *data structures* of the problem.

The (form of the) input of the program has to be defined; in most cases the data structures determine or at least influence the form of input and thus *restrict* the possibilities of processing.

It is implied that each processing step can be comprehended insofar as it is explicitly (i.e., in natural language) describable. Each step in the course of the program has its equivalent in the domain of the linguistic description (d_x) and in most cases in x.

As shown in Figure 5, we can differentiate between three domains (of representation): the environment itself (x), the linguistic domain of descriptions in natural language (d_x), and the "computational representation space" (p_x); we have seen that an isomorphy between the problem or phenomenon x, its description d_x, and its representation in a computer program p_x is assumed in the traditional com-

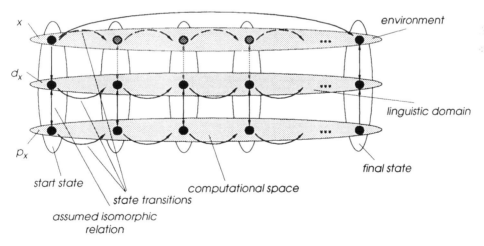

Figure 5 A quasi-isomorphic relation between the problem or phenomenon x, its description d_x and its representation in a computer program p_x.

puter science paradigm. This implies that the solution of the problem x or the processing of knowledge x is *reduced* to the processing of its description, or, to be more exact, to the result of a mapping of its *description d_x* (i.e., p_x). Of course, it is very tempting for us as human beings to use natural language descriptions and manipulation of natural language as a basis for processing knowledge or for solving problems. How is this exclusive and monopolistic use of natural language as a basic representation system justified? It can not really be justified—the only argument is the "common sense" argument that it is our impression that we are thinking by making use of or by manipulating natural language. The problem of language itself is completely ignored, implying the assumption (not reflected on) that language (meaning, etc.) is "given." Natural language is *not* the "ultimate" structure for knowledge representation, but rather represents the tip of the iceberg of a more general representation system that is not based on linguistic categories. We have to look back to the results of *cybernetics* (as suggested by *Varela*, 1990), investigating the basic processes of processing at the level of "primary representation." By "primary representation" I understand the direct physical representation of the environment (item, etc.) that is not linguistically describable. It is placed between the environment itself (we will never have direct access to it) and its (abstract) linguistic description.

The concept of the *von Neumann* architecture, however, supports the assumptions that problems can be broken down into small "explicit linguistic process pieces" and that an equivalence exists between the three domains in Figure 5. One reason for this seems to be that the structure of the *von Neumann* architecture itself is based on these assumptions. Thus, the application of this very flexible and powerful instrument implicitly reinforces them. As an implication of this dominance we have to analyze this superficial assumption of the isomorphy of environment, linguistic domain, and computational representation space (of programming languages). As we have seen in Section IV.A, we have to differentiate between the domain of meaning, the domain of syntax, and the domain of the environment, which are closely related to the different domains discussed in this section. Traditional cognitive science, AI, and computer science do not really make such distinctions and mix up these domains by reducing the whole problem to the manipulation of symbols, instead of asking how these symbols emerge from more basic representational structures.

2.   The Representation of the Representation System

The problem gets even more complicated if we apply the "explicit processing paradigm" to the problem "x is a cognitive system." It is often forgotten that *this* represents the basic problem in cognitive science. One often has the impression that the central questions being investigated by traditional cognitive science concern the problems of manipulation of syntactic or "pseudosemantic" structures in an abstract space of a formal language, rather than the basic processes involved in the representation of knowledge. This means that we have to investigate the problem of knowledge representation on a *metalevel*. The problem of knowledge representation has become twofold:

First-order representation: we have to find an adequate, very general representation system, capable of physically representing its environment (e.g., the nervous system).[3]

Second-order representation: this first-order representation system itself must be represented in the computer.

We have seen that most orthodox AI and traditional cognitive science approaches err by mixing up or even equating these two domains; first-order representation is assumed to provide the generality of representing and processing of all kinds of knowledge. This is due to the restriction to the superfratal and exclusive use of natural language as a basis for processing knowledge. Instead, we must look at language as an *emerging* result of physical processes in first-order representation. Symbol-manipulating systems as these are used in the traditional approaches do *not* provide the means for representing such physical processes—there are two mixed-up categories.

The alternative approach of *computational neuroepistemology,* however, makes use of a very general representation mechanism, inspired by biological ideas: artificial neural networks (parallel distributed processing, connectionism, etc.). We do *not* follow the traditional approach of interpreting the in put/output as symbols. As shown in *Peschl* (1990 a,b), we think rather of a cognitive system *directly* coupled to its environment via sensors and effectors. By moving around in its environment, it builds up its own representation, which is determined by the structure of its nervous system, by its periphery, and by its experiences.

In this approach a linguistic description can no longer be found, since the system has to build up its representation by itself. This autonomous behavior is based on the ability to learn and adapt to the environment. Parallel distributed processing offers many very powerful learning algorithms (*Hinton,* 1987)—we restrict this approach to various forms of *Hebb*ian learning, because of biological plausibility. Language may emerge by looking at how these simple cognitive systems learn to make use of simple quasi-symbolic structures. Hence, we have to investigate cognitive phenomena in a *bottom-up* manner to achieve an adequate view of the problems. It is clear that such an approach is limited by today's computational resources; it seems, however, more valuable to understand very basic and fundamental processes than to speculate in the traditional top-down manner.

---

[3]In the case of traditional cognitive science, this general representation system is represented by natural language.

V. COMPUTATIONAL NEUROEPISTEMOLOGY: RETHINKING AND REORGANIZING COGNITIVE SCIENCE

As mentioned above, the conception and organization of traditional cognitive science seems to be inadequate for answering the difficult questions concerning the investigation of cognitive processes. That is why we are trying to *reorganize* this discipline, using the approach called *computational neuroepistemology* (*CNE*). The participating and contributing disciplines in cognitive science are restricted to *philosophy* (*epistemology*), *neuroscience,* and *computer science.* What are the reasons for this restriction?

1. On the one hand it seems to be very problematic to restrict the contributions from many different disciplines to a minimum. As *Feyerabend* claims (1983), (cognitive) science must always apply a *great variety of methods* to avoid coming to a standstill; many results, methods, and contributions from many different disciplines seem to guarantee an "objective" description of a phenomenon. From a constructivist point of view, however, we will never be able to call anything "*objective.*" An "objective" description does *not* exist at all! Even if we were to collect all the knowledge we have, we would *not* be able to state that this knowledge "is" the "reality." We must always be aware that we are *constructing* our very personal reality in our cognitive domain. The results provided by different disciplines are determined by their methods, being themselves the result of a process of construction (theories, assumptions, hypotheses, etc.).

2. Of course we have to allow (and force) contributions from many different disciplines in such a sophisticated problem of investigating cognitive processes. As we have seen, however, this "interdisciplinarity" does not work by just increasing the number of participating disciplines. It seems to me that the main problems are as follows: *lacking consequent integration* of results of the discourse of the participating disciplines; *lacking reflection* of one's own results; and *different levels of discussion.* The first two points were discussed in Section III. The point of interest here is the problem of different levels of discussion. As we have seen, many different disciplines—each of them acting on a *different level* of abstraction and description—are involved in traditional cognitive science. Neuroscientific results, for example, can be compared only with great difficulty to results from orthodox AI (e.g., chess playing) or to linguistic investigations. The lack of interest in the other disciplines' results is due to the absence of connections between the disciplines—the gap between the levels of abstractions is too large to permit us to find a useful link between the results. That is why we have to think of an alternative, which allows successful communication and integration of the participating disciplines.

The computational neuroepistemology approach tries to "purify" traditional cognitive science by reducing the participating disciplines to epistemology, computer science, and neuroscience, to achieve a common level of discussion in the interdisciplinary discourse. We understand such a discourse as a cybernectic feedback loop, a *dynamical process* of interactions (Krohn et al., 1987; Krohn and Küppers, 1988, 1990). This process can reach a *stable equilibrium* only if all constraints are "satisfied." For our approach to cognitive science, this means that an equilibrium can be found only if the participating disciplines are integrated in such a way that they can formulate common results that satisfy the claims of each of them. In the following paragraphs I am going to show how such an equilibrium can be found by these three disciplines by discussing their roles and contributions in the interdisciplinary discourse:

Neuroscience. Neuroscience represents the *empirical* part of our approach. It provides the empirical evidence for epistemological investigations. As the brain is the substratum (material basis) of our cognitive processes, neuroscience investigates physical (and physiological) processes (and behavior correlated with them); epistemology must integrate these (empirical) results into its theories, hypotheses, etc., interpret and examine the applied methods and empirical data, to value and perhaps qualify or revise them. Neuroscience, on the other hand, must examine the plausibility of the epistemologists' theories. This mutual examination, revision, and correction of methods, empirical data, theories, hypotheses, etc. ensures a well-balanced cooperation between philosophy and neuroscience, which have *one* goal, but completely *different* methods, approaches, and means.

Epistemology and philosophy. I restrict philosophy to *naturalistic epistemology* and *philosophy of science*; *epistemology* is understood as the discipline investigating the question, What is *knowledge*? This means that this conception of epistemology always has one root in the natural sciences, to avoid misleading, inadequate, purely speculative, and unsuitable developments (for natural sciences, as they are well known from literature). *Churchland* (1986, 1989, 1990; see also Churchland and Sejnowski, 1989, and Oeser and Seitelberger, 1988), for instance, are exponents of this approach called *neurophilosophy* and/or *neuroepistemology*. In the (CNE) approach to cognitive science of consequently integrating epistemology into cognitive science, philosophy/epistemology plays a *speculative* role, which is constrained but *not* determined by the empirical results. It also plays the role of reflecting these results and the methods of computer science as well as of neuroscience with respect to their relevance and context.

Computer science. Computer science provides the *generative* aspect of *computational neuroepistemology*. This means that CNE makes use of computer science's simulation techniques and, thus, is capable of artificially generating cognitive phenomena. As discussed above, computational neuroepistemology does *not* apply the traditional methods of symbol manipulation, but rather the alternative (quite young) concept of *artificial neural networks*. Computers play an important role as simulating instruments for artificial *connectionist networks*, with a view to achieving a deeper understanding of cognitive processes in an interdisciplinary context. The PDP approach provides "compatibility" to neuroscience and philosophy by having similar (and more realistic) assumptions concerning knowledge representation (e.g., distributed representation), learning, etc., and by providing similar process structures (e.g., parallel processing, spreading activations).

By restricting cognitive science to these three disciplines, the basic *boundary conditions* for a successful dialogue are created. The level of discussion is well defined; epistemology, computer science (connectionism), and neuroscience assume the same level of abstraction. Neural processes represent the basis for the investigations and for the discussions about cognitive phenomena.

As an implication of this approach, a cognitive model is suggested (compare Fig. 1). An artificial organism is simulated in an (artificial) environment (*Braitenberg*, 1984; *Peschl*, 1989, 1990a, b; *Beer*, 1990). It is coupled to its environment by sensory and effector devices—no direct (symbolic) interaction can be found in this model. The aim is to achieve a deeper understanding of basic problems:

By investigating how this artificial organism adapts to its environment, we can learn a great deal about the *constructive* aspects of *knowledge* and *knowledge representation.*

Very simple forms of *behavior* are generated by simulations—they verify as well as stimulate epistemology and neuroscience investigations and results. Of course, we cannot offer such spectacular results as a machine playing chess or solving formal problems; rather we offer a *very general* mechanism for representing and constructing knowledge, and for adapting to and behaving adequately in an ever-changing dynamic environment.

By studying interactions with the environment or with other organisms, the development of symbols and language (in a very general sense) can be investigated. As mentioned, symbols and language evolve by making common use of certain patterns of reference—these investigations will have a strong influence on epistemological issues.

The speculative ideas of epistemology can be tested and verified in simple simulation models, which are constrained by neuroscience.

Neuroscientific results influence greatly the artificial generation of cognitive phenomena by making use of connectionist networks. Neuroscience as well as computer science can profit by the interdisciplinary results made available by this approach.

It seems that we are standing at the beginning of a (*scientific*) *revolution* in the sense of *Kuhn* (1967), in the investigation of cognitive phenomena, of knowledge, etc. We have to give up the naive and superficial assumptions of looking at cognitive processes as symbol manipulation; rather, we must *consequently* integrate the results coming from the disciplines that are doing research in the field of *basic* problems. *Computational neuroepistemology* represents such an alternative approach to cognitive science—*convergence* can be observed in computer science and epistemology, as well as in neuroscience (Sejnowski and Churchland, 1989): by investigating very fundamental and basic processes of cognition, such phenomena as language, symbols, and complex problem solving can be rather understood as *emerging* properties rather than being predetermined by the method (of simulation) itself. It turns out that this *bottom-up* approach is capable of spanning the wide gap between very simple forms of behavior and highly complex forms of knowledge. As mentioned at the beginning, we understand cognitive science in such a way; of course computational neuroepistemology stands at the very outset—the concepts, however, promise not to lead to such a dead end as traditional symbol manipulation.

REFERENCES

Anderson, J. R. (1988). *Kognitive Psychologie*. Heidelberg: Spektrum der Wissenschaft Verlag.

Beer, R. D. (1990). *Intelligence as Adaptive Behavior. An Experiment in Computational Neuroethology*. New York: Academic Press.

Braitenberg, V. (1984). *Vehicles. Experiments in Synthetic Psychology*. Cambridge, MA MIT Press.

Chomsky, N. (1980). *Regeln und Repräsentationen*. Frankfurt am Main: Suhrkamp, 1981. (First published as *Rules and Representations*, Columbia University Press, New York, 1980.)

Churchland, P. S. (1986). *Neurophilosophy. Toward a Unified Science of the Brain*. Cambridge, MIT Press.

Churchland, P. M. (1989). *Neurocomputational Perspective—The Nature of Mind and the Structure of Science*. Cambridge, MA: MIT Press.

Churchland, P. S., and Sejnowski, T. J. (1989). "Neural Representation and Neural Computation" in A. M. Galaburda (ed.), *From Reading to Neurons*. Cambridge, MA: MIT Press, pp. 217-250.

Churchland, P. M. (1990). "Cognitive Activity in Artificial Neural Networks," in Osherson, D. N., et al. (eds.), *An Invitation to Cognitive Science,* Vol. 3. Cambridge, MA: MIT Press, pp. 199-227, 1990.

Clark, A. (1989). *Microcognition. Philosophy, Cognitive Science and Parallel Distributed Processing*. Cambridge, MA: MIT Press.

Eco, U. (1972). *Einführung in die Semiotik. Uni-Taschenbücher UTB 105*. Munich: Wilhelm Fink Verlag.

Eco, U. (1973). *Zeichen. Eine Einführung in einen Begriff und seine Geschicht,* Suhrkamp: Frankfurt am Main, 1977.

Feyerabend, P. (1983). *Wider den Methodenzwang (Against Method)* Frankfurt am Main: Suhrkamp.

von Foerster, H. (1973). "Das Konstruieren einer Wirklichkeit" in Watzlawick, P. (ed.), *Die erfundene Wirklichkeit.* Munich, Piper Verlag, 1981, pp. 39-60.

von Foerster, H. (1984). "Erkenntnistheorien und Selbstorganisation" in Schmidt, S. J. (ed.), *Der Diskurs des Radikalen Konstruktivismus.* Frankfurt am Main: Suhrkamp, 1987, pp. 133-158.

von Glasersfeld, E. (1976). Sprache als zweckorintiertes Verhalten: Zur Entwicklungsgeschichte," in *E. v. Glasersfeld, Wissen, Sprache und Wirklichkeit,* Braunschwieg/Wiesbaden, Vieweg, 1987, pp. 63-79.

von Glasersfeld, E. (1981). "Einführung in den radikalen Konstruktivismus," in Watzlawick, P. (ed.), *Die erfundene Wirklichkeit.* Munich, Piper Verlag: pp. 16-38.

Hinton, G. E. (1987). "Connectionist Learning Procedures," Technical Report CMU-CS-87-115, Carnegie-Mellon University, Pittsburgh.

Hubel, D. A., and Wiesel, T. N. (1962). "Receptive Fields, Binocular Interaction and Functional Architecture in the Cat's Visual Cortex" *J. Physiol., 160*: 106-154.

Hubel, D. A., and Wiesel, T. N. (1965). "Receptive Fields and Functional Architecture in Two Nonstriate Visual Areas, *J. Physiol., 195*: 215-243.

Hubel, D. A., and Wiesel, T. N. (1968). "Receptive Fields and Functional Architecture of Monkey Striate Cortex" *J. Physiol., 195*: 215-243.

Krohn, W., Küppers, G., and Paslack, R. (1987). "Selbstorganisation—Zur Genese und Entwicklung einer wissenschaftlichen Revolution, in Schmidt, S. J. (ed.), *Der Diskurs des Radikalen Konstruktivismus.* Frankfurt am Main: Suhrkamp, pp. 441-465.

Krohn, W., and Küppers, W. (1988). *Die Selbastorganisation der Wissenschaft.* Frankfurtam Main: Suhrkamp.

Krohn, W., and Küppers, G. (1990). "Science as a Self-Organizing System. Outline of a Theoretical Model, in Krohn, W., et al., (eds.), *Selforganization. Portrait of a Scientific Revolution.* Dordrecht: Kluwer, pp. 208-222.

Kuhn, T. S. (1967). *Die Struktur wissenschaftlicher Revolutionen.* Frankfurt am Main: Suhrkamp Taschenbuch.

Mandl, H. and Spada, H. (eds. (1988). *Wissenspsyochlogie,* Munich: Psychologie Verlagsunion.

Marr, D. (1982). *Vision: A Computational Investigation into the Human Representation and Processing of Visual Information.* San Francisco: Freeman.

Maturana, H. R. (1970). "Biology of Cognition," in Maturana, H. R., and Varela, F. J. (eds.), *Autopoiesis and Cognition.* Dordrecht: Reidel, (1980), pp. 2-60.

Maturana, H. R., and Varela F. J. (1975). "Autopoiesis: The Organization of the Living," in Maturana, H. R., and Varela, F. D. (eds.). *Autopoiesis and Cognition.* Dordrecht: Reidel, 1980, pp. 63-134.

Maturana, H. R., and Varela, F. J., eds. (1980). *Autopoiesis and Cognition. The Realization of the Living.* Drodrecht: Reidel.

Maturana, H. R. (1983). What Is It to See? *Arch. Biol. Med. Exp., 16*: 255-269.

Newell, A., and Simon, H. A. (1976). "Computer Science as Empirical Inquiry: Symbols and Search," *Commun. ACM, 19*(3): 113-126.

Newell, A. (1980). "Physical Symbol Systems," *Cognitive Sci., 4*: 135-183.

Oeser, E., and Seitelberger, F. (1988). *Gehirn, Bewußtsein und Erkenntnis.* Darmstadt: Wissenschaftliche Buchgesellschaft.

Osherson, D. N., ed. (1990). *An Invitation to Cognitive Science.* Cambridge, MA: MIT Press.

Peschl, M. F. (1989). "An Alternative Approach to Modeling Cognition," in *Proceedings of the Man & Machine Conference.* John von Neumann Society for Computing Sciences. Budapest, Hungary, pp. 49-56.

Peschl, M. F. (1990a). "Cognition and Neural Computing—An Interdisciplinary Approach, in *Proceedings of the International Joint Conference on Neural Networks, Washington.* Hillsdale, NJ: Erlbaum, pp. 110-113.

Peschl, M. F. (1990b). "A Cognitive Model Coming Up to Epistemological Claims: Constructivist Aspects to Modeling Cognition," in *Proceedings of the International Joint Conference on Neural Networks 1990,* Vol. III, Hillsdale, NJ: Erlbaum, pp. 657-662.

Peschl, M. F. (1990c). "Aufdem Weg zu einem neuen Verständnis der Cognitive Science (On the Way to a New Understanding of Cognitive Science), *Inf. Forum, 4*(2): 92-104.

Posner, M. I., ed. (1989). *Foundations of Cognitive Science.* Cambridge, MA: MIT Press.

Rumelhart, D. E., and McClelland, J. L. (1986). "On Learning the Past Tenses of English Verbs, in McClelland, J. L., (ed.), *Parallel Distributed Processing,* Vol. 2., Cambridge, MA: MIT Press, pp. 216-271.

Sejnowski, T. J., and Rosenberg, C. (1986). NETtalk: A Parallel network That Learns to Read Aloud," Johns Hopkins University Electrical Engineering and Computer Science Technical Report JHU/EECS-86/01.

Sejnowski, T. J., and Rosenberg, C. (1987). "Parallel Networks That Learn to Pronounce English Text," *Complex Syst., 1*: 145-168.

Sejnowski, T. J., and Churchland, P. S. (1989). "Brain and Cognition," in Posner, M. I. (ed.), *Foundations of Cognitive Science.* Cambridge, MA: MIT Press, pp. 301-356.

Sejnowski, T. J., Koch, C., and Churchland, P. S. (1990). "Computational Neuroscience," in Hanson, S. J. et al. (eds.), *Connectionist Modeling and Brain Function.* Cambridge, MA: MIT Press, pp. 5-35.

Simon, H. A., and Kaplan, C. A. (1989). "Foundations of Cognitive Science," in Posner M. I. (ed.), *Foundations of Cognitive Science.* Cambridge, MA: MIT Press, pp. 1-47.

Stillings, N. A., Feinstein, M. H., Garfield, J. L., et al. (1987). *Cognitive Science, An Introduction.* Cambridge, MA: A Bradford Book, MIT Press.

Varela, F. J. (1990). *Kognitionswissenschaft—Kognitionstechnik. Eine Skizze aktueller Perspektiven (Cognitive Science),* Frankfurt am Main: Suhrkamp.

Winograd, T., and Flores, F. (1986). *Understanding Computers and Cognition, A New Foundation for Design.* Reading, MA: Addison-Wesley.

17

Active Seismic Response Controlled Structure: Cybernetic–Active Control Philosophy

Takuji Kobori   Kajima Corporation, Tokyo, Japan

I. INTRODUCTION

In conventional seismic resistant design, most structures are designed to withstand elastically earthquakes of moderate intensity (allowable stress design) and to prevent collapse during a severe earthquake, thereby avoiding loss of human life. However, in many urban areas not only individual buildings, but also entire city functions are becoming intelligence oriented. Therefore, it seems unwise to cling to a design philosophy designated for severe earthquakes, in which a barely prevented collapse at the ultimate structural limit is recognized as acceptable, provided there is no loss of human life. Is such thinking still acceptable? The conventional philosophy, which is several decades old, can result in a decrease in an individual building's function and loss in its financial value, as well as preventing reuse of the building after severe earthquakes. This should not be tolerated in the coming age. A technology is required that will not only suppress the vibrations of individual buildings, but will preserve the information and communication function that sustains a city's life.

It is anticipated that the seismic response controlled structure will fulfill this requirement in the twenty-first century. With a system based on this new concept, the building itself functions actively and continuously to act on earthquake ground motions. In Japan, there have been many recent technological advances in this field, and various technologies that were not conceivable a decade ago have now become possible.

This chapter presents a general view of current research and development into active and hybrid control systems relevant to the seismic response controlled structure being conducted in the research institutes of private firms and universities in Japan and the United States. Reports are presented, in particular, on active and hybrid control devices actually being utilized, focusing on those that have already been installed and those that are in the experimental stage with the objective of practical application.

II. CONCEPT OF A SEISMIC RESPONSE CONTROL

A. Background of the Concept

The relationship among the seismic resistant, base isolation, and active seismic response control systems is shown in Figure 1. Both the earthquake-resistant structure and the base isolation system, however, are endurance and passive types that simply wait for an earthquake to happen and are unable to take positive action against earthquake motions. In view of the uncertainty of earthquake motions, anxiety regarding safety cannot be dismissed.

Despite continuous research, the waveforms of earthquake motions are quite unpredictable.

For example, in the Mexico earthquake of 1985, great damage was caused by earthquake motions that far exceeded predictions. These large ground motions

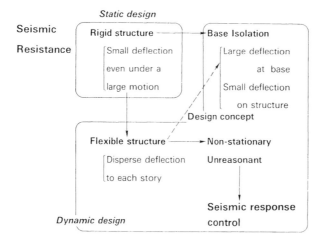

Figure 1   Relation between conventional aseimic design and new seismic response control concepts.

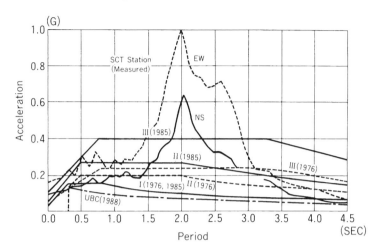

Figure 2 Response spectra for design and measured earthquake in Mexico.

were in turn caused by the particular ground conditions. The damage occurred in spite of revisions to the seismic design criteria (regulation) as shown in Figure 2.

The reliability design method, founded on probabilistic theory, is a design method that involves uncertain elements. However, at present it is difficult even to determine qualitative allowable criteria.

To ensure the safety of buildings subject to highly unpredictable earthquake waveforms, nonlinearity is applied to their structural elements, and the path to the nonstationary and nonresonant state is the starting point of the concept of the seismic response controlled structure. Since a definite prediction of an input earthquake waveform is impossible, the only alternative for maintaining safety is to control the building structural part when it receives such input.

In applying this concept, a computer installed in the building performs appropriate recognition and judgment of information transmitted from ground motion sensors and response sensors, and functions to counteract the destructive force of earthquakes. To achieve this, the building selects and changes its own structural dynamic characteristics or induces a controlling force. Thus, damage of the building, including internal information and communication facilities, is prevented even in large earthquakes, and the building is not only maintained in a completely usable state but also offers a pleasant living space in a high residential environment characterized by frequently occurring earthquakes of moderate intensity.

In strong winds, the response of the structure is mainly of low mode, its duration time is long, and the control does not need to cope with severe, instantaneously changing conditions. Therefore, the function of the vibration control system designed for the seismic response controlled structure will be appropriate for strong wind disturbances.

B. Types of Seismic Response Control

A seismic response control system is defined as a system that fortifies the structure by imparting its particular characteristics or a control device that controls the earthquake motions. The procedures are as follows:

1. Cut off the input energy from the earthquake ground motions,
2. Isolate the natural frequencies of the building from the predominant seismic power components,
3. Provide nonlinear structural characteristics and establish a nonstationary state nonresonant system,
4. Supply a control force to suppress the structural response induced by earthquakes,
5. Utilize an energy absorption mechanism.

Item 1 above is the original concept of the ideal goal of a base isolation system. If this could be completely realized, procedures 2–5 would become unnecessary. However, as this is impossible at present, the currently applied base isolation system is based on 2 with assistance from 5, which offers the building a longer natural period to evade resonance. Obviously, the conditions in which this procedure can be applied are limited. Next, items 2, 3, and 5 are nothing but the theoretical backbone for realizing the safety of highrise buildings, which is possible only where the supporting soil base is hard and also where the long period components of the input earthquake ground motion are not predominant.

Seismic response control originated in an approach to the maintenance of building safety against the unpredictable earthquakes without such limited conditions. In seismic response control, the function of controlling the earthquake ground motions should be given to the structure by adding item 5 to 3 or 4. Furthermore, the subject buildings must be of general nature, including those from the low tiered to the highrises.

C. Application of Seismic Response Control System

Figure 3 shows examples of applications of the seismic response control system. They can be roughly divided into three categories: passive, active, and hybrid.

The base isolation system is positioned under the passive classification. Next Figure 3 shows the dampers: the tuned mass damper, the sloshing liquid damper, the oil damper, the friction damper, the elastoplastic damper, and the others function as energy absorbers and therefore correspond to item 5 in the list presented in Section II.B. These dampers are also categorized as passive devices, but when the

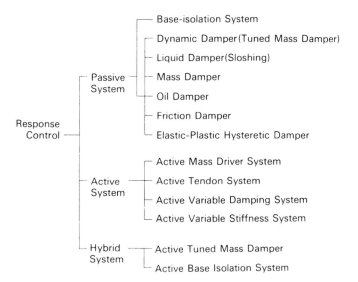

Figure 3 Application of passive, active, and hybrid control systems.

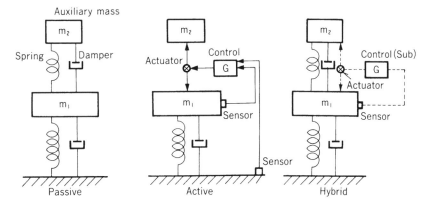

Figure 4 Model of three types of control system with auxiliary mass.

seismic response control of the structure is considered, it is practical to incorporate them in the system as much as possible.

The active control system may be of the response control force type or the nonresonant type. The former is based on item 4, above. In addition to the AMD, which provides a seismic control force by actively operating the installed mass device, various other methods have been contrived. In these methods, variable tendons are used, the pulse force is applied, or seismic control force is provided by a variable damping force, which can be generated by the device used in the active variable stiffness (AVS) system. All are categorized as types that provide a seismic control force. The AVS system is based on item 3, above, in which a nonstationary nonresonant system is established. It provides nonlinear characteristics to the structure by making stiffness variable.

The hybrid control system combines the merits of the active and passive control systems and utilizes the best features of both. Figure 4 is a conceptual drawing of a seismic response controlled structure that uses auxiliary mass of three control types, namely, passive, active, and hybrid. The differences among these types are also shown.

III.   ACTIVE SEISMIC RESPONSE CONTROL SYSTEM

The research regarding active seismic controlled structures in the United States was started in 1972 by J. T. P. Yao, who first applied the control theory from control engineering to civil engineering and building structures. In the past two decades, such work has been promoted steadily by S. F. Masri, J. N. Yang, T. T. Soong, et al.

In the meantime, in Japan, full-scale research into practical applications of the active seismic response control system commenced in 1985. The history of active control systems does not go back too far, and yet, in the past few years the research in this field has been expanding rapidly. This was induced only because the author stressed its importance. Moreover, at the present, the joint Japan–U.S. research effort on seismic response control systems is being promoted extensively and in varied forms [1–7].

The research and development process for seismic response control is divided into its initial philosophy and five subsequent steps, as shown in Figure 5, which indicates that current development in industrial companies and various research institutes is completely uncoordinated. However, as in the development of any new technology, the initial concept must be clearly understood before development is commenced.

Needless to say, careful study and experiments are necessary to achieve a successful combination of theory and practical application. Above all, the hardware requirements in the practical application are all specific to the respective seismic

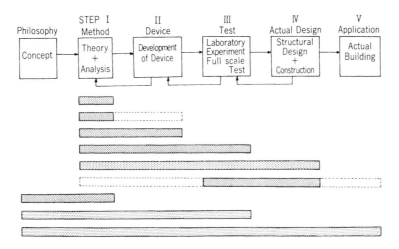

Figure 5 The research and development process on active control.

response control devices, and they must all be verified by experiment and resolved before success can be attained.

Therefore, this chapter reports on research up to step III of Figure 5, which is to conduct a controlled experiment in the laboratory. The algorithm, which is discussed later, is also referred to in the analytical research of step I.

As shown in Figure 3, active seismic response control systems can be roughly categorized into the seismic response control force type and the nonresonant type. These are reviewed next.

A. Control Force Type Seismic Response Controlled Structure

The seismic response controlled structure of the control force type provides a control force to the structure by operating the auxiliary mass installed in the structure by means of an actuator, thus reducing the response of the structure to earthquakes and strong winds. There are various systems,—for example, active mass damper (AMD, Fig. 6) [8], active mass driver (AMD, Fig. 7) [9], and active dynamic vibration absorber (DVA, Fig. 8) [10]. Some of these have already been applied to buildings. Others are in the experimental stage with the intention of future application. Next, as tendon-type systems, there are experimental examples (Fig. 9) [11] and examples of application to an actual viaduct on the Metropolitan Expressway in Tokyo (Fig. 10) [12]. Finally there is the system that applies the pulse force by a pulse generator (Fig. 11) [13].

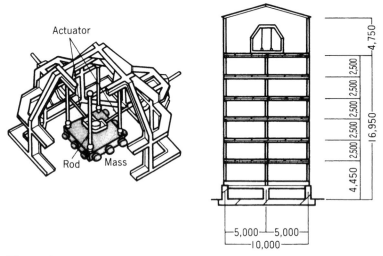

Figure 6 Active mass damper system [8].

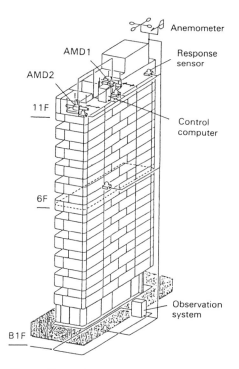

Figure 7 Active mass driver system [9].

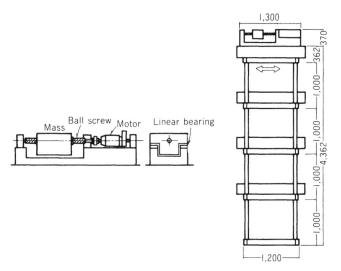

Figure 8 Active dynamic vibration absorber [10].

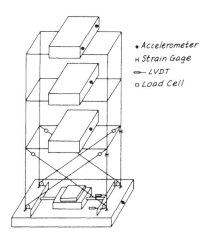

Figure 9 Active tendon system [11].

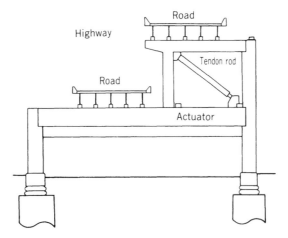

Figure 10   Active tendon system [12].

The problem with these auxiliary mass methods is that they must be constantly prepared—even for large earthquakes that seldom occur—with an applicable energy source that can provide appropriate large control forces.

1.   Subject Buildings

Subject structures include a 6-story experimental building, an 11-story office building, and a 15-story office building (under planning). These structures are all of steel framing. Their weights range from several hundred to several thousand tons.

The contemplated external disturbances are earthquakes of moderate intensity and strong winds, and the measures described are aimed at improving the comfort of people in the subject buildings. These external disturbances occur frequently, and the target is to reduce the response of the uncontrolled state by two-thirds. The direction of control is determined in accordance with the shape of the particular building. Control may be in the transverse direction and the torsional direction, or in the two horizontal (transverse and longitudinal) directions. In the case of the steel bridge (Fig. 10), the main objective is to suppress vibration induced by traffic.

2.   Seismic Response Control Devices

In the earlier stage, electrohydraulic-type actuators were mainly used as seismic response control devices. However, with rapid progress in motor technology, large capacity ac servomotors are now under development. The merits of the servomotor are that its maintenance is simple, its response capability is excellent, and hydraulic tank space is not needed. If its power can be improved, it could become

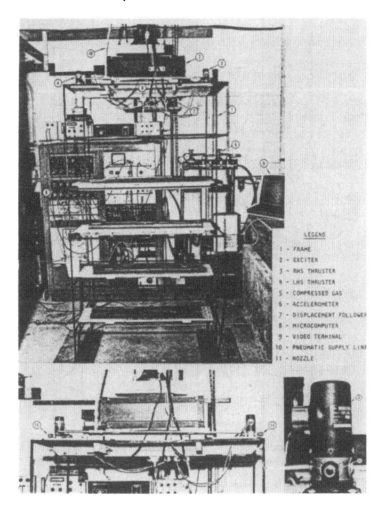

Figure 11 Pulse control system [13].

more widely used. All the seismic response control devices are placed on the top floor. The sensors are placed according to various planning requirements. In some cases they are installed only on the top floor, while in others they are distributed on intermediate floors. The weight of the auxiliary mass ranges from 0.5 to 1.0% of the building's weight, and their vertical support varies (e.g., pendulum type, sliding-on-rail type). In all cases, to facilitate the drive function, the vibration period of the auxiliary mass system is set at a longer period than the fundamental period of the building. Also, the pulse generator utilizes the compressed air stored in the accumulator.

3. Problems for Study

The current objective of the seismic response control device of the control force type is to improve the daily comfort of the occupants of medium-scale buildings in strong winds and frequently occurring earthquakes of moderate intensity. The efficiency of these structures has been verified. However, it would be difficult to apply these systems in their current form to large-scale buildings for controlling the effects of severe earthquakes. If it were possible to make available an auxiliary mass weight of 0.5–1.0% of the entire building weight, an actuator with a large stroke and an enormous control force would be required. Furthermore, a tremendous energy source would be required for its operation. Thus, it is evident that a limit exists in the building scale and its subject external force level. At this point, a semiactive concept should be given serious consideration.

B. Nonresonant-Type Seismic Response Controlled Structure

In the nonresonant-type seismic response controlled structure, the system actively controls the vibration characteristics of the building so that resonance with the continuously arriving earthquake motions can be avoided and the building's response can be suppressed. To achieve this objective, the active variable stiffness (AVS) system (Fig. 12) [14,15] actively controls the stiffness of the building to ensure nonresonance. Model tests of this system have been finished, and it is now in the practical application stage.

1. Outline

The subject structure is composed of a three-story steel frame. It is designed to be safe during earthquakes of severe to moderate intensity and typhoon winds. The seismic response control device is a two-ended, rod-type hydraulic closing cylinder (cylinder locking device). A switch valve is installed in the connecting tube that joins two separate cylinder chambers. The joint between the brace and the frame is fixed or freed by opening or closing this valve. Thus, the damping factor as well as the stiffness of the entire building can be altered. The necessary energy for this operation is only the 12 V of electricity needed to operate this switch.

2. Special Features and Problems

So far, the control efficiency of the nonresonant-type system has been confirmed by shaking table tests and is being applied on a trial basis to an actual building. An excellent feature of this system is that the device can operate adequately with only enough electricity for emergency sources, thus contributing to power (energy) saving. Therefore, unlike devices of the seismic control force type, this system can

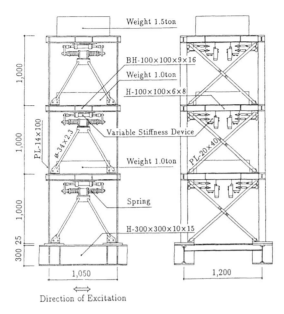

Figure 12 Active variable stiffness system [14,15].

operate during large earthquakes. This is confirmed to be effective against earthquake waves that contain comparatively clear specific peaks in the predominant period. Research and development is being promoted so that adequate effective nonstationary state nonresonancy can be attained also for earthquake waves that are irregular and do not have a special predominant peak. Clearly, it is important to comprehend the system's dynamic characteristics (system identification) by conducting vibration tests, as well as the verification of the control system.

IV. HYBRID CONTROL SYSTEMS

The passive systems shown in Figure 3 do not require special electrical power and are therefore maintenance free and mechanically simple. However, with the base isolation structure a certain fundamental period exists, and large deformations can occur in parts of the base isolation device, which evidently limit its capacity. Also, it is ineffective against strong winds. The damper-type systems function effectively only after the structure begins to shake, which means that it has the shortcoming of slow start-up in its effect. To supplement this deficiency of passive systems, a trial is being made to combine a passive with an active control system. It is recognized, however, that depending on the ratio of active to passive portions, the hybrid system can become meaningless. Up to the present, the systems that have been developed or currently are under research include the active tuned mass damper, which combines the tuned mass damper with the actuator, and the active base isolation system, which combined the base isolation device with the actuator. These systems are described below.

A. Active Tuned Mass Damper

The method of controlling the response of structures with a passive-type tuned mass damper has been applied in numerous actual cases: to observation towers, tall chimneys, and main towers of bridges. However, when applied to large-scale structures, the following factors must be considered.

1. An enormous auxiliary mass is needed.
2. The period of the mass damper system must be synchronized to the structure. If the period becomes unsynchronized, the vibration effect is reduced tremendously.
3. Since such a damper is based on natural vibration characteristics, it takes time to get started.

On the other hand, the active vibration control device of the control force type by itself would have difficulty in controlling large-scale structures. However, with the active tuned mass damper, the merits of both features are combined and effective vibration control is improved by using a small actuator. Typical examples are the powered passive mass damper (Fig. 13) [16] and the hybrid-type mass damper (Fig. 14) [17].

1. Subject Structures

The subject structures featuring active tuned mass dampers are large-scale structures such as the main towers of long, large bridges and highrise buildings, whose weights range from several tens of thousands of tons to several hundred thousand tons. In particular, the powered passive mass damper system is already planned for installation in a 70-story highrise building. The main external force to be suppressed is strong wind with a return period of about 5 years, and the objective is to maintain a certain level of habitant comfort.

2. Vibration Control Device

The vibration control device consists of a tuned mass damper and a control drive unit. Tuned mass dampers include the pendulum type and the type in which a curved auxiliary mass is swung over a roller. Both are set to synchronize with the natural period of the building. The weight of the auxiliary mass is about 0.5% of the structure's weight. Both control drive units use an ac servomotor, but there are two systems for transmitting the force to the auxiliary mass: the ball screw type and the rack-and-pinion type.

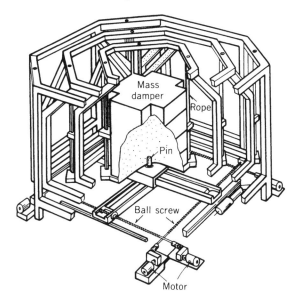

Figure 13   Powered passive mass damper [16].

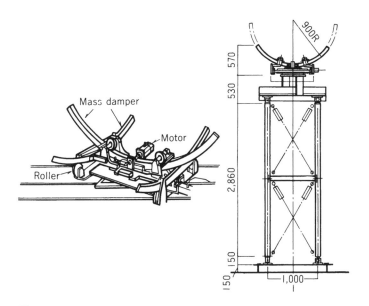

Figure 14   Hybrid-type mass damper [17].

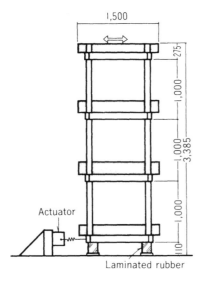

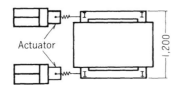

Figure 15   Absolute vibration control system [18].

B.   Active Base Isolation System

The earthquake response acceleration of the building with a base isolation system was reduced as a result of lengthening the natural period by supporting the structure on laminated rubber bearings.

In recent years, many buildings have used this system because its mechanism is quite simple. However, this isolation system often has problems because of its limitations with respect to relative displacement. Even so, demand has increased for industrial facilities and sophisticated information-oriented buildings with reduced absolute acceleration response, even with allowance displacement relative to the ground. In response to this demand, active control systems are expected to be added to the base isolation structures. An example of this development is the absolute vibration control system (Fig. 15) [18].

1. Subject Structures

The system is being tested in the laboratory to verify its basic characteristics, but no plan is yet available for application to a specific building. However, its anticipated future use is in ultraprecise fabrication plants and sophisticated information-oriented buildings. Also, under consideration is application in important heavy buildings such as nuclear fusion reactor plants.

C. Problems for Study

For highrise buildings, there may be cases in which the external wind forces exceed the assumed seismic forces in structural design, depending not only on their weight, but also on their shape. Therefore, it is important to plan on response wind loads by means of passive control only, and experiments must be conducted to verify that enough vibration control effect can be obtained. However, as the subject building has a long natural period, the devices will not commence effective operation until the building has reached a state of considerable vibration. Therefore, they are ineffective in earthquakes whose main seismic wave components (principal shock) appear in a short period of time, making them unsuitable from the standpoint of seismic response controlled structures. To counter this shortcoming, various trials are being continued to supplement the active control methods. However, effective devices have not been developed.

V. CONTROL ALGORITHM

Depending on the utilization of the measured information, the control algorithms are classified as follows: feedback control, feedforward control, and feedback and feedforward control. In feedback control, the active control forces are determined by the measured feedback responses. In feedforward control, however, the active control forces are computed from measured external excitations. In feedback and feedforward control, the active control forces are regulated by measured results of both external loads and structural responses. Various control algorithms have been investigated, including optimal control, modal control, and pole assignment.

A. Feedback Control

The feedback control algorithm is usually used in actual systems because it does not require a term of the external load and it is easy to design the circuit and ensure stability.

The algorithms adopted in the control force type system described in Section III.A (excluding the pulse generator), and the hybrid control system described in Section IV, are classified as feedback control. In the system, various researchers have contrived to adopt the feedback responses and evaluation feedback gains. The control force u is expressed as follows:

$$u = G_b x$$

where x is a state vector.

In the active mass damper system, the biaxial control forces are computed by the feedback gains that correspond to the displacement and velocities at every floor containing an auxiliary mass. The optimal G_b values are evaluated by optimal control theory. In the active mass driver system, the control forces in the transverse and torsional directions are evaluated by simplified feedback gains that have an effectiveness equivalent to the optimal gains obtained from optimal control theory. The feedback responses are only the velocities at the center and edge of the top floor. In the active dynamic vibration absorber system installed in the four-story test model, the feedback gains G_b corresponding to the displacements and velocities at all floors are evaluated from the optimal control theory.

The powered passive mass damper and the hybrid mass damper can control only one modal response, so the feedback responses are the displacement and velocities of the system-installed floor and the mass damper.

B. Feedback and Feedforward Control

Various types of feedback and feedforward control are investigated, mainly by numerical analyses. In general, the control force u of this type can be expressed as follows:

$$u = G_b \cdot x + G_f \cdot y$$

where x is a state vector and y is an external disturbance (ground motion).

In the classical optimal method when obtaining a Riccati matrix, there were comments at the time that the external disturbance term had been disregarded. Therefore J. N. Yang et al. proposed instantaneous optimal control [19], which determines the control force by using the present tense and the prior external disturbance. If this method is used, the nuisance of computing the Riccati formula is avoided, and it is said that because external disturbance information is being used, speaking theoretically, the control effect is better than the classical optimal method.

Yamada, Iemura, and their colleagues [20] indicated that future ground motion can be predicted as an output of one degree of freedom under a white noise input using the Kalman filtering technique; then the structural response is predicted when the earthquake ground motion y has a predominant frequency. Feedforward gain is multiplied by the predicted ground motion, and feedback gain is multiplied by the predicted response x to obtain the optimal control force u.

Sato and Toki [21] proposed the instantaneous closed–open algorithm derived by minimizing the sum of the quadratic time-dependent performance index and the seismic energy input y to the structural system. Since only the responses x and observed ground motions y up to the present were used in this algorithm, the effect of time delay to apply the control force was a problem and is under review. The authors emphasized that the control law provides feasible control algorithms that can easily be implemented for applications to seismically excited structures.

Kawahara and Fukazawa [22] investigated a solution algorithm for the tracking problem of discrete time linear quadratic control based on dynamic programming to evaluate the feedforward term. In the solution, all earthquake loads y are known at the beginning. Since, however, this is impossible in actual control, a subtracking control system was proposed in which only a part of the earthquake load is known in advance.

Shimogo and Yoshida [23] present a feedforward control obtained by assuming that the shaping filter possesses the same natural frequency as a primary building in the frequency range of the input disturbance. The optimal control force is obtained by gains that minimize the performance index containing the absolute acceleration responses. Furthermore, to improve reliability, a control system consisting of a feedback control and a feedforward control is synthesized.

C. Other Algorithms

The objectives of active control are structural safety and living comfort. Bounded state control [24] endeavors to restrict the response value by providing pulse forces so that it does not exceed the allowable value determined by the foregoing demands.

S. F. Masri explains the physical meaning of the seismic control effect by such seismic force as "the seismic control force breaking up the condition to attain resonance." This control method is rather simple when compared with the others, and the external energy required for control is small.

VI. FUTURE DEVELOPMENT

Development of the technology required to realize a seismic response controlled structure has progressed steadily, and the very first one has been realized in Japan. But because of restrictions in the current Japanese building codes, a building with a seismic response control system simply offers living comfort during strong winds and earthquakes of moderate intensity. This has given us the opportunity first, to make many observations of seismic response effects during the indicated external disturbances, and second, to verify the system's effectiveness from actual experience. In fact, the control system presently being planned is going to be designed in accordance with a similar philosophy. The final purpose of the system, however, can be truly described as realization of a structure that will not suffer any large damage, and not only will be able to maintain the building's function but will also prevent panic by occupants during severe earthquakes. To attain this final target, it will probably be necessary to pass over several higher hurdles.

Essentially, the selection of the most appropriate devices and systems depends on the type of external disturbance, the type of subject structure, and the aim of control. In particular, to realize the final purpose of safety and functional integrity of building structures in severe earthquakes, innovative ideas are required to combine a high capacity energy absorber with a highly efficient active seismic response control system of the energy-saving type.

Before such a system can be realized, several factors must be debated. If the passive control system alone can effectively suppress the responses of building structures to unknown ground motions of future earthquakes, there would be no need to expend our research and development efforts with respect to an active control system.

The active mass driver system has been verified by the building with the first installation of a fully active system in Tokyo. However, if the scale of the structure is large and the earthquake is of large magnitude, the amount of energy required to control is very large. Thus, there are problems in applying such a system to this kind of large-scale structure. Therefore, we should opt for a variable damping capacity or a variable stiffness system, both of which are nonresonant control type and energy-saving system. We are also considering a tuned mass damper system, which provides active operation only at the beginning of earthquakes. This system may be considered to be a semiactive system.

It is important that we set aside energy-saving measures and economic considerations for the time being and concentrate on pure engineering considerations to research and develop a system that will be effective in earthquakes of all magnitudes, from small to large. Only after these steps have been taken, should we consider energy saving, economics, and simplification to achieve a practical system. That is the principle of research, development, and implementation.

We do not doubt that with the development of advanced technologies such as computer science technologies, an active response control system will prove to offer the ultimate and perfect design for an earthquake-resistant structure in the near future.

REFERENCES

1. G. W. Housner, T. T. Soong, and S. F. Masri, "An Overview of Active and Hybrid Control Research," presented at the meeting of U.S. and Japan Panels on Active Structural Control, March 27-28, 1990, Tokyo.
2. T. T. Soong, "State-of-the-Art Review: Active Structural Control in Civil Engineering," *Eng. Struct., 10*: 74-84 (1988).
3. S. F. Masri, "Seismic Response Control of Structural Systems: Closure," in *Proceedings of the Ninth World Conference on Earthquake Engineering*, Vol. VIII, pp. 497-502, 1988.
4. T. T. Soong and T. Kobori, "Outlook of Passive and Active Protective Systems for

Seismic Safety of Structures," presented at the American Society of Civil Engineers Structures Congress, Baltimore, 1990.

5. T. Kobori, "State-of-the-Art on Dynamic Intelligent Building system," in *Proceedings of the Eighth International Congress of Cybernetics and Systems*, New York, June 1990.

6. T. Kobori, "Technology Development and Forecast of Dynamical Intelligent Building (D. I. B.)," in *Proceedings of the International Workshop on Intelligent Structures*, Taipei, July 1990.

7. T. Kobori, H. Kanayama, et al., "A Proposal of New Antiseismic Structure with Active Seismic Response Control System—Dynamic Intelligent Building," *Proceedings of the Ninth World Conference on Earthquake Engineering*, Kyoto, August 1988.

8. S. Aizawa, Y. Hayamizu, et al., "Study on Active Dual Axis Mass Damper," *Proceedings of the Annual Meeting of the AIJ*, October 1990, pp. 861–866 (in Japanese). Summaries of technical papers of the annual meeting of the AIJ, structure I.

9. T. Kobori et al., "Study on Active Mass Driver (AMD) System—Active Seismic Response Controlled Structure," presented at the Fourth World Congress of Councils on Tall Buildings and Urban Habitat, Hong Kong, November 1990.

10. T. Shimogo, K. Yoshida, T. Suzuki, et al., "Active Vibration Control System for High-Rise Buildings," *Proceedings of the Annual Meeting of the AIJ*, October 1990, pp. 867–872 (in Japanese). Summaries of technical papers of the annual meeting of the AIJ, structure I.

11. L. L. Chung, A. M. Reinhorn, and T. T. Soong, "Experiments on Active Control of Seismic Structures," *ASCE J. Eng. Mech., 114*: 241–256 (1988).

12. K. Yahagi and K. Yoshida, "An Active Control of Traffic Vibration on the Urban Viaducts," *Proc. JSCE*, No. 356/I-3 (April 1985) (in Japanese).

13. R. K. Miller, S. F. Masri, T. J. Dehghanyar, and T. K. Caughey, "Active Vibration Control of Large Civil Structures," *ASCE J. Eng. Mech., 114*: 1542–1570 (1988).

14. T. Kobori et al., "Shaking Table Experiment of Multi-Story Seismic Response Controlled Structure with Active Variable Stiffness (AVS) System," presented at the Eighth Japan Earthquake Engineering Symposium, December 1990 (in Japanese).

15. T. Kobori et al., "Experimental Study on Active Variable Stiffness System—Active Seismic Response Controlled Structure," presented at the Fourth World Congress of Councils on Tall Buildings and Urban Habitat, Hong Kong, November 1990.

16. T. Matsumoto, H. Abiru, et al., "Study on Powered Passive Mass Damper for High-Rise Building," *Proceedings of the Annual Meeting of the AIJ*, October 1990, pp. 881–884 (in Japanese). Summaries of technical papers of the annual meeting of the AIJ, structure I.

17. K. Tanida, Y. Koike, et al., "Development of Hybrid-Type Mass Damper Combining Active-Type with Passive-Type," in *Proceedings of the Dynamics and Design Conference*, Kawasaki, July 1990 (in Japanese).

18. M. Kageyama, A. Nohata, et al., "A Study on Absolute Vibration Control System of Structures," in *Proceedings of the Dynamics and Design Conference*, Kawasaki, July 1990 (in Japanese).

19. J. N. Yang, A. Akbapour, and P. Ghaemnaghami, "New Optimal Control Algorithms for Structural Control," *ASCE J. Eng. Mech., 113*: 1369–1386 (1987).

20. Y. Yamada, H. Iemura, A. Igarashi, and Y. Iwasaki, "Phase-Delayed Active Control of Structures Under Random Earthquake Motion," presented at the Fourth U.S. National Conference on Earthquake Engineering, 1989.

21. T. Sato and K. Toki, "Active Control of Seismic Response of Structures," in *Proceedings of the International Workshop on Intelligent Structures*, Taipei, July 1990.

22. M. Kawahara and K. Fukazawa, "Optimal Control of Structures Subject to Earthquake Loading Using Dynamic Programming," *Proc. JSCE*, No. 404/I-11 (April 1989) (in Japanese).

23. T. Shimogo, K. Yoshida, et al., "Optimal Active Dynamic Vibration Absorber for Multi-Degree-of-Freedom Systems (Feedback and Feedforward Control Using a Kalman Filter)," *Trans. JSME, 55*(517): 88–1358A (September 1989) (in Japanese).

24. S. F. Masri, G. A. Bekey, and F. E. Udwadia, "On-Line Pulse Control of Tall Buildings," in H. H. E. Leipholz (ed.), *Structural Control*. North Holland: Amsterdam, pp. 471–492, 1980.

Index

Printed and bound by CPI Group (UK) Ltd, Croydon, CR0 4YY

23/10/2024

01777916-0001